MortgageMatters®

DEMYSTIFYING THE LOAN APPROVAL MAZE

"The most comprehensive book about the mortgage process I
have ever read. It is accessible, smart and informational."
— **Amy Tierce, Mortgage Professional**

SYLVIA M. GUTIÉRREZ

MortgageMatters

Mortgage Matters: Demystifying the Loan Approval Maze is a work of nonfiction. Nonetheless, some stories, corporations, and personal characteristics of individuals or events have been changed in order to disguise identities. Any resulting resemblance to persons, living or dead, and/or corporations, open or closed, is entirely coincidental and unintentional. While the author has made every effort to provide accurate telephone numbers, Internet addresses, and contact information at the time of this publication, neither the publisher nor the author assumes any responsibility for errors or for changes that occur after publication. Further, the publisher does not have any control over and does not assume any responsibility for author or third-party websites or their content.

For more information about this book, visit MortgageMattersBook.com. For information about special discounts for bulk purchases, please contact RealWorks Press at publicity@ RealWorksPress.com.

ISBN 978-0-9904004-0-0 English ebook
ISBN 978-0-9904004-1-7 English paperback

information or resources. All logos, trade marks, service marks, and copyrighted words and/or titles used in these pages, including but not limited to text fields, meta tags, within frames, or otherwise, remain the intellectual property of their owner(s) and are used herein for identification purposes only and/or to assist topic searches. This material could be inaccurate or become inaccurate as a result of certain developments occurring after the respective dates of publication of the material contained in this website. RealWorks Press undertakes no obligation to verify or maintain the currency of such information.

Certain links in this book may lead to resources located on servers maintained by third parties over whom RealWorks Press has no control. Certain outside links from servers maintained by third parties over whom RealWorks Press has no control may lead to resources located within MortgageMattersBook.com. Accordingly, RealWorks Press makes no representation as to the accuracy, completeness, appropriateness, or any other aspect of the information contained on such servers. Inclusion of a link does not imply or constitute an endorsement by RealWorks Press, of the referenced site or of those associated with such sites. The jurisdiction for any cause of action shall reside in the state of Florida and the country of the United States. You hereby release RealWorks Press, the author, MortgageMattersBook.com, and everyone associated in any manner with Mortgage Matters: Demystifying the Loan Approval Maze, or the information contained therein, from any liability whatsoever.

Without limiting the above-mentioned, RealWorks Press, and everyone associated in any manner with this book or accompanying website do not warrant that the site, or the information contained therein, will be free of errors, fit for any particular purpose, accurate, complete, or current, or that any use of the site or communication with any participants in the site will be secure or confidential. Also, there are no warranties as to the results that might be obtained from using the information provided in the book, MortgageMattersBook.com, or the information contained therein. Persons acting under color of governmental authority, which authority is later decided to be lacking by a court of competent jurisdiction or legislatively, shall be considered individuals for purposes of this disclaimer.

You agree to indemnify, hold harmless, and defend RealWorks Press its members, directors, officers, employees and agents, from and against any action, cause, claim, damage, debt, demand, or liability, asserted by any person, arising out of or related to: (i) these Terms of Use; (ii) your use of this book and the accompanying website, including any date or work downloaded, transmitted or received by you; and (iii) any libelous, slanderous, indecent or other statement concerning any person made or republished by you. This disclaimer is in addition to, and does not override or otherwise modify or supersede, the terms and conditions that apply to the products or services offered by the links contained within or the accompanying website and other companies throughout the book.

DEDICATION

For those envisioning the American dream of sustainable homeownership

AS A VETERAN of the mortgage industry since 1993, I've found myself struggling to find a balance between lenders' policies and federal regulations that seemingly contradict one another and make it effectively impossible for the mortgage industry as a whole to deliver great service to consumers. There is deep frustration on all sides with polarizing views on what is right for consumers, what is safe for the investor, and what is profitable for the lender. In very few situations are all these objectives aligned. Transparency is challenging to achieve, but there is a commonality of issues that affects most originating organizations.

With the 2013 industry-wide success rate of converting applications to originations (closed loans) at a mere 58% (according to Ellie Mae's January 2015 Origination Insight Report)—a failure by any measure—there is much room for improvement. There are many barriers of entry into homeownership; the loan application process shouldn't be one of them. As with any high-risk transaction, education is key and success begins with financial readiness and a strong lender match. It's on the consumer to be a savvy shopper. But how can we expect anyone to learn what it is they don't know they need to learn.

With over two decades of experience as a residential mortgage loan officer, I've compiled an actionable plan to prepare consumers for the process of mortgage financing. My opinions are my own. I am not giving legal advice; I am not a lawyer. I am a primary market participant, having functioned in every origination capacity as a banker, a mortgage banker, a mortgage broker, and as a private money lender. I have filled these roles at every level of the industry: as a top producer for one of the big three, as well as at a mid-size bank, a community bank, a mortgage banker, and a small mom-and-pop shop. I've worn all hats, so to speak. No matter the title, the work is the same. Loan officers uncover needs, provide options, and guide the borrower through the loan approval maze. You will need to partner with a lending professional who can review your specific financial situation and help you define options that are best for you. Listen carefully to what they have to say and ask plenty of questions.

There are many lessons to learn from the recent collapse of the mortgage market. At the beginning of 2007, I was one of many industry professionals logging onto Aaron Krowne's website The Mortgage Lender Implode-O-Meter www.ml-implode.com on a daily basis, where the collapse of the mortgage market was documented in real time. The site is still up and running, acting as a historical record of the meltdown. All around us, good people, hard workers, were brought to their knees, most through no fault of their own. So much sadness and confusion everywhere, it didn't make sense to any of us. Housing could not fail—everything depends on housing. And still, we burned.

Fear makes people act in irrational ways; there is plenty of fear in the mortgage community and rightfully so. I am a mortgage professional; there are hundreds of thousands like me who serve the mortgage industry. By "our community," I don't just mean loan officers. I mean everyone involved in mortgage banking. We are still reeling from the fires that burned. We are afraid. We are afraid of making mistakes, missing details, misrepresenting, violating regulations, getting fired, losing our licenses, losing our livelihood, closing our doors, costing stakeholders millions of dollars, going to prison, creating homelessness, breaking up families. How does this fear translate to you, the consumer? It makes the process all that more challenging to document. Eight years later, regulations are in place that, through the practice of safe and sustainable lending, aim to never allow for another catastrophic event. While they are still being modified to fit and make sense, it's up to all of us to embrace them and move forward.

Know this: Everyone within our community wants to do a remarkable job for you.

Visit the Mortgage Matters companion website, MortgageMattersBook.com, to access downloadable resources that support the material in the book. You'll find valuable resources such as a comprehensive mortgage documentation checklist, generic condo questionnaire form, modifiable budget calculator, income worksheet, mortgage payment calculator, amortization schedule, instructions for completion of forms 4506-T, SSA-89, and VOE, and sample letters of explanation, credit, bank, and employment reference letters and industry resources designed to make the lending experience more accessible and less stressful.

A special note to my peers: I encourage you to expand your occupational knowledge by participating in our trade associations and make your voice heard. It is only when we speak up that we can effect change. Maintain the integrity of the profession. Invest in your education. Make the connections that will make a difference. Collaborate. Share your best practices. Hold your leaders accountable to delivering excellence in service. Serve your communities. Hold educational seminars. Mentor someone. Teach responsible finance.

ACKNOWLEDGMENTS

I AM DEEPLY grateful to many people, whose contributions on this project have been invaluable. Most especially I want to thank my husband Luis, whose love fosters my creative goals, carries me through uncertainties, and empowers me to take bold risks.

A woman will have many roles in her life. Being Jason's and Ryan's mother is my most treasured endeavor by far. Sons: Thank you for your patience when dinner wasn't always ready when you needed it to be. Always trust your instincts; if something doesn't feel right, it probably isn't. To every situation there is a silver lining; find it. Set goals and achieve them, have dreams and follow them, and always remember you must first believe it before you can see it.

For my sister Lydia Ruidiaz, my greatest fan and toughest teacher: Thanks for requiring that I navigate AllRegs before you'd entertain answering my questions and for demanding I articulate my arguments as an "underwriter" instead of as a "loan officer." These things made me a better loan officer to my clients.

Speaking of which, I've been blessed to have the most amazing, diverse, and loyal clientele who consistently inspire me to do better. Thank you for your patience in what is a challenging process.

I'd also like to thank my editors Jane Friedman and Melissa Wuske for narrowing my focus to the intended audience; René F. Rodríguez, whose guidance on influence, delivering value and identifying triggers set the right tone; and my fellow mortgage professionals who offered great insight— Lourdes Ojeda, Ed Wilburn, Carlos Lastres, James Venney, Stacy McGinty and Melva Garcia. Being an active member of the Mortgage Banker's Association and NAMB-The National Association of Mortgage Professionals has expanded my education beyond the classroom and frontline sales concerns. Through participation, I have connected with industry executives with the power and resources to effect significant and necessary changes, and I am grateful for their welcoming me into leadership roles that allow for expanded communication. I'm also grateful to many more subject matter experts representing the industry who will remain anonymous: Thank you for your honesty.

And thanks finally to my elders, for showing me there is only one direction and that is forward.

TABLE OF CONTENTS

THERE ARE FEW investments in our lives that will be as significant as the purchase of a home, and few events in our lives that will be as stressful as the mortgage application process. Death, divorce, and moving are often considered the three highest stressors in a person's life. Planning a move due to a death or a divorce is stress raised exponentially. Moving is much more than the physical act of packing up your life and transporting it from Main Street to Broadway; it is also a time of mourning the neighbors you're leaving behind with whom you've shared experiences. As you are struggling with these emotions, you are also charged with focusing and navigating through the land mines on the mortgage highway. You're probably looking forward to your mortgage experience much as one would a colonoscopy: You may need the results, but you certainly aren't looking forward to the process.

There is no easier client to serve than one who is ready. Mortgage Matters is written to share with you, the borrower, the things that matter and that are within your control, from beginning to end. While there is no way to completely remove the stress, what we'll be doing is preparing for loan application, to shorten the length of the decision-making phase of your loan request, and in turn, shorten the length of time you will feel stressed.

First Things First

Before the mortgage crisis, I used to tell everyone what I did for a living, as this always paved the way for future referrals. After the meltdown, I gradually stopped. So many people needed to share their story of job loss or underemployment, and while it was evident that they were angry at their lender for not providing better assistance and communication, it was very clear to me that they couldn't keep the losses attributed to the recession from defining how they viewed themselves as providers for their families. They didn't understand why the government was willing to bail out the banks but not them. They wanted answers.

This doesn't have anything to do with the nature of this book, but I wanted to start with this because I think it needs to be said. For all of those who were affected by the financial crisis and lost their home, you are not defined by that event. The Great Recession brought mass unemployment and underemployment that made it difficult for many to make their mortgage payments or repair and maintain their homes, and many suffered the negative psychological emotions of foreclosure that include anxiety, stress, fear, hopelessness, depression, and embarrassment. But you must remember that you didn't cause the Great Recession and your self-worth isn't tied to homeownership. Home is defined by what takes place within our four walls. Let it go. Take this opportunity to move forward.

Will I Have to Earn a Ph.D. in Mortgage Banking?

No matter who you are or how much you earn, all homebuyers share the same fears, concerns, and anxieties. You're nervous, and rightly so. Generally speaking, people aren't all expected to know the same things, we don't all learn in the same way, and we're not all equally interested in the same forms of knowledge. Yet most of us, at some point in time, are expected to know about the mortgage process and how to get through it—and we're expected to do that without any training whatsoever or by relying on partial information given by misinformed people. You may only want to learn about the things that apply to you and this is understandable, but you'll find that most everything in this book applies to you in some way, so there are no shortcuts. The key to success in the mortgage process is preparation. This is going to require a significant investment of your time, but the financial rewards are well worth the time spent.

There are a few sections of the book where I discuss topics that aren't really about how to best prepare for the loan application process, but are necessary for your overall understanding of the workings of the mortgage industry and the issues you may face. You will learn about how the primary and secondary mortgage markets work together to deliver mortgage products, the different designations for institutions that are authorized to originate mortgage loans, the relationship between originating organizations, creditors, aggregators, investors, and the government-sponsored enterprises (GSEs), the necessity for better communication between borrowers and servicers and homeowners associations, and an overview of some key things to keep in mind during the servicing of your home loan. I share my insights on the impact of federal and state laws on the mortgage industry and the effect of lenders' policies that are designed to protect their stakeholders and how those polices determine the types of loan products you are offered by a particular lender.

You may be going into this believing that all lenders offer the same loan products and follow the same set of strict guidelines—and that's the second biggest mistake that you'll make. The first and largest mistake most people make is not putting their finances in order before beginning the mortgage application process. In the face of these facts, you have lots of doubts and are unsure how to formulate your questions. Does a particular lender offer the loan products that best suit your particular needs? Can your loan officer be trusted to accurately represent your financial profile? Will you be offered the best pricing? Will the flow of your loan application be properly directed so that you can receive a timely loan approval and meet your closing requirements by contract date? Will your kids be able to hang their posters on the walls of the bedroom they selected? I get it.

Storytelling

Your loan officer is the storyteller, the person you've retained to write your biography. The representation of your life story will only be as true as the information you give the biographer. Whether or not your loan request is approved is 95 percent attributable to how your story is told. Guidelines are guidelines, facts are facts, and in today's mortgage banking environment, what you don't reveal at application, and is later identified, greatly affects the comfort level of the underwriter who is tasked to make a decision on your creditworthiness.

Know that you are selecting a loan officer, not a lender. Just as not all lenders offer the same products, not all lending platforms offer you the most beneficial service nor do all loan officers have the same skill set. You'll learn how to identify the better loan officers. Although this isn't a term I really like to use because it implies that one person is better than another, the term helps you identify those attributes that a stronger loan officer will have and whose value will undoubtedly increase your likelihood of a successful process.

Guidance and Policy

As unusual as this may sound to you, loan officers aren't allowed to tell you exactly what you need to do to get your loan approved. Organizations put policies in place that prohibit us from telling you how submitting one document over another would be easier for loan approval, as doing so may imply coaching, and prohibit us from having any discussion of loan eligibility requirements, as doing so may imply that we are discouraging you from making loan application that violates Fair Lending laws, or suggesting one product over another, as it may imply steering. So this book is a seasoned loan officer's voice for conversations that time, regulations, and policy may prevent most loan officers from having with you. Here you'll learn how we assess your creditworthiness, and how you can prepare accordingly and ask the right questions

The topics follow the general guidelines of conventional and government underwriting standards at the time of publication. Throughout, the word agency is often used to describe the authority issuing these guidelines under which we evaluate your creditworthiness when deciding a loan. In practice, the term *agency* generally refers to the accepted minimum credit standards for loans delivered to mortgage giants Fannie Mae, Freddie Mac, or Ginnie Mae that are government-sponsored enterprises (GSEs). Just as the Generally Accepted Accounting Principles (GAAP) or standard accounting practices refer to the standard framework of guidelines for financial accounting used in any given jurisdiction, agency guidelines include the standards, conventions, and rules that mortgage lenders generally follow when reviewing loan underwriting criteria in anticipation of delivering your loan to a government-sponsored enterprise for guaranty.

Not all lenders follow agency guidelines and instead institute their own set of policies. Lenders use the term policy to mean one of two things: the specific business practices of anyone involved in the mortgage lending process or a lender's particular rules surrounding their appetite for risk. Keep in mind that policy is specific to each lender and guidelines set by the GSEs are fluid. When a lender has stricter rules on top of agency guidelines, we call these overlays.

I will not spend time educating you on the pros and cons of a fixed-rate mortgage versus an adjustable rate mortgage—there are plenty of free materials available at hud.gov to address the benefits of each. I am fluent in the languages of English, Spanish, and Mortgage and can pick up on conversational Portuguese and Italian. Google Translate is my friend. I've sat across from a Brazilian borrower, typed my questions in English, had them translated to Portuguese, flipped my laptop over to the applicant who read the question in Portuguese, responded in Portuguese, and then Google Translate gave me their responses in English (although not with grammatical perfection). Unfortunately, Google Translate does not support Mortgage Speak, and that's the impetus for this book. I can't help but speak in Mortgage, but I am told I'm very good at interpreting our language so that you will understand. As you read along, foreign terms are introduced and defined. The "Learn the Lingo" section presents a glossary of mortgage industry terms.

I'll leave you with these tips on being a savvy mortgage consumer:

- Decide in advance the maximum monthly housing payment you can afford.
- Know your credit score.
- Follow the recommendations provided identifying creditworthiness.
- Gather current market information about prevailing interest rates.
- Speak with at least two different lenders to get advice on several loan programs and compare their features.
- Get preapplication cost estimates and know the variables used in their calculations.
- Make sure that your loan officer has all appropriate licenses.
- Read and understand any legal document you are asked to sign.
- Don't commit to anything on impulse or under pressure.
- Ask whom to contact if you have a question or problem and your loan officer isn't available.

Sustainable homeownership remains the single best idea for building family wealth and growing the middle class. Housing has been suffering death by a thousand cuts ... It's time to change the dialogue of distrust to a dialogue of confidence.

—David H. Stevens, 2014 President and CEO of the
Mortgage Bankers Association

01 Steps Toward Homeownership

Homeownership is a goal for many of us. But how will you know when you're financially ready to meet this responsibility? What's it going to take to get you ready to make the commitment? And what can you do today to ensure the best mortgage products and pricing are available to you when you are ready?

If you are the perfect borrower—a mystical, magical being—employed in the same profession for two or more years, have received a salary with no bonus or overtime compensation, consistently show only deposits into your checking/savings account from employment compensation, have accumulated savings of 25 percent or more of your purchase price, have no prior marriages, have no minor children residing outside of your household, have no off-the-credit-report debt obligations, have not cosigned a loan for anyone, and have no derogatory information on your credit report, then you are the unicorn of loan applicants. You exist only in fairytales. Everyone needs direction to support a successful outcome.

B Y THE TIME you finish this book, you'll have more answers than questions, a clear understanding of available loan programs and products within those options, an awareness of how individual loan pricing is determined, command over documentation requests, proficiency in the steps that are necessary to get you to the closing table, and an appreciation of what you can expect during the servicing of your home loan. The student who gets an A isn't always the smartest—he or she may just be the one who did all of the homework, turned it in on time, and stayed up late to study for the exam. The very wise Ben Franklin shared, "By failing to prepare, you are preparing to fail." By reading this, you are taking the first step in preparing for mortgage success. Congratulations!

I believe there are two signs of readiness that will help you identify if you are prepared for homeownership. The first is knowing exactly why it's beneficial for you to own a home; and the second is having a fair sense of whether or not you have financial responsibility.

Benefits of Owning Your Home

Home calls to mind family, community, friends, relationships, and a shared history. Where we live affects our self-esteem, the control we have over our environment, and our perceptions over financial security. Being a homeowner is seen by most as a sign of accomplishment and success. Buying a home takes a lot of thought, hard work, and sacrifice.

Whether you are a single person or have a family, you need to decide whether or not owning a home is right for you. There are many things to consider, including where you want to live, how much you can reasonably afford, and what you are willing to do to make sure your new home maintains its value. How will you know when and if you're ready to become a homeowner? Sure, financial security is one measure of readiness, but why buy when you can rent? Many choose to rent to maintain ease of mobility.

Here are just a few of the financial benefits of owning your home: (1) mortgage payments are a sort of forced savings with a portion of your monthly payment going to reduce the principal balance, (2) the U.S. tax code allows homeowners to reduce mortgage interest from tax obligations, (3) real estate property taxes paid are also fully deductible from tax obligations, (4) if you live in the home for more than two years and then decide to sell it, up to $250,000 of the profit gained from the sale is excluded from capital gains taxes for single persons and up to $500,000 for married persons, and (5) price appreciation helps build home equity, which is the difference between the market price of the house and the remaining mortgage payments.

There are also social benefits of owning a home. Generally speaking, there is greater residential stability for homeowners than for renters. A Harvard study, "Reexamining the Social Benefits of Homeownership after the Housing Crisis" (http://www.jchs.harvard.edu/sites/jchs.harvard.edu/files/hbtl-04.pdf) found that despite the sufferings of foreclosure, owning a home remains an important desire for many Americans. Aside from historical equity appreciation, an even greater benefit of homeownership may be the achievements realized by children whose parents maintain a foothold in the community. This benefit was identified in several ways:

- Children of homeowners do not change schools as often. Children who change schools often have been found to do considerably worse in school.
- Residential stability may increase parent participation in local civic organizations, thereby building social networks that are supportive of positive child behaviors.
- Homeownership may require parents to learn home repair, financial, and interpersonal skills that they then pass along to their children.
- Improved self-esteem and reduced financial stress among home-owning parents may positively impact children's behaviors.
- The children of home-owning parents had math achievement test scores that were nine percent higher and reading achievement scores that were seven percent higher than the children of renters.
- Children of homeowners are generally less likely to drop out of school than those of renters.

Responsible Personal Finance

Home buying can be an intimidating process, particularly for first-time homebuyers. A household's ability to obtain ownership is in part a function of the resources available to them and the personal circumstances that make homeownership a desirable outcome. Many people are simply unfamiliar with the significance of credit management, the need to build an emergency fund, and the importance of having a steady and reliable income source. Personal financial education isn't specifically taught in our high schools (the first time I learned how to write a check was in a college mathematics class), and some people lack familial role models who educate on budgeting and the consequences of financial mismanagement. There is much to be learned.

Know Your Budget

Most of us know that we need to budget our money, put some aside for the future, and stay out of debt, but many of us still struggle to follow these three principles consistently. At any income level, the surest road to responsible finance is spending less than we earn. If planning a monthly budget has never been on your priority list, you probably have no idea where your money goes. Knowing where each dollar goes is essential to building opportunities for savings. The key to achieving any goal is to set a date.

For many of us, the word budget conjures up the same feelings of self-induced torture and deprivation that we get when we hear the word diet. Those who live a healthy lifestyle never have to diet. Healthy eaters tend to make meal plans ahead of time and keep a daily journal of what they put in their mouths. If you apply these basic concepts to tracking your income and expenditures for about a month, you'll be able to pinpoint extra funds. We call these extra funds discretionary income. Discretionary income can be used on fun things like a night of bowling or happy hour with your friends at the local pub, or it can be set aside for a future vacation or a down payment on a home. (Visit www.MortgageMattersBook.com to download a Monthly Budget Spreadsheet to help you get started and is easily modifiable to meet your specific profile.)

Begin by identifying and listing fixed costs such as housing, auto loan/lease payments, student loans, utilities (telephone, cell phone, Internet, electricity, and water), cable, parking, commuter expenses, auto insurance, health insurance, life insurance, day care, and tuition. Then add variable expenditures such as minimum payments on credit cards, groceries, meals outside the home, and entertainment. Remember to include allocation for clothing and the nonessentials such as iTunes, gaming memberships, health club memberships, and grooming. Once you have created a clear picture of where your money goes throughout the course of a month, you can begin to spot trends and problem areas and identify where you can cut back and by exactly how much. Just by having the mindset to track expenses, you'll automatically start to think twice about frivolous expenditures, and it'll become easier to hold off on an unnecessary purchase when you have set a timeline for achieving your dream of homeownership.

Gaining Access to Credit and Maintaining Proper Management of Debts

Credit cards can be used as an easy way to track expenses and provide for ease of payments. In the U.S., credit scoring models utilize payment histories on loans and lines of credit to determine a borrower's creditworthiness by assigning a score. Ideally, mortgage applicants will have four active trade lines with a minimum twenty-four-month history of payments. While lenders prefer that the trade lines are ones that report to the credit repositories such as credit cards, auto loans or mortgages, we will accept histories on nontraditional credit accounts, including housing and utilities such as gas, telephone, electricity, water, and cable. Additionally, we may accept payment histories on auto insurance, renters insurance, and daycare and school tuition, to name a few. Here are some things we look for in evaluating credit risk:

a. Older, established accounts generally represent lower credit risk.

b. Revolving accounts with a low balance-to-limit ratio (a term describing how much of your available monies you've used) generally represent a lower credit risk, while those accounts with a high balance-to-limit ratio represent a higher credit risk.

c. Recent late payments represent a higher credit risk than late payments that occurred more than twenty-four-months ago.

d. Mortgage delinquencies within the preceding twelve-month period indicate high risk.

e. Significant derogatory events such as foreclosures, deeds in lieu of foreclosure, and public records information, such as bankruptcies, judgments, and liens, represent a higher credit risk.

Going forward, do not make late payments on any of your debt obligations. You may have made mistakes in the past, but you have to keep your eye on your future goals. Keep track of payment due dates and ensure timely payments. Your credit score determines the price you pay for a mortgage or rent, an auto loan, and homeowners insurance. So let's take a close look at how we manage our access to credit.

Building credit doesn't mean you have to build debt. An effective way to manage this is by following this simple rule: If it isn't a necessity, and if you can't afford to pay for it with the money you currently have, don't buy it. When you buy a nonnecessity expecting money you will receive at some point in the future, you risk accruing debt and increasing the cost of that nonnecessity by incurring interest costs.

For example, if we earn $100 and spend $110 we're now in the red by $10. With credit access, that $10 of borrowed money comes with the additional cost of interest payments. This means we're actually on the hook for more than ten dollars. If this happens on a regular basis, month after month, and with large dollar amounts, it's easy to see how someone can get into thousands of dollars of debt. This is the reason most people feel as if they don't have any money to save.

Only use credit to buy items that have lasting value. For example, it's perfectly normal to buy a car with credit. Or a dishwasher, stove, or other big-ticket items you need to live. On the flip side, avoid credit spending for things like dining out and vacations, because while they may bring you immediate pleasure, they have no long-term value. Use cash for those types of expenses, and make room for them in your family budget.

Establishing an Emergency Fund

Financial emergencies can come in many different forms. Job loss, significant medical expenses, home or auto repairs, or something we've never before imagined can force us to rely on access to credit that could compound the problem. The best we can do to prepare for emergencies that require quick access to cash is by establishing and maintaining an emergency fund.

I understand that many people go through their entire lives just barely making ends meet and this can be very stressful. However, we need to learn how to establish responsible financial habits. Ideally, we should be keeping between three and six months worth of our living expenses set aside in an emergency fund. Living expenses include not only the amount for housing, but also include your entire monthly expenses. A sudden job loss will require some time to find suitable re-employment and a medical emergency may keep us bedridden for a while, and we need to be prepared for these emergencies as our bills won't stop coming in simply because we don't have income. By planning for the bigger emergencies, we get to easily deal with the smaller emergencies such as replacing the hot water heater.

If you currently don't have an emergency fund or find it difficult to save money, the key is to start small. Accumulating one month's worth of expenses will take some time, saving three to six months may seem like a daunting task, but it is achievable. By setting immediate goals to be small and manageable, we have a better chance in reaching them.

Where to Keep Your Savings

While it is most certainly your right to keep your money hidden away underneath your mattress or in a coffee can, the best way to document your savings is through your bank. If this will be your first banking experience, enjoy walking into your local bank and open up a new savings account. The next step is to get into the habit of making regular deposits into this account. Whether it is weekly, biweekly, or monthly, create a schedule and stick to it. Once you make saving automatic, you won't even have to think about it. Many employers offer direct deposit and allow you to deposit money into separate accounts.

Accruing Down Payment and Closing Costs

By building on these steps, you'll eventually reach the place where your financial house is in order, and you'll begin to find a feeling of comfort within a specific range allocated for monthly housing expenses. This is the point where you can identify how much house you are willing to buy. What you are willing to spend can be very different from what a lender says you can afford.

When a new client comes to me to see how much house he can afford to buy, I always begin the analysis with this question instead: What amount are you comfortable spending each month on your total housing expenses? I've gotten into this habit because, nine times out of ten, how much house a person can afford is greater than the amount he or she is willing to expend on housing monthly. Total housing expense includes the monthly amount paid for principal and interest on the mortgage loan, property taxes, insurance, and homeowner association dues, if any. We refer to this as your PITIA or your front-end ratio when we are analyzing your loan file and calculating debt-to-income (DTI) ratios. DTI represents a very important measure of risk and is a determining factor in program eligibility.

A simple rule of thumb says that you should be able to afford a mortgage that is two and a half times your yearly gross income (pretax dollars). For example, if you have yearly household income of $40,000, you should be able to obtain a loan approval in the amount of $100,000. When we say household income what we really mean is the income of those persons who will be qualifying for the mortgage loan. Keep in mind, every individual on the loan transaction will have their income, credit, and liabilities scrutinized during the mortgage approval process.

That said, much more goes into determining how much home you can afford beyond the loan amount you qualify for. You need to take into account a lot of other things that consume your discretionary income. Do you have young children at home requiring daycare? Do you have a college age child that you wish to support while they're in school? Do you help support your parents? Do you like to take lavish vacations? Do you enjoy taking your family out to dinner once a week? Do you have an expensive hobby? Do you invest in a private school education for your minor children? Your choice of how much home you can afford should take into consideration your expectations for quality of life. Monthly expenses tied to daycare, primary, and secondary school tuition are not included in debt-to-income ratios because these are choices and not obligations.

Let's not commingle the emergency fund with the down payment and closing cost fund. Keep the emergency fund active, separate, and ongoing, and instead, open a separate savings account to build the money you'll need to get you moved in to your new home. A positive aspect of keeping that emergency fund separate is that at the time of loan application, you will disclose it to your lender on the application, and it will serve the dual purpose of qualifying as your reserve money that may be needed for mortgage qualification. Reserves are not used in the loan transaction, but they serve as a cushion, and excess reserves can act as a compensating factor to your lender when another aspect of your loan file may be weak.

The Six Basic Steps to Mortgage Approval

Whether you are a first-time homebuyer or a long-time real estate investor, everyone needs to understand and prepare for each step of the loan approval process in order to avoid missteps, miscalculations, misunderstandings, and unintentional misrepresentations that cause delays. There are a total of six steps. The first two steps are completed without the involvement of your lender and will require a significant investment of your time, attention to detail, and effort in making corrections where necessary. The remaining four will have you working closely with your lender.

We are going to prepare your loan file so that we don't give an underwriter a reason to think. If you've given them cause to think, you're in trouble, because their thinking leads to questions, which leads to more documentation requests, which leads to more questions, which leads to various submissions, which leads to closing delays, which leads to frustration and disappointment. By addressing all potential issues upfront, you and the loan officer can work together to minimize delays.

Here's an overview of the steps that pave the path for a successful loan approval process:

1. Obtain a Copy of Your Tri-Merge Credit Report
2. Gather Supporting Documentation
3. Meet with a Loan Officer for Prequalification
4. Make Application for Preapproval
5. Obtain a Conditional Loan Commitment
6. Satisfy Lender's Requirements to Obtain a Final Loan Commitment

Step 1: Obtain a Copy of Your Tri-Merge Credit Report

Knowing your credit profile is key in determining loan eligibility. Step one is to get a copy of your credit report and dissect it confirming accuracy and looking for errors. You can obtain a free copy of your credit history annually at AnnualCreditReport.com or call 1-877-322-8228. While this version is a good place to start, it doesn't provide your credit score that loan officers will need as a guide to prepare your preapplication cost estimates and have discussions around loan programs during the prequalification phase. For a monthly fee, service providers such as MyFICO.com provide tri-merged credit reports that provide raw data from all of the major credit repositories: Equifax, TransUnion and Experian. These services have options to help you monitor credit activity, prevent identity theft, and model the impact of changes to your credit profile. Follow the guided review instructions in chapter 6 and immediately begin working on correcting any errors.

Step 2: Gather Supporting Documentation

In Step 2 you will gather all supplies as listed on the supply list in the "Resources" section, organize them as instructed, and review them for possible issues.

Step 3: Meet with a Loan Officer for Prequalification

Sometimes people use the words prequalification and preapproval interchangeably, but as they apply to mortgage financing, they have quite different meanings. In the prequalification phase, we take a look at your mortgage financing options. You'll likely have a discussion with a loan officer in which you'll share how much you have available for down payment and closing costs, your monthly income and recurring monthly debts, and a calculated guess of your credit score. Using your estimations, the loan officer will perform quick calculations that suggest how much home you can afford and discuss options for loan programs you may be eligible.

At this point, your credit report has not been run by the lender, no formal loan application has been made and you should have no expectation of seeing any written loan disclosures. You should, however, request to be provided with loan comparisons identifying features and benefits and preapplication cost estimates. You'll also learn what documentation is needed to support your loan application and have a general expectation of the timeline for when you should make formal application and the fees required to do so.

While prequalification is an important step in the process, you need to remember that a prequalification letter means absolutely nothing. The reason why a prequalification alone doesn't work is that the amount you tell the loan officer as your monthly income is rarely the exact amount of income that the lender can use as your qualifying income. Qualifying income isn't identified in the prequalification step because the process of prequalification doesn't require the review of any supporting documentation. It naturally follows then if all you have is a prequalification letter, you don't have a solid commitment to lend from a creditor.

Note: A creditor is the entity that funds your loan. It could be a bank, a nonbank mortgage company, or a private investor. Within each of these classifications, there are hundreds of entities providing different loan product options, adhering to different underwriting guidelines, lending on only certain types of housing, and pricing their loans based on assessed risk and desired profit margins. All are necessary in the free market to provide the housing industry with funding options. You can make an application directly with a representative of any of these creditors, or you can engage with a loan officer at a mortgage broker firm who searches for a creditor that matches your specific needs. For purposes of clarity throughout this book, and unless otherwise noted, the word lender is consistently used to describe a creditor.

Step 4: Make Application for Preapproval

The difference between a prequalification and a preapproval is that in a preapproval, a formal loan application is made (with no subject property listed), a credit report is pulled and your estimations of income and assets are run through an automated underwriting system. There are six elements that define when loan application is made; receipt of your name, social security number, income, purchase price, loan amount, and property address. A lender is required to issue loan disclosures within three business days of receiving these six details that trigger a loan application.

With preapproval, you and your loan officer complete a full mortgage application with all the elements, except to be determined (TBD) is used as the subject property address along with an assumption on the type of property (single family, condo, planned unit development, multifamily). At this point, some money may be collected for the credit report and underwriting fees, and this depends on the lenders policy. Your loan officer will then obtain your consent to run your credit report, review with you the liabilities listed on the report to assert accuracy, exclude duplicate listings, match mortgage liabilities to their corresponding property and review derogatory items such as slow pays, collections or judgments. Pricing is rerun based on your usable credit score. Subsequently, the data on your loan application is run through an automated underwriting system. A lender will typically use Desktop Underwriter or Loan Prospector, the proprietary underwriting systems for Fannie Mae and Freddie Mac, respectively. These automated underwriting systems provide lenders a comprehensive credit risk assessment that determines whether a loan meets eligibility requirements. Sometimes a lender will use their own proprietary underwriting system to accommodate their specific portfolio lending programs or additional overlays (restrictions) to agency guidelines. Based on the initial findings, the loan officer will receive a recommendation and a list of conditions that need to be satisfied.

While a preapproval is significantly better than a prequalification because credit history is reviewed and a recommendation of approval is received, the recommendation is based on an assumption that the data you gave to your loan officer about your employment, assets, income, and debts is correct, so preapproval still doesn't confirm your loan eligibility. Only after an underwriter reviews your supporting documentation can you be fairly certain that you've secured financing.

Tip: While with successful preparation and no extenuating circumstances, you could realistically expect to close your transaction within thirty days of making loan application, rarely are there no hiccups. The time to make formal application and request a conditional loan commitment is within three months of buying a home. This is critical. Loan documents have expiration dates. If you apply too early and loan documents expire before the loan funding date, new documents will be requested. Significant changes on the loan application can impact loan eligibility and prior approvals.

Step 5: Obtain a Conditional Loan Commitment

Sellers are far more receptive to purchase offers supported by a lender's conditional loan commitment as this signals that you're a serious buyer who is ready to make your move. Once you've reviewed the loan disclosures and agree with the lender's terms, you must issue your consent to continue with the loan application. Once consent is recorded, application fees collected, supporting documentation is gathered, and the data on your loan application is updated to reflect actual data as evidenced by your supporting documents, only then is your entire loan file submitted to an underwriter. The underwriter is the decision maker in this process and takes a deep dive into your loan file to ensure the data on the application is supported by documentation and is submitted in compliance with lending guidelines. If it does, a conditional loan commitment is issued.

You may be wondering how long it will take to get your loan conditionally approved: it mostly depends on you. Your loan officer can work to get your conditional loan commitment issued within three days to three weeks from loan application—depending on the lender's capacity for review of new files and assuming you've provided all the supporting documents on day one. If you can't be bothered with gathering all necessary supporting loan documentation so that an underwriter can make an informed decision quickly and you don't have the funds to pay for the property in cash, then you're not really serious about the buying process.

Based on my experience, the greatest point of contention between you and your lender will be the lender's calculation of qualifying income as it relates to declarations made on your income tax return for unreimbursed business expenses and rental income. We get that nobody wants to pay more taxes than they absolutely have to pay and will use the benefit of a tax break whenever applicable. What you need to know is that your lender can only use the income as reported to the IRS for loan qualification. For those who are self-employed, receive bonuses, or whose commission income exceeds 25 percent of their total income, an analysis of a two-year average of reported income is required. In chapter 10, I go into the detailed industry standards for calculating qualifying income.

Step 6: Satisfy Lender's Requirements to Obtain a Final Loan Commitment

Once you have found a property and negotiated a sales contract, your lender then orders a property appraisal or valuation report and sends a title request to your selected settlement agent. The settlement agent is a real estate attorney or title agent who conveys the orderly transfer of legal title from the seller to the buyer through the closing process. When the appraisal comes in, you are given a copy and you will begin working with your insurance agent to secure adequate property insurance coverage and provide evidence of that coverage through a certificate of insurance sent to your lender. When the lender receives all documentation you submitted to comply with the preliminary loan conditions and the appraisal is in, the file goes back to the underwriter. Once the documentation submitted satisfies the underwriting conditions, a final loan commitment is issued. The final loan commitment will list any prior to loan funding conditions that can only be satisfied at closing, so you'll never receive a final loan commitment that is completely free of conditions.

As a result of all these possible complexities, it's extremely important for you to remember the steps in the process. While its good to know where you stand, don't make the mistake of pausing at prequalification and jumping into contract negotiations. Know your credit, gather your supporting documentation, research lending programs, and shop pricing.

Bumps in the Road

Even with a lender's conditional loan commitment in hand, things can go wrong once there is a property. If a lender denies your request for preapproval, keep in mind this doesn't exclude you from buying a home. Maybe the amounts estimated for property taxes and insurance are higher than the actual amounts, maybe you wanted a fifteen-year term but only qualify for a thirty-year term. Those are things that can easily be fixed. Fair Lending laws, discussed further in the appendix, apply to preapprovals as well. If you're deemed ineligible for the terms you've requested, in all likelihood, the lender is not going to come back to you to tell you what you can be approved for unless you specifically ask them to rework the numbers. Have a meaningful conversation with your loan officer to determine where you can make adjustments to improve the likelihood of approval.

Here is a short list of some of those things that can go wrong:
a. The amounts estimated on the loan application for property taxes, insurance, and homeowner association dues are less than the actual fees for the property selected and now your debt-to-income ratio is higher than the loan program allows. Does the lender offer another loan program that allows a higher debt-to-income ratio? Do you have additional assets to pay off installment debt or provide a higher down payment? Will doing so bring your debt-to-income ratio inline?
b. The condo association has a high investor concentration, thereby classifying the project

as nonwarrantable. Does the lender offer a financing option for nonwarrantable condos? If not, can they refer you to a lender who does?

c. Loans for nonwarrantable condos carry higher risk and are therefore priced higher than loans for warrantable condos. If you have to change the loan program to meet the condo requirements, that loan program may have a higher interest rate thus possibly making your debt-to-income ratio excessive. Explore the adjustable rate mortgage option beginning with an initial fixed interest rate of seven years amortized over a thirty-year term. This option allows you to qualify at the much lower initial offered interest rate (typically at least .5 percent lower than the thirty-year fixed rate option) instead of the higher fully indexed rate.

d. The final appraised value is less than the contract sales price. Are there comparable sales that support a greater value that were not considered in the appraisal? Is the seller willing to drop the sales price to match the appraised value? Can you access additional funds to make up the difference between sales price and appraised value at closing? Does your selected loan program allow for a higher loan-to-value? Is there sufficient time to change your program selection for one that offers a higher loan-to-value and still meet your contract closing date? Will the seller agree to a contract extension?

e. The selected property differs from the property type listed on the initial loan request (e.g., changing from a single family to a 2-4 unit, planned unit development, condominium, or co-operative) thereby requiring a higher down payment or a change from reviewing the most recent year's tax returns to reviewing the average of two years' tax returns which may produce lower qualifying income. Do you have access to additional assets for down payment or for reducing installment debt to bring your debt-to-income ratio inline?

f. Your credit report expired and a re-pull indicates a derogatory item that lowers your usable credit score or identifies an increase in monthly recurring debts. A lower credit score may raise your initially offered interest rate. Having more debt will increase your debt-to-income ratio.

Tip: Do you already have a particular property in mind? Get the property tax bill and have the loan officer use that amount for their property tax estimate. Some lenders use the current tax bill in their qualification of your loan request while other lenders use the estimated future tax cost based on your sales price and the millage rate as determined by the property tax appraisers office in the county. Because of this, loan eligibility from one lender to another lender may vary.

Tip: To prevent last minute blowups, be sure your settlement agent quickly provides the title commitment, which is an insurance policy on title and will list among other things, the amount due on yearly property taxes. If the property taxes shown on the commitment differs from that listed on your loan application, ask your loan officer for an update to your file reflecting the amount of property taxes as listed on the title insurance commitment. Updating this at the last minute may impact your loan eligibility based on your debt-to-income ratio.

Tip: Instead of letting the lender estimate homeowners association dues, if you have a particular community that you are interested in, provide your loan officer the correspondent monthly homeowners association fee for the unit model that interests you and use this information to have her run the numbers.

Tip: If your income alone is insufficient to qualify and are considering adding a cosigner, be sure to ask if the loan program you applied for has the option of a nonoccupant co-borrower. If not, ask your loan officer to review which loan program allows for it.

Tip: If it appears you are short cash-to-close, double check that you have disclosed all of your asset accounts (not just checking and savings) and think about other possibilities. Do your parents have you listed as a co-owner on one of their accounts? Do you have retirement accounts? Is there a cash value on your life insurance policy? Is a family member planning on giving you funds for the transaction?

Tip: Shop insurance providers. Reduce your insurance costs by obtaining a four-point property inspection to take advantage of the many property insurance discounts available based on the age and structure of your property.

The point here is this: The time to explore possibilities is before you sign a purchase agreement so that you can relieve the stress and anxiety of the mortgage process. If you and your loan officer have done your jobs well in documenting your loan file, you should generally expect this conditional commitment to be issued subject only to appraisal, title insurance, and evidence of property insurance. Only now, are you really good to go shopping for a home.

When You're Simply Not Ready

Sometimes no is a good answer, because it is an answer. Think of it this way: Would you rather hear a no today or be fiddled around with for months on end with conditions and review and then more conditions and more review and then subsequent submission of new documentation to replace expired documentation and more conditions and so on? No means your road to approval with that lender is over; pick up the pieces and move on. Don't give up on the approval process, but do learn what was in your control and could have been done better, and then fix it and try again. Be persistent.

The Language of Mortgage

My goal in preparing you for mortgage application is to have your initial, conditional loan commitment issued with very few conditions. Conditions are additional supporting documents requested and reviewed by your lender either prior to scheduling loan closing or at loan closing. You can achieve this goal by submitting the proper documentation to satisfy most loan requirements at the time of loan application. The number one reason this doesn't happen is because a borrower doesn't receive a complete list of required documentation upfront or doesn't understand exactly what is being asked. By following these pages and preparing your loan file for delivery, you can prevent delays due to lack of detailed instruction. As for understanding exactly what is being asked—well, that's a completely different story. Mortgage Speak is filled with a lot of acronyms. We tend to get caught up in our own language and forget that our listeners aren't familiar with our jargon. Whenever possible, clarify with the lender what exactly they're asking of you to avoid breakdowns in communication that lead to closing delays. The language of mortgage begins with an understanding of how credit markets work. For this, we'll take a brief look at the mortgage market.

02 The Mortgage Market

People generally tend to concern themselves with only those things that directly affect them, but if you want to make sense of why the mortgage industry does the things it does in mortgage, you'll need a high level overview of how the U.S. housing finance system functions. These aren't topics that you need memorize or take notes on, but they are essential to your broad understanding of and interaction with the mortgage markets. The language and concepts are sometimes challenging, but I will provide clarity in this chapter. For those who are interested in a more in-depth analysis of the challenges within the mortgage industry, the "Appendix" addresses these topics with references to key studies and reports that are available to the general public.

The U.S. Housing Finance System

THE U.S. HOUSING finance system is composed of the primary and secondary mortgage markets consisting of banks, thrifts, credit unions, and nonbank mortgage companies that deal directly with you on the origination of your home mortgage loan. Primary market institutions typically sell the mortgages they originate to participants in the secondary market. This means that your lender may sell your loan in the secondary market to recapture their investment and increase their liquidity. Liquidity allows a lender to originate new mortgages or to set aside reserve funds for capital requirements as imposed by our regulators. Regulators are governmental entities at either federal or state levels that are tasked with supervising the players in the financial markets.

Fannie Mae and Freddie Mac are two government-sponsored enterprises (GSEs) that were set up as privately owned corporations chartered by the U.S. federal government. Their purpose is to support the secondary market for residential mortgages by promoting access to mortgage credit, increasing liquidity of mortgage investments, improving distribution of capital, and they are among the largest nonbank financial institutions in the world. Ginnie Mae is wholly owned by the U.S. government and is a part of the Department of Housing and Urban Development (HUD). Fannie Mae was created in 1938, Ginnie Mae in 1968, and Freddie Mac in 1970. Collectively, we refer to these as the Enterprises. The Enterprises function to support the housing sector and assist refinance activity by ensuring that residential mortgage lenders in all regions of the country have continual access to funds on comparable terms.

The Enterprises are in the business of insuring mortgage-backed securities (MBS)—which are single and multi-class securities whose cash flows are derived from groups of residential mortgages or MBS. This means that the Enterprises generate revenue by charging the MBS guarantee fees (premiums). In exchange for the fees collected, the Enterprises give their guarantee to MBS investors (people and organizations that buy MBS) that they will continue to receive timely principal and interest payments regardless of the performance of or the credit risk associated with the mortgages underlying the MBS. Investors are not subject to individual loan-specific credit risk, but only face interest and prepayment risk, which is the risk that homeowners will refinance the loan when rates are low. Traditionally, investors have perceived an implicit federal guarantee of those obligations backed by the Enterprises. However, prior to November 25, 2008, the U.S. government provided no explicit legal backing for them.

Fannie and Freddie almost ceased to exist in 2008. The recession that began in 2007 hit many U.S. homeowners very hard. When borrowers began defaulting, the GSEs and many other investors found themselves holding essentially worthless mortgage-backed securities. To prevent a widespread panic and market crash, Fannie and Freddie were placed under conservatorship, and the U.S. government pledged to temporarily guarantee principal and interest payments on all such GSE securities. As of this printing, Fannie and Freddie remain in conservatorship and their future is uncertain.

Evaluation of Credit Risk

Credit risk is evaluated on several underwriting standards and represents the risk that a homeowner will default on the mortgage that serves as the collateral for the MBS. It assesses the probability that the homeowner will stop making payments altogether or fail to deliver them regularly on time. The term agency guidelines is used throughout this book to refer to the Enterprises' evaluation of credit risk or underwriting standards. Secondary market participants act as aggregators when they pool together several mortgages into packages labeled either mortgage-backed securities (MBS) or private-label mortgage-backed securities (PLMBS) for sale to investors. The mortgages that comprise PLMBS securitizations generally do not meet agency guidelines.

The Enterprises are generally restricted by law to purchasing single-family mortgages with loan amounts below a specific amount known as the "conforming loan limit." Loans above this limit are known as nonconforming or jumbo loans. The loan limits are established under the terms of the Housing and Economic Recovery Act of 2008 (HERA) and are recalculated each year. For 2015, the conforming loan limit is $417,000 for one-unit properties in most areas of the contiguous United States, although it can increase to a maximum of $625,500 in specific high cost areas. (Find out conforming loan limits for all counties at www.fhfa.gov/DataTools/Downloads/Pages/Conforming-Loan-Limits.aspx.) Conforming loans must also observe the underwriting standards of the Enterprises through agency guidelines. Most primary market institutions originate both conforming and nonconforming loans.

Government Insured and Guaranteed Mortgage Markets

Primary market lenders may also originate mortgages that are insured or guaranteed by the federal government. These include the Federal Housing Authority (FHA), U.S. Department of Veteran's Affairs (VA), and Rural Development (RD) loans. The FHA insures single-family mortgages through approved private lenders against losses from defaults on mortgages that meet FHA underwriting criteria. Homebuyers pay premiums to FHA that are used to compensate lenders for their losses associated with defaults or foreclosures. The VA guarantees against losses on a portion of the principal balance on loans made to eligible veterans, active duty service members, surviving spouses, and members of the reserve components. RD-guaranteed loans provide lenders a guarantee against losses on mortgage loans provided to low-to-moderate income borrowers in rural areas.

Ginnie Mae, which operates as a unit of the U.S. Department of Housing and Urban Development, provides a secondary market for government insured or guaranteed loans. Ginnie Mae does provide an explicit guarantee (backed by the full faith and credit of the United States government) on MBS that is collateralized by FHA, VA, or RD mortgages. However, unlike the Enterprises, Ginnie Mae does not issue its own MBS. Rather, it relies upon approved financial institutions to pool and secure the eligible mortgages and issue Ginnie Mae–guaranteed MBS. Ginnie Mae's guarantee is limited to the risk that issuers may not fulfill the required monthly principal and interest payments to investors. For this guarantee Ginnie Mae charges MBS issuers a guarantee fee.

How Enterprise Guarantee Fees Are Structured and Collected

Each Enterprise uses their own proprietary financial models to establish the price at which to set guarantee fees (g-fees) to cover the credit risks associated with a particular MBS issuance. This is achieved by modeling, among other things, the rate at which the underlying mortgages will default (i.e., the mortgage default rate) and the average losses on those that default (i.e., the loss severity rate). The mortgage default rate is a probability measure, and it is based upon particular loan characteristics, such as credit scores and loan-to-value's, as well as macroeconomic variables, including collateral value and interest rate projections. (Find the Enterprises' matrices for calculating risk-based upfront fees at https://www.fanniemae.com/content/pricing/llpa-matrix.pdf and www.freddiemac.com/singlefamily/pdf/ex19.pdf.)

G-fees are generally assessed as ongoing monthly payments; however, the up-front fees for loan level price adjustments are paid at the time of loan acquisition. The effective g-fee is not the same for every seller. In general, g-fees are quoted as a fraction of a percentage of the outstanding principal balance of a particular MBS issuance. Typically, these fractions are referred to as basis points of the unpaid principal balance (i.e., 1/100 of 1 percent). Suppose, for example, that an

Enterprise issued an MBS security with an average unpaid principal balance of $100 million. If the g-fee was 33 basis points (or 33/100s of 1 percent), then the upfront guarantee fees collected for that particular MBS would be $330,000. Although Fannie Mae and Freddie Mac have used financial model outputs and business judgment to set guarantee fees, the Federal Housing Finance Authority (FHFA) and others have argued that federal financial support for the Enterprises has allowed them to set their guarantee fees lower than would otherwise have been the case.

How Mortgage-Backed Securities (MBS) Function and What They Provide

MBS purchases are primarily made as "to be announced," where the pool identity is unknown at the time of the purchase. The pool identity refers to the specific details that compose the underlying credit risk of the totality of the mortgages held in the pool; the pool is the aggregate of several loans that are sold together to form a particular MBS offering. Upon announcement, the contract tells only the average maturity and coupon of the underlying mortgage pool, and by which GSE the MBS is backed (or guaranteed). The precise pool information isn't released until forty-eight hours prior to the established trade settlement date at which time the investor is made aware of the exact underlying risk of the mortgages that are included in that pool.

For example, let's say you have one million dollars sitting in a savings account earning 1 percent interest at your local bank and are looking for options to earn a greater return on your money than the 1 percent that you're currently earning. Through a broker or an investment bank, you could purchase an MBS that offers a return on your investment of 8 percent through the issuance of thirty-year Fannie Mae MBS. You like the idea that your money is going to earn 8 percent instead of 1 percent and you feel this poses little risk because Fannie Mae is guaranteeing your investment. You feel there is little risk because you know that Fannie Mae is a government-sponsored enterprise and you interpret this to mean that your investment is fully backed by the U.S. government, but it isn't. You've made an assumption based on your understanding of an implicit guaranty. Prior to conservatorship, Fannie Mae was not explicitly guaranteed by the U.S. government.

The investor's commitment to buy an MBS issuance allows a lender to lock in the interest rate they can offer by having presold its loans to the investor, and thus the lender assures it will have available funds to secure their origination pipeline. If investors lose their appetite to invest in MBS, lenders will have no one to buy their mortgages in the secondary market. If lenders have no one to buy their mortgages, they tie up their capital. If their capital is tied up, they can't make new mortgages. If no new mortgages can be made, the housing market collapses because it becomes limited to cash only buyers, and housing prices plummet.

Financial Reform

The Dodd-Frank Wall Street Reform and Consumer Protection Act, known throughout the financial industry as Dodd-Frank, was signed into federal law by President Barack Obama on July 21, 2010. It represents the most comprehensive financial regulatory reform measures taken since the Great Depression. This act created the Consumer Financial Protection Bureau includes 2,319 pages of new law affecting nearly all aspects of mortgage lending and requires implementation of 243 new regulations with the hopes of preventing another financial crisis. These regulations are fluid and new proposals and modifications are constantly being assessed and pushed through the industry. For the past few years, the mortgage industry as a whole has directed a large investment of resources to try to make sense of these new rulings, and interpretation of the law is left up to compliance officials for each lender. Because such a large overhaul has never before been attempted and its required implementation must take place in a very short period of time, there is a high risk of unintended consequences resulting from the implementation of conflicting rulings.

Qualified Mortgage and Ability-to-Repay Rule

During the financial crisis, it was identified that many of the defaulted loans contained certain product features or required no income or no asset verification, and many loans were funded without validating that borrowers earned the income that was stated on the loan application. As a result, many borrowers ended up in risky loans they could not afford. While a lender's assessment of a borrowers ability to repay a loan is a very commonsense presumption that we all have, lenders are able to make judgment calls on differing factors other than IRS reported and validated income. As part of the final rule of the Dodd-Frank Act, in January 2014 new laws were implemented that require a lender to confirm your ability to repay a loan and the implementation of this law has greatly altered the landscape of lending products and tightened income eligibility standards.

What Does It Mean to Be Given a Qualified Mortgage?

A qualified mortgage (QM) is a category of loans as defined by the federal government that have certain, more stable features that help make it more likely that a homebuyer will be able to afford the loan that is given to them. If a lender provides a QM loan, it means that the lender met certain requirements and it's assumed that the lender followed the Ability-to-Repay rule. The Ability-to-Repay (ATR) rule requires most mortgage lenders to make a good-faith effort to determine that a borrower is likely to be able to pay back the loan. The "good faith effort" is determined by our regulators if we follow their acceptable methods to calculate your qualifying income as defined by "Standards for Determining Monthly Debt and Income" (appendix Q of the Consumer Financial Protection Bureau's regulations) or list our methods for determining your monthly debt and income in our product guidelines. Doing that allows future investors in private label mortgage-backed securities to have an accurate depiction of the credit profile of loans that are included in a particular issuance. Appendix Q contains detailed requirements for determining recurring debt and qualifying income for the purposes of the debt-to-income calculation based on the definitions of those terms set forth in the HUD Handbook.

A QM loan gives the lender a safe harbor (for non-higher priced loans) or a rebuttable presumption (for higher-priced loans) against a legal claim that the borrower didn't have the ability to repay the loan that was provided. The lender gets certain legal protections when showing it made sure the homebuyer had the ability to repay the loan. We show a person's ability to repay a loan by validating and considering income, assets, employment, credit history, and monthly expenses. If a lender chooses to calculate income outside of the rules set by ATR, the loan is not deliverable to the GSEs for guaranty.

Why Are Lenders Encouraged to Comply with QM?

Lenders' violations of the Ability-to-Repay rule are enforceable by the Consumer Financial Protection Bureau's authority to impose cease-and-desist orders or impose civil money penalties for violations. But an interesting thing about this new law is that it also allows you, the borrower, through private action, to file a claim against a lender for violating the requirements of the Ability-to-Repay rule, just because or through your defense to a foreclosure action under the Dodd-Frank amendment to the Truth in Lending Act. This amendment has presented all sorts of challenges to the mortgage industry requiring that we develop reliable processes to ensure that we are being compliant with the law and that we maintain the documentation evidencing that we were compliant when we decided your loan. How this information will follow the note— through its subsequent sales in the secondary markets—presents a challenge in and of itself.

Characteristics of Qualified Mortgage (QM) Loans

Qualified mortgages exclude certain loan features that were identified during the financial crisis as bearing a high risk of default, such as:

- An interest-only period, when your minimum required monthly payments include only the interest costs with no portion of the minimum monthly payment assigned to paying down the principal balance.
- Negative amortization, which can allow your principal balance to increase over time, even though you're making payments, because the required monthly payments may only include a portion of the total interest cost. Any interest cost that was not paid

in the monthly payment is accrued to the loan balance. These are also known as Option ARMs because the interest rate is variable and the monthly statement gives the borrower options for payments. Some example would be:

o   The minimum payment is based on the initial interest rate (usually below market and known as a teaser rate); this option may accrue interest to the loan balance.

o   Interest-only payment, based on the fully indexed interest rate; this option does not accrue interest, and it does not pay down the principal balance—it's effectively the same as paying rent.

o   The fully amortized payment based on the current, fully indexed interest rate, and the remaining loan term.

- Balloon payments, which are larger-than-usual payments at the end of a loan term. The loan term is the length of time over which your loan should be paid back.
- Loan terms that are longer than thirty years.
- A limit on the maximum percentage of your income that can go towards your monthly debt, including your mortgage and the combination of all other monthly debt obligations with more than ten months remaining. The final rule calls for a debt-to-income ratio not to exceed 43 percent.
- Pass a points and fees test. If you get a qualified mortgage, there are limits on the amount of certain up-front points and fees your lender can charge. These limits will depend on the size of your loan. Not all charges, like the cost of a credit report, for example, are included in this limit. If the points and fees exceed the threshold, then the loan is not considered a qualified mortgage.
- Full verification of all income, assets, and liabilities, etc.

Not All Loans Have to Follow ATR

Only loans that are regulated by the Truth in Lending Act (TILA) must conform with the Ability-to-Repay rule. As investment properties are not regulated by TILA, lenders are not required to document your ability to repay a loan on a property that is owned as an investment. However, when setting their internal policies, many lenders are not distinguishing between occupancy and investment when applying methods to calculate your monthly debt and income and are inadvertently creating more roadblocks to credit access.

ATR Exemptions

Not all originating organizations are required to abide by the Ability-to-Repay rule. These exceptions include:

a. Community Development Financial Institutions. These groups are certified by the U.S. Department of the Treasury to provide credit and financial services to underserved populations.

b. Community Housing Development Organizations or Downpayment Assistance Providers of Secondary Financing. These are nonprofit service groups that receive aid from the Department of Housing and Urban Development (HUD) to help provide affordable housing in their communities.

c. Nonprofit organizations that lend less than two hundred times a year and provide credit to low-to-moderate income consumers only. These groups have to follow their own written procedures to determine that consumers have a reasonable ability to repay their loans.

d. Housing Finance Agencies, which are state agencies that offer a certain amount of mortgages with low rates for low and moderate-income borrowers.

e. Loans made through programs under the Emergency Economic Stabilization Act. These programs help those communities hardest hit by the financial crisis of 2007 and 2008.

Not Only QM Loans Exist in the Marketplace

While the Qualified Mortgage rule doesn't prohibit a lender from offering high-risk loan products, many lenders have completely stopped offering loans with features such as interest-only payment, option ARMs, stated income/stated asset loans, and loans with terms greater than thirty years because these loans are no longer deliverable to the GSEs for guaranty or sale. Loans that don't abide by QM still exist in the marketplace today and we refer to these as part of non-QM lending or portfolio lending options.

It was in the news that Ben Bernanke, now former Chairman of the Federal Reserve System, was unable to refinance his personal mortgage. It appears that when migrating from a salaried position in the public sector to self-employment in the public sector, earning variable income in the speaking circuit, he failed to meet the income qualification requirements, even though Bloomberg reports he earns as much as $200,000 per speech. The presumption is that he did not meet the two-year average qualifications for acceptance of variable income, and therefore, with exclusion of this very real income, he fails to be within the maximum debt-to-income requirements restricted by QM. If I were a betting person, I would wager that there are several non-QM lenders itching to provide the former Chairman with a stated income loan with terms based on the lender's overall risk assessment of whether the Chairman would meet his monthly obligations. This loan would not be deliverable to the GSEs because it doesn't meet QM standards, and it would still need to be properly labeled if the lender wanted to package it for sale in a private label mortgage-backed securities issuance. But I'm inclined to think the lender would hold the note in their portfolio just to lay claim to the bragging rights.

03 Originator Engagement

Your interaction with a mortgage provider will vary according to entity type, distribution channel, location, and originator product offerings. Here you'll learn about the different types of originating organizations, their distribution channels for delivering mortgages, the distinguishing factor that identifies mortgage loan originators as either loan officers for creditors or loan officers for mortgage broker companies, the role of your loan officer, and a framework for your expectations of the loan application process.

Originating Organizations

THE MAJORITY OF us will most likely make application for a mortgage loan through either a depository institution (commercial bank, community bank, credit union, or thrift) or a mortgage company. A mortgage company can be an independent nonbank mortgage company or the subsidiary of a commercial bank dedicated to mortgage lending. Here are some differences in how these organizations operate:

- Commercial banks take your deposits and lend you money, and they may operate other business lines such as business banking, investment banking, and credit card operations.
- Credit unions are member-owned, not-for-profit financial cooperatives that provide savings, credit, and other financial services to their members. Credit unions pool their members' savings to finance their loan portfolios rather than relying on outside capital.
- Thrifts, also called savings and loans, are primarily organized to promote savings and home mortgage lending, as opposed to commercial lending practices. However, they generally possess the same depository, credit, and account transactional functions as commercial banks.
- Nonbank mortgage companies specialize in the origination, sale, and/or servicing of real estate mortgage loans. This business generally relies on short-term funding resources, such as lines of credit from commercial banks to close mortgage transactions.

A loan officer can work for a bank, a nonbank mortgage company, or a mortgage broker. An example of a bank originator is Wells Fargo, a nonbank originator is Quicken Loans, and a mortgage broker originator is Mom & Pop's Local Mortgage Shop. Banks generally rely on the deposits of their customers to loan money and nonbanks generally rely on their stakeholders' capital or on warehouse lines of credit to immediately fund their loans while they prepare them for delivery to the investor in their post-closing efforts. Once delivered, they receive funds from the investor to replenish their own funds or to pay down the warehouse line that was used to front the money for the loan, freeing up their resources to lend more money, continuing the cycle.

A mortgage broker does not use his funds to loan you money. Instead, he delivers your loan to a creditor through its wholesale channel, and your loan is funded in the creditors name. A creditor is the entity that funds your loan whether it is a bank or a nonbank. An organization that operates as a nonbank mortgage company can deliver your loan through two channels. It can either submit your loan for review through one of their wholesale relationships to a creditor (bank or nonbank) or it can fund your loan in the name of their organization and then quickly deliver it to the investor to recapture their funds. When a nonbank mortgage company funds your loan in their name, they are acting as correspondents of the investor and are considered the creditor. Ultimately, it is the creditor who holds the risk in evaluating your creditworthiness and who is subject to various perils such as repurchase, default, foreclosure, and litigation.

Creditors can either hold your loan in their portfolio or they can sell it to investors in the secondary market including the GSEs, other creditors, or private equity firms. If an auditor of the investor identifies an error, oversight, or misrepresentation, it can delay or deny the delivery of your loan; that will then cause the creditor to hold or buy back your mortgage. If a creditor is forced to buy back a loan, it will hold that loan in its portfolio until it can cure the defect. Smaller companies that don't have a lot of capital in reserves or who have limited access to warehouse lines can easily be forced to cease originations when buy backs limit their liquidity, which is exactly what we witnessed during the recent financial crisis.

The servicing of your mortgage (the handling of your monthly mortgage payments) can remain with the creditor, be transferred to the investor, or assigned to a third-party servicer, whichever the investor prefers. Knowing who your investor is isn't generally of importance to you, except when consideration is given on refinancing options. Loans sold after funding can present some challenges for you if you're not paying attention to your mail delivery providing notification of an upcoming servicing change. Throughout the life of your loan, be sure to read your mail for any notifications regarding changes of servicer or payment mailing address as these can happen at any time.

Distribution Channels

Amazon, Zappos, and Apple are companies that have spoiled us. Because of their superior service and swift execution, we now have the expectation that all organizations deliver their products just as seamlessly. We all want intuitive interfaces, around-the-clock availability, personalized treatment, zero errors, and the lowest costs for everything we buy. You want your mortgage request to be preapproved in minutes. You expect us to have automated access to all the data you've provided earlier, and you don't want us to ask the same questions over and over again or to request the same documents over and over again. You wonder why we need a copy of your pay stub as proof of income when your money is being directly deposited into your checking account at the same bank where you made loan application. It doesn't make sense to you how we do the things we do and to some extent, you're right. There should be a better way.

While the mortgage industry has made some significant strides in digitization over the past twenty years, the complexity of the loan transaction and its subsequent servicing, make it very challenging for us to meet these borrower expectations. While dealing with regulatory issues and fraud concerns, the industry is trying to overhaul the entire process by specializing, cutting the number of manual steps required, and shortening turnaround times. While these changes in operating models, skill sets, and organizational structuring are attempting to allow for a better customer experience, roles are being redefined to match the reinvented processes. All of these changes are mostly happening in the backend of mortgage banking and are invisible to you. But you may be affected based on your interaction with mortgage distribution channels.

Distribution channels are the different ways we can originate a mortgage loan. In practice, many organizations use a mix of different channels that complement the direct, on the ground, foot soldier loan officers who are mostly dedicated to originating purchase transactions. In a refinance boom, distributed channels can easily pick up the volume on the less time-sensitive refinance transaction, leaving in-market loan officers to work with and support local purchase market activity by partnering with realtors to provide counseling and coaching to prospective homebuyers.

How Does the Distributed Business Model Affect You?

Back in the olden days, you'd be able to walk into a banking center and meet with a mortgage loan officer who would be able to offer you all the loan products that organization had available. Today, you walk into a banking center and you may not be able to even find a mortgage loan officer. When you do connect with one, that person may not be best able to match a loan product to your particular needs because that loan officer may have a limited set of product offerings to provide to you.

In their effort to supply best in class service, minimize overhead costs, and contain errors, many lenders have opted to specialize their loan officers based on the type of transaction. For example, if you call in and request a VA loan, which is a mortgage program offered by the U.S. Department of Veteran's Affairs available to current or prior members of the U.S. Armed Forces or their surviving spouses, you'll be transferred to a loan officer who specializes in VA loans. If you are moving because your employer is transferring you to another city and is picking up your relocation costs or has negotiated with a particular lender to provide you with expedited loan approval, you'll be transferred to a loan officer that specializes in corporate relocations. If you say that you are a foreign national buying a second home or an investment property in the U.S., you may be transferred to a loan officer who only handles foreign national loans. If you're looking for a reverse mortgage, you may be transferred to a loan officer that specializes in reverse mortgages. That's all wonderful because those particular loan programs have their specific nuances that require special handling of your loan request. But what if you call in and aren't sure about what you want and want to learn which loan programs or products you may be eligible? Who is going to see to it that you are placed into the right loan product for you?

While the distributed channels really took off with Internet banking and the refinance boom and can certainly be a profitable channel for the business, strict adherence to passing off a mortgage referral to another loan officer 2,000 miles away doesn't exactly sit well with you or your realtor because face-to-face meetings and local market knowledge are greatly valued by referral partners. And, for in-market loan officers who work on a commission basis and are unable to service their referral partners needs, although their institution does advertise a particular loan program but they themselves can't offer it, they will eventually lose those relationships to loan officers who can contain the relationship.

The Impact of Technology on Mortgage Banking

In a 2001 study by the Group of Ten on the impact of consolidation in the financial sectors, it was revealed that customers do not seem to view Internet banking as a substitute for banking with an institution that has physical branches (the full report is available online at www.bis. org/publ/gten05.htm). Households overwhelmingly select banking services from institutions located within a few miles of the customer. For some high-value and infrequently purchased banking products, you demand more than just online service, however personalized it may be. The evolution of the Internet has effectively made it so that all financial services can be supplied by electronic means. Without the need for physical branch offices, geographic limits to credit accessibility have essentially disappeared. Have you ever heard the phrase "All real estate is local"? Areas such as provinces, rural counties, cantons, or metropolitan areas usually approximate local markets. According to Inside Mortgage Finance Publications, many realtors express frustration when their clients deal with ecommerce lenders (full article available at http://cdn.insidemortgagefinance.com/media/pdfs/Campbell_08_22_14.pdf).

With more and more financial institutions offering multiple financial service products, there is an attempt to sell bundles of their products to its customers through cross-selling. In your loan disclosure set—which you'll be provided within three business days of making loan application— you'll be given a document that asks if you want to opt-out of marketing promotions from your lender or its affiliates. It's important to note here that while you may not want to be bombarded with sales solicitations, you need to know that your mortgage lender will routinely mine through their database to identify opportunities for refinancing existing customers into a lower interest rate product and if you have elected to opt-out of solicitations, you will not be contacted by the lender with their offer; the same applies for credit cards. For these reasons, you may want to opt-in.

Call Center Originations

Being convenient doesn't always equate to being simpler. If you live in California, how comfortable are you hiring an accountant that you've never met before who lives in Rhode Island? Not very, I imagine. If there are no accountants in California, then you have no choice. But if there is an accountant in your city of Los Angeles, would you really forego the benefit of sitting face-to-face with this financial service provider to save a few hundred bucks? Probably not.

A big part of the sales process is reading body language. In this fast-paced digital age, more and more people are making buying decisions without regard to locality. In a retailing study (available online at http://home.tm.tue.nl/ajong/JRarticle.pdf), it was found that the delivery of nonroutine financial services, such as mortgage consulting, is more likely to lead to a positive customer experience through a face-to-face interaction than routine services, such as credit applications, for which customers increasingly use Internet banking.

When in the initial discovery phase—where you and your loan officer are getting to know one another and your loan program options—if communication is handled solely via digital methods, this presents challenges for both your loan officer and you. Conducting financial service sales in this manner makes it very difficult to build trust in an environment that mutes body language, tone, and inflection. If an email is sent, word meanings are subject to the kind of day the receiver is having because words don't carry tone or inflection. If a text message is sent and doesn't receive an immediate reply, the sender assumes the message was read and gets upset about lack of response.

In addition to the trust building challenges of not having a face-to-face discovery meeting, most call center loan officers do not collect or review supporting documentation at application because doing so isn't in their business model. Without reviewing documentation prior to submission to loan processing, how can they possibly, accurately and completely, describe the loan characteristics of the file and help you select the right loan product, address potential issues, and minimize processing times? The same challenges apply to in-market loan officers who submit applications to back-office operations without first collecting and reviewing all required documentation.

Basing your selection of loan officer solely on who is advertising the lowest interest rate may not be the most effective way to decide your best representation in this high dollar transaction. If what you are really looking for is credible representation, then take the time to find the right match for you. As most loan applications require the collection of an application fee, I doubt that you'll want to apply with too many lenders. Consider your choices carefully. Is telephone convenience more important than a thorough review of your financial data and presentation of solutions for your specific challenges?

Internet Mortgage Banking

The Internet is filled with all kinds of information, some good and some bad. Avoid the trap of mortgage offers that claim to give you a loan approval within thirty-seconds. It's understandable that these offers can be quite appealing, and you may be enticed to give it a shot on your own because it sounds quick, easy, and cheap. But remember that there are few things in life that are quick, easy, cheap, and good for you. The thought process for selecting a financial service provider shouldn't be the same as the process we use when selecting the provider of a hairbrush.

While I've done my very best to present you with a plan of action to execute on whichever delivery channel you wish to pursue, if you decide that Internet mortgage banking is for you, and if you fail with this delivery channel, don't give up. Regroup and try again. Seek and obtain at least two recommendations to a specific loan officer from a trusted advisor. Your trusted advisor doesn't necessarily have to be related to the housing industry. This person should be someone of integrity whose opinion you value, who you trust or admire. Keep your ears and eyes open in the lunchroom. If you happen to overhear someone who is either going through or has just completed a mortgage transaction, ask them how their experience went, and whether they would recommend their provider to you. Be ready for an earful, good or bad.

Mortgage Loan Originator Distinctions

As it relates to the mortgage industry, the Dodd-Frank Act was enacted to protect the consumer from many things, including receiving loan-related information from persons unauthorized to represent the lender. By law, if a bank employee is not registered with the National Mortgage Licensing System (NMLS), he cannot discuss interest rates with you, period. So don't get mad if you walk into a bank lobby and ask what today's rate is on a thirty-year fixed rate loan, and they instruct you to schedule an appointment to speak with the loan representative.

Those who work for an insured depository (bank), or its owned or controlled subsidiary that is regulated by a federal banking agency, or for an institution regulated by the Farm Credit Administration, are required to have their loan officer's simply register with the NMLS. All other nonbank mortgage loan originators are required to be individually licensed by the states in which they wish to transact business. One of the things that should matter to you in the process of applying for a mortgage is that the person to whom you give your loan data is the same person whose NMLS identification is listed in Section X—Information for Government

Monitoring Purposes on your loan application (find out more about Section X in chapter 10). If it doesn't match, this is an indication that you've fallen into the hands of a person who is not licensed or registered to discuss loan options or that your loan was re-assigned by your lender to another loan officer. To verify whether the person you are communicating with regarding a home loan is authorized by law to do so, conduct a search for them by name or using their NMLS identification at www.nmlsconsumeraccess.org.

Loan Officer Compensation

Generally speaking, loan officers work on a base salary or hourly wage and receive commission income on a per transaction basis. Through the Qualified Mortgage Rule under the Dodd-Frank Act, compensation is prohibited under any term of the mortgage loan that can be altered, amended, or omitted by the loan officer. Basing compensation as a percentage of the loan amount is the acceptable and, in fact, the recommended way to establish compensation plans. Minimum and maximum flat dollar amounts are also acceptable and customary on a compensation plan that is otherwise based on loan amount. Therefore, the loan officer's earned income on your transaction is predetermined based on their employment contract and does not vary based on the loan program you choose. This provides you with a greater comfort level in knowing that your selection of loan program is not biased based on the loan officer's compensation. If your loan application does not close, the loan officer receives no compensation on your transaction.

Whether you are dealing directly with a creditor or through a mortgage broker, know that all loan related charges on a qualified mortgage are capped by law. The dollar limits are adjusted annually for inflation and published each year in the commentary to Regulation Z. (See § 1026.43(e)(3)(ii) and accompanying Commentary available at: http://www.consumerfinance. gov/eregulations/1026-43/2013-30108_20150718#1026-43-e-3.)

Mortgage Broker vs. Direct Lender

A mortgage broker is a company with channels to many different lenders. A loan officer is either an employee of a creditor (direct lender)—whether a bank or a nonbank, or an employee of a mortgage broker. For consistency and clarity of position, the law requires the profession be addressed as mortgage loan originators (MLOs) but throughout the book, I will refer to an individual loan originator as "loan officer".

Quite frankly, the functions of a loan officer are no different whether we work for a creditor or for a mortgage broker. Having worked at banks, nonbanks, and a brokerage, I can tell you that where we hang our license is irrelevant to the level of support that we provide to our clients when evaluating loan programs, completing the loan application, and shepherding them through the loan approval maze. As a matter of fact, the Consumer Financial Protection Bureau doesn't distinguish between what you should look out for when working with either a creditor or a mortgage broker. (You can find their prospective borrower expectations at http:// files.consumerfinance.gov/f/201401_cfpb_mortgages_consumer-summary-new-mortgage.pdf.)

The Value of the Broker Model

Loan officers for mortgage brokers take your information and shop your loan with different creditors. As such, they are able to offer you a wider array of loan products, eliminating your need to make application with different lenders, pay several application fees, or miss out on the home buying experience altogether because you've been declined by the restrictions of one particular lender's policies through overlays. They do the homework for you. Brokerages typically can't duplicate the cost efficiencies of larger lenders and as a result, their fixed costs are slightly higher. Are you willing to pay extra for their service?

When you need a gallon of milk, do you drive to Costco to get the best cost per gallon of milk, or do you make the decision to drive up to the window of your local farm store and ask the attendant to deliver it to your car even though it costs more? When you need to find a pair of shoes to match the dress you just bought for an event coming up in three days, do you spend a full day at the mall carrying your dress with you to find the perfect pair at the lowest price; or do you log on to Zappos.com at 10p.m., find five that you like—priced at retail—and have them delivered to your home the next day with "guaranteed free shipping and returns" in the hopes of choosing one and returning the rest? We make financial decisions based on the perceived value of the service provided. Your choice of mortgage provider should not be exclusively cost driven.

Mortgage Industry Complaints

The newly formed Consumer Financial Protection Bureau (CFPB) began collecting consumer complaints about the mortgage industry on December 1, 2011. Between December 1, 2011, and June 30, 2014, the CFPB received approximately 134,300 consumer complaints related to mortgages. Fifty-six percent of these complaints involved problems consumers face when they are unable to make payments, such as issues relating to loan modifications, collections, or foreclosures. Twenty-six percent of these complaints address issues related to making payments to include loan servicing, payments, or escrow accounts. Eight percent of these complaints addressed mortgage application issues related to interest rate-lock agreements, such as lenders refusing to honor rate-locks or assessing penalties when the loan does not close. (See the July 2014 full report here: http://files.consumerfinance.gov/f/201407_cfpb_report_consumer-complaint-snapshot.pdf)

As we'll learn in chapter 5, in the section titled, "Why Do I Keep Receiving Copies of the Good Faith/Loan Estimate?" there are many unknown variables at the time of mortgage application that affect final loan pricing. Without understanding these variables, one will undoubtedly become frustrated when final pricing offered changes substantially from an initial quote received—when no lender explanation is provided. There is no penalty charged for not closing a loan. However, a lender will expect payment for third-party fees disclosed at loan application and agreed upon by the applicant through their issuance of consent to proceed. These fees typically include credit report, application, and appraisal fees. In the "Issuing Your Consent" section in chapter 9, you'll learn specific events for which the lender is required to record your approval in order to proceed with the next step in the loan process.

The Value of Discovery

Let's flash forward a bit to a time where you've read through this book, gathered all your documentation, reviewed loan programs, and scheduled an appointment with a loan officer. You have a pretty good idea of the loan program you want and are ready to make application. You don't want to waste your time being "sold to" because you've already done your research. All that you want to know is how much it's going to cost to go with a particular lender. I'm going to share with you why this line of thinking would be a mistake.

Entrepreneur, author, lawyer, business consultant, and Realtor, Stacey Alcorn shares the value of discovery. In her March 9, 2014, blog post, "Your Customer Has No Idea" (www.staceyalcorn. com/customers) she writes about the experience of shopping for a new pair of sneakers to train for a marathon. When she arrived at the store, she knew exactly what she wanted, or at least she thought she did—something "sleek, colorful, and comfortable." By allowing herself to engage with the sneaker salesperson, she shared her intended use for the sneakers and was educated on the different options based on tread, materials, and price range. When it came time to make her buying decision, Stacey felt confident she had selected the right pair of sneakers—even though they were completely different from what she had walked in thinking she needed.

The point is this: There may be something better for you than what you think you need, but you won't learn about it if you close yourself off from being "sold to." While loan officers are salespeople, our value isn't tied to interest rates and neither is our compensation tied to your selection of loan program. The true measure of our value is based on whether or not we are able to establish a rapport that allows you to share your needs and concerns, and allows us to bridge the gaps between what you think you need and what is available to you, presenting possible solutions and educating you on the features and benefits—thereby allowing you to make an informed decision.

Mortgages are high-ticket items and the cost of selecting the wrong program can be in the tens of thousands of dollars. But this is important for you to know, you can only make application under one loan program with any specific lender. Ideally, you could submit a general application for a mortgage loan and selection of a particular program would be determined by an analysis of your loan data and you'd be provided a list of features, benefits and costs to base your loan program selection. Unfortunately, the complexity of a mortgage combined with regulatory compliance on the timing of delivery of loan disclosures and adherence to fee tolerances, make it effectively impossible for lenders to apply the technological advances that would automatically identify your available program options and signal the benefits and costs associated for your analysis. So how will you know which program is right for you?

Hopefully, you've connected with a loan officer who listens more than they speak. In most relationships, it takes some time for people to get to know one another because you're both looking to see whether the other person can be trusted. With your loan officer, your journey of trust doesn't have the benefit of time so don't doubt revealing too much about yourself up-front. If you think something about you is important for the loan officer to know, say so.

When we hear you tell us about something that is unfavorable—which every file has at some level—we acknowledge your fear about how it might present an issue in the mortgage process, but we attempt to do so without passing judgment on the behavior. This is critical, because if at the first sign of a possible issue, we stop the flow of the conversation to address the behavior, we've inadvertently made you feel anxious about communicating other possible issues and we don't want that to happen. It is for this same reason that psychologists never sit directly in front of their patients; they don't want their natural bodily reactions to negative comments to interrupt their patients sharing of information. If you've found yourself one of the better loan officers and had an effortless conversation, by the end of the initial discovery appointment, I bet 95 percent of your questions will have been answered without your needing to ask them.

In the interest of time, I prefer to begin the process of discovery with potential clients by scheduling a ten-minute telephone interview where I ask several questions to get a general depiction of their needs and their employment, income, and asset profile. I pretty much ask for everything except their Social Security number and date of birth, as these are only relevant if they are ready to proceed with loan application. When I identify a red flag or something that will bring an underwriter pause, I'll pry a little deeper to develop a better understanding of how to properly document the concern so that little room is left for the underwriter to question anything. Before we hang up, I give them a general idea of the supporting documentation they will need to have ready for loan application. Often they're eager to deliver these documents right away, but I put off delivery until they've had the opportunity to review loan solutions and are ready to move forward. With their general information at hand, I'm able to research program options and put together a few preapplication cost estimates for their review.

Once the client has reviewed program features, benefits, and costs, selected a loan program, and is ready to proceed with loan application (usually within forty-eight hours), I then ask for the Social Security number and date of birth along with the delivery of the supporting documentation. This method has provided my clients with the fewest discrepancies between the initial and the final loan application and the least downtime between initial discovery, formal application, delivery of conditional loan commitment, and issuance of final loan commitment. Once you've followed the suggestions on the Supply List and the Comprehensive Documentation Checklist found in the "Resources" section, you're ready for loan application.

Tip: Whenever a discovery interview is scheduled, be certain that your attention is 100 percent dedicated to the topic at hand. If either of you interrupt the flow of the conversation to pick up a call or return an email or handle any kind of interruption, your attention is distracted and you may forget to go over a very important step in the evaluation of your needs.

Owner of the Client Experience

Loan officers don't actually sell a thing; we sell a concept. We sell you on the concept that we are going to place you in the right loan product, make ourselves available throughout the process to expedite the deciding of your loan, and meet your anticipated closing date. No loan officer can promise you a loan approval; it isn't within their power to do so, and there are too many variables at the time of loan application that can delay the decision.

According to the CFPB, as many as 70 percent of borrowers for home purchase choose their lender or broker before deciding on a type of loan (see the full report here: http://files. consumerfinance.gov/f/201501_cfpb_consumers-mortgage-shopping-experience.pdf).   This makes sense as without expert guidance, borrowers find it very difficult to know what loan programs are available to them. In choosing your lending partner, there are many factors to take into consideration. Sure, advertised interest rates are a compelling factor, but you don't yet know all the loan level pricing adjustments that come into play and what interest rate you're eligible to receive, which will undoubtedly be different from what is advertised.

Loan officers don't set interest rates; we can only influence your preparedness for the process. Partner with someone who offers clear explanations, has a credible reputation (testimonials are key), and offers personalized support. Be vocal about your mortgage concerns and your past lending experiences, because this helps us identify what really matters to you. Keep in mind that you're developing a relationship with a loan officer and not with a brand.

Realtors are excellent sources of information for assessing neighborhood trends and connecting service providers within the housing industry. If you're not already working with a realtor, do your due diligence and start a connection. With the constant fluctuation of interest rates and changing underwriting guidelines, realtors and homebuyers need the educational assistance of loan officers more than ever. Realtors are loyal to loan officers who provide value, performance, and superb communications, above all else. Ask any realtor for a referral, and they will give you the name of a loan officer and not that of a bank or of a mortgage company. The distinction might seem benign to you, but it is loan officers, after all, who typically return their calls.

What Can You Expect?

Hands down, the loan officer owns the client experience. Our relationship with you is much like an intense love affair at first. For a good three weeks or so, we are running at full throttle, with high touch and high trust. As with any relationship, when you each understand what you want from the other, the excitement wanes. When the initial loan commitment is issued and review of those conditions indicates a full commitment is on the horizon, less communication is needed between you and your loan officer, but more is needed between you and the loan processor. Typically, loan officers re-engage with their borrowers when the appraisal comes in, when the conditional loan commitment is issued, when the closing has been scheduled, and when the final settlement statement is approved. When the transaction is closed, the affair is over. We may see each other out on the town and exchange niceties and updates on the family, but otherwise, we typically only reconnect every three to five years for a mortgage check up unless you send us a referral for a new client, and we'll certainly reconnect with gratitude.

According to PricewaterhouseCoopers, fees and terms only drive 10 percent of positive memorable mortgage experiences, while the loan officer drives almost half. No matter if your loan file is approvable or not, the number one thing you want is consistent and timely communication. This is the factor that absolutely determines your impression of the mortgage process. Good news, bad news, or no news, you want to know. Some issues require a longer period of resolution and frequent updates help everyone stay on task. Sometimes loan officers avoid making difficult calls because, quite frankly, who wants to? The better loan officers may opt to sit on an issue for a little while until they can investigate all options before calling you with challenging news. If at all possible, they try to find resolution without involving you. However, many times a simple phone call to address an underwriting concern provides clarity, and together you can brainstorm how to properly document your loan file to support resolution.

Everything Begins with a Date

Our favorite way to meet a potential new client is through the introduction of a mutual acquaintance. The majority of mortgage leads come to us from referral partners such as realtors, accountants, commercial bankers, financial advisors, and attorneys. It turns out that most people who rely on the advice of the preceding group of professionals are also savvy business owners or senior level managers. Here's the interesting thing about that: While this group of people is usually more educated on financial products and services, they know that they can find a reputable loan officer on their own, but instead they use their connections to gain a recommendation from a trusted advisor to expedite the selection process. How is this helpful to you?

The hardest thing that we must overcome in our initial contact with you is your fear that we are trying to sell you something that you don't really need or want. So if someone else tells you from personal experience that a loan officer is awesome and is great and is going to get you to closing on time, it saves you both time spent on removing the barriers of sales resistance. As a result, you can have an effortless conversation, allowing your loan officer to uncover your true needs and present you with options that will satisfy those needs.

While it is impossible for us to truly educate you about every single challenge that you might face along the way, it is within our control to mitigate your exposure by doing a better job of making sure your particular situation is properly represented on the loan application. By taking a complete and thorough loan application and requiring you to submit supporting documentation within forty-eight hours of application, your loan officer is empowered to uncover potential hazards and address these up front. Without the documentation, we can't review potential issues with usable assets, we can't calculate qualifying income, we can't cross reference program eligibility, and we can't effectively communicate your story to the underwriter. To paraphrase Jerry Maguire, "You must let us, help you."

The better loan officers are up-front and honest about the process and will set proper expectations on timeliness with you. Do they provide you with qualifying remarks based on their preapplication cost estimates by stating the variables that will affect final pricing such as usable credit score, valuation of property, property type, and debt-to-income ratio? Do they set the expectation as to when you will hear from them again? Your homework as a loan applicant is not to seek out the cheapest advertised interest rate; it is to seek your storyteller.

Tip: While you are interviewing potential loan officers, pay attention to whether they are predictable. Do they meet with you at the designated time? Do they call you back by end of business? Do they provide you with preapplication cost estimates within the timetable they set? Do they follow up to address any questions? Predictability shows a respect for your time, and it naturally follows that if both of you have a respect for each others time, in all likelihood, your partnership will get your loan decided quickly and to the closing table on the date anticipated.

Methods of Communication

In any business transaction, and especially in the mortgage process, all important communications are best handled in person. That said, we must rely on digital communications to expedite action to keep the constraints of distance from eating up time. As a loan officer's network expands, so does the physical distance between them and their connections. As I began exploring the psychology of trust in a digital world, I felt the need to be seen by my own advisors. I know that to establish trust and uncover needs, there are things in our advisor/client relationships that we use to build rapport and chemistry, and we want to be sure our trusted advisors are able to read our body language, hear our tone and the inflection in our voice so that there are no miscues. If at all possible, really and truly, meet with your loan officer for a face-to-face conversation. If it is not physically possible for you to do so, then try Skype.

Years ago when I had a client meeting and saw that they pulled out a list of questions, I would sigh in agony thinking it was going to be a very long appointment. It wasn't until I began partnering with my own mentors, coaches, and advisors—reversing my advisor/client role—that I realized this list was not an indication of ignorance, but an indication that they respected my time. When working with your advisors, you have questions or ideas that pop up throughout the day, and while you may be inclined to quickly jump to communicate, resist that temptation to drop a quick note or text message. Manage your need to communicate by keeping notes until your next scheduled meeting. Here are some tried and true processes that seem to work for both my clients and me:

1. Schedule appointments to communicate (either in person or teleconference).
2. Define communication preferences.
3. Acknowledge receipt of an email/voicemail, even if we don't have the answer.
4. Send a test email before sending critical information.
5. Provide instructions on how to access documents that are sent via the lenders secure email delivery system.
6. Always deliver sensitive documents via a secure system.

On Expectations

Let's face it, loan officers are not cardiothoracic surgeons. That said, we understand that your loan file is of critical importance to you—and to us. Our daily functions have activities both inside and outside of the office, so recognize that we may not pick up the phone on each ring and we may not respond to every email within ten minutes of receiving it. A realistic expectation is that your loan officer or loan processor returns your call by the end of the business day, even if they don't have the answer to your question. Unresponsiveness is usually attributed to not having your answer, and unresponsiveness is what leads to most customer service issues in mortgage lending.

In many instances, the answer you're waiting on is coming from a third party (underwriter, appraiser, closer, etc.) we have no control over, and we are just as annoyed by the lack of response as you are. Still, we are the face of the organization, and we are expected to make that call even if it's just to say, "We have nothing."

Loan officers are trained to be über-effective planners of our day. For many years, I was a faithful user of the FranklinCovey planning system and carried my planner everywhere. Every aspect of my life was in it, including rate sheets, a one-sheet for each pending transaction that listed all parties involved and important contract dates, contacts, business and personal goals, favorite quotes, timelines for yearly exams, school schedules, national and international time zones, sales activities, and production reports. There was visual confirmation at the end of every day that all tasks were completed and I was able to prepare the next day's to-do list after I'd followed up on pending new business. I time-blocked every activity and planned out each day, each week, each month, and each year.

In 2009, I bought my first smartphone and that was the end of smart time management for me. We can all get easily distracted by shiny objects. With information and alerts coming at us in all directions, it makes it very difficult for any of us to slide on the smartphone and do the one thing that we picked it up to do. The telephone rings or we receive a text message, and now that the phone is in our hands, we scroll through emails, then we look at social media, and then we start surfing the net and order something we didn't really need.

Because of these constant distractions, there is a part of the loan officer's day where all communications are shut down. We do this either when we are with a client or when we are knee deep in structuring a complex file. In either of these two scenarios, if we divert our attention to a phone call or a text or an email or a walk in client, we will invariably miss an important detail of your loan file. For this reason, we schedule bursts of time for client contact throughout the day, and we strive to get back to your communication by end of business.

On Texting

In mortgage, please forget that texting is an option, even if it is offered. Much can be misinterpreted in texting and delays are costly. If you text us a question in the regular course of a business day, you may inevitably become upset by the lack of an immediate response, but don't.

On Email

Very few people resort to email to communicate important information in your personal relationships. I avoid it for business transactions as well, and here's why: My greatest breakdowns in communications have always come from failing to clearly deliver my message in an email.

What I thought was a cut and dry communication was interpreted by the reader as something completely other than what I intended. Or I fail in delivering my message because I become so determined to be understood that I wrote a fifteen-page essay that no one wants to read. Knowing this, I use email to document conversations I've had instead of using email to have conversations.

I've encountered a few people who hide behind email to avoid real conversations and this can also be extremely unsettling and disruptive to workflow. We all have busy schedules. If the answer isn't yes, no, or maybe, we're better off picking up the phone. If we need ten minutes of someone's time, send a quick email asking to schedule a teleconference and state the topic of the call and the expected time needed.

In mortgage operations, there is constant email frenzy throughout the day and well into the night. Our industry has resorted to this method of internal communication so that every conversation can be documented and we don't interrupt our partners' focus. Because we try to limit flowery words in business communication, we often sound abrupt in our emails. If you receive an email you don't understand, pick up the phone.

On Voicemail

I love voicemail when used properly because it conveys tone and inflection. That said, playing phone tag is a horrible waste of everyone's time. When you reach someone's voicemail, do your best to leave a clear message identifying the nature of the call and provide your availability for a return call. Don't be that person who calls nine times, doesn't leave a message, and then is angry that you didn't receive a call back. If there is no message, understand that the recipient may not have caller identification and there should be no expectation of a return call.

04 Basic Concepts of Mortgage Lending

In this chapter, you'll learn about how mortgage loans are priced, how lenders assess risk, key differences between loan eligibility and loan pricing, the definition of mortgage and note, and options for low down payments.

Interest Rates and Loan Pricing

EVERYONE WANTS TO receive the lowest terms on their mortgage, but unfortunately, not everyone manages their finances in a way that enables them to qualify for the best terms or meet the lending requirements of the GSEs. Loan officers don't set interest rates. There is an entire world of secondary market professionals who are dedicated to following market movements. When shopping for a home loan, you will typically call a lender and ask for current interest rates. Our response isn't a simple read off a chart.

The initial interest rate quoted is based on several initial facts and assumptions that include your assumed credit score, intended occupancy, desired loan amount, and the expected valuation of the property to determine the loan-to-value ratio. This is subject to change by market movements up until the point you lock in the interest rate and by the subsequent verification of previously assumed data. In the section "Why Do I Keep Receiving Copies of the Good Faith/ Loan Estimate?" found in chapter 5, I provide scenarios that impact the final pricing of your loan.

Interest rates are expressed in increments of 0.125 percentage points. Origination points, which represent the cost of a particular interest rate, are expressed as a percentage of the loan amount and can range from positive to negative. Higher origination points provide a lower interest rate; low or negative origination points equate to a higher interest rate. When positive, you will pay the fee at closing; when negative you will receive a lender credit towards your closing costs.

Interest rates offered vary based on credit score and loan eligibility standards. The interest rate you are charged is referred to as the primary mortgage market rate and consists of both set and variable factors. The variable factor is the intraday fluctuation of interest rates in the secondary mortgage market. Using the base secondary market rate at the starting point, your lender will add the fee for the GSE insurance (g-fee), loan level pricing adjustments, a servicing spread to cover the cost of servicing your mortgage loan through its term, and an originator spread, which is the lender's revenue.

Many lenders will allow you to lock your interest rate at loan application, while a few only allow you to lock the interest rate upon full loan approval. When we lock your loan and you don't close the transaction with us either through loan denial or your withdrawal, we call this measure fall-out. Fall-out presents a risk for creditors as we try to hedge the delivery of your loan to our investors. As we learned in the overview of the U.S. housing market, through forward commitments investors trade promises to deliver mortgage-backed securities at fixed dates into the future. Fall-out affects our ability to deliver on our commitment.

As these forward commitments are traded in the to-be-announced market, the intraday value of the coupons affects the price you are quoted at any particular time during a given day. While interest rates typically remain stable for extended periods of time, what changes is the number of origination points that you will be asked to pay to obtain the quoted rate. For this reason, it's unreasonable to compare an interest rate and points that you were quoted by one lender on Monday with that of another lender whose quote was received on Thursday. You need an instant quote from both lenders to truly compare apples to apples.

Mortgage Eligibility: The Five Cs of Underwriting

Whether you are eligible for a mortgage is primarily dependent on five equally important measurements. The five Cs of underwriting are the cornerstone to lending philosophy. Each loan request is measured by evaluating the condition of the collateral (property) you wish to finance, your capital investment into the transaction (down payment), your credit habits in meeting your past debt obligations (credit score), your capacity to repay the debt (income), and the overall stability of your financial character.

An underwriter performs a comprehensive evaluation of the five Cs of credit, weighing each factor based on the amount of risk it presents the likelihood that you will repay your debt on a timely basis. When we look at your creditworthiness, we are reviewing credit history, delinquent accounts, mortgage accounts, revolving credit utilization, public records, foreclosures, collection accounts, and inquiries. When we evaluate your noncredit risk factors, we are looking at the equity and loan-to-value, liquid reserves, loan purpose, loan term, loan amortization type, occupancy type, total expense ratio, property type, and co-borrowers.

Not all lenders are alike, not all lenders offer the same loan programs, and not all lenders can accommodate your request. Each has overlays that are more conservative guidelines than what the GSEs require. For example, HUD will guaranty an FHA loan with a credit score as low as 500. If mortgage stakeholders make the determination that they believe that a person who manages their credit history with a resulting FICO score below 640 is bound to be delinquent on their mortgage payment, then that lender will place an overlay to FHA's guidelines on their internal program guidelines to state they restrict lending to borrowers with a credit score above

640 or 620 or 700 or whatever score the stakeholders feel is a safer, more manageable risk for their organization. It is for this reason, that a borrower can be denied by one lender and approved by another when nothing about the borrower has changed.

Tip: Ask your loan officer what credit overlays the loan product you are considering has and how they may affect you. If their credit overlays will negatively impact your ability to obtain a mortgage with that particular lender, seek a referral to another lender that doesn't have such stringent overlays, or ideally take the time to improve your credit profile if your eligibility has been impacted by a low credit score.

Collateral

Collateral is the strength of the property itself. The better shape the home is in and the higher the value of the home compared to the amount you are paying for it, the better. The amount you are borrowing compared to the value of the home or purchase price (whichever is less) determines your loan-to-value ratio. An appraisal is one of the tools that will be used to assess the value of the property. Lenders look at whether the property is owner occupied (do you/will you live there?) or if it is to be an investment and rented for income purposes. Is the property a single family residence, condominium, or townhome? Is the property located in a metropolitan neighborhood or a rural area? Is it a single-unit or multifamily dwelling? The lender considers all these factors when assessing the marketability of your property. Marketability of the home tells a lender how long it will take them to find a new buyer should they have to take back the property in foreclosure.

Capital

Capital is the value of liquid assets (cash or funds that are easily converted into cash) that you currently hold. When purchasing a home, your capital investment along with the property valuation determines your loan-to-value ratio, which takes your loan amount and divides it by the value of your property. Your down payment, or really the amount of skin you have in the game, identifies how much you personally have at risk should you default in your payments to the lender. Capital in excess of down payment and closing costs, demonstrates that you have a propensity to save and accumulate assets and that you are more likely to keep up with your mortgage payments. The more capital you have, the less risk you represent.

Lenders view your investment in capital as your commitment to the stability of homeownership. A lender's maximum allowable loan-to-value ratio varies by loan program and is based on a number of factors, including the representative credit score, the type of mortgage product, the number of dwelling units, and your occupancy status. The higher your down payment, the more flexible a lender can be with other aspects of your loan file, because it is believed that you are less likely to walk away from an investment that you have placed your own hard-earned funds into. For example, let's say you've had some recent job changes that would indicate instability of employment. The loan program you are requesting allows up to a minimum down payment of 5 percent, but you are electing to place an initial down payment of 25 percent. That additional amount is considered a compensating factor and will provide some comfort to offset the weakness of instability of employment.

After you've made the capital investment, a lender will identify what money remains. We call the money outside of the loan transaction reserves or post-closing liquidity. Having reserve funds gives the lender some peace of mind in knowing that should you encounter financial hardship for a brief period of time, you'll be able to dip into your savings to meet your monthly financial obligations and avoid falling behind. Without reserves, you present a higher risk to the lender, but this doesn't exclude you from homeownership because some loan programs don't require that you have any reserves at all.

Credit

Because a mortgage is a considerable amount of money, it only makes sense that a lender will review how well you've responded to your past debt obligations by reviewing your credit history. What are your payment habits? Do you pay your bills on time? Aside from whether you make your payments on time, some other factors that affect your credit rating are how much of your available credit you use. We call this measure credit utilization. If your card balances are greater than 85 percent of the total credit available on all revolving accounts, if an account has gone to collection, or if there have been multiple inquiries into your credit, these occurrences will result in a lower credit score. We use your credit score to indicate the likelihood you will make your mortgage payment on time. The higher your credit score, the more favorable you appear to the lender.

A credit score is simply a snapshot in time. Higher credit scores will allow your lender to provide you with the lowest offered interest rate because you present a lower risk of making late payments, and you will reap the benefit from having maintained an excellent credit history by having lower interest costs over the life of your loan. There are challenges for those with no credit histories or with poor credit histories and we take a closer look at how to best handle those situations in the section "Why Managing Your Credit Matters Most" in chapter 6.

Capacity

Your capacity to repay the debt is determined by assessing your qualifying income or debt-to-income ratio and identifying the residual income that remains. A lender believes that the more money you have left over at the end of every month (i.e., your disposable or residual income), the more likely you are to build sound financial habits by setting aside a portion of those extra funds for savings. The lender's focus here is on how you receive your income. Whether you are salaried, commissioned, self-employed, full time, or part time are factors used to determine what types of documents are required to confirm your stable earnings which are likely to continue to assess the probability—as a measure of your capacity—to successfully repay the mortgage.

Qualifying ratios are basic mathematical formulas that we use in the loan approval process. Maximum qualifying ratios will vary from lender to lender, and by simply selecting a more risk-averse lender, you may be making the mistake of inadvertently disqualifying yourself from homeownership. The GSEs post their guidelines publicly on their websites, but individual lending organizations do not. Lenders only release their guidelines and overlays to licensees who are authorized to conduct business with them, and this is unfortunate for you. Lenders who offer application services through the Internet make the presumption that you, the consumer, will know whether you are eligible for a loan product, and yet they don't tell you their guidelines. Excluding the advising function only has the potential to benefit the lender (through reduced origination costs) and not the consumer, simply because you aren't made aware of their specific credit guidelines and may make application for a loan program you aren't qualified for, and you won't be made aware of another loan program that might be a better fit for you.

Qualifying ratios are made up of two numerical values: the front-end ratio and the back-end ratio. The front-end ratio takes your monthly principal, interest, taxes, insurance, and association dues (PITIA), if any, and divides this by your monthly qualifying income. The back-end ratio takes your PITIA plus your recurring monthly liabilities and divides this amount by your monthly qualifying income. As a rule of thumb, the most conservative approach to qualifying ratios says debt-to-income ratio's should not exceed 28/36 percent—meaning that your total housing payment could not exceed 28 percent of your gross monthly income and the total of your recurring monthly debts (including the housing payment) could not exceed 36 percent of your monthly gross income. For a lender to meet the eligibility standards of the Qualified Mortgage rule, it may allow a maximum back-end ratio of 43 percent. Many loan programs are available as non-QM programs, which may allow for a much higher debt-to-income ratio.

Tip: As you begin conversations with your referred loan officers and preliminary calculations are made, ask what their maximum qualifying ratios are on the loan program they are reviewing with you. If you don't fall under a 43 percent back-end ratio, ask if they have another loan program that you may be eligible for.

Character

Character is a little misleading; it actually involves an overall subjective review of your loan application and credit history to assess your ability and willingness to meet your financial obligations in a timely manner. In other words, we are looking to determine your financial character—just like you would when a friend asks you to loan him $200 until the end of the week. Your education and work experience will be factors, along with job stability, career trajectory, length of time at your current residence, and how well you've managed the timely payments on the access to credit you have been given in the past. Additionally, maintaining a life insurance policy indicates that you care about the burden your financial obligations present to the heirs of your estate. Different lenders evaluate character differently.

Mortgage Underwriting Processes

Mortgage underwriting is the process of evaluating the five Cs of underwriting and approving or denying a loan. In today's world, there are two types of underwriting methods. The traditional method of review is considered manual underwriting; it is performed exclusively by humans and was considered the gold standard for many years. The second method is an automated underwriting process. Automation changed mortgage banking, and I'd like to share with you the progression so that you can have a better understanding of where we sit today.

A Little History on Loan Officers

The term loan officer no longer means what it used to as recently as the 80s. Back then, you would walk into your local thrift and make application with a bank officer who typically held a college degree and had the credit authority to underwrite your loan and decide whether you were creditworthy. That person—the loan officer—would take your loan application, review your loan documents, make a decision, and fund your loan. At that time, lenders strictly adhered to a debt-to-income ratio of 28/36. In the late 80s, many depository institutions decided to separate the loan application function from the underwriting function and loan officers became a designation for salespeople while underwriters were tasked to review the creditworthiness of applicants.

When I joined the business in 1993, there was only manual underwriting in existence. Loan production offices had in-house processors, underwriters, closers, sales managers, and operations managers. Typewriters were used and desktop computer software programs were limited to word processing functions. All clients required face-to-face meetings and these would typically last one to two hours because we would look at all documentation together. The client would have to bring original documents, and I would make copies from the originals and stamp them "True and Certified" and add my initials. All loan disclosures required original signatures in blue ink. Processes are very different today.

At that time, mortgage brokers were also in existence, but they dealt primarily with the subprime market in hard-money lending. That is, they connected borrowers who didn't qualify for prime loans (saleable to the GSEs) with private investors who were willing to lend them money at a much higher interest rate with terms that usually included prepayment penalties and a balloon payment after five to seven years, as these were typically considered short-term funds. And then something interesting happened. Depository institutions decided to further their reach by having retail channels and wholesale channels. While their loan officers would offer depository clients mortgages through the retail channel, lenders began allowing mortgage brokers to bring them new prime rate–worthy business through wholesale channels. The mortgage broker was no longer limited to subprime offerings. Then and now, the mortgage broker must be licensed to conduct business within the state where they are originating loans and loan officers employed by depository institutions are authorized to conduct business in any state where their employer is licensed.

Technology Changed Everything

With the introduction of FICO scoring and technological advances in 1996, automated underwriting systems (AUS) were developed by the GSEs using their guidelines and computer-based algorithms to speed processing, remove subjective human judgment, apply uniform standards of creditworthiness, and evaluate the layering of risks. Fannie Mae's system is called Desktop Underwriter and Freddie Mac's is Loan Prospector. These systems employ artificial intelligence with a predictive model that assigns a quantitative risk factor to individual mortgage applications. Based on the application data and the credit report information, the system generates a findings report. AUS does not approve or disapprove loans; it merely determines a risk classification and some loans may be referred back to manual underwriting. Introduction of AUS dramatically changed the way lenders processed the financing of homes.

Much faith is placed upon the accuracy of the data entered on the loan application, and following AUS recommendations, the system allows for documentation waivers based on risk classification. We call this lender-directed reduced documentation. To utilize AUS, a lender first enters your data from the loan application into its computer system. The information is then transmitted to a central computer, which integrates your credit report. The automated underwriting system weighs all information to determine the likelihood that the loan will repay as agreed, based on the way similar mortgages with comparable borrower, property, and loan characteristics have performed in the past. Default probabilities grow when multiple risk factors are present in an application, which we refer to as "layering of risk."

The approval recommendation issued by AUS is a binding commitment on the part of the GSEs, provided that the information that is in their systems is validated or determined to be accurate and documented by an underwriter. With an initial findings report, one can feel fairly confident that their loan will be funded if their loan data is accurately represented and supported by factual documentation. But even when AUS offers a recommendation for approval, it is always up to the lender's underwriter to make the final decision as whether to approve or deny a loan.

Mortgage Professionals vs. Data Entry Clerks

With the simplicity of automation, many depository institutions began allowing nonmortgage professionals within their organization to originate loans. This meant that the person who opened your checking account was also deemed qualified to take your mortgage application after completing an online course in data entry for the lender's mortgage origination software. Lenders determined that they could save thousands of dollars in origination costs by having clerks offer reduced documentation loans instead of having mortgage professionals conduct a thorough analysis of the borrower's financial profile, but boy oh boy, did we ever pay the price.

As the industry moved from a customer-centric model to a manufacturing model where you, the client, are just one small piece of the bigger picture, risk was elevated. Bill McBride runs CalculatedRiskBlog.com and offers commentary on many finance and economic topics. During the financial crisis, mortgage industry insider Doris Dungey contributed several incisive and accurate articles to the blog under the pseudonym Tanta (you can read them at www.calculatedriskblog.com/p/doris-tanta-dungey.html). She wrote biting commentary on the complicated motivations of primary market participants and secondary market participants who placed an irrational faith in both borrowers and originators to tell the truth when every incentive in the system encouraged participants to misrepresent. She shares that, "Had we insisted on knowledgeable, well-trained, fiduciary loan officers and brokers, that would have been OK." Instead, the industry switched to a manufacturing model. "If you're brave, you can go to a website and take your own application (be sure to give yourself good advice), after which you will have contact not with a broker or a loan officer but with a "customer service representative" who may or may not share your continent." (Read the full article at: www.calculatedriskblog.com/2007/09/mortgage-origination-channels-for.html.)

Lenders who changed the business model certainly increased their volume, but at what long-term costs? Not only did they suffer through buybacks for misrepresentation and fraud, but they also subjected themselves to the sufferings from reputational risk. Reputational risk refers to the risk that a company is not socially responsible, fails to comply with governance, or lacks transparency to its community and stakeholders. While automation certainly produces volume in a refinance environment, this manufacturing model doesn't take into account the value of relationships. Purchase-oriented business is driven by relationships within communities.

AUS: Choosing Freddie or Fannie

Some lenders only sell their conforming loans to Fannie Mae, others sell their conforming loans only to Freddie Mac, and others still, sell to both. When the lender is selling to both, a loan officer will register your loan for delivery to either Freddie or Fannie so that they can price their forward commitments. For you, this is blind: All you would know are the terms of the mortgage that is being offered (interest rate, amortization type, term, and cost).

Many times, a loan officer will register your loan with whichever agency has the best pricing on the product with the selected loan terms for that day (i.e., fifteen-year fixed or thirty-year fixed). But selection of product only on price, may impact your ability to receive a loan approval. Aside from some subtle differences in how these two GSEs price their loans, there are some differences with the underwriting criteria by which they each evaluate your loan.

One of their differences is that on a Fannie Mae product, only manually underwritten loans can utilize the income of a nonoccupying co-borrower when the loan-to-value ratio is below 90 percent. Freddie allows equal consideration of income for all applicants on the loan file— whether they occupy the property or not—regardless of whether the lender follows manual or automated underwriting guidelines.

Tip: If you need a nonoccupant co-borrower's income to meet loan qualification, ask your loan officer to review the features and benefits of conventional financing through Freddie Mac or government loan programs. If your lender only sells to Fannie and not to Freddie, seek a referral to another lender that sells to Freddie.

An underwriter validates AUS findings. This means that the underwriter (the decision maker) reviews the documentation that is in your loan file against the data entered into your loan application. This is why it's so critical to deliver your loan documentation up-front to your loan officer. If you've given your loan officer the opportunity to review your loan documents against what you tell them, then they will be able to enter accurate and usable data onto your loan application. Typically, it is your loan officer who runs the initial AUS findings. With these findings, we can issue a preliminary loan approval at application that lists the conditions you'll need to satisfy before the lender issues a final loan commitment. If you come unprepared to the loan application, qualifying income and usable assets may not be properly reflected on your initial loan application, and the preliminary loan approval can quickly be replaced with a loan denial once proper review of your loan documentation takes place.

Note: Each time that you submit new loan documentation that differs from data on the loan application, AUS findings must be re-run. This means that in each of these times, you run the risk of having a significant difference in loan conditions or even your loan approval.

Most lenders only allow underwriters to make changes to the loan application once the file has an initial decision. This is an important quality control step for the lender as any changes to the loan application can greatly impact the loan decision. For this reason, even though you submitted updated loan documents to the loan officer or loan processor on a Monday, you will not receive an updated conditional loan commitment or final loan commitment until the underwriter has reviewed the new documentation, updated the origination system and re-run AUS. Upon review of loan documents, an underwriter may identify that your documentation doesn't support the data that was entered into the system by the loan officer or updated by the loan processor. That's when an initial loan approval can change. And this can happen at any time during the processing of your loan request.

Eligibility Versus Qualification

Many times, you have the complete credit profile that makes you a qualified borrower, but you won't get a mortgage loan approval because you simply aren't eligible under the particular loan program under which you made application. Eligibility and Qualification mean two very different things. Eligibility refers to whom the loan program is intended for and qualification refers to whether or not that borrower meets the underwriting criteria of the loan product. Here are a few examples of those situations.

Mortgage Insurance Providers' Guidelines

If you have less than a 20 percent down payment, you may be required to have private mortgage insurance. There are differences between mortgage insurance (MI) providers' underwriting guidelines. Many lenders employ a policy of round robin assignment to the MI providers once an underwriter receives your loan, so as not to appear to steer loans to any particular MI provider. You won't typically have any say in which provider a lender chooses because this insurance covers the lender and not you. However, your loan officer does have the ability to request a loan be assigned to a particular MI provider if he is able to provide documentation to justify why one MI vendor is better suited to your needs. A better loan officer will know the differences in underwriting guidelines of the MI companies with whom their lender transacts. Typical differences between MI providers relate to:

- Maximum allowable debt-to-income ratio
- Minimum allowable credit scores
- Maximum loan-to-value variances based on usable credit scores
- Requirements for qualifying income when a nonoccupant co-borrower exists

HARP Refinance When LTV Is Below 80 Percent

If the property valuation shows that you have at least 80 percent equity in your home, you aren't eligible under the Home Affordable Refinance Program. You won't know this until the valuation comes in, so when it does and your loan request is denied, simply make application under the lender's regular refinance program. Valuation criteria for the new program may require a different measure of value so be prepared to possibly pay an additional appraisal fee.

Ineligible Condominium Project

If the condominium project does not meet the requirements for delivery to Fannie or Freddie, the project is deemed nonwarrantable. If your lender does not have a loan product that serves nonwarrantable condominium projects, your loan request will be denied. If you seek and qualify for an FHA loan, but the property is located in a condominium project that is not approved by the FHA, your loan request will be denied. These two denials don't mean that you don't meet the credit criteria for homeownership; they simply mean the property you were looking at doesn't meet the investor's criteria.

Cash-Out Refinance

Loan programs have limitations based on whether they allow you to tap into the equity of the home by cashing-out. These limitations can be based on occupancy, credit score, and the length of time since you purchased the home. Delayed financing is a term the agency uses to describe when a borrower has paid for a property in cash (without any financing) and within the first year of purchase, decides to take a home loan. Sometimes, a lender will call this transaction a technical refinance. If your loan request doesn't meet the agency's waiting period for allowing for access to equity, you may be eligible under Fannie Mae's delayed financing option; under certain circumstances, it allows you to cash-out sooner than the regular refinance program. Under delayed financing, additional scrutiny is placed on where the funds came from to make the initial purchase transaction.

Non-Arm's Length Transactions

Non–arm's length transactions are purchase transactions in which there is a relationship or business affiliation between the seller and the buyer of the property. Fannie Mae allows non–arm's length transactions for the purchase of existing properties unless specifically forbidden for the particular scenario, such as if you are seeking delayed financing. For the purchase of newly constructed properties, if the borrower has a relationship or business affiliation (any ownership interest or employment) with the builder, developer, or seller of the property, Fannie Mae will only purchase mortgage loans secured for a primary residence. Fannie Mae will not purchase mortgage loans on newly constructed homes secured as a second home or investment property if the borrower has a relationship or business affiliation with the builder, developer, or seller of the property.

Mortgage Versus Note

Very often people mistakenly equate the terms mortgage and note. When we say, "the note" we are referring to a promissory note. It is a contract whereby you make a promise to pay a sum of money to a lender under specific terms. The note has virtually nothing to do with the property itself and can technically exist without any collateral at all. A typical note will include the below information:

1. Name(s) of the borrower
2. Property address
3. Interest rate (fixed or adjustable)
4. Monthly payment
5. Late charge amount
6. Amount of the loan
7. Term (number of years)

A mortgage, on the other hand, is a transfer of interest in a property. While a mortgage is tied to the underlying debt created by the note, it is not a promise to repay the debt. The mortgage contains granting language, like a deed, which gives the lender the right to foreclose property if you don't pay according to the terms of the note. The key difference is who signs each document: the people who agree to pay the debt sign the note and the owners of the property sign the mortgage. For example, a husband and wife jointly own their primary residence, but when applying for a loan, only the husband made application. At closing, the husband will sign both the note and the mortgage and the wife will only sign the mortgage.

Additionally, the mortgage needs to be recorded in the county records, but the note does not. The note gets filed directly with the lender. When the note is fully paid, the lender will mark the original note "paid in full" and return it to the borrower. The lender will also record a release (or satisfaction) of mortgage in the county land records when the note is fully paid. Some states use either a mortgage or a Deed of Trust to secure a loan. When a Deed of Trust is utilized, a Deed of Reconveyance releases the claim.

The mortgage or deed of trust contains an acceleration clause that permits the lender to demand that the entire balance of the loan be repaid if you default on the loan. If you do not pay according to the terms on the promissory note, then the property can be taken in foreclosure and sold to satisfy the debt. Generally, the lender must provide notice to you before it can accelerate the loan. If you do not cure the default (bring the loan current) within the time specified, the lender may begin foreclosure proceedings. Foreclosure is the legal process where real estate secured by a mortgage or deed of trust is sold to satisfy the underlying debt as evidenced in the promissory note.

There are differences between the mortgage and the note as they relate to filing bankruptcy as well. The mortgage is not dischargeable in a bankruptcy filing while the note (your personal obligation for the debt) is. Although you are no longer personally liable for the note, the mortgage remains a valid lien that has not been avoided (i.e., made unenforceable) in the bankruptcy case and will remain after the bankruptcy case. Therefore, a creditor may enforce the lien to recover the collateral that is secured by the lien. What this means in the case of a mortgage loan is that although the loan was included in the bankruptcy discharge by court order, and you are no longer required to make payments on the note, and the repositories are required to stop reporting the mortgage as delinquent, the creditor can and will still hold a lien against the property in order to recover their investment at the time of future sale or refinance. When you file for bankruptcy and include the note, this limits the lender's ability to sell the property and delays the foreclosure proceedings. The lender will then petition the court to be removed from the bankruptcy and to proceed with a foreclosure sale.

If your property is sold in foreclosure or through a short sale, and the lender receives less than what it is owed from the proceeds, you may be on the hook for income taxes on the difference between the amount you owed and the amount generated from the sale. We call this difference the deficiency. If the deficiency amount is forgiven or cancelled by the mortgage lender, the IRS or state taxing authority might treat the forgiven debt as income, and then you'll have to pay income taxes on this difference (the deficiency judgment).

The IRS learns of the forgiven deficiency debt when it receives an IRS Form 1099C from the lender. This is a form on which an investor reports income derived when repayment of a loan is no longer feasible—which would be the case in a short sale or foreclosure, or when the investor writes off a debt. When the investor files this form, it will also send you a copy of it, and you will need to declare it as income in your federal income tax return. For more specific details on handling this issue, consult both a certified public accountant and a real estate or tax lawyer.

The Misnomer of First-Time Homebuyer

While a person who has never owned a home before certainly counts as a first-time homebuyer, those who have previously owned a home can also qualify as first-time homebuyers under certain circumstances. In Mortgage Speak, a first-time homebuyer is someone who has not held title to a property or held a mortgage within the preceding three years. That said, be mindful that although you in particular may have never owned a home, if your parents added you to the title of their home for estate planning purposes, you are now technically, a homeowner. There are many loan programs and grants that cater to first-time homebuyers, especially on the state and local levels.

The FHA considers someone who has only owned a home with a spouse as a first-time homebuyer (when only the spouse was on the mortgage). This includes single parents who are now divorced from their spouses or those who are displaced homemakers. Generally speaking, a single parent is defined as the parent of a minor child that is unmarried or legally separated. A displaced homemaker is an unemployed homemaker who has been dependent on the income of a relative and is no longer being supported by that person. Many of these individuals have been on the deed for a home without being on the note. Those who have only owned a mobile home that is not permanently attached to a foundation are also considered first-time homebuyers.

Any person who has not owned a principal residence in three years qualifies as a first-time homebuyer under FHA guidelines. It does not matter if the person has recently owned an investment property. If a person does not qualify on their own, but his or her spouse does, then they both qualify as first-time homebuyers.

Use of Retirement Funds for Purchase

In many cases, the IRS allows first-time homebuyers to borrow against their IRAs without paying the standard 10 percent penalty. These homebuyers may also borrow against their Roth IRAs tax-free if the account has been open for five years. The money must be used for a down payment or acquisition costs on a principal residence for the IRA owner or close family member.

By IRS standards, a first-time homebuyer is anyone who has not owned a home for at least the previous two years. If the buyer or spouse has owned a home within the previous two years, IRS guidelines do not consider them to be first-time homebuyers. Agency or lender specific underwriting definitions and not IRS definitions are considered in determining first-time homebuyer status for a mortgage application.

Down Payments Less than 20 Percent

Coming up with the required down payment can be one of the biggest hurdles to homeownership. Back in the 1950s and 60s, lenders required a minimum down payment of 20 percent of the home's purchase price. Today, lenders will approve riskier mortgages with much smaller down payments if the mortgage is covered by mortgage insurance or explicitly guaranteed by the federal government. If you have less than a 20 percent down payment when purchasing your primary residence, you will most likely be required to make an additional monthly payment for mortgage insurance in excess of your PITIA (principal, interest, taxes, insurance, and HOA).

Mortgage Insurance for Government-Backed Loans

To obtain a low down payment loan through the Federal Housing Administration, Veterans Affairs, or Rural Development, you must apply through an originating entity that is an approved lender. These programs have an up-front mortgage insurance premium and an annual insurance premium that is paid monthly. The specifics to these government lending programs are identified in chapter 8, "Comparing Loan Program Options."

Mortgage Insurance for Conventional Loans

Private mortgage insurance (PMI) is the private-sector alternative to government-backed low down payment options. Generally speaking, on a conventional loan, a lender will require a minimum down payment between 3 and 5 percent of a home's value. PMI is also available when refinancing and your loan-to-value ratio exceeds 80 percent. PMI protects the lender on a conventional mortgage in the event you default (stop making payments) and the lender forecloses on the property. PMI is not to be confused with a mortgage life insurance policy that, in the case of your death, protects the beneficiaries of your estate by paying off the remaining balance owed on your note. For this type of insurance coverage, seek assistance from a financial planner.

Tip: When considering mortgage life insurance, also take a look at your options for a term life policy. With a term life policy, the death benefit is for a specific period of time and payout is based on the amount of coverage purchased (not the remaining mortgage balance). Additionally, funds can be utilized in whatever manner the beneficiaries choose instead of going specifically to pay off the mortgage.

Can You Choose the Mortgage Insurance Provider?

Currently, there are fewer than ten national mortgage insurance providers. Although the monthly premium for PMI is paid for by you and included in your monthly mortgage payment, you don't select which provider insures your loan; the lender makes the selection. Most lenders are signed up with two to five providers, each having their own set of guidelines. The cost of PMI can be anywhere from half of 1 percent to almost 6 percent of the principal amount of the loan, depending on the down payment, the type of loan (fixed or adjustable interest rate), term of the loan, as well as your usable credit score.

If the conventional loan was set up with a monthly premium, coverage may be canceled once certain conditions are met. Your loan servicer is required to provide annual notification of the conditions that need to be met for cancellation (usually time and growth of equity). This notification is usually included with the information provided in the yearly escrow analysis regarding the amount of interest you paid on the mortgage and the disbursements from your escrow account for taxes and insurance.

05 Answers to Your Most Common Questions

You will have many questions in the mortgage process. Here I've compiled those that are frequently asked by my borrowers and those with important responses that a borrower rarely knows to ask. The answers will provide greater clarity about the process, may allow for consideration of other loan programs, or can save you a lot of time by finding the right lender upfront. Take notes and be prepared to review your questions at your first meeting with your loan officer.

Who Should I Expect to Be Contacting Me Throughout the Process?

THIS IS A big one. With some lenders, you will only speak to the loan officer and the loan processor. With other lenders, you may be shuffled through ten or more people. Be sure to ask your loan officer what method you can use to verify that the person who is calling is actually representing the lender.

How Can I Track the Status of My Loan Application?

Some lenders have technology set up that allows you to see exactly where the loan is in the process. While this is an excellent tool, it should not be the only method of status tracking. At the very least, you should expect a weekly status call with your loan officer or loan processor to review outstanding items and monitor loan progress. When turnaround times are slow, documentation may expire. Be sure your loan file contains the most up-to-date documentation to ensure no further delays.

What Other Loan Programs Might Work for Me?

It's good to know you have options, and it's important to review the different options as some organizations instruct their loan officers to only review the loan programs you inquire about. So ask. Maybe an adjustable rate mortgage (ARM) might be a better fit for you and will save you money in interest costs if you don't plan on holding the mortgage for an extended period of time. Maybe the lower monthly payment option will get your debt-to-income ratios in line. Maybe the loan program you applied for doesn't allow a nonoccupant co-borrower but another one does. By not asking this question, you are potentially missing out on an opportunity to own a home.

What Is the Minimum Credit Score Requirement for the Loan Program We Are Considering?

Credit score requirements vary by loan product, loan-to-value, and lender. Therefore, it isn't only people with poor credit histories that should be concerned with the lender's minimum credit score requirements. Some loan programs have very high credit standards, and most programs lower their minimum credit score requirement as you place larger down payments. You are going to want to know what expanded criteria are available to you with increased down payments and reductions to loan-to-value in increments of 5 percent.

Does the Condo Project Where I Am Buying a Unit Currently Appear on Your Approved Condo Project List?

The answer will vary depending on what type of loan program you are seeking. Is it yes for conventional? Yes for FHA? Or yes for VA? Subsequent questions to ask:

1. If it does appear on your approved list, when does the approval expire? If it expires before your anticipated closing date, ask which updated documents the lender's condo project review team needs to ensure continued approval status and get those documents to your lender right away.

2. What forms and documents are required to ensure project eligibility? Usually, the lender has a specific condo questionnaire that will need to be completed by the homeowner association property manager. Receipt of this along with a copy of the master certificate of insurance is standard practice and some lenders require additional documentation.

3. What is the turnaround time for review of condo documents? The review of condo documents is completely separate from the review of your credit, income, and assets. As each is reviewed separately and both are required for a full loan commitment, be sure to get your lender the documentation necessary as quickly as possible. If issues arise, be sure you have enough time to work through them with your lender and the property manager.

4. If the project is found to be nonwarrantable, do you offer financing for nonwarrantable projects? If the lender does not, ask for a referral to a lender they know who might. If they are unable to provide you with a referral, contact the property manager and ask which lenders have provided financing in the project in the last six months.

Tip: When faced with a possible loan denial, ask your loan officer this question: With borrowers of similar issues, what have you seen happen to clear this issue? This is a very different question than, "What do I need to do to get my loan approved?" Here, you are giving the loan officer an opportunity to share what has worked in the past and you are not boxing them in to say that if you do this same thing, you too will receive a loan approval. You don't want to back your loan officer into a corner because he is not the decision maker. You want to phrase your question to allow him to think of possibilities, then you take those possibilities and consider applying them to your specific situation so that you too can achieve resolution.

What's Your Thirty-Year Interest Rate?

There's no simple response to this question. Pricing options are based on many variables, including the type of loan transaction (purchase, cash-out or rate and term refinance, delayed financing), occupancy of property (primary residence, second home, investment), residency status (U.S. citizen, permanent resident, nonpermanent resident alien, nonresident alien), property type (single family residence, condominium, townhouse, multifamily, manufactured home), appraised value, loan-to-value, usable credit score, and most recently added to the pricing matrix, whether the loan meets the definition of qualified mortgage and ability-to-repay, which is reviewed in the, "Qualified Mortgage and Ability-to-Repay Rule" section in chapter 2. A loan officer can provide a preapplication cost estimate for your particular scenario, but always remember that final pricing will be determined based on a number of variables that only reveal themselves during the processing of your loan request.

What's It Going to Cost Me to Close?

Cost estimations can be provided through three different forms: a preapplication cost estimate, which is non-binding to the lender; a good faith estimate that is subject to certain tolerance restrictions; and in August 2015, we introduce the new loan estimate that replaces the good faith estimate in certain transactions. A preapplication cost estimate will usually detail the amount of cash you are required to bring to closing and this amount varies by loan program, loan-to-value and interest rate selection and is based on many assumptions including the assumption of credit score.

A big failure of the 2010 revision to the good faith estimate is that it doesn't clearly identify funds needed to close. While the 2015 loan estimate is designed to clearly identify the amount, if any, you will need to bring to closing, there are still transactions where a good faith estimate will be used in place of the loan estimate. For these, you can identify estimated funds needed for closing on the loan application. In the "Section VII – Details of Transaction" of chapter 10, we find a detailed breakdown of total transactional costs and credits and the elusive cash-to-close amount.

Why Is the APR Different from the Interest Rate I Was Quoted?

The interest rate is the nominal, annual representation of the percentage rate that is used in the calculation of your monthly interest charges. This percentage cost of interest is listed on the loan application in "Section I. Types of Mortgage and Terms of Loan". It is also found on the good faith/loan estimate and on the promissory note that is signed at closing. The annual percentage rate (APR) is intended to give you more information about what you're really paying. The APR represents the nominal rate of interest charged on your loan plus prepaid finance charges that reflect the total cost of the loan with a particular lender. Oftentimes, borrowers interpret a lower offered interest rate as a better value, but that isn't necessarily true. To know for sure, compare one loan's APR with another loan's APR to get a fair representation of total costs associated with procuring the loan. And be sure to analyze the long-term costs of interest rates, mortgage insurance premiums, and prepayment penalties on each loan program as well, as these relate to actual dollars over the lifetime of the loan.

Lenders are mandated by the Truth in Lending Act to disclose the APR on every consumer loan agreement and all lenders must follow the same rules for calculating APR to ensure the accuracy of this tool as a loan comparison. The APR includes prepaid finance charges such as: loan origination, loan discount, underwriting, processing, life of loan tax related service (to monitor the county that is receiving property tax payments), buy-down (to lower the interest rate), per diem interest calculation (this is the amount from the date of loan funding to the end of the month), flood life of loan coverage, upfront mortgage insurance premium, condominium questionnaire, attorney, settlement/closing/additional closing fees, notary, overnight mail/courier, processing of a subordination agreement, payoff request to your existing lienholders, tax certification, miscellaneous title fees, title endorsement, charges for completion of verifications of deposit, mortgage or rent, and property inspection waiver (by the GSEs).

A mortgage payment differs from a rental housing payment in that a mortgage payment is paid in arrears while a rental housing payment is made in advance of utilizing the property. Insurance premiums are also paid in advance of the coverage period. Unless your loan has a prepayment penalty, if you prepay your mortgage, you will not be charged for future interest due on the prepaid balance. You will know if your loan has a prepayment penalty because it is disclosed on the good faith/loan estimate and would also be listed on the promissory note signed at loan closing.

To Float or to Lock, Who Decides?

In a refinance boom, some lenders will not accept anything other than applications where the interest rate is locked. This is done to protect pipeline integrity in case the market drives interest rates up while your loan is being processed and with the new, higher market rate, you find there's no benefit to refinancing and cancel your loan request. In a purchase transaction, it is always your option to lock or float the interest rate at application. That said, it isn't on your loan officer to provide you with market updates. The market risk is always on you, and unless you have a magic crystal ball, no one ever knows market direction with certainty.

My advice to my clients is always this: At the interest rate that provides you with a comfortable housing payment, lock, and don't look back. Once you lock, and rates go down, you can't get a lower rate without additional costs. If you choose to float your rate, you risk that rates may go up. How much higher than today's rate are you willing to go? The answer is usually, "I don't want to go anything above today's rate."

To weigh the pros and cons of floating or locking, ask your loan officer to provide you with details that can help you quantify that risk. Market fluctuations can impact loan approval. A slight movement of just .5 percent can potentially price you out of a loan amount. If you are considering floating your interest rate up until before closing, you need to calculate your risks by knowing two things. First, you need to know the current market rate and the interest rate at which your lender is going to evaluate your loan file. Some lenders will issue their loan commitments on floating rates at .5 percent above market rate to give them some protection in issuing a commitment. (This practice can potentially price someone out of a purchase price if the debt-to-income ratio is slightly above program guidelines due to a lender-imposed cushion on a floating interest rate. Ask your lender if you were to lock at today's rate, what your debt-to-income ratio would be. If it's tight, don't risk it.) The second thing you should know is your potential housing payments above and below the current rate because knowing your payment difference can help you decide your risk tolerance. With this information in hand, 99.5 percent of the time, my clients will lock at application.

If I Lock and Rates Go Down, Can I Get a Lower Rate?

At loan application, you are given the option of either locking in the interest rate typically for a term of thirty, forty-five, sixty, or ninety days (longer lock periods may be available by your lender and carry an additional cost) or letting the interest rate float and risk variances with market fluctuations. Some factors to consider when deciding your rate lock period are: contract closing date, lender turnaround times, and your vision of the direction of the interest rate market. These things matter because there is a cost related to the rate lock period. If you decide to float the interest rate, many lenders will require that it be locked at least seven days before your anticipated closing date at which time you may be offered a fifteen-day lock period.

The longer you hold the rate lock, the greater the cost for the same interest rate. For example, let's say a fifteen-year fixed rate is priced at 4 percent. To hold the rate for a thirty-day lock period, the cost is zero points at closing. Points referred to here are listed as either origination or discount points on the good faith/loan estimate. The same 4 percent locked in for forty-five days has a cost of 25 basis points at closing. For example, on a $100,000 loan, 25 basis points equates to a $250 charge that is collected at loan closing. If your purchase contract calls for a closing no sooner than thirty-five days, at minimum you would select the forty-five–day lock option at loan application.

If you chose to lock the interest rate and the market takes a dip, some lenders will allow you a one-time option to re-price to market rate under certain parameters. These could be something like this:

- All loan conditions have cleared
- At a minimum, your locked rate must be .5 percent higher than the current market rate given the same price (basis points)

For example, let's say you locked at 5 percent with zero points. The market dropped to 4.25 percent with zero points but you haven't provided the lender with all loan conditions. You won't be allowed to re-lock, just yet. If you have satisfied all loan conditions, and at your request, the lender will take a look at the cost of the rate of 4.25 percent on lock in day and split this difference with you. If the rate of 4.25 percent cost 150 basis points on the original lock date, you will be charged 75 basis points at closing to have the lender reduce the rate to market. Remember, they have a forward commitment to sell your loan to an investor and the re-lock isn't free to them either.

Should I Hire a Real Estate Attorney or a Title Agent?

To help my clients define this for themselves, I ask a few questions to assess where they are in the process and their comfort level with the transaction to help them determine their needs. The one thing I make sure to always clarify is that if they choose to hire an attorney to represent them at loan closing, I suggest they hire an attorney who specializes in real estate law and not their cousin who practices bankruptcy law and offers them her services at a lower cost. Evaluation of true cost is skewed by a person's level of competence in any particular subject matter.

Both real estate attorneys and title agents provide the service of settlement to ensure the legal transfer of title and that all parties are accurately compensated in a real estate transaction. They are agents for procuring title insurance against any prior liens or encumbrances. An encumbrance impacts the transferability of property and can restrict its free use until the claim against ownership is removed. Both title agents and real estate attorneys secure a title insurance policy to protect the lender and you (should you purchase a separate owner's policy) through a national insurance provider such as The Fund, Old Republic, or First National Title. Additionally, the settlement agent will order a property survey when one is required.

Selection of a settlement agent is generally up to you and based upon your particular needs. In cases where you are buying new construction, the developer may require or incentivize you to use their particular settlement agent for the ease of the seller/developer, closing multiple transactions simultaneously. In the state of New York, the lender will select an attorney to represent the lender at closing. If you are a borrower in the state of New York and you wish to use the same attorney to represent you at closing, you may. If not, you may hire another real estate attorney of your liking—at your own expense to represent your interests.

Tip: The time to engage a real estate attorney is before you sign a purchase contract. You are retaining a real estate attorney to represent your best interests. If you don't give this person the opportunity to review the contract you are about to enter into—for what is most likely the biggest investment of your life—then what's the point of hiring them in the first place? Be smart about your choices and their timing.

The only time a forced settlement agent (selected by the seller) is required is when a GSE is selling foreclosed property and will be paying for title insurance. I have heard of mortgage lenders whose policy it is to require the use of a national title vendor for closing on a loan under the Home Affordable Refinance Program. In those cases, if you prefer not to use that lender's third-party service provider, you have the right to seek financing with another lender. National title vendors hire local notaries to meet with you at settlement to sign the closing documents.

If you are refinancing a loan transaction, you may want to consider selecting a title agent. Title agents may or may not have a real estate attorney on staff. If they don't, they will rely on the staff attorneys of the master fund for issues that require review, analysis, or recommendations.

Can I Pay my Own Taxes and Insurance?

Unless someone regularly receives yearly bonuses or has income variations on a monthly basis, for financial planning purposes, including the collection of taxes and insurance in your monthly payment to the lender is widely recommended. Families with varying monthly income may want to exercise the lender's escrow waiver option to minimize monthly debt obligations and hold off on paying the full bills for property taxes and insurance until year end or when due, if the lender allows. Sometimes a borrower will request to have his or her monthly mortgage payment include only principal and interest and pay the county directly for property taxes and the insurance agent directly for homeowners insurance. The lender's ability to grant this request depends on the loan product chosen and the loan-to-value. In most cases, if the down payment is at least 20 percent, the loan product selected may have the option of waiving the collection of monthly escrow for taxes and insurance. Most lenders typically charge a one-time fee at closing for waiving escrows. Loans to nonresident aliens usually require the collection of monthly escrows.

Beginning January 1, 2016, for loans on properties located within a special flood area, the Homeowner Flood Insurance Affordability Act of 2014 mandates that flood insurance be escrowed. (Find out more about the law at: www.fema.gov/media-library-data/1396551935597-4048b68f6d695a6eb6e6e7118d3ce464/HFIAA_Overview_FINAL_03282014.pdf.) This means that even if your lender allows you to waive the collection of taxes and homeowners insurance with the monthly mortgage payment, the government requires the lender collect for flood insurance in your monthly payment.

Why Do I Need Flood Insurance?

Flood insurance is mandated on improved real property (land with a building on it) for all federally backed mortgages and for mortgages obtained through federally insured and regulated financial institutions by the Flood Disaster Protection Act of 1973 (FDPA). This act, and subsequent revisions, makes it the lender's responsibility to determine which properties are in areas most prone to flooding and enforce the purchase and maintenance of flood insurance protection.

The FDPA covers loans as described above, who are in a flood hazard area and for who flood insurance is available. All areas that have been mapped by the Federal Emergency Management Agency (FEMA) for flood status have a designated zone. The designations for all special flood hazard areas begin with the letters A or V. The National Flood Insurance Program (NFIP) provides federally subsidized flood insurance for owners of properties located in designated flood hazard areas within communities that participate in NFIP. To participate in NFIP, a community must be mapped and flood zones designated.

If a community does not participate in NFIP and insurance is not available for the property, it is your lender's decision whether to make the loan and whether to require private flood insurance. If you know your property is located in a community that does not participate, ask your lender up front how they will handle your particular situation. Don't wait until you're four weeks into the process to find out they can't make the loan based on their policy regarding flood insurance coverage.

After making loan application, you will receive a set of disclosures from your lender. In this set, you will receive notification if the subject property is in a flood hazard area and whether flood insurance is available to you. If it is, you must obtain evidence of coverage prior to scheduling loan closing. The lender is also required to ensure coverage remains in force for the life of the loan.

The FDPA requires that lenders make a flood determination any time it is making, increasing, renewing, or extending a loan on your property. Lenders will contract with a vendor to do this; the vendor guarantees the accuracy of their determination, affirming they have access to current flood maps as published by the NFIP. Use of current flood determination is important as occasionally, areas are remapped to better reflect current conditions. For this reason, many homeowners who are refinancing an existing mortgage are surprised to learn their lender is requiring flood insurance where none was previously required.

In 2012, the Biggert-Waters Flood Insurance Reform Act was signed into law and provided requirements for lenders to hold escrow for flood insurance and to accept private flood insurance policies that meet defined criteria. Because these and other items included in the law presented many challenges for bankers and the insurance industry, the Homeowner Flood Insurance Affordability Act of 2014 (HFIAA) was signed into law. HFIAA clarifies that mandatory escrow only applies to loans that are originated, refinanced, increased, extended, or renewed on or after January 1, 2016.

Determination of minimum coverage is based on the lowest of these criteria:
a. The outstanding principal balance of the loan
b. The maximum amount of coverage available under the NFIP for the particular type of structure
c. The full insurable value of the structure and its contents, better known as replacement cost value, which is not measured by market value, but rather the cost to rebuild

For clarification, given that the maximum available coverage for single-family residences under NFIP is currently $250,000, a loan in the amount of $400,000 secured for a single-family dwelling with a replacement cost of $230,000 would have a minimum required flood insurance coverage of $230,000.

If your property is in a flood zone, your lender will condition for evidence of flood coverage prior to releasing the loan to closing. In order to comply with this condition, you will need to provide to your lender three things:
1. A copy of the declarations page of the flood insurance policy showing the lenders mortgagee clause and your particular loan number
2. A copy of the flood insurance application
3. Evidence of premium payment

After loan closing, your lender will monitor flood insurance coverage for the remainder of the loan term. If at any point in time the lender determines a lapse of coverage has occurred, it will send you a written request to provide evidence of insurance within forty-five days. If after forty-five days you have not provided evidence of insurance coverage, your lender is required by law to force place a policy. A force placed policy is usually much higher in cost than what you can obtain for yourself and you will be required to pay it.

You may be wondering, "How could there be a lapse of coverage when my lender is collecting an insurance escrow with my monthly mortgage payment?" This could very easily happen if your lender does not receive the renewal notice from your insurance company with the correct mailing address for the loan servicer, the correct mortgagee clause for the loan servicer, and your particular loan number. From time to time, your lender may change their servicing information (and even your loan number). It is your responsibility to inform your insurance agent of any changes in servicing from your lender to avoid presumed lapses in coverage. I hear a collective moan. From the consumer standpoint, I can see how one might believe it to be more effective to have the servicer notify the existing insurance provider of important changes. However, you are the owner of the insurance policy and not the servicer. Therefore, the servicer is unable to modify your policy.

Why Do I Keep Receiving Copies of the Good Faith/Loan Estimate?

Within three business days of loan application, you will receive the lender's initial good faith or loan estimate that is based on the loan program chosen. The written estimate includes a summary of loan terms and estimated settlement charges. It also includes information about key dates such as the expiration date of the interest rate quoted and when the estimate expires. On the good faith/loan estimate, settlement charges are broken down into eleven categories of costs, and the loan estimate lists the costs alphabetically. An originator is not required to provide a good faith estimate if, before the end of the three-business-day period, the application is denied or the borrower withdraws their loan application. The originator is bound, within certain tolerances, to the settlement charges and terms listed, unless a new estimate is provided prior to loan settlement. Initially quoted fees can, and most likely will, change.

There are several factors that can cause the lender's initial offered terms to change when certain previously assumed data is validated. We call these instances a change of circumstance. When a change of circumstance occurs, the lender is required to re-issue the revised good faith/loan estimate. When the 2010 version of the good faith estimate was released, lenders were required to re-issue a good faith estimate with any changes in fees or loan terms. This is the reason an applicant will receive multiple estimates while their loan is in processing.

While the lender is required to record the reason for the change of circumstance, borrowers don't receive a written explanation highlighting what fees exactly were affected; they simply receive a new estimate. This is extremely confusing to the borrower. Until lenders change this policy, you will need to either communicate with your lender to define what caused the change in terms and what fees are affected or comb through the original and revised estimate—line-by-line—to figure it out for yourself. With the new loan estimate form being released in August 2015, the Consumer Financial Protection Bureau has proposed that lenders will only reissue the loan estimate where the tolerance level exceeds 10 percent. A tolerance level indicates by how much the estimated charges can increase at closing. Here are some examples of events that allow for changes in fee estimates:

- Acts of God, war, disaster, or other emergency
- A borrower chose to lock the interest rate on a loan where disclosures were issued when the initial rate quoted was floating (unlocked), the lock period on the initial rate quoted expired and a re-lock includes a fee for rate extension, or an adjustment to market interest rates and fees
- Information particular to the borrower or to the type of transaction that was relied on in providing the previously issued estimate changes or is found to be inaccurate
- A change in the representative credit score
- A change in the loan amount
- Property valuation is different from the value listed when the previously issued estimate was prepared
- An upgraded appraisal type or additional review is required
- An occupancy change
- New information particular to the borrower or transaction that was not relied on in providing the original estimate or other circumstances that are particular to the borrower or transaction such as a requirement for flood insurance, environmental inspection, or pest inspection
- Parties are added or removed from title or the property is moved into or out of a trust
- Transaction changes from a fixed rate loan program to an adjustable rate loan program (or vice versa)
- A co-borrower is added to the loan
- After the original estimate is issued it is determined that a party will be using a power of attorney to sign loan documents, which may require additional review by the lender or additional fees
- A discovery of previously undisclosed circumstances affecting settlement costs such as unreleased liens (only the increase in recording fees may change on the estimate all other charges must remain the same)

Common Issues that Can Cause Loan Terms to Change

Property valuation: Changes in property valuation may affect your final pricing if the change significantly impacts loan-to-value. If your appraisal comes in higher than anticipated on a purchase transaction, this does not affect final pricing at all because on a purchase, the lender will accept lower of purchase price or valuation. On a refinance transaction, a higher than expected valuation may provide a better interest rate if it represents at a minimum, a 5 percent improvement in LTV. When the appraisal comes in, ask if your pricing is benefitted by the final valuation.

If the valuation comes in lower than expected, again depending on LTV, your interest rate may be affected along with your ability to meet loan eligibility guidelines. In either a purchase or refinance transaction, if the valuation is less than anticipated, and the LTV doesn't meet the loan program requirements, your loan request may be denied. You can preemptively avoid this denial by reducing your requested loan amount or by exploring other loan program options that will allow for a higher LTV. A lender will not make the adjustment for you unless you specifically ask them to. If it is a purchase transaction, you can use the appraisal to go back to the seller and negotiate a price reduction to market value. If the seller refuses to lower the sales price and you are willing and able to come to closing with money to cover the gap between sales price and lender valuation, you still have the option of buying the property at the price you and the seller agreed to. The lender will only finance that portion that is based on its valuation and within its loan-to-value guidelines.

Final debt-to-income (DTI) ratio: At loan application, I've never had a client ask me what the guidelines are for DTI. Once the general public has an understanding of the Qualified Mortgage (QM) and Ability-to-Repay (ATR) rules, I believe more loan officers will be asked this question. If a lender only offers loan products that comply with QM lending, this means that your DTI is capped at 43 percent for all loan programs with that lender. If the lender offers a combination of QM and non-QM loan programs, your loan will be registered under one or the other available loan products.

If your loan was initially registered and locked under a QM loan program where it was assumed that your DTI would fall below 43 percent, and your final calculated DTI exceeds 43 percent, you may be denied under the registered QM loan program (depends on some allowable exclusions). If this happens to you, ask your lender to review possible exclusions to the rule or the possibility of your qualifying under a non-QM loan program. If you will need to change your loan program, your lender may allow a simple program change and re-disclose the terms of the new loan program. If you are switching between conventional and government program options, you will be required to submit a whole new loan application because the disclosure set is different for each. When switching between a QM loan program to a non-QM loan program, you should expect your loan terms (interest rate and fees) to be higher with a non-QM loan than with a QM loan. Since the GSEs will only guaranty loans that qualify under QM guidelines, without that guaranty, a non-QM loan presents a higher risk to the final investor and higher risk loans will carry higher premiums.

Switching loan programs: You may exercise your option of switching loan programs at any time during the processing of your loan; however, when you switch loan programs on a locked loan, you will be subjected to worst-case pricing, not market pricing, on the newly selected loan program. This means that the lender will evaluate the current day pricing on the new program and compare it with the pricing for that same program on the day you locked your loan on the existing loan program. Whichever pricing is worse, that's the pricing that will apply to your changed loan program. The reason for this is that creditors secure interest rates by committing to delivering mortgage notes at a future date for issuance of mortgage-backed securities. If they break their commitments, they risk being cut off by the investor. If no investors buy their loans, origination activities cease and they are out of business.

Switching between same day interest rates and fees: When shopping for your loan program, your loan officer may provide you with preapplication cost estimates showing different pricing options for the same loan product. For example, you may be shown how your monthly payment is affected by slight variations in interest rate with pricing at zero points, half a point, one point, or one and a half points paid at loan closing. Let's say that on the day you locked in your interest rate, you selected a fifteen-year fixed rate with a 4 percent interest rate, paying zero origination points at loan closing. Three weeks later, you decide that you would prefer the same fifteen-year fixed rate loan program, but priced at the 3.75 percent paying a 1 percent origination fee at closing that was offered on the day you locked the 4 percent at zero points. This is okay. No worst-case scenario pricing applies here because nothing about your change affects the lenders forward commitment to deliver your loan. If you were originally qualified under a lower interest rate and are considering making a change to a higher interest rate (maybe you'd rather not pay origination points), ask your loan officer to review how the pricing change will affect your debt-to-income ratio.

How Can I Avoid Paying Mortgage Insurance?

It's understandable that you'd like to avoid paying a premium on an insurance policy that protects the lender and not you directly. If you have less than a 20 percent down payment and want to avoid paying monthly mortgage insurance, you can explore these options:

1. Are you a veteran of the United States military? Be sure to notify your loan officer if you are, as you may be entitled to receive the benefits of a VA loan with zero down payment requirements and no monthly mortgage insurance.

2. Have you considered all of your asset options for down payment? Do you have retirement accounts? Most 401(k)s allow for an early distribution or a loan up to $50,000 for the purchase of a primary residence without a penalty. Review your options with your plan administrator so that you may consider those funds for the transaction. A benefit of using those funds is that your debt-to-income ratio will be significantly lower because you won't have the monthly mortgage insurance payment, and because if you decide to take a loan against any financial asset, that loan payment is not included in debt-to-income calculations because it is a secured asset.

3. Will there be anyone on the loan application who is a recent college graduate? If it applies, seek lenders who may offer loan programs for recent college graduates with low down payment options and no requirement for mortgage insurance.

4. Review the benefits and features of FHA financing versus conventional financing with private mortgage insurance in chapter 8, "Comparing Loan Program Options."

Can You Make my Loan Stay With You?

I understand why loan servicing is a concern. What happens after closing is just as important as what happens before closing. Unfortunately, you have no control over whether a lender chooses to service your loan or to sell the note in the secondary market, transferring loan servicing. We acknowledge that the mortgage servicing industry was inundated with an unprecedented amount of defaults during the financial crisis, and though everyone expects to be dealing with knowledgeable representatives when they call in with standard questions, this didn't always happen.

While most people are naturally reluctant to deal with the consequences of their financial struggles, their first and best option is always to go directly to their mortgage servicer and explain the circumstances. If you find yourself in this situation, you may think that you are doing a good thing by sending in a partial mortgage payment for the amount you can afford, but unless you've been preapproved for a short-term reduction in payments by your servicer, the receipt of any partial loan payment may be rejected and returned and you will be reported to the credit bureaus as delinquent on your account. To seek approval for a short-term reprieve, you will be asked to document extenuating circumstances that are beyond your control and make it impossible for you to keep up.

In the years following the financial crisis, I saw and heard a lot of advertisements from companies claiming to be able to help you with a loan modification. I've seen people begin delivering their mortgage payments to a third-party with the hopes of that third-party handling a loan modification on their behalf. People have told me that they've been told by people who claim to be "in the know" to purposefully withhold payment of their mortgage so that your lender will pay attention to you. A strategic default is a negative reflection of your financial character. A strategic default means that you had the resources to make timely and full mortgage payments but chose not to. I've had people say to me, "Why should I keep paying the mortgage when the value has gone down by so much? Let the bank take it." Well, the reason you should is that you can and because by signing a promissory note, you promised that you would. By creating more losses, people who committed strategic defaults further exacerbated the financial crisis.

I Already Have an FHA Loan; Can I Get Another One?

Sometimes a borrower will seek the financing assistance of an FHA loan when they already own a property that is insured by an FHA mortgage. Typically, any person individually or jointly owning a home covered by an FHA mortgage may not purchase another principal residence that is covered by FHA mortgage insurance. However, there are some exceptions to this rule. (See additional information in the HUD Handbook at: portal.hud.gov/hudportal/documents/ huddoc?id=40001HSGH.pdf.) Considerations used by your lender to determine your eligibility for one of these exceptions will include the length of time for which you owned the property secured by the FHA loan and the circumstances that compel you to purchase another residence. If you do not meet the below listed FHA exceptions to this rule, you will need to either pay off your existing FHA loan or terminate ownership of that property and satisfy the existing lien before acquiring another FHA insured mortgage.

Exceptions that will permit you to obtain a new FHA loan while currently obligated on another FHA loan must be documented by your lender and follow these guidelines:

a.   Relocations: If you are relocating and re-establishing primary residency in another area that is not within reasonable commuting distance from your current principal residence, you may obtain another mortgage using FHA-insured financing and are not required to sell the existing property covered by an FHA-insured mortgage. The relocation need not be employer mandated to qualify for this exception.

b.   Increase in family size: You may be permitted to obtain another home with an FHA-insured mortgage if the number of legal dependents increases to the point that the present housing no longer meets your family's needs. You will need to provide your lender with satisfactory evidence of the increase in dependents and your current property's failure to meet the family's needs. Additionally, FHA will require that you pay down the outstanding FHA lien mortgage on your present property to a minimum loan-to-value of 75 percent based on current valuation. A current residential appraisal must be obtained on the departure residence to determine compliance with loan-to-value requirements.

c.   Vacating a jointly owned property: If you are vacating a residence that will remain occupied by a co-borrower, you are permitted to obtain another FHA-insured mortgage. Acceptable situations include instances of divorce, after which the vacating ex-spouse will purchase a new home or one of the co-borrowers will vacate the existing property.

d.   Nonoccupying co-borrower: A nonoccupying co-borrower on a property being purchased with an FHA mortgage as a principal residence by other family members may have a joint interest in that property as well as in a principal residence of their own with an FHA-insured mortgage.

The FHA does not allow financing to private investors to acquire rental properties. If the FHA concludes that a loan transaction was designed for obtaining an investment property, even if the property to be encumbered will be the only one owned using FHA mortgage insurance, it will not insure the mortgage. FHA does allow refinancing an existing FHA loan into a new FHA loan. This is especially helpful when considering a reduction to your monthly housing costs in times where market interest rates have dropped significantly.

Tip: When refinancing an existing FHA mortgage and the loan-to-value exceeds 80 percent, consider application for an FHA Streamline mortgage (this has reduced documentation options for your lender). If you have at least 20 percent equity in your home (compared to current market value not original purchase price), you may want to consider conventional financing where you will not need to carry mortgage insurance in the new loan. If your new loan-to-value is at least 95 percent, and you meet the financing requirements of a conventional loan, you may want to consider private mortgage insurance that is cancelable after your principal balance drops below 80 percent of the original value. This option may prove more beneficial to you as FHA insurance is currently mandated for the life of the loan with few exceptions.

06 Why Managing Your Credit Matters Most

Credit scoring has become the standard measure of U.S. consumer credit risk. The absolute most important thing you can do to influence the cost and approval of your loan is having and maintaining an exemplary credit history. Very simply, loan pricing and loan eligibility are credit-score driven. The number one thing you can do to ensure you get the best possible interest rate is to review your reported credit history and scores: correct any errors and learn how to effectively utilize open trade lines to increase the value of the scoring models. Do not wait until you apply for a loan to know your credit score, and don't allow yourself to be completely oblivious to the information that is being reported about you.

A CREDIT REPORT SIMPLY represents a snapshot in time; it is the ultimate selfie. It contains identifying information such as address, social security number, and name variations, lists credit accounts or trade lines that are reported to the credit repositories, information about companies that have pulled an inquiry on you, and provides details on public records such as a short sale, bankruptcy, foreclosure, judgment, tax lien, and collections information. Credit reports do not include arrest records.

Some people equate high credit scores with higher income. I can tell you there seems to be no correlation with income and credit score. Some people simply prioritize their payment due dates and some people are really disorganized, regardless of income level.

Let's Put a Value on It

If you're wondering why paying all your creditors on time consistently matters, I'm going to share with you a very typical scenario. Let's say that on the same day, you and a coworker both make an appointment to visit the loan officer at the bank across from your office and each of you decide to make application for a thirty-year fixed rate loan and lock the interest rate in for sixty days. Both of you are pleased with the experience because you did your homework and selected one of the better loan officers.

You get back to work the next day and you share the interest rate offer you received, thinking that it was fantastic. But you learn that your coworker received a better rate at a better price than you did. You feel that your loan officer put one over on you, so at lunchtime, you head back over to the bank and you accuse your loan officer of overcharging. You demand that she match the rate she quoted your buddy.

Each loan application is different and pricing is specific to each borrower's particular loan scenario. Although she can't discuss the elements of your buddy's loan transaction, she can go into detail as to what affected your particular pricing. The GSEs publicly post the loan level adjustments that affect your particular loan pricing (you can find them at https://www.fanniemae.com/content/pricing/llpa-matrix.pdf). But don't spend too much time reading that matrix because the only takeaway is that the only thing you can control is the information that is being reported by the repositories.

With all other loan characteristics being the same, here's an idea of how your credit score affects the pricing the lender can offer you. On a thirty-year fixed rate mortgage for $100,000, borrower A has a representative credit score of 745 and will receive an interest rate of 4 percent, which provides a monthly principal and interest payment of $477.42. On the same loan amount, borrower B has a representative credit score of 650 and will receive an interest rate of 5 percent with a monthly payment of $536.82. That credit score difference costs borrower B an additional $59.40 per month over thirty years. That's $21,384 over the life of the loan.

Sometimes, a creditor is technically right that you owe them money, but in your opinion, you should not be responsible for a certain fee. Think twice before you let them place your account in collections because you simply refuse to pay that $30 charge on the basis of principal. I see this happen often with medical collections. The borrower usually believes that their medical insurance should cover a certain charge. The doctor's office sends the bill to the insurer, but the insurer denies coverage, or in the case of out-of-network providers, makes payment based on the schedule that they pay in-network providers. If it was your choice to go out-of-network, then it's your responsibility to pay the provider the portion of their fee that was not covered by the insurer. If you had no choice but to go out-of-network, then you can dispute the payment with your insurer or you can negotiate a lower fee from the provider. In either case, you can't simply ignore the bill. At some point, you're going to have to weigh the cost/benefit of not making payment. If no one budges—and they have a legitimate claim against you—just pay it. Otherwise, it's going to cost you a lot of more money in higher interest charges with every other creditor because that derogatory account will drop your credit score.

Risk-based Pricing

Under the amended Fair and Accurate Credit Transactions Act, effective January 1, 2011, lenders are required to adjust loan pricing based on your individual risk profile. Risk-based pricing means lenders use your credit score, which reflects your risk of nonpayment and credit utilization, in setting the price and other terms of credit offered. It's no surprise that lenders offer more favorable terms to borrowers with better credit histories. While negative information contained on a credit report may not result in loan denial, it may result in your loan costing you more than it otherwise would.

As part of your lenders responsibility to ensure the credit information it uses to determine loan eligibility is accurate, if your loan is priced with terms that are considerably less favorable than what your lender provides to other borrowers, you will receive written notification via a risk-based pricing notice indicating that you are receiving worse terms due to information contained on your credit report. Some lenders choose to utilize the credit score exception notice instead on all files, which is an alternative way of complying with the rule, regardless of the terms on which you were granted credit.

Currently, federal law does not mandate that mortgage applicants receive a copy of the credit report that is used by the lender to decide the loan. I think it's crazy that you don't get to see the single most important piece of information that determines your loan eligibility. Years ago, federal law mandated that only credit-reporting agencies could give you a copy of your credit report. As your lender is not a credit-reporting agency, it was not allowed to provide you with a copy of the report that is being used to determine loan qualification. That issue has since been clarified with our regulators, and while lenders are no longer forbidden to share with you a copy of the credit report they are using, it is not mandated by federal law that they do.

Tip: Knowing how important an accurate depiction of your credit profile is in determining loan eligibility and pricing, obtaining and reviewing a copy of a mortgage credit report at least six months prior to making a loan application is your number one priority in preparing for a successful mortgage loan approval process. If there are errors on the report, you need to give yourself ample time to work with the creditors and repositories to fix the errors. Access your free report at www.AnnualCreditReport.com.

Tip: Know your credit score to avoid having unnecessary credit pulls while shopping for a mortgage. You can access this through a paid service provider such as MyFico.com. When interviewing potential lenders, provide them with your estimated credit score so they can present you with fairly accurate pricing options.

Tip: Monitor the monthly reporting of your credit history while you're working through the corrections, throughout the mortgage process, and up until loan funding by subscribing to a monthly service such as Identity Guard® or LifeLock® that sends you alerts for all new inquiries and reporting of derogatory items.

Look Out for These Things on the Credit Report
Print a copy of your tri-merged credit report. Sit down in a quiet space with no telephone interruptions and go line-by-line identifying errors. Credit accounts usually list the following items on your report:
- Name of account—look for name variations

- Comment on the account, including whether it's current or delinquent and for how long its been delinquent
- Account status: positive or negative
- Date account opened
- Monthly payment amount
- Date of last payment
- Type and terms of account
- Payment history for past twelve, twenty-four, or thirty-six months
- Original loan amount, credit limit, historical high balance
- Balance owed, balance date, and amount past due (if applicable)

Here are a few examples of things I look for when helping a client prepare for loan application:

- Closed accounts with current balances: Do you still owe the money listed? Do you have evidence of payment?
- Accounts listed as in dispute: Remove the dispute (see below, "Handling Disputed Accounts," for more information).
- Credit card balances: Keep your available credit at 50 percent or more. This means that if your creditor grants you a line of $5,000, at no point in the month should your balance exceed $2,500. This is a huge factor affecting credit scores.
- Filed bankruptcy: Check to make sure accounts included show no derogatory items from the date of final discharge forward.
- Paid collections: Do they show a zero balance?
- Open collections: Depending on their age, it may or may not be a good idea to pay them off because "date of last activity" is updated and will affect credit scoring. The service of rapid rescoring by the credit repositories can provide you with an indication of how payment of an old account will affect scoring.
- Negotiating with collection agencies: Collection agencies are accustomed to settling an account for less than what is owed. For example, you may have an open collection for $1,000 and the creditor is willing to take 25 cents on the dollar, so to settle the account you'd pay $250. After the account is settled and the debt is extinguished, it stays on your credit report as a closed collection. Some collection agencies will entertain completely removing the reporting of the collection account in its entirety if you pay the account in full. Whatever happens, be sure to obtain a paid receipt and a letter from the agency confirming the dispute is resolved.

Credit Scoring Variances by Provider

The FICO credit score is the most commonly used scoring model in the mortgage industry. Have you ever experienced your credit being pulled within a short time frame and your credit score is significantly different from one lender to another? Here's an example of how this can happen. You walk into a bank and apply for a credit card and they tell you that your FICO score is 728. Then, on the same day, you walk into an auto dealership and they say your FICO is 723. You keep walking into a mortgage company and they say your FICO is 719. Why the variations?

FICO has close to fifty different scoring models that it makes available to each lender with scores ranging from 300 to 850. Each formula weighs the credit factors that are of importance to a particular industry. You want to know what the formula is? Me too, so that I could share it with you; however, this formula, along with the Coca-Cola recipe, is kept under lock and key. Additionally, each bank or other institution may be pulling your score from only one repository: Equifax, TransUnion, or Experian. Not all creditors report to all three repositories. So it's very likely there will be variations between the three. This is why lenders select the middle score of the three repositories as the representative score for making a decision on your loan.

In 2006, the three major repositories got together and formulated VantageScore, a model in which they all agreed to follow the same weighting system. The VantageScore ranges from 501 to 990. It has yet to knock down the FICO scoring system as lenders' preferred model because, among other reasons, the GSEs haven't requested it. When looking at your credit report, be sure to identify which scoring model the analysis is based on, as an 800 on FICO does not signify the same as an 800 on Vantage.

What Does Your Credit Score Indicate?

Borrowers with a representative FICO score of 619 or less demonstrate to lenders that they are a high risk for nonpayment or for delays in receipt of payment, and they are often excluded from traditional lending options. Typically, these borrowers' only available option is a hard equity loan with private lending institutions, where they will be charged interest rates between two and four times the prevailing primary market interest rates. Borrowers with representative FICO scores in this range are strongly urged to make the investment of time and effort to repair their credit history as the long term costs associated with not doing so can be quite hefty.

While they may be eligible for lending through loan programs offered by the Federal Housing Administration, borrowers with credit scores ranging between 500 and 619 will find that many traditional lenders have their own credit overlays that prohibit lending to borrowers with a representative FICO score less than 620. Traditional lenders will likely approve loans with representative scores ranging from 620 to 659, but these borrowers should anticipate a higher cost mortgage. Credit scores between 660 and 739 are considered average; scores between 740 and 799 demonstrate to your lender that you are a very dependable borrower; and FICO scores above 800 demonstrate to your lender that you are an exceptional borrower.

Credit Utilization

Credit utilization represents a big portion of your total credit score. Revolving accounts that have a low balance-to-limit ratio generally represent a lower credit risk, while revolving accounts with a high balance-to-limit ratio represent a higher credit risk. Your balance-to-limit ratio is calculated by dividing the total of the balances on your credit cards by the total of the credit limits on your credit cards. A high balance-to-limit ratio warns creditors that you may be experiencing financial difficulty or using credit to live beyond your means.

The lower your utilization rate, the better. Reducing your credit limits will cause your utilization rate to increase because your existing balances will become a higher percentage of your reduced total available credit limits. Reducing your credit limits will, most likely, hurt your credit scores because of this mathematical reality. Try to keep your individual account balances below 50 percent of the total availability of that singular account during the entire course of the billing cycle. If you find yourself exceeding the 50 percent mark at any point during the billing cycle, send in an early payment on the account—because you don't know at what point in time the provider of credit will report your usage to the credit repositories.

While you may be someone who pays off their bill in its entirety at the end of each month, if your balance exceeds the 50 percent mark when it is reported, your high usage will be reflected in your credit evaluation and you will be at risk of obtaining a lower credit score. As a lower credit score generally indicates that you are a higher risk to the lender—and as we learned in high school Economics 101—higher risk demands a higher rate of return, so you should expect to be charged a higher interest rate. When your interest rate is higher, your interest costs are higher. It can be a heavy price to pay for simply mismanaging your credit access even with timely payments; be mindful of this during the months leading up to loan application.

Should You Close an Account?

Many people wonder whether their credit score will improve if they close an account. Some people will close an account that has an open balance because they want to limit their access to credit while paying down their bill. Not a good idea. If at your request, you limit your access to credit, what is a future lender to infer? The lender sees this as your inability to trust your usage of credit. It defeats your intended purpose. In establishing and maintaining credit accounts, your sole objective is to show you are creditworthy.

Having access to credit isn't a bad thing. Using your credit access on unimportant things you can't afford is a bad thing. In a credit analysis, one of the important factors we look at is how long an account has been open so that we can have a measure of your ability to make timely payments. Open accounts carry more weight than dormant accounts in a credit analysis. If you want your excellent payment history to be better reflected, use the account. I'm not saying to go out on a shopping spree, I'm suggesting you view it as a cash account for your necessities, and pay off the bill in full at the end of every month.

Credit card accounts are not like bank accounts. If your credit card information has been breached, you may have been told to immediately close the account. Instead, what you may want to do is ask the provider to issue a new number, so your account history remains intact.

Credit Inquiries

When the credit report indicates that recent inquiries took place (usually as far back as ninety days), your lender will ask you to write a letter of explanation addressing whether or not any new credit has been obtained that is not yet reflected as an open account on the credit report. The section "Letter of Explanation" in chapter 14 presents a model form to submit to your lender. To prevent delays in loan processing, work with your loan officer at loan application to remit this letter so that the underwriter doesn't have to condition your loan file for an explanation.

Tip: Be prepared to write a letter of explanation addressing all credit inquiries identified on your credit report. If no new credit was obtained, you will need a written explanation of why you allowed your credit to be pulled or what type of credit you were seeking, and clearly identify whether any new credit was opened. If additional credit was obtained, provide the lender with a copy of the terms of credit and the most recent billing statement, along with your signed and dated letter of explanation.

Addresses Reported

Your creditors may report any address they have on record to which you have your mail delivered and any address associated with an account that has your name on it. This means that work addresses and P.O. boxes may be listed, even though you never actually lived there. The same applies to temporary mailing addresses. If you are a joint account holder or an authorized user on an account with a friend or a family member, their address could be associated with you and subsequently their address may appear on your credit report as well. An address you do not recognize could be a sign of fraud, particularly if there are other identifying elements you don't recognize or accounts that aren't yours appearing in your report. Be sure to contact the repository that is reporting the account to learn methods of handling the issue.

For all addresses reported on your credit file, the lender will require that you provide a signed and dated letter of explanation disclosing whether you have ever maintained residence at the address reported and whether you have any ownership interest in each of the addresses reported. Additionally, some repositories report partial addresses or variants of the same address. Your lender will need you to identify your relationship with each address listed on your credit report. The section "Letter of Explanation" in chapter 14 provides a model form to submit to your lender. To prevent delays in loan processing, work with your loan officer at loan application to remit this letter so that the underwriter doesn't have to condition your loan file for an explanation.

Handling Disputed Accounts

The account history for a credit item listed as "in dispute" on the credit report is not included in the repositories scoring algorithm. While you may think this is good for you on accounts reporting derogatory events, it certainly is not good for your lender—which at the end of the day, is not good for you either. If an account has a derogatory history, some lenders will require that you remove the dispute so that your credit score can accurately reflect your payment history with that creditor. Once the dispute is removed, the lender will do a hard pull of your credit. The new usable credit score on the credit report may affect your loan pricing and loan eligibility. To your disfavor, an account maintained in good status that you've placed in dispute, let's say for an erroneous charge, will also be excluded from the credit scoring algorithm.

Some lenders have a policy in place that only allows for a credit re-pull when you can prove substantial error. I'll share with you a story about a wealthy applicant who used only three credit cards and had no mortgages and no auto loans. Although he had no slow pays, because he used limited credit, his credit score was average and this affected the pricing made available him, and the maximum loan amount he could be offered due to loan-to-value (LTV) eligibility standards. We reviewed the credit report together and identified that one of his credit cards was listed in dispute. He had forgotten that he had placed a dispute on the account at a time when a vendor had incorrectly billed him for a service that he had not authorized. The account in question had an excellent payment history and was excluded in the repository scoring algorithm. We believed his score would be improved if this account were included in the repository review. I asked the borrower to contact the repository and remove the dispute.

Once removed, we went back to the underwriter and asked for a new hard pull. Because the borrower could not prove there was a substantial error in the credit report and because the underwriter's risk manager felt inclusion of the account in the scoring algorithm would not significantly impact the FICO score, a business decision was made not to allow a hard pull. Their argument was that because of Fair Lending, we could not re-pull credit because, unless there was an error, the borrower's intent was to improve his usable credit score. As there was no error, just that the account remained "in dispute," I argued credit policy for weeks to allow the underwriter to re-pull credit because in not permitting this, I felt we were the one's committing a violation of Fair Lending. Finally, credit policy conceded with the warning that no matter what the new credit score would be, the borrower needed to know that it would be the final score used for loan pricing and eligibility.

I went back to the borrower and explained the risk. I asked him to confirm he had made all payments (on all accounts) on time since our original credit pull and that current balances on all accounts were less than 50 percent of available credit. We took a deep breath, notified the underwriter of his decision to proceed, lit a candle (if you're of Latin descent, you'll know what that implies), and waited. The borrower's credit score improved by fifty-six points. Whew! The loan closed at best pricing and the borrower's requested loan amount.

Manual Underwriting Downgrades

Aside from disputed accounts providing an inaccurate depiction of your credit score, an additional concern in underwriting an FHA loan is that FHA policy recommends a manual downgrade from an AUS approval of "Approve/Accept" to a "Refer." With a refer status, your loan file is automatically subjected to tighter restrictions for most underwriting guidelines. If this happens to you, an initial, conditional loan approval may easily be replaced with a denial because the manual downgrade requiring more stringent underwriting guidelines now prohibits you from obtaining a loan approval at the more aggressive credit criteria of AUS. If you didn't thoroughly review the results of your credit report with your loan officer, you will not have an accurate depiction of loan eligibility until an underwriter reviews your file.

For FHA analysis, disputed derogatory credit accounts are defined as follows:

- Disputed charge-off accounts
- Disputed collection accounts
- Disputed accounts with late payments in the last twenty-four months.

Nonderogatory disputed accounts include the following types of accounts:

- Disputed accounts with zero balance
- Disputed accounts with late payments twenty-four months or older
- Disputed accounts that are current and paid as agreed.

If you are disputing nonderogatory accounts, the lender is not required to downgrade the application to a "Refer." However, the lender must analyze the effect of the disputed accounts on your ability to repay the loan. If the dispute results in your making additional payments, that amount will also be factored into your debt-to- income ratio, making the new DTI ratio higher than what was originally indicated.

Tip: If your loan file is submitted with a credit report indicating disputed derogatory accounts, you will need to provide a letter of explanation and documentation supporting the basis of the dispute. The underwriter will analyze the documentation provided for consistency with other credit information in the file to determine if the derogatory credit account should be considered in the underwriting analysis. If the loan file is submitted without addressing the dispute, no consideration will be given to following the recommended findings of an AUS approval.

Tip: To avoid a headache and documentation hazard, resolve your disputed account before making loan application and contact the credit repositories to update their status upon resolution.

How Long Do Derogatory Credit Events Stay on the Credit Report?

Derogatory credit events will stay on your credit report for a definite period of time. Slow pays usually become less impactful to your credit scores after 24 months have passed. Here are some significant events and how long, by law, they are allowed to stay on your report:

- Chapter 7 bankruptcy (the type of bankruptcy where a person does not repay any of the debt included in the filing) will remain on the credit report for up to ten years from the filing date.
- Chapter 13 bankruptcy (the type of bankruptcy where a person at least repays a portion of their debt) remains on the credit report for at least seven years from the filing date.
- Any unpaid tax liens can remain on the credit report for up to ten years from the filing date and any paid tax liens can remain on the credit report for up to seven years from the date it was paid.

What Is Your Total Overall Cost of Credit?

Let's go to the accordion folder and pull out the most current billing statements for your revolving charge accounts. Grab a highlighter and comb through the billing statement to find your annual percentage rate (APR). Mark it. Your APR is your annual cost of credit. Unlike installment loans, revolving credit accounts allow the interest rate charged by the provider to change over time. Many credit card companies offer you a very low introductory interest rate to compel you to open an account. Over time, they can change your billing rate as they perform routine checks of your credit history and will adjust the terms of your existing revolving credit account based on the current information it receives from the credit repositories, even if you've never made a late payment on their account. Yikes! Do you know what rate of interest you're currently being charged?

Some credit cards begin charging interest at the moment you make the purchase. Others begin charging interest only on the balance that is not paid in full at the end of every month. Some charge an annual fee, others don't. Read the billing statement to determine how each of your accounts imposes their fees. Go to your Monthly Budget Spreadsheet (a customizable model form is provided at www.MortgageMattersBook.com) and next to each account, write the APR, the annual fee, and a running total of all interest charges billed over the previous twelve months.

If you are a current homeowner and are considering refinancing your mortgage, have equity in your home, and are struggling to payoff accrued debt, you may want to consider converting some of the equity in your home into cash to pay off the high interest credit cards or student loans. Don't use debt consolidation as a tool to extend payment of the debt over a thirty-year period: that would be a mistake in financial planning. Instead, select a term that's commensurate with your remaining term, take advantage of the lower interest charges and prepay the mortgage with the additional disposable income realized from the interest savings.

No Credit?

According to TransUnion, in 2013, roughly twenty-two million persons or 9 percent of the U.S. population has no credit file, fewer than one in five persons have had their reports checked, and forty-two million Americans have errors on their credit reports. (See the full report at: http://www.urban.org/uploadedpdf/413191-delinquent-debt-in-america.pdf.) The U.S. credit markets are a new concept for many people. Many of our grandparents have traditionally refused to buy on credit. For them, cash-only was the way to go: "If you can't afford it, you don't buy it." While that attitude is still held as a virtue by many, in today's world it can cause problems for people who need to borrow, especially for a high-ticket item like a mortgage. I see this often with recent immigrants as well: In their homeland, credit markets aren't as developed as the U.S. credit market, and they don't understand why we encourage them to use credit when they have cash available.

The reason lenders want to see how you've responded to borrowing money is to make a determination as to whether you will repay your mortgage on time, and without an existing credit history, that's difficult to estimate. So for those with no traditional credit histories, before making loan application, consider two options. The first option is to build a nontraditional credit history, which can help you obtain a mortgage even if you don't have four traditional credit accounts. A nontraditional credit history can be built with things like utility bill payments, rent, telephone bills, and daycare expenses—anything that does not normally appear on a credit report. To build this nontraditional credit report, work with your creditors and your lender to provide credit reference letters. Review the "Credit Reference Letter" section in chapter 14 for lender requirements of letters to validate account existence and payment history.

The second option, if time is on your side, is to apply for a standard credit card or store charge account. If you choose this option, be careful. The idea is not to build debt. The idea is to use the cards as if they were cash and pay them off every month as you budget your spending. You can do this very easily by only using the charge cards for small-ticket items such as gasoline, groceries, or clothing.

A Special Note to Women

According to the Federal Trade Commission, under the Equal Credit Opportunity Act, not having a credit history reported under her name can hurt a married, separated, divorced, or widowed woman. Typically, there are two reasons women don't have credit histories in their own names: either they lost their credit histories with utility companies when they married and changed their names, or creditors reported accounts shared by married couples in the husband's name only. When making loan application, be sure to provide your loan officer with all of your name variations used for gaining credit access.

Tip: If you're married, separated, divorced, or widowed, contact the three repositories and all utility companies to make sure all relevant bill payment information is in a file under your own name. The repositories sell the information in your report to creditors, insurers, employers, and other businesses that, in turn, use it to evaluate your applications for credit, insurance, employment, or renting a home.

One Borrower Has Traditional Credit and the Other Doesn't

When one borrower has traditional credit represented by a FICO score and the second borrower (or co-borrower) is using nontraditional credit history with no representative credit score, this presents challenges for the lender. The agency's provide guidance for the lender on how to use the scores for determining eligibility and calculate pricing (you can find Fannie Mae's borrower resource on this topic at https://www.fanniemae.com/content/job_aid/uldd-quick-guide-borrower.pdf). In assessing loan eligibility, the representative credit score for the borrower with traditional credit is the representative credit score for the transaction for eligibility purposes. However, when pricing the loan, the guideline is to use the lowest representative credit score of all borrowers and pricing add-ons are enforced as listed in the Loan Level Pricing Adjustments (LLPA) Matrix. This means that your loan will receive worst case pricing based on the lack of a representative score for the nontraditional credit borrower. Additionally, some lenders have overlays that require that both borrowers have usable scores and that the lowest of those scores is what is used for both setting pricing and meeting eligibility. Ask your loan officer how you are affected by the lenders overlay, if at all.

Authorized Users

An authorized user of a credit account is not the owner of the credit account and therefore, a lender typically excludes the credit history on that account from your profile. However, if you have a limited credit profile or are attempting to build a nontraditional credit history, you may be able to request that your lender include the history on that account in their credit review. For consideration, the lender will need a written request from you and this would require documentation (e.g., canceled checks or payment receipts) to support that you have been the actual and sole payer of the monthly payment on the account for at least twelve months preceding the date of the application.

Tip: If you are an authorized user on a revolving credit account that you don't use where the primary account owner is not making timely payments, you may want to consider removing yourself from this account, as activity will be held against you.

Fraud Alerts and Security Freezes Can Help Protect Your Credit

The credit repositories provide these two tools to help mitigate fraud on your credit report. Fraud alerts signal credit grantors that you may have been a victim of suspicious activity. They also provide indicators for creditors to take extra steps to verify the legitimacy of a request for new credit. The repositories update their alert databases based on indicators that are cause for concern. The lender pays special attention to alerts that may indicate misrepresentation. (You can find Equifax's alerts on their Consumer Information Solutions page at www.equifax.com/pdfs/corp/EFS-937-ADV-IdentityScan_4page.pdf.)

A security freeze will prevent the information in your credit file from being reported to third parties, such as credit grantors and other companies. This means that it's unlikely that an identity thief would be able to open a new account in your name. Many (but not all) states allow you to place a security freeze on your credit file for free or for a reduced fee. To see if a security freeze is available in your state, what your state requires, how to request it, and what fees may apply, visit Consumers Union (http://consumersunion.org/research/consumers-unions-guide-to-security-freeze-protection).

As you head into securing a mortgage loan request, you must review your credit and take certain actions when you have fraud alerts and security freezes. Your cell phone number should accompany a fraud alert so that potential creditors can contact you to confirm your identity before granting new credit. If you don't have a cell phone, provide the telephone number where you can be reached during business hours. Additionally, a security freeze must be lifted in order for the repository to release information to a lender. When either of these things is not taken care of before loan application, you will have delays in the processing of your loan request, guaranteed.

There are three main types of fraud alerts and each has their own length of effectiveness:

1. Initial fraud alert: 90 days
2. Active duty alert: 1 year
3. Extended fraud alert: 7 years

If you believe that you may have been a victim of fraud or are at risk of being a victim you can put an initial fraud alert on your credit file. With an Initial fraud alert on your credit report, you're entitled to order one free credit report from each of the three repositories, and if you ask, only the last four digits of your Social Security number will appear on your credit reports.

You may be eligible to place an active duty alert if you have been called to active duty military service away from your usual duty post. This type of alert is similar to the initial fraud alert, except that it will remain on your file for twelve months, and it removes your name from prescreened offers of credit for two years.

If you discover evidence of fraud or know that you are a victim, you may place an extended fraud alert, which stays on your credit file for seven years and requires creditors to verify your request by contacting you on the telephone number(s) you provide to the credit-reporting agency when you requested the extended fraud alert. To place an extended fraud alert, you will need to write to one of the nationwide credit-reporting agencies and provide a valid police report showing that you have been the victim of identity theft (called an Identity Theft Report) as well as a day and evening telephone number to include on your credit file. The requirements for an Identity Theft Report are listed on the Federal Trade Commission website, which can be found at https://www.consumer.ftc.gov/articles/0277-create-identity-theft-report. With an extended fraud alert, you may request two additional free credit file disclosures, and your name is removed from prescreened offers of credit or insurance for five years.

Filing with one repository is usually sufficient, as the expectation is that each will automatically forward any of your fraud or active duty alerts to the other two credit-reporting bureaus, and they will generally be placed on your credit file within twenty-four hours. Make sure to monitor activities on all three repositories.

07 Documentation Standards

I would venture to say that the number one reason mortgage transactions are delayed or abandoned is that frustration sets in with the overwhelming amount of documentation that is required. I don't want you to be a person who walks away. We can minimize the number of touches your file receives by properly preparing and submitting loan documentation that supports what the underwriter needs to satisfy loan conditions. All documents have expiration dates. You'll learn how to identify them as they relate to your loan application and funding date.

WITH MY BORROWERS, I lay down the rules upfront and in a rather dictatorial fashion. During our initial discovery interview, I take notes, and at the end, I give the borrower the laundry list of supporting documentation that the underwriter is going to require to complete the analysis of the loan request. Some clients are turned off by the long list and either express their frustration or call up another loan officer who doesn't request so many items upfront. Choosing to make application with "an easier" loan officer, does not provide for an atmosphere of quick decision-making. Whether you want to or not, at some point along the processing of your loan request, you will hand over all the documents that are asked of you. The longer it takes you to hand them over, the longer the processing period of your loan request.

Here's a question that causes regular delays in loan processing: Do you really need the last page of my bank statement, because its just blank? My answer is always, "Well, if you really need a loan commitment by contract date, yes." All numbered pages of bank statements are required to be reviewed by a decision maker. Documentation requirements are nonnegotiable.

Underwriting decisions are expedited when the underwriter has all the facts at hand. The initial review of a loan application is typically made within the first seven days of submission. The second (and hopefully) final review isn't made until the requested conditions from the initial review are all in. If the initial submission was missing critical loan data that wasn't identified until the second review was completed, additional supporting documentation will be required and the deciding of your loan could be delayed another two weeks. To minimize this period of indecision, its best to provide to your loan officer all requested loan documents within forty-eight hours of loan application. In this section, I've highlighted information on supporting documentation that will require explanation, correction, or additional documentation.

It's essential that you prepare right now—even if you're not quite ready to make loan application. Here's why: By gathering your loan documentation and reviewing it as we go along, you'll be able to identify gaps and create opportunities, just as I would do when working with my clients. Dedicate a Saturday to gathering all that you need in one shot. Start by getting your supplies and making a copy of the Comprehensive Documentation Checklist found in the "Resources" section or download a printable version at www.MortgageMattersBook.com.

Identification Documents

Your lender will require review of typical documentation that confirms your identity and will use all methods available to verify authenticity to prevent identity fraud. Have available your driver's license or government issued ID and Social Security card. If you are a permanent or a nonpermanent resident, provide your alien registration card or permanent resident card (INS Form I-551). If you are a nonresident alien, provide your valid U.S. nonimmigrant visa and unexpired passport from your country of origin.

Here are some common issues to address with your lender at loan application to prevent unnecessary delays:

1. Does your driver's license have your current address? Why not? Be prepared to write an explanation listing where you actually currently reside.
2. Does your driver's license list your full legal name? Is this name how you wish to title the property? If not, address titling options with your loan officer.
3. Does the name on your driver's license match the name on your social security card, tax returns for the preceding two years, W-2s, and bank statements? If not, be prepared to write an explanation of name variances.
4. Do you go by a nickname?
5. Does the name listed on your social security card match identically to that listed on the loan application? If not, you may be subjected to additional verifications of your identity. See section in chapter 14 on proper execution of form SSA-89.

Address History

Each loan applicant is asked to list the addresses where they have resided for the preceding two years. Have ready a list with the complete addresses. If you use a mailing address, let your loan officer know that although you reside at 123 Main Street, you prefer to have all postal service mailed documents delivered to 456 Elm Street. If you were renting at any time over the preceding two-year period, have available the complete contact information for your landlord as the lender will need to verify the timeliness of your payment history. You may also need to give the lender evidence of rental payments to include front and back copies of cancelled checks. If you're making rental payments to a management company, the lender may not require you to evidence rental payments as it can verify payment history through a third party; it depends on the lender's policy. Have evidence of payments ready anyway.

Employment Data

For each employment you've held over the preceding two-year period (and including all income sources as reported in the last two years of tax returns), come prepared to loan application with the contact information for the person who can verify your income, position, and employment dates. This is typically not your direct supervisor, but your human resources director. If it's a small business, sometimes the owner or their accountant provides this information. If the employer is now defunct just write, sign and date a letter of explanation stating this fact.

Employment gaps longer than one month need to be documented by a signed and dated letter of explanation. Some major corporations use The Work Number service to provide verification of employment and income data. If this is what your employer uses, be sure to obtain the authorization code from your human resource director to share with your lender so that your lender can access the verification system. The Work Number will not release information to a third party without your confirmation and consent.

We are looking for a two-year employment history as this helps us assess your income reliability. That said, it is still possible to document stable earnings that are likely to continue without having established a stable employment history in one position or job. It is not unusual for some borrowers to change jobs frequently, even changing lines of work. Many times, a person simply has to go where there is available work. To offset a lack of employment stability, where there is documentable continuance of income, provide a signed and dated letter of explanation addressing why income sources vary.

Generally speaking, a lender will require a full two-year history of employment, but not always. Is your new employment salary based? If so, much leeway is given here if you are able to document extenuating circumstances. For example, were you a full-time student and recently graduated? Are you a lawyer returning to the workforce after seven years? Provide explanation through a signed and dated letter of explanation and provide supporting documentation as requested to help your lender justify its decision.

Documentation to Support Income

Determination of qualifying income is based on many, many variables. To document your income, you will provide copies of W-2s, federal income tax returns, paycheck stubs, or other documentation to support the income claimed on the loan application. Multiple combinations of scenarios exist that can affect how qualifying income is determined: using one pay stub and one

W-2; four pay stubs and one W-2; four pay stubs, two W-2s and two personal tax returns; four pay stubs, two W-2s, two personal tax returns, and two business tax returns (for all businesses); or four pay stubs, two W-2s, two personal tax returns, two business tax returns, a profit and loss statement, a balance sheet, a Schedule K-1, and a partridge in a pear tree. If there is ever a time a loan officer can expect "it depends" as an answer to their underwriting question, it's when we are unsure if the analysis will be based on a one year or a two year history or reported income. Minor updates to the loan application can drastically change the documentation requirements. We can have gone from requiring only the most recent years tax return to averaging the two most recent years tax returns. Averaging income can significantly reduce the amount eligible for use in qualifying income.

Pay Stubs

The pay stubs provided should cover the most recent pay periods, including at least thirty days of income, at the time of loan application. For loan applications that take longer than four months to close, updated pay stubs will be requested as they can be no older than four months from the date the note is signed at loan closing. If you make loan application too early or if your loan closing is delayed, be ready to provide updated pay stubs prior to loan closing, so keep collecting copies in your accordion folder.

The number of pay stubs needed varies depending on your pay schedule. If you are paid weekly, you will deliver to your loan officer the most recent four pay stubs. If you are paid biweekly, you will deliver to your loan officer the most recent two pay stubs. If you are paid monthly, you will deliver to your loan officer one pay stub. If your pay stubs do not include a running year-to-date total (many small businesses don't) the lender will need to send a written verification of employment request form to the person authorized to release this information by your employer. Often this person is the small business owner or the bookkeeper or the company accountant. If you work for a family-owned business, in addition to the completion of the verification of employment form, your lender may require that you submit personal tax returns for the preceding two years.

Tax Returns: Yes or No? If So, One or Two?

Sometimes, your lender may not require review of your income tax returns at all. That decision typically depends on GSE recommendations for your income structure and the lender's individual policies on documentation review standards. For example, for a self-employed borrower, automated underwriting system recommendations could call for a review of just the most recent year's filed tax return, but the lender you are working with is requiring a two year review of tax returns because their risk appetite is less aggressive than the agency's. This difference in documentation standards could lead to receiving a denial from one lender and an approval from another lender when nothing about you has changed. This may occur in instances where a self-employed borrower reports greater income on their most recent year's federal income tax return, but the previous year's reported income is much lower.

When the review of two year's federal income tax returns is required, the lender will typically use the average of both years if the most current year income is the same or better than the previous year's income. If the most recent year return shows a decline in income from the previous year, the lender may choose to not average the two-year income. In this case, the lender may use only the most recent year's lower reported income—unless you can explain and document extenuating circumstances.

You may or may not be asked to provide your personal tax return; it depends on a lot of things. Whether you are asked to present your lender with your personal tax returns or not, they have the right to validate the income you reported to the IRS separately through IRS Form 4506-T. Knowing that your lender can get your reported income directly from the IRS, you may be wondering why they would still require you give them a copy of your income tax return: This a precautionary measure to protect you, itself, and future investors against identity theft by someone who has accessed your identifying information such as a driver's license and social security card, and is seeking financing under your name.

Generally speaking, for salaried borrowers qualifying income can be determined by reviewing pay stubs covering the most recent thirty-day period. While we usually request W-2s for the preceding one or two years, we do not base your qualifying income on W-2s. We use the W-2s to document stability of income. That said, we may or may not ask you for personal federal income tax returns in addition to the W-2s. In all cases where the lender has validated federal income tax returns, the calculation of qualifying income for salaried borrowers will be reduced by deductions taken for unreimbursed business expenses.

If you own a 25 percent or more share of a business, you are considered self-employed for underwriting purposes and will be asked to provide your personal income tax returns as well as your business income tax returns. If you are a salaried employee who receives 25 percent or more of your income from commissions or bonuses, you will be asked to deliver your personal income tax returns and the lender will need your employer to confirm bonus and overtime income over the preceding two year period.

When federal tax returns are used in the calculation of qualifying income, generally speaking, only income validated by the IRS can be used for underwriting decisions. This means that if you prepare your federal income tax return, but do not submit it to the IRS for processing, your lender is unable to give consideration to the income reported. However, with evidence of payment of your estimated tax liability, your lender may give consideration to the income reported. Maybe.

If you filed your return and it shows you owe money to the IRS, the lender will require evidence that you've made payment on your tax liability or it will deduct from your usable assets the amount you owe, if any, to the IRS. Foreign income earned and not reported on U.S. tax returns presents specific challenges for mortgage underwriting and the determination of qualifying income. Read the section "Foreign Income Earned" in chapter 11 to learn your unique challenges.

Determining If You Need to Provide Federal Income Tax Returns

While you may be a salaried borrower and your loan officer may initially tell you that you will only need to deliver W-2s and not income tax returns, you will be required to submit signed federal income tax returns for the most recent two years if any of the following situations apply to you:

- Earn 25 percent or more of your income from commissions
- Are employed by a family member
- Are employed by interested parties to the purchase
- Receive rental income from an investment property
- Receive income from temporary or periodic employment (or unemployment) or employment that is subject to time limits, such as that of a contract employee or a tradesman
- Receive income from capital gains, royalties, real estate, or other miscellaneous nonemployment earnings reported on IRS Form 1099
- Receive income that cannot otherwise be verified by an independent and knowledgeable source
- Use foreign income to qualify
- Use interest and dividend income to qualify
- Receive income from sole proprietorships, limited liability companies, partnerships, corporations, or any other type of business structure where you have a 25 percent or greater ownership interest. (If you have a 25 percent or greater ownership interest, you are considered self-employed for that entity. The lender must document and underwrite the loan application using the requirements for self-employed borrowers found in chapter 4.)

Allowable Age of Federal and State Tax Returns

There is often confusion about which year's tax returns a lender needs to review in order to make an underwriting decision. This may happen when a filing extension is requested or when a business uses fiscal year reporting versus calendar year reporting. The list below offers some clarity. In all cases where your lender requires review of your tax returns, it will confirm the validity of the tax returns submitted by exerting its right to execute IRS Form 4506-T. Regardless of whether tax returns were submitted or not, the lender can exercise its right to verify income reported to the IRS through Form 4506-T and the subsequent investor can elect to verify the same as part of its auditing processes.

The requirement for the most recent year's tax return is defined by a combination of the IRS filing deadlines and the scheduled funding date of your loan. (The funding date is the loan disbursement date. Disbursement means that the creditor delivered the funds to the settlement agent and the settlement agent disbursed the loan proceeds according to the items listed and approved on the HUD-1 or Closing Disclosure.) Depending on the funding date of the loan, this is the documentation you'll need to provide to your lender:

1. If the funding date is between October 15 and April 14 of any year, you will need to provide the most recent year's tax return.
2. If the funding date is between April 15 and June 30 of the current year, you'll be asked whether you've completed and filed your tax return with the IRS for the previous year. If the answer is yes, the lender must obtain copies of that return. If the answer is no, the lender will obtain copies of tax returns for the preceding two years or one year, as applicable. Although not required, it is the lender's prerogative to execute IRS Form 4506-T, confirming your claim that no tax return was filed for the most recent year.
3. If the funding date is between July 1 and October 14, the lender must obtain the most recent year's tax return, or an executed IRS tax transcript confirming "No Transcripts Available" for the preceding tax year and copies of the two prior years' returns.

If the loan funding date is: Then, IRS defined most recent return is:
February 15, 2015 2013
April 17, 2015 2014
December 15, 2015 2014

If You Filed an Extension for Your Taxes

Filing an extension of the IRS deadline for reporting doesn't relieve you of tax liability for income earned, nor does it exclude its analysis by the underwriter. While its possible that you were unprepared to file your tax return by the IRS tax filing date of April 15, and subsequently submitted a filing extension (IRS Form 4868), if your lender requires the review of the tax return and it is not available nor filed, the lender will request a copy of the IRS application for extension of filing in place of the most recent year's tax return.

It will review the total tax liability reported on IRS Form 4868 and compare it with your tax liability from the previous two years as a measure of income source, stability, and continuance. If the estimated tax liability on the current year extension form is less than line 61 on the prior year return, then the income is declining, and the current year's return must be used for calculating income. You must not only provide all pages of the federal income tax return, but also must also provide proof that returns were filed. An estimated tax liability that is inconsistent with previous years may make it necessary for the lender to review the most recent year's income tax returns in order to proceed.

Tip: If you are self-employed and you expect to report a significant increase in income compared to the prior year's income tax return, or if the prior year's income tax return was significantly higher than the return filed in the penultimate year (i.e. 2015 will be higher than 2013), hurry up and provide your information to your accountant and file your return right away so that the lender can use your most current, higher reported two-year average for determining qualifying income.

Filing Amendments to Tax Returns

If you have filed an amendment to previously reported income in the prior two-year period (or for any period that you presented tax returns to your lender) there are extra steps both you and your lender will need to take. You will need to write a letter of explanation regarding what specifically caused a change in reporting, and you will need to provide both your original income tax return and the amended tax return. Your lender will in turn, verify the validity of reporting for both the original and the amended return. Here's the thing: Amended tax returns don't automatically appear on the tax transcripts as requested by IRS Form 4506-T. If you have filed an amended return, be sure to point this out to your loan officer at application so that IRS Form 4506-T can be properly executed by marking section 6B Account Transcript or 6C Record of Account. Otherwise, the lender will only receive the tax transcript for the originally submitted return, and this will cause a delay for you in the processing of your loan, as it may appear that you've submitted fraudulent reporting of income.

Documentation to Support Assets

The more usable assets you report on your loan application, the lower the risk you present to the decision maker (usable assets are defined in chapter 10 in the section on assets and liabilities). This is because lender's view post-closing liquidity or reserves as one of the highest indicators of the likelihood that you will make your mortgage payments on time. Post-closing liquidity is the money available to you after loan closing, calculated by taking your verified assets and reducing them by your down payment and closing costs.

To prove usable assets, standard business practices are to deliver the most recent two months of bank, brokerage, and retirement account statements that include all numbered pages (include two monthly statements or one quarterly). Yes, even the page that has nothing on it and the page that is provided to help you balance your checkbook. If it is numbered, give it to the lender. In all cases, the most recent statement is the one your lender needs. Avoid transferring money between accounts that are not linked to one another on bank statements within the three months preceding your loan application. Many, many, many times, the lender mishandles updating asset information on the loan application when it receives an updated bank statement or a transaction history to document the movement of monies, and we inadvertently lose track of previously documented funds and the borrower—now appears to be short on funds for closing. Typically, this occurs when the second escrow deposit has been paid and we haven't provided you with a credit for this amount. See "Section VII: Details of Transaction" in chapter 10.

If at the time of loan application you've already provided your initial escrow deposit and it has cleared your bank account, disclose this information to your loan officer so that the loan application will show a credit for the first deposit. Additionally, identify this transfer of funds on bank statements or a transaction history by circling or highlighting it to indicate these funds will apply as credits on your closing statement. If they haven't cleared your account at application, the lender will ask for an updated statement to show that the first escrow check cleared your account or a transaction history from the date of the last statement through the date the escrow funds cleared your account. Be mindful that while we may be looking to verify that initial escrow payment, we aren't looking for any additional withdrawals that would indicate you made the second escrow payment—unless you specifically tell us that you paid the second escrow deposit and you give us a copy of the front and back of that check as well.

Sometimes, initial AUS recommendations will require the loan officer to collect only one bank statement to validate the assets as listed on your loan application. It is very common to be asked to provide additional bank statements, as there are many variables that no one can predict with certainty. As verified data is updated on your loan application to include such things as the value of the property, type of property, final determination of qualifying income, recurring debts, or cost of homeowners insurance, the underwriter will re-run AUS and the system will issue new recommendations. The new findings may require the review of a two-month history of bank statements instead of the one originally requested month. This happens quite often and it is neither a defect of your loan officer nor that of your lender, it simply is the way loans are underwritten.

If a second month is required, and from the time of the originally submitted statement ending date (provided to the loan officer at application) a new bank statement has been issued, you will need to provide the lender with that new statement instead of the one you are holding in your accordion file that preceded the statement you provided at loan application. For this reason, its important to add new statements to your accordion file as your loan file is in processing so that you'll be ready to provide them if your lender subsequently requires them.

With new construction, you will also be required to show evidence of your initial escrow payments and these additional bank statements may not be from the most recent month. They will be as old as when you initially entered into contract and are generally required to evidence each escrow payment.

Tip: It's very, very, very important to point out to your loan officer or loan processor all money that is given prior to settlement to ensure these funds are properly reflected in your required cash to close figures. This information is discussed in "Section VII—Details of Transaction" in chapter 10.

Tip: For all real estate owned, put together a spreadsheet that includes the following categories: complete property address, year acquired, initial purchase price, yearly tax bill, yearly insurance premiums, monthly homeowner association dues, and rental income, if any. For each lien holder (first mortgage, second mortgage, equity line), list the following: name of lender, account number, current balance, current interest rate (fixed or adjustable), monthly principal and interest payment, and portion of monthly payment to lender that is for escrows (tax and insurances), if any.

08 Comparing Loan Program Options

Every lender has a different set of loan programs that it can offer, and you should expect slight pricing variations from one lender to another even in the same program and same scenario presumptions. Most importantly, each lender has different underwriting guidelines for their product offerings. When comparison shopping, ask plenty of questions. Aside from getting a quote for the standard thirty-year fixed rate loan product that most people initially perceive to be their best choice, make it a point to seek your loan officer's opinion on other loan options that may present a better match based on your specific financial objectives.

THE CONSUMER FINANCIAL Protection Bureau conducted a survey asking consumers how many good faith estimates they received before making an application, the study found that about 77 percent of borrowers stop the mortgage shopping process after making their first loan application. (See the full survey here: http://files.consumerfinance.gov/f/twentyfifteen01_cfpb_consumers-mortgage-shopping-experience.pdf.) With this information, it was deduced that most consumers do not spend sufficient time exploring their options. What was not asked is how many preapplication cost estimates they received prior to making a decision to make loan application. That is the true measure of the shopping experience. Few people will make an application with more than two lenders as applications fees can be upwards of $300.

Ask for preapplication cost estimates based on different programs, different terms, different down payment options, and different origination points. A preapplication cost estimate is not the same as a good faith/loan estimate—those are binding. A preapplication cost estimate is provided based on many assumptions. First of which is an estimation of your usable credit score, since at this point, your lender has not yet pulled your credit. Final loan pricing will depend on many factors.

Comparing Lenders

Unless you can instantly access a mortgage quote based on your particular criteria within minutes of each other, you won't really have an accurate method of comparing lender pricing. With today's technology, the secondary market—where mortgages are priced and sold—constantly provides updates to lenders in real time. Lenders in turn, will issue pricing updates to their sales force throughout the day to protect themselves against losses or to take advantage of price reductions in the marketplace. It's important for you to keep timing in mind when obtaining price quotes.

If you spoke to a loan officer you liked on Monday and then on Thursday you received a price quote from another loan officer that was better than the quote received from Monday's loan officer, but you felt more comfortable with the Monday loan officer, do yourself a favor and call back the Monday loan officer and ask him to update his preapplication cost estimate for you based on today's rates. In all likelihood, his rates will be just as favorable as the Thursday loan officer quoted.

Tip: It is wisest to choose to make loan application with the loan officer that you feel will most effectively represent your needs rather than focusing only on getting the lowest preapplication rate.

Homebuyer Counseling

Many low down payment loan programs require you to go through homebuyer counseling. If obtaining a conventional loan with mortgage insurance, the mortgage insurance providers offer online course options your loan officer can set this up for you. Then your loan officer will be notified and provided a completion certificate to document your loan file. If seeking a loan in conjunction with a county or city grant, many lenders require receipt of a HUD homeownership counseling certificate prior to accepting your loan application. Check with your lender and check with the county or city grant provider. HUD provides online tools and in-person seminars here: www.consumerfinance.gov/find-a-housing-counselor.

Conventional Versus Government Loan Products

Any loan not guaranteed or insured by the U.S. government is considered a conventional loan. Any loan guaranteed or insured by the government is considered a government loan. Conventional loans are broken down into conforming and nonconforming loan amounts. Currently, conforming loan amounts are those that do not exceed $417,000. Any loan amount above $417,000 is considered a nonconforming or jumbo loan amount.

Loan limits are the maximum allowable loan size for a mortgage delivered to the GSEs and will vary by loan product and region. Loan limits for both government and conventional loans are established annually using the permanent authority under section 203(b)(2) of the National Housing Act, as amended by Congress in the Housing and Economic Recovery Act of 2008 (HERA). The National Housing Act also sets loan limits in high cost areas at 115 percent of the median home prices for the area. Limits for government insured loans vary by metropolitan statistical area. For example, the Federal Housing Administration enforces loan limits for FHA loans, and the Department of Veterans Affairs maintains loan limits for VA loans. Loans that exceed an FHA loan's local loan limit cannot be insured and loans exceeding the VA loans local limit cannot be guaranteed. (To learn FHA loan limits in a specific area, visit https://entp.hud.

gov/idapp/html/hicostlook.cfm. To learn VA loan limits in a specific area, visit www.benefits. va.gov/homeloans/purchaseco_loan_limits.asp.)

New Loan Disclosures

As part of the implementation of the final rules of the Dodd-Frank Act, there will be a combination of various Real Estate Settlement and Procedures Act (RESPA) and Truth-in-Lending Act (TILA) regulations to create all-new disclosure documents designed to be more helpful to consumers, while integrating information from existing documents to reduce the overall number of forms. The rule will replace the traditional good faith estimate and the HUD-1 settlement form for certain loan transactions, but not all. These rules apply to most closed-end consumer mortgages. They do not apply to home equity lines of credit (HELOCs), reverse mortgages, or mortgages secured for a mobile home or by a dwelling that is not attached to real property (i.e., land). Oddly enough, for these loans, the old forms will continue to be used which will create a slew of issues for both lenders and settlement agents. Real estate transactions paid in cash will still use the HUD-1 settlement form.

Implementation of this new rule goes into effect August 1, 2015 and impacts two processes of the mortgage transaction and affects everyone involved in real estate. Key features of the TILA/ RESPA Integrated Disclosure rule include:

- When applying for a loan, the new loan estimate document replaces the Truth-in-Lending disclosure and the good faith estimate.
- At loan closing, the new closing disclosure replaces the final TIL and HUD-1/ settlement form.
- Loan applications taken prior to August 1, 2015, require the use of the traditional GFE and HUD-1. As such, lenders will be telling closing agents for months to come whether to use the HUD-1 or the new closing disclosure.

The Loan Estimate

The Consumer Financial Protection Bureau (CFPB) has designed the new loan estimate as a comparison tool intended to provide financial uniformity for borrowers with which to shop different lenders and aims to provide them with a better way to understand the information being given. Uniformity of the loan estimate throughout the marketplace also applies to timing. The loan estimate must be delivered to you within three business days of taking a loan application. No fees can be collected by the lender and no consent to proceed can be requested by you until you have received the loan estimate—much as is required in today's operating environment with the good faith estimate. The closing disclosure must be delivered to you at a minimum of three business days prior to loan consummation.

The CFPB governs implementation of the rules that define a loan application as information taken from you to include a minimum six components. These are: (1) borrower name, (2) borrower Social Security number, (3) borrower income, (4) property address, (5) estimate of property value, and (6) mortgage amount requested. Once these six items are collected, the law identifies the lender has a loan application, and this sets in motion the clock for issuing loan disclosures.

Note: For the reasons reviewed in the "The Six Basic Steps to Mortgage Approval" section in chapter 1, although a lender can't require it, it is in your best interests to deliver to your loan officer supporting documentation at the time you disclose your Social Security number. The time to release your Social Security number is when you've narrowed down your loan options and are ready to make application. Program eligibility will be subject to credit score minimums. Be prepared to evaluate different options once your lender has identified your representative credit score from their service provider (not a report you give them).

Overall, the loan estimate is intended to give you more helpful information about the key features, costs, and risks of the loan for which you are applying. Certain costs on the loan estimate are binding to the lender and any changes from estimated fees to final fees are subject to tolerance variances. If a lender exceeds a tolerance variance, it must absorb the cost or risk consequences of a compliance violation. A lender is required to keep records of when the loan estimate was issued to ensure it is in compliance. For this reason, many lenders will prohibit the issuance of the loan estimate to only instances where all six components of a loan application are received (much as they do currently when issuing a good faith estimate).

Here's where this may get tricky for you: When you're at the shopping stage of the loan process, all you want to do is review loan programs that may satisfy your financial needs and objectives and shop interest rates and fees with different lenders. You don't want to make full application with any lender just yet. What you really need at this point is a preapplication cost estimate, which is nonbinding to the lender. To provide a preapplication cost estimate, a lender needs only three of the six components that define a loan application—borrower name, estimate of property value, and mortgage loan amount requested. Therefore, providing preapplication cost estimates does not trigger the issuance of regulatory disclosures for loan application. Preapplication cost estimates are nonbinding to the lender because they are based on certain variables that will only reveal themselves during the processing of your loan that may include:
- Credit score
- Property type (single-family, condo, PUD) and number of units
- Value of property

- Loan amount
- Intended occupancy (owner-occupied, second home, investment)
- Assumption of debt-to-income ratio of 43 percent or less
- Date and time of interest rate lock request

As scheduled for release, a fault of the proposed loan estimate is that it doesn't specifically list all assumptions the lender has made in its calculation of pricing, which would aid clarity for borrowers who are comparison shopping between lenders.

Today, there is no rule that prohibits a lender from issuing a preapplication cost estimate prior to your making full loan application. After August 2015, there still will be no rule that will prohibit this activity. After August 2015, a preapplication estimate is prohibited to look like either the new loan estimate or the existing good faith estimate and will need to include specific language that it is not to be considered either a loan estimate or a good faith estimate. If you've contacted a lender who only provides written cost estimates using the loan estimate and does not design preapplication cost estimates for their sales force to use to assist potential applicants in viewing program options, then essentially, you will have to make application with a lender in order to receive the loan estimate—which is counterintuitive to the intent of the loan estimate, which is to provide a consistent method to compare loan options prior to making application.

The Closing Disclosure

The second component of the TILA/RESPA integrations is the closing disclosure, which is intended to reduce surprises regarding the amount of cash you will need to bring to the closing table. The new closing disclosure is a blend of the existing Truth-in-Lending disclosure and the HUD-1 settlement statement. It's important to note that the Truth-in-Lending Act, not the Real Estate Settlement Procedures Act, governs the new closing disclosure. TILA provides different accuracy expectations and enforcement provisions than RESPA, as well as some differences in definitions, with associated risks and penalties that are much more severe than RESPA.

The biggest change that will come from the TILA/RESPA Integrated Disclosure rule is that you must receive the closing disclosure at least three business days prior to consummation as opposed to the current one-day requirement for delivering the HUD-1 settlement statement. TILA defines consummation to be: "The time that a consumer becomes contractually obligated on a credit transaction." Each lender is left to decide at what point it considers that a borrower has become contractually obligated on a transaction. Although a three-day right of rescission rule applies when refinancing owner-occupied properties, many lenders are choosing to define the consummation date as the date the borrower signs the loan documents even though technically, the borrower still has three days to rescind the offer.

While its effect is no doubt a positive for all parties, its implementation is creating major challenges for lenders and settlement agents alike. Traditionally, settlement agents prepare the HUD-1 settlement statement. In this new environment where lenders are required to show compliance of delivery of the closing disclosure to the borrower, there is much debate and concern over who is responsible for the preparation, accuracy, and timing of the closing disclosure. Lenders can only guarantee their fees. Settlement agents are responsible for ensuring all other fees are accurately represented on the closing statement. This marriage of responsibilities is requiring lenders and settlement agents to open better lines of communication much earlier in the process.

TILA/RESPA Integration Details

Each of these two new forms consists of three pages. The Consumer Financial Protection Bureau offers excellent tools to help you understand the new loan disclosures. For borrowers, please visit the CFPB mortgage page at www.consumerfinance.gov/knowbeforeyouowe. For lenders, the CFPB has also issued a detailed ninety-six-page explanation of these two new forms, which can be viewed online at http://files.consumerfinance.gov/f/twenty1409_cfpb_tila-respa-integrated-disclosure-guide-to-form.pdf.

Conventional: Conforming Versus Nonconforming or Jumbo

A conforming loan is currently capped at a loan amount of $417,000. Any loan amount above this is considered nonconforming or jumbo. Within each conforming or nonconforming categories, there are several options of loan products available to you. For starters, these include ten-, fifteen-, twenty-, twenty-five- or thirty-year fixed rate terms and many fully amortizing adjustable rate mortgage options starting with a 3/1, 5/1, 7/1, or a 10/1 loan product—the first part of the combination designates the number of years the initial interest rate is fixed. The second part designates how often the interest rate will be adjusted after the initial, fixed-rate period.

Each adjustable rate mortgage can be offered with a different term. For example, you can get a 5/1 adjustable rate mortgage with a fifteen-year term. This means that you will be amortizing your loan over fifteen years. Of the first five years, the interest rate you are charged will be fixed based on your selected rate/pricing option. For every year after the first five years and up until you've paid off your loan at the end of fifteen years, your interest rate will be adjusted to market and is limited to variations only within the terms of your adjustable rate mortgage note.

Tip: While it is generally true that a shorter term offers a lower interest rate, sometimes a fifteen-year note is priced better than a ten-year note. This has to do with secondary market conditions. Ask your loan officer to quote both for you. As typically the fixed rate options have no prepayment penalties, you may be better off taking the fifteen-year term and scheduling your payments based on a ten-year amortization so that you meet both objectives of paying the note within ten years and obtaining the lowest possible interest rate.

Tip: Clients purchasing a home valued above the conforming loan limit will often come in telling me they don't want a jumbo loan, without even asking the pricing difference on the loan products or stating that they're willing and able to pay a higher down payment to meet the conforming loan limit. But avoiding a jumbo loan isn't the only way to elude a possible higher interest cost. Before making that demand, ask your lender what the price difference is on both products. While it is true that jumbo loans are typically priced higher than conforming loans, sometimes a lender markets specifically to the affluent market and will offer their jumbo loans at a price that is as competitive, if not better than, the pricing on their conforming loans to deposit account holders. By knowing the price difference, you'll be able to make an educated decision as to whether or not you wish to use your money for a higher down payment or not. If that lender has their jumbo loans priced higher than conforming loans, ask if they offer piggyback financing. Piggyback financing gives you two mortgages. The first mortgage is available up to the conforming loan limit of $417,000 and the second mortgage for the remaining balance up to the total amount your selected loan product allows.

Refinancing and the Net Tangible Benefit

Just like everything else in mortgage banking, the benefit of refinancing depends on many variables. I've often heard people say that a determining factor in whether it makes sense to refinance your existing mortgage or not is that it's not worth it unless your interest rate drops by at least 2 percent. I have no idea where they are getting this misinformation. Determining whether or not you should refinance requires a lot more research than just the mortgage interest rate reduction.

If you find that you've overextended yourself and your total cost of credit is very high, there may be great benefit in refinancing your home mortgage to reduce your total monthly overhead. If you are considering cashing out some of the equity in your home to pay other debts, you will want to ask yourself a few questions. What do you need the money for? A major renovation or debt consolidation? Are you carrying monthly balances on credit cards and being charged well over current mortgage rates? What is your total interest cost exposure including interest charges from installment and credit card debt? Will you be utilizing the freed up monthly funds to prepay the mortgage and re-build your equity? Or will you go on continuing to accrue debt where maybe you shouldn't? Would you be better off leaving a low-interest first mortgage in place instead of refinancing into a larger loan amount that carries a higher interest cost, by obtaining a subordinate home equity line of credit or a second mortgage? Subordinate liens will usually carry a higher interest cost than a first mortgage. Check the tax laws that pertain to interest deduction benefits at www.irs.gov. Mortgage interest is tax deductible, but credit card interest is not.

While a 2 percent or greater interest rate reduction may be perceived as a good thing, it may not be worthwhile to refinance if you have a relatively short period left of repayment. In an effort to prevent what we call "churn and burn," which is the unethical practice of recommending a refinance that only benefits the originator, for consideration of a rate and term refinance (where no cashing out is taking place other than the inclusion of closing costs), regulators came up with the net benefit rule.

By law, your lender must perform an analysis to determine that you receive a minimum net tangible benefit of either a reduction in interest rate by .5 percent or a reduction in minimum monthly payment of 4 percent. For consideration of a rate and term refinance, when any of the below existing loan features are combined with the below listed new loan features, the new loan must be tested by an underwriter to ensure that you receive a minimum reduction of the your total principal, interest, and monthly mortgage insurance payment by at least 4 percent of the existing loan payment. Existing to new loan features:

- Existing fixed-rate to new fixed-rate
- Existing fixed-rate to new hybrid ARM (3/1 or 5/1 ARM)
- Existing one-year ARM to new one-year ARM
- Existing hybrid ARM that is currently in its initial fixed-rate period to new fixed-rate
- Existing hybrid ARM that is currently in its initial fixed-rate period to new hybrid ARM (3/1 or 5/1 ARM)
- Existing hybrid ARM that is currently in its adjustable-rate period to new one-year ARM (3/1 or 5/1 ARM)
- Existing fixed-rate to new one-year ARM (for rate/term refinance loans only)

Meeting the net tangible benefit rule is not required if the new transaction:

- Converts an existing one-year ARM or hybrid ARM financing to a fixed-rate loan
- Converts interest-only financing to fully-amortized financing (rate and term refinance loans only)
- Reduces the amortization of the existing loan
- Rate and term refinance is the result of a court-ordered divorce buyout (court documents, such as divorce decree, are required)
- Converts balloon loan to a fixed-rate loan (rate and term refinance loans only)
- Consolidates a first mortgage with a purchase-money second or seasoned second (rate and term refinance loans only)

The new payment divided by the previous payment must be 96 percent or less or .96 on a rate and term refinance loan. Additionally, a loan requiring more than forty-eight months to recoup the closing costs will not be approved. To calculate the time period to recoup costs, your lender will take your total closing costs and divide this by the monthly decrease in total mortgage payment from the old loan to the new loan. These lender calculations and restrictions are a precautionary benefit to borrowers who may not be financially savvy.

Custom Built Construction Loans

Designing and building your dream home can be an exciting adventure. It can also be a time of great conflict and tension between you and your partner. Someone is usually very excited about the opportunities to design their "perfect home" and someone else is usually managing the checkbook and busting the excited person's bubble. The first step in planning your new home is structural design. You'll meet with an architect and work together on the basics that are important to you. Before meeting with your architect, do a little research on www.houzz.com where you'll find many design ideas that you can incorporate into your plans.

At this time, you may or may not already have the land on which to build your home. If you do—great, if you don't, that's okay too. A construction loan can be used to finance the land or lot as well as the construction of the property. Once you decide on the building plans, you'll meet with a few general contractors who will review the plans and provide you with a spec sheet. The specifications sheet is a detailed itemization of the estimated costs of construction including the soft costs and hard costs. Soft costs include things such fees as permits, engineering, architectural, and inspections. Hard costs include such fees as labor and materials associated with the project, including roof tiles, cabinets, floorings, bathroom fixtures, door hinges, base boards, tiles, paint, etc., and all costs associated with completion of the structure.

Before you decide on the general contractor (GC), you'll meet with your lender. Your lender will review not only your creditworthiness and your ability to repay the loan, but will also review the GC's credentials, check their references, and confirm they have sufficient liability coverage. In addition to the usual financial information, your lender will request the following:

- If applicable, a land purchase contract for the lot on which your house will be built
- A deed to the lot, if you already own it
- Floor plans
- Specification sheet
- Builder's package to include (resume, credit/bank/jobs references, liability coverage, list of subcontractors and suppliers, and signed authorization to obtain credit references)
- Construction agreement between you and your builder, including construction timeline and materials description

Typically, lender's who finance custom built homes only offer financing to those who will occupy the residence or for whom the residence will be a second home. Some lenders restrict the type of housing to a one-unit, single-family detached home. All lenders will require that you contract with a licensed builder in the construction of your home. A little known fact that makes the dream of building a home achievable, is that during the construction period, many lenders do not require that you make any payments for principal or interest. Some, instead, tag onto the loan balance the estimated costs of interest payments. Others, begin billing interest-only payments on the portion of money drawn. In either situation, you aren't making two housing payments. Additionally, most lenders who offer construction loan programs provide rate-lock options that protect against interest rate changes while your home is being built, regardless of market fluctuations. Some lenders only offer financing during the short time period of construction, and you will be required to pay off that loan once the property is completed (usually by obtaining a permanent loan). In this case, you'll have to go the approval process twice.

In a one-time close construction-to-permanent financing arrangement, you'll only have one loan closing and at the end of the construction period, you'll automatically convert into a permanent loan. Loan programs are usually available on government, conventional, conforming, and nonconforming fixed and adjustable rate loans. Typically, the interest rate lock period will hold up to twelve months on conforming loan amounts and up to twenty-four months on jumbo loans. If the overall interest rate increases, your interest rate remains protected through the rate-lock period. If the overall interest rates decrease, you are generally allowed to exercise a one-time float down to the current rate. Many lenders will also allow you to switch from one loan program to another within sixty days of loan closing, but be careful with this, as it would require a new review of loan documents.

In addition to standard closing fees, you will pay for several home inspections. Generally, a lender will require, at a minimum, four to six inspections of your home during the construction phase. Before a request for disbursement can be approved, following a draw schedule, your lender will send out an inspector (usually an appraiser) to view the property to ensure it is moving according to plan. In addition to all the anticipated costs you have recorded, most lenders will require that you budget in the loan amount for a contingency reserve. Depending on the complexity of the plans, this amount varies by lender between 10 and 20 percent of the anticipated costs.

Prior to the first draw on your loan, you must provide evidence of prepaid homeowners insurance, which must include builder's risk coverage. This coverage protects you from financial responsibility for any damage, theft, or liability that may occur while your home is under construction. Construction delays due to weather and material/labor availability are fairly common. Be sure to build some allowances for this into the construction timetable.

While you're eager to make selections for everything you want, you'll also be forced to make decisions about things you care nothing about. Choosing cabinets and fixtures is a lot more fun than choosing door hinges, floorboards, and grout. It's not uncommon to make modifications or upgrades to the original plans when building a new home. When this occurs, know that these cost overruns can't be added to the loan amount midterm. If you run under the estimated costs, the original loan amount can be reduced prior to modification into your permanent loan.

The construction period concludes when the lender receives the final completion certificate and occupancy permit or equivalent from the local governing jurisdiction, and when your lender performs a final inspection of the property. Shortly after your home is completed, your one-time close construction-to-permanent will be modified into the permanent phase of the loan program you have chosen. Escrow accounts for real estate taxes and insurance will be established after your home is completed and after your loan modifies to the permanent loan. If you had selected a straight construction loan, you would need to pay that off once the certificate of occupancy has been issued in either cash or through a regular mortgage loan.

VA Loans

Loans guaranteed by the U.S. Department of Veteran's Affairs (VA loans) help service members, veterans, and eligible surviving spouses become homeowners. VA home loans are provided through authorized private lenders, such as banks and mortgage companies, and are not directly available through the VA. For information on eligibility, supporting evidence, and instructions for application to receive confirmation of benefit eligibility to present to your lender, visit Certificate of Eligibility (http://benefits.va.gov/homeloans/purchaseco_certificate.asp). At your first meeting with your loan officer, be sure to tell them if you may qualify for VA home loan benefits as nine times out of ten, this program will be the best priced, require the least out-of-pocket funds and offer the most flexibility in underwriting standards. As complex as mortgages can be, there are many additional intricacies that apply exclusively to VA loans. Here are some clarifications over common misconceptions about VA loans:

- You don't have to be a first-time homebuyer
- You aren't limited to a maximum purchase price of $417,000 (check http://benefits. va.gov/homeloans/purchaseco_loan_limits.asp to confirm current amounts)
- You can reuse the VA benefit through reinstatement
- VA-backed loans may be assumable

VA home loans can be used to:
- Buy a home, townhome, or a condominium unit in a VA-approved project
- Build a home
- Simultaneously purchase and improve a home

- Improve a home by installing energy-related features or making energy efficient improvements
- Buy a manufactured home and/or lot

Tip: If VA financing is for you, it's important that you seek and connect with both a realtor and a mortgage professional that are fluent in the workings of the VA home loan eligibility standards. If you fall into the hands of someone who isn't schooled in the intricacies of VA financing, you may find yourself locked out of an opportunity.

The Benefits of a VA Loan

- Zero down payment is required for a purchase transaction when the sales price doesn't exceed the appraised value, the amount financed doesn't exceed four times your entitlement benefit, and the loan amount is $417,000 or less. In cases where the valuation is less than the sales price, you can choose to proceed with the purchase at the higher price as long as you make up the difference between the sales price and the appraised value.
- There is no requirement of monthly mortgage insurance premiums.
- VA loans typically provide the lowest total monthly payment when compared to FHA financing and conventional financing with mortgage insurance.
- There are no prepayment penalties.
- They are assumable by a buyer. Assumability means that the buyer may be eligible to take over payments on the VA loan regardless of whether they are civilian or military. A word of caution: Unless you obtain written approval from the VA (not the mortgage servicer), a veteran will remain liable on the assumed loan even after the sale of the property. Be sure to go through this extra step to protect yourself against possible future financial mismanagement by the buyer.
- Up to 100 percent of the valuation may be available on a rate and term refinance.
- Up to 90 percent of the valuation may be available on a cash out refinance.
- Financing is available with credit scores as low as 620.
- They allow a maximum debt-to-income ratio (DTI) of 60 percent with automated underwriting approve/eligible findings. A manual underwrite will require a maximum DTI of 41 percent; however, allowances can be made given residual income, employment, and credit histories. At the maximum DTI of 60 percent, only fixed-rate loans are allowed. If your credit score is less than 640 and the loan-to-value is greater than 95 percent, your DTI will be capped at 45 percent.

Tip: When presenting an offer for purchase, ensure the agreement includes an addendum for the VA Option Clause. Here's a sample of a VA Option Clause:

"It is expressly agreed that, notwithstanding any other provisions of this contract, the purchaser shall not incur any penalty by forfeiture of earnest money or otherwise be obligated to complete the purchase of the property described herein if the contract purchase price or cost exceeds the reasonable value of the property established by the Department of Veterans Affairs. The purchaser shall, however, have the privilege and option of proceeding with the consummation of this contract without regard to the amount of the reasonable value established by the Department of Veterans Affairs."

Understanding the Intricacies of VA Loan Guaranty

The VA loan guaranty is insurance that the Department of Veteran's Affairs provides the lender. The VA will guaranty loans up to 100 percent of the value for owner-occupied homes. The VA guarantees a portion of the loan, which enables the lender to provide you with more favorable terms. Guarantee simply means the lender is protected against loss in the event of a foreclosure and replaces the protection the lender would normally receive by requiring a 20 percent down payment and/or private mortgage insurance. This guarantee allows the veteran to obtain more favorable financing terms.

VA Funding Fee

The VA charges a funding fee to pay for this insurance. The VA funding fee is required by law and can cost you anywhere between zero and 3.3 percent of the loan amount depending on your eligibility status, whether you've used your VA benefit in the past, the size of your down payment (if any), and whether you qualify as a service-connected disabled veteran or are the surviving spouse of a veteran who died in service or from a service-connected disability. The fee is intended to enable the veteran who obtains a VA home loan to contribute toward the cost of this benefit, and thereby reduces the cost passed on to taxpayers. When refinancing a VA loan with a new VA loan, the new loan is eligible for a reduced funding fee of .5 percent.

Entitlement

The VA provides each qualified veteran with at least $104,250 in entitlement and extra entitlement in select high cost counties as determined by HUD. Entitlement requires that 25 percent of the loan amount be guaranteed to the loan. With that, a portion of the entitlement is charged to the loan as a guaranty to the lender in the event of default. All qualified veterans start out with $36,000 in basic entitlement and $68,250 in bonus entitlement or $120,375 bonus in Alaska and Hawaii. With the basic amount provided, the veteran receives $104,250 in entitlement and we count this as 25 percent of the guaranteed loan amount of $417,000. With all bonuses available, the maximum guaranteed loan amount can be as high as $1,500,000. (The VA provides its yearly updated list of home loan limits online at http://benefits.va.gov/homeloans/purchaseco_loan_limits.asp.)

The 2015 VA loan limit for Miami-Dade, Florida, is $417,000. This means that if the veteran has full entitlement, the VA will provide a 25 percent guaranty on the loan up to $417,000. If a veteran has a contract to purchase a home in the amount of $480,000, the lender may require the veteran to make a down payment of 25 percent of the $63,000 difference, which would be $15,750, providing the lender a full 25 percent guaranty. In the same example, a borrower not using VA benefits and instead opting for using a conventional loan product, may have to place a traditional down payment of 20 percent of the total purchase price which in this case, would be $111,000.

Understanding entitlement benefits can be a little tricky. If a veteran purchased a home using his VA entitlement (in full or in part), the mortgage on that loan is assigned a portion of his entitlement as guaranty. Because VA loans are assumable, a veteran can sell a property and have the existing VA mortgage assumed by the new buyer. If that new buyer is an ordinary citizen with no VA entitlement benefits, the seller's VA entitlement stays with that mortgage and the veteran is not released from liability. If on the other hand, the new buyer is active military or a qualified veteran and has entitlement benefits that he can assign to the existing VA mortgage, the seller can take back his entitlement and be released from future obligations on the existing note. With release, veterans can use the home loan benefit multiple times. Release is requested through the VA.

Restoration of Entitlement

Veterans can have previously used entitlement restored to purchase another home with a VA loan by completing VA Form 26-1880 and submitting a request through the VA Eligibility Center if one of these things happens:

a.   The property purchased with the prior VA loan has been sold and the outstanding loan has been paid in full.

b.   The property is sold to a qualified veteran-transferee (buyer) who agrees to assume the existing VA loan and substitute his or her entitlement for the same amount of entitlement that was originally used by the veteran seller.

c.   If the veteran has repaid the initial VA loan in full but has not sold the property purchased with his initial entitlement under a VA loan, he can still place a request for restoration and use his restored entitlement to gain the benefits of a new VA loan.

Condo Project Approval

If VA financing is the only way to go for you, be sure to not waste your valuable time by selecting a property that is not eligible for financing with a VA guaranty. Resale of existing homes doesn't require any special approval, however, new construction, condos and PUDs will. Prior to 2009, if a condominium project was FHA certified, the VA would accept the FHA approval for VA loans. As of December 7, 2009, the VA no longer accepts newly added FHA condominium approvals in lieu of an independent VA approval. FHA and VA maintain separate approval lists on their respective websites.

Tip: Narrow your property search by selecting a condo project, planned unit development, or builder of new construction that is already on the VA approved list before you enter into contract. You can search the VA database at Veterans Information Portal Condo/PUD Search Tool (https://vip.vba.va.gov/portal/VBAH/VBAHome/condopudsearch).

Searching this site is not exactly user friendly. You will find that city names are abbreviated and the system is not searchable by zip code. For example, a search for condos in Rancho Santa Margarita, California, has four results; however, a search for Rancho Santa Ma, California, returns twenty-one results. Projects can be listed under original tract numbers, parcel maps, or lot lines, and the project name is often abbreviated. This can preclude the searcher from finding accurate results.

Once you locate your community on the search site, you will find one of three statuses:

1. Accepted without conditions: These communities are 100 percent accepted for VA loans and lenders can use the condo ID with no issues.
2. HUD accepted: This community was accepted under the pre-2009 reciprocity agreement with HUD where FHA approved projects were automatically eligible for VA Guaranty. For the most part, these communities are still accepted by VA, however it is recommended that the lender call the regional VA office that is assigned to the state where the community is located to verify. Current FHA status is not relevant to HUD-accepted VA designations.
3. Unaccepted: VA loans are not permitted in these communities.

Limitations on Borrower-Paid Closing Costs

There are certain customary closing costs that the VA does not allow the borrower to pay for, and therefore, must be applied to either the lender or the seller and reflected accordingly on the GFE/loan estimate and subsequent HUD-1/closing disclosure. These fees include administration, underwriting, processing, tax related service, any courier/mail fees, and attorney services that are exclusive of title work.

Additionally, specific purchase transactions, seller concessions, or credits from the seller to the buyer at closing are capped at a maximum of 4 percent of the purchase price or valuation, whichever is less. The 4 percent cap excludes normal and customary closing costs or discount points of up to 2 percent. The 4 percent does include:

- Paying over 2 percent in discount points
- Paying down the veterans debt to qualify for the loan
- Paying off of veterans judgments
- The VA funding fee
- Prepayment of property taxes and homeowners insurance

Notes on Delinquency and Foreclosure on VA Loans

No one wants to lose their home in foreclosure. If you can no longer afford it, consider selling it. If foreclosure is eminent, know that aside from ruining your credit profile and having higher interest costs on every other item you finance until you restore your credit, you may still be liable for the debt on a VA loan. If your loan closed on or after January 1, 1990, you will owe the government in the event of a default if there was fraud, misrepresentation, or bad faith on your part.

Refinance Transactions

VA loans aren't exclusively for purchase transactions. A VA Interest Rate Reduction Refinance Loan (IRRRL) is a VA-to-VA loan, meaning you are only eligible for this loan program if you are refinancing an existing VA loan into a new VA loan. An IRRRL requires less documentation that provides for quicker loan decisions and carries a lower VA funding fee limited to .5 percent. When considering an IRRRL, keep in mind:

- Only the veteran and their spouse may be on loan and title.
- Nonoccupant co-borrowers are prohibited.
- Co-borrower must be married to the veteran. (Same-sex marriages are now allowed in certain states. The VA must approve eligibility prior to submission to underwriting.)
- In the debt-to-income calculations, we must include childcare expenses for all children under age twelve.

VA Jumbo Loan Program

The VA limits the loan amount it guarantees, but that does not mean you can't buy a home that is valued at greater than your full entitlement benefit insures. To learn what the current limits are in the county where your property is located, visit: https://entp.hud.gov/idapp/html/hicostlook.cfm.

For counties where the VA maximum loan amount is $417,000:
- You don't need to make any down payment on the first $417,000.
- When the purchase price is greater than $417,000, your lender may require only a 25 percent down payment on the amount greater than $417,000.
- For loan amounts between $417,000 and $1,000,000, you aren't able to finance the funding fee, so it must be paid in full at closing either by you or by the seller.

In counties determined to be of high cost by HUD, when the VA loan amount exceeds $417,000, the following applies:
- You don't need to place a down payment on the portion below the high cost county loan limit.
- You will need to place a minimum down payment of 25 percent on the portion of the loan amount that exceeds the high cost county limit.
- For loan amounts exceeding the high cost county limit and up to $1,000,000, you aren't able to finance the funding fee so it must be paid in full at closing either by you or by the seller.

Additionally for any VA jumbo loan that exceeds the county limits set by the VA, the following overlays apply:
- Minimum credit score of 640 for loan amounts above $650,000
- Manufactured homes are not eligible
- Two-to-four unit purchase transactions are capped at $417,000
- Only fixed rate loan products are allowed

Federal Housing Administration Mortgages

The Federal Housing Administration (FHA) provides mortgage insurance on loans made by FHA-approved lenders throughout the United States and its territories. FHA insures mortgages on single family and multifamily homes including manufactured homes. It is the largest insurer of mortgages in the world, insuring more than thirty-four million properties since it was created by congress in 1934 as a means to revive the devastated post-Depression housing market.

The Federal Housing Administration and its parent organization, the Department of

Housing and Urban Development (HUD), manage loans explicitly guaranteed by the U.S. federal government. The federal government's promise to pay in the event of homeowner default gives mortgage lenders the confidence to lend to higher-risk borrowers, such as those with less-than-perfect credit or those with no established credit history. A one-to-four unit is financed under section 203(b) of the program, a condominium is financed through section 234(c), and a unit in a cooperative is financed under section 203(n).

A main distinction between FHA and conventional loan programs is that the FHA allows for down payments as low as 3.5 percent with much lower credit score requirements than conventional underwriting allows. For a while after the Great Recession, the GSEs stopped offering loan programs in excess of 95 percent financing. With the reintroduction of 97 percent financing for conventional loans in 2015, the FHA program is now seen by most as a lending program of last resort typically benefitting those who lack a traditional credit history or who have not managed to repair or maintain favorable credit ratings above a representative credit score of 660. This may be attributed to recent changes in the FHA program that mandate permanent coverage of mortgage insurance over the life of an FHA loan. With conventional underwriting, private mortgage insurance can be cancelled after the original loan balance falls below a 78 percent loan-to-value.

When the housing market crashed and conventional loans began having tighter credit guidelines, many borrowers—especially first time homebuyers—resorted to FHA financing. To avert being heavily invested in housing, the FHA decided to increase their insurance premiums, lower their limits on loan size, and tighten their credit score minimums. These changes brought down the number of loans originated for FHA and heavily restricted entry into homeownership for first-time homebuyers. FHA guidelines, like all guidelines, are constantly changing. Here is an overview of FHA loan requirements and standards for 2015:

- It is not limited to first-time buyers, contrary to popular belief.
- All FHA borrowers are required to make at the very least, a minimum down payment equal to 3.5 percent of the property valuation or sales price, whichever is less. Where sales price is greater than valuation, you are required to make up the full difference if you choose to make purchase above market value.
- To qualify for the 3.5 percent down-payment option, you must have a credit score of 580 or higher. Lender overlays may apply.
- Borrowers with a credit score between 500 and 579 may be eligible for FHA financing, but are required to put at least a 10 percent down payment. Again, lender overlays may apply.
- There are debt requirements as well, but these are a bit more lax when compared to the credit scores above. Generally speaking, a borrower's total monthly debt load should account for no more than 43 percent of his or her monthly income. HUD allows

borrowers to have higher debt-to-income ratios if the lender can identify and document significant compensating factors. Such factors might include a long history of timely mortgage payments, excellent credit, or significant cash reserves.

- Borrowers with credit scores below 620 and total debt-to-income ratios above 43 percent may encounter additional scrutiny during the application and approval process. Borrowers in this bracket may have to undergo manual underwriting. The underwriter will be looking for compensating factors to make up for the low-score/high-debt situation.

Tip: Often, FHA loans are offered with lower interest rates than conventional loans because they are explicitly guaranteed by the U.S. government, and therefore, present a lower risk to your lender. Because of the lower interest rate, you may automatically think that this loan program is the lowest cost option, but you must also take into account the upfront mortgage insurance premium and the annualized monthly mortgage insurance dues and weigh these against the costs and benefits of a conventional mortgage where the interest rate may be higher, but mortgage insurance costs are generally less and cancelable.

Tip: If you have limited funds for down payment and no traditional credit history (credit cards, auto loans, etc.), FHA is the way to go. If you have nontraditional credit (telephone, gym membership, auto insurance, day care, etc.) and can work with your lender to build a third-party verified credit report with at least four accounts, you may be eligible for conventional loan financing even without a usable credit score. Ask your loan officer for details. Review the "Credit Reference Letter" section in chapter 14 to learn the details of validating a nontraditional credit account.

Tip: When searching for an FHA-approved condo at HUD's condo search tool (https://entp.hud.gov/idapp/html/condlook.cfm), only enter the zip code for your area of interest. If you enter too many variables, you may inadvertently exclude available options. Pay special attention to the approval expiration dates on the far right column. Loans must be funded prior to FHA's project approval expiration date.

Tip: Although the FHA allows for very low credit scores, your particular lender may have an overlay that restricts the credit score to one that meets your lender's risk tolerance. If you have a low credit score, (a) make the effort to repair your credit starting right now, (b) if you can't wait to buy a home and are willing to pay much higher costs over the life of your loan because of your low score, ask your lender how low they are willing to go on credit score. If their overlay exceeds your score but is still within FHA's guidance, ask for a referral to a lender with less restrictions/overlays.

Tip: If your credit score is above 660, you may be better served by selecting a conventional loan with private mortgage insurance assuming you meet all other guidelines of the lender and the mortgage insurance company. Ask your loan officer for alternatives. Know that just like lenders, mortgage insurers have different guidelines and pricing. Although you don't have the option to select a particular mortgage insurance provider, you should at least ask your loan officer to be sure your loan profile meets the eligibility standards of the mortgage insurance provider that the lender will assign it to. Oftentimes, provider assignment is based on round robin selection with no regard to difference in eligibility standards. If your loan file requires a particular mortgage insurance provider, your loan officer can request assignment.

Mortgage Insurance Premiums and Seller Credits

There are two kinds of mortgage insurance that apply to the FHA loans: upfront mortgage insurance premium (UFMIP) and monthly mortgage insurance premiums (MIP). UFMIP is the one time mortgage insurance premium collected at closing and is sent to HUD to insure the loan. UFMIP may be paid in cash at closing and may be paid by the borrower, seller, or lender. UFMIP may be financed into the loan amount. If financed, the UFMIP is added to the base loan amount to arrive at a greater total loan amount. The total loan amount is the principal amount that you repay in the mortgage payment each month. The total loan amount may exceed FHA's statutory (locality) lending limit only by the amount of the financed UFMIP. If you refinance into another FHA mortgage within the first three years of the term, a portion of the UFMIP will apply to the new loan. If the loan is paid off and/or not refinanced to another FHA mortgage, there will be no refund of the UFMIP.

Adding the UFMIP to your loan balance may be the most efficient way to structure the payment because it reduces the amount of cash needed at closing (if you had the additional resources, you may want to look at a conventional financing option instead). In addition to financing the UFMIP, you can select an interest rate option that provides you with a credit from your lender that is applied to your closing costs to further reduce the amount of cash you need to bring to closing.

Tip: In the initial interview with your loan officer, be sure to review the terms of the sales contract to identify whether any seller credits/sales concessions have been negotiated. With this information in hand, review your interest rate options with your loan officer to determine if it makes sense to increase the interest rate and receive a lender credit for closing costs on the closing statement. This option may make sense if you have limited cash available for the transaction and the additional money will help meet the lender's cash-to-close and reserve requirements.

Tip: It's important to note here that obtaining a preliminary HUD-1/closing disclosure from your settlement agent is a best practice before selecting your interest rate option. This is necessary so that you have a very close estimate as to the actual closing fees, as oftentimes lenders will inflate their estimated fees on the original good faith/loan estimate to avoid potential losses for under-disclosing.

Tip: If you select an interest rate that provides a lender credit for your closing costs and the bottom line figure on the HUD-1/closing disclosure (cash required for closing) is less than the amount of the lender credit plus any seller credits or sales concessions (meaning that you would be walking away from the closing table with extra cash in hand) the lender will reduce the amount of credit they are giving you. If you catch this early on, you can have the lender reduce the closing credit by reducing your interest rate. If you've waited until you receive the preliminary HUD-1/closing disclosure and if you must close within seven days, you may elect to forfeit the excess credits and still be charged a higher interest rate. The reason a borrower typically closes with the higher interest rate and forgoes lowering the interest rate to reduce lender credits is because when a last minute change is made to the interest rate or origination points that exceed the tolerance levels of the annual percentage rate (even when the rate is reduced), the loan must have a mandatory wait period of four days prior to closing (plus three more days if the revised good faith/loan estimate is mailed). This was one of the initial rulings of Dodd-Frank intended to protect the consumer from last minute changes in loan terms.

Options for Canceling FHA Monthly Mortgage Insurance

For FHA loans predating June 3, 2013, monthly mortgage insurance can be removed when the following conditions are met:

- Thirty-year loan term: Monthly mortgage insurance premiums are required for the first sixty payments. Beyond this, premiums will be automatically canceled once the loan reaches a 78 percent loan-to-value.
- Fifteen-year loan term: Monthly mortgage insurance premiums are not required for the full sixty months and will automatically be cancelled once the loan reaches a 78 percent loan-to-value.

For FHA loans funded after June 3, 2013, monthly mortgage insurance is no longer automatically eliminated for most loans when they reach 78 percent of their original value.

- For all mortgages regardless of their amortization terms, any mortgage involving an original principal obligation (excludes portion added of UFMIP) less than or equal to 90 percent loan-to-value, the monthly mortgage insurance premiums will be assessed until the end of the mortgage term or for the first eleven years of the mortgage term, whichever occurs first.

- For any mortgage involving an original principal obligation (excludes portion added of UFMIP) with a loan-to-value greater than 90 percent, premiums are assessed until the end of the mortgage term or for the first thirty years of the term, whichever occurs first.

Note: FHA calculates loan-to-value as a percentage by dividing the loan amount (prior to the financing of any UFMIP) by the lesser of the purchase price (if applicable) or appraised value at origination (new appraised values will not be considered). This differs from conventional financing where cancellation can occur with a current market appraisal that meets the lender's loan-to-value guidelines and is what makes conventional financing a better option for those with higher credit scores. For streamline refinances without appraisals, FHA uses the original appraised value of the property to calculate the loan-to-value.

Here's a helpful chart to compare cancellation options for FHA loans issued before and after June 3, 2013:

Term	LTV (%)	Before June 3, 2013	After June 3, 2013
15 years or less	78% or less	No annual MIP	11 years
15 years or less	78-90%	Cancelled at 78% LTV	11 years
15 years or less	more than 90.00%	Cancelled at 78% LTV	Loan term
More than 15 years	78% or less	5 years	11 years
More than 15 years	78-90%	Cancelled at 78% LTV and 5 years	11 years
More than 15 years	more than 90.00%	Cancelled at 78% LTV and 5 years	Loan term

FHA Renovation Loans

There are many people who can benefit from the features provided through an FHA renovation loan. A few examples include those who have outgrown their current home and wish to build an addition instead of moving, those whose property needs major repairs and haven't amassed the money to pay for these costs, and those who are entering negotiating a purchase contract to buy a home that is in need of major repairs or renovations.

The renovation loan process is very similar to standard loan processing except the assessed value that is used by the lender is different. In this scenario, we will base our loan-to-value calculations using the market value of the property based on future improvements. To assist the appraiser in determining future value, you will need to provide your lender with the specification sheet for the improvements to include planned repairs, materials, and total costs. Additionally, the lender will evaluate the contractor selected to ensure experience and expertise. The loan amount can include hard and soft costs, a contingency reserve, closing costs, and payment reserves. With payment reserves, you will not need to make principal and interest payments during the renovation period.

The standard program requires that at least $5,000 be utilized for required improvements that are necessary for the safety of the inhabitants. Beyond that minimum, you can add funds for the following:

- Structural alterations
- Replacing roof or windows
- Enhancing accessibility for disabled persons
- Eliminating obsolescence (such as replacing well water with septic)
- Reconditioning plumbing
- Replacing flooring
- Updating bathroom or kitchens
- Upgrading energy conservation

The FHA renovation program has three different product options: standard, streamline, and disaster reconstruction). The standard FHA 203(k) is an option for that fixer-upper purchase. The benefits and features of this program include:

- You can borrow up to 110 percent of the future value of the home (appraisal based on improvements).
- It has the same FHA qualifying requirements as a FHA mortgage, such as down payment, credit and debt-to-income.
- Owner-occupied properties, one-to-four unit buildings, and FHA-approved PUDs and condos are all eligible.
- The loan size is determined by the maximum FHA loan amount in your area, the repair budget, and your debt-to-income qualifications.
- Work must begin within thirty days of loan closing and must be completed within six months.

In an FHA streamlined refinance 203(k), you can include the payoff of the existing loan balance, closing costs, pre-paids such as homeowners insurance premiums, and up to $35,000 of the cost of renovation.

The 203(h) reconstruction program was designed for when disaster strikes. It helps disaster victims whose primary residence, located in a President-declared disaster area, whether owned or rented, was destroyed or damaged to such an extent that reconstruction or replacement is necessary. The mortgage may be used to finance the purchase or reconstruction of a one-unit single family home or FHA-approved condominium that will be the principal residence of the displaced borrower. To determine if a property qualifies, visit the FEMA Disaster Declarations website (www.fema.gov/disasters).

There are many benefits specific to a 203(h) loan. You may relocate anywhere within the U.S., the new home does not have to be in the same area as the previous home, and 100 percent financing is available up to and within the FHA loan limits (value determined by sales price or appraised value, whichever is less). Here are the eligibility details for the program:

- You must prove your residence was located in a President-declared disaster area (such proof may include a valid driver's license, voter registration card, or utility bills).
- You must provide evidence of destruction of the property (such proof may include insurance reports or appraisal paperwork).
- You must exercise your right to participate within one year from the date of the President's declaration of disaster (which may not be the same as the date of the disastrous event).
- Standard FHA income and asset qualification guidelines apply. If the credit report indicates satisfactory credit prior to the disaster and any derogatory credit subsequent to that date can be related to the effects of the disaster, FHA will consider, for its underwriting standards, that you are a satisfactory credit risk.
- Not all property types are admissible for financing under the 203(h) program. Ineligible properties include: single-unit attached primary residence, attached PUD, two-to-four unit primary residence, second homes, investment properties, co-ops, and manufactured homes.
- Additionally, for these loans, closing costs and prepaid expenses must be paid by you in cash or paid through premium loan pricing through the lender or by the seller (subject to a 6 percent limitation on seller concessions).

In addition to standard loan documentation, you will need to provide your lender with the following items:
- Plans and specification sheet
- Contractor agreement
- Itemized materials and costs

Reverse Mortgage: Home Equity Conversion Mortgages

As people begin to age, homeowners start considering options of lowering their overall monthly payments. If you are sixty-two years or older, you may be eligible for a reverse mortgage that allows you to convert a portion of your home equity into cash. In a traditional mortgage, you make monthly payments to your lender over the life of the loan. With a reverse mortgage, you will receive money from your lender, and generally don't have to pay interest or principal on the loan for as long as you live in your home. You will still be required to make payments on property taxes, homeowners insurance and HOA payments, as necessary. The loan is repaid when you die, sell your home, or when your home is no longer your primary residence.

Funds from a reverse mortgage can be used to finance a home improvement, pay off your current mortgage, supplement your retirement income, pay for healthcare expenses, or purchase a new home. The proceeds of a reverse mortgage are generally tax free, and many reverse mortgages have no income restrictions. No matter what type of reverse mortgage you're considering, it is recommended that you seek professional advice to thoroughly understand all the conditions that would make the loan due and payable and to assess whether or not this is the best option for you.

How It Works

The amount you owe on a reverse mortgage grows over time. Interest is charged on the outstanding balance and is added to the amount you owe. That means your total debt increases as the loan funds are advanced to you and as interest costs on the loan are accrued over time. Although some reverse mortgages allow for fixed rates, most are offered with a variable rate option that is tied to a financial index. This means that the cost of interest will vary with market conditions.

A reverse mortgage loan allows you to choose among several advance payment options. Your payment options are selected at origination, and they can be changed at any time during the life of your loan for a fee of approximately $20. You may select:

- A term option with fixed monthly cash advances for a specific period of time.
- A tenure option with fixed monthly cash advances for as long as you live in your home.
- A line of credit that lets you draw down the loan proceeds at any time in amounts you choose until you have used up the amount available on the line of credit.
- A combination of monthly payments and a line of credit.

Three Types of Reverse Mortgages

- Single-purpose reverse mortgages are offered by some state and local government agencies, and nonprofit organizations. These have income and use restrictions.
- Home Equity Conversion Mortgages (HECMs) are federally insured and backed by the U.S. Department of Housing and Urban Development (HUD).
- Proprietary reverse mortgages are private loans that are backed by the companies that develop them.

Choosing a Reverse Mortgage Option

A single-purpose reverse mortgage may be your least expensive option, but it may not be your most beneficial option. These are not available everywhere and proceeds can only be used for one purpose, which is usually to pay only for home repairs, improvements, or property taxes. HECMs and proprietary reverse mortgages may be more costly than traditional home loans, with higher up-front fees, but these have no income or medical requirements and funds distributed can be used for any purpose. All HECM lenders must follow the minimum HUD guidelines. And while the mortgage insurance premium is the same from lender to lender, total loan costs will vary among lenders. Obtain preapplication cost estimates from at least two or three lenders to compare pricing and program options.

Before applying for a HECM loan, you will be required to meet with a counselor from an independent, government-approved housing counseling agency who will explain the loan's costs and financial implications, and possible alternatives to a HECM, like government and nonprofit programs or a single-purpose or proprietary reverse mortgage. (For a list of counselors, visit www. hud.gov or call 1-800-569-4287.) You can also circle back to the counselor with preapplication cost estimates from different lenders, and they can help you compare the costs of different types of reverse mortgages and tell you how different payment options, fees, and other costs affect the total cost of the loan over time. Most counseling agencies charge around $125 for their services. The fee can be paid from the loan proceeds, but you cannot be turned away if you can't afford the fee.

How Much Can You Borrow?

The maximum loan amount of a HECM or proprietary reverse mortgage depends on several factors, including your age, the type of reverse mortgage you select, the appraised value of your home, and current interest rates. In general, the older you are, the more equity you have in your home and the less you owe on it, the more money you can get. HECMs generally provide bigger loan advances at a lower total cost compared with proprietary loans, but if you own a higher-value home, you may get a bigger loan advance from a proprietary reverse mortgage. If you live in a higher-value home, consider a proprietary reverse mortgage that allows for financing above the conforming loan limit (currently $417,000).

Important Things to Consider with a Reverse Mortgage:
- Reverse mortgage loan advances are not taxable, and generally don't affect your Social Security or Medicare benefits.
- You retain the title to your home, and you don't have to make monthly repayments of principal or interest. The loan must be repaid when the last surviving borrower dies, sells the home, or no longer lives in the home as their principal residence. It's important

to note here that loan repayment will come due if the borrower dies and the spouse, who did not sign the mortgage, wishes to remain in the home.

- Long-term care options should be carefully considered with family members and/or a financial advisor. In the HECM program, a borrower can live in a nursing home or other medical facility for up to 12 consecutive months before the loan must be repaid.
- Reverse mortgages can use up all or some of the equity in your home and leave fewer assets for you and your heirs. Most reverse mortgages have a nonrecourse clause, which prevents you or your estate from owing more than the value of your home when the loan becomes due and the home is sold. However, if you or your heirs want to retain ownership of the home, you usually must repay the loan in full—even if the loan balance is greater than the value of the home.
- If you fail to make payments on property taxes, carry homeowners insurance, or maintain the condition of your home, your loan may become due and payable.
- Interest on reverse mortgages is not tax deductible until the loan is paid off in part or whole.
- If you plan on staying in your home through end of life care, you may want to consider your income options such as an annuity or long-term care insurance. In this planning stage, you may wish to consider who will manage your estate when you no longer have the ability to do so. Speak with a trust attorney to gain valuable advice based on your specific needs.

A Word of Caution

Elder abuse is very tragic. Some family members or friends may suggest a reverse mortgage so that funds can be distributed for their own personal use. Out of sympathy or fear, some borrowers feel obliged to appease those who they think are looking out for their best interests, but this should never be the use of loan proceeds. You should never feel pressured to gain any mortgage you are not comfortable with. With most reverse mortgages, you have at least three business days after loan closing to cancel the deal for any reason without penalty. This is called the rescission period. For assistance, seek help from a HUD counselor, your lender, police authorities, the Federal Trade Commission (www.ftc.gov), your state attorney general's office (www.naag.org), or your state banking regulatory agency (www.csbs.org) if at any time you feel pressured to complete the transaction against your will.

Sources of Additional Information
- U.S. Administration on Aging, visit www.eldercare.gov or call 1-800-677-1116
- Reverse Mortgage Education Project AARP Foundation, visit http://www.aarp.org/money/credit-loans-debt/reverse_mortgages/ or call 1-800-209-8085

- National Reverse Mortgage Lenders Association, visit www.reversemortgage.org
- U.S. Department of Housing and Urban Development (HUD), visit http://portal. hud.gov/hudportal/HUD?src=/program_offices/housing/sfh/hecm/hecmhome or call 1-800-CALL-FHA (1-800-225-5342)
- Federal Trade Commission, visit https://www.consumer.ftc.gov/articles/0192-reverse-mortgages or call toll-free, 1-877-FTC-HELP (1-877-382-4357)

USDA Rural Development Mortgage Loans

U.S. Department of Agriculture (USDA) Rural Development mortgage loans are offered in certain rural areas to help borrowers, who meet income guidelines, gain access to home loans at low mortgage rates. Rural areas are defined as open country and communities with populations of 10,000 or less. Towns and cities with populations between 10,000 and 25,000 may also be considered as rural, under certain conditions.

While the term rural may immediately call to mind areas located in the Great Plains, you'll find many qualified rural areas along the coastlines. Over 90 percent of the U.S. land mass is USDA-eligible (based on the 2000 census information), which represents housing for over 100 million people. Many properties in what may traditionally be considered suburban areas may be eligible for USDA financing. To check eligibility guidelines and if a particular address is eligible for USDA financing, visit the USDA website at http://eligibility.sc.egov.usda.gov/eligibility/welcomeAction.do.

USDA rates are typically priced lower than non-USDA mortgage rates because the USDA provides the full faith and assurance of the U.S. government that any financial loss resulting from servicing the loan will be reimbursed in full up to an amount not exceeding 90% of the original loan amount. Property types that may be eligible for USDA loans include single-family homes, condominiums, planned unit developments and manufactured housing on a permanent foundation. Eligibility requirements will vary depending on the property location, and loans offered only to individuals whose income is within the rural-development county limits based on the number of members in the household (not to exceed 115 percent of the area's median income). Eligible applicants may build, rehabilitate, improve, or relocate a dwelling in an eligible rural area.

An important distinction between USDA mortgages and all other types of mortgages is that the USDA issues the final loan approval and not individual lenders. So your loan file will be processed by an approved lender and then submitted to the USDA for final approval. This process can take a little longer to complete than a regular mortgage application, but the benefits to qualified applicants are substantial. Aside from the up-front mortgage insurance fee collected at loan closing of 2 percent of the loan amount, USDA loans also carry a monthly mortgage insurance premium of .5 percent, which is lower than the traditional cost of private monthly mortgage insurance. To learn which lenders are currently approved to accept USDA mortgage applications, visit the USDA website at http://www.rd.usda.gov/files/SFHGLDApprovedLenders. pdf. Important benefits of USDA mortgages include:

- No money down, and up to 103.5 percent financing.
- Not exclusive to first-time homebuyers.
- Nontraditional credit references are available.
- Loans insured are only available under a thirty-year fixed rate term, but have no prepayment penalty.
- The USDA assesses a 2 percent mortgage insurance fee to all loans and the cost may be added to the loan amount at the time of closing, as can the costs of eligible home repairs and improvements. The USDA uses a calculation that includes 2.0 percent of the entire financed loan amount so borrowers who finance the upfront mortgage insurance premium of 2 percent will actually be assessed on the loan amount plus 2 percent. For example, on a $200,000 mortgage the total guarantee fee is $4,080 or about 2.04 percent of the original loan amount.
- Available for purchase and no-cash-out refinances of primary residences (no second homes or investment properties are eligible for financing).
- Gifts and/or grants are allowed to cover payment of closing costs.
- The seller is allowed to pay for the borrower's closing costs.
- Where the appraised value is higher than the purchase price, borrowers can increase their loan size (up to appraised value) to cover closing costs.

Home Affordable Refinance Program

When your existing mortgage is underwater—meaning that you owe more than the property is worth, and your loan was delivered to investors Fannie Mae or Freddie Mac before May 2009, refinancing under the Home Affordable Refinance Program (HARP) may provide you with instant savings. During the financial crisis, many clients came to me complaining that they'd been trying to get a loan modification for years and kept getting denied. All they wanted to do is reduce the interest rate on their current loan. When property values declined and they found they were upside down on their debt, lenders told them they weren't eligible for regular refinancing options because they didn't meet loan-to-value minimum requirements. When they contacted their loan servicer to be considered for a loan modification, they learned they were not eligible for a loan modification because they had not undergone financial hardship, were making timely payments on their mortgage, or didn't meet any of the other criteria for loan modification. While the rest of the country was able to refinance into new loans with lower monthly payments, these borrowers in good standing were stuck with higher interest costs. They'd ask, "What are we supposed to do? Stop paying our mortgage so that we qualify? This doesn't make sense." No, it didn't make sense.

HARP aims to solve that problem. If you are not currently delinquent on your existing home loan and owe more than your home is worth, you may be eligible to refinance your mortgage to receive the benefit of today's lower interest rates or to convert your adjustable rate mortgage into a fixed rate mortgage under HARP. The HARP program has enabled many borrowers who traditionally would not have had credit access to refinance to obtain low rates and significantly reduce their monthly interest costs. The program has helped over 3.2 million refinancing borrowers since its inception and through August 2014 according to Freddie Mac. Homeowners who have refinanced through HARP have benefited from an average interest rate reduction of 1.7 percentage points. For a $200,000 loan this means homeowners saved an average of more than $3,400 in mortgage interest payments during their first twelve months or about $280 every month.

Most, if not all lenders offer the HARP program. However, not every lender can offer you the most aggressive underwriting criteria because each lender adds their own overlays to the guidelines as set forth by the GSEs. The HARP program has many, many benefits and loan eligibility is structured so that it makes it a whole lot easier for you to get approved for refinancing with your current lender/mortgage servicer. The servicer of your mortgage is the company to whom you write the monthly checks. The investor on your mortgage is the company that actually holds the note. You can make application directly with the servicer, or you may use the services of a mortgage broker to submit your loan request to the servicer.

Borrower Benefits Under HARP

- If your mortgage is underwater and you are seeking a fixed rate loan, there are no limitations to loan-to-value if you apply with your current servicer. That means if you owe $400,000 and your home is worth $200,000, your current mortgage servicer won't care about current value because they already hold the debt.
- When you are refinancing with your current mortgage servicer, there is no minimum credit score required to establish eligibility. When you are refinancing with another lender, and your payment is increasing by more than 20 percent, you must have a minimum representative credit score of no less than 620.
- Significant derogatory events such as bankruptcy, foreclosure, and judgments are not considered in eligibility. However, the mortgage delinquency policy must be met for the subject property. This means that you could be delinquent on a loan for another

property and still be eligible for HARP on the subject property where you've not been delinquent for, at a minimum, the preceding twelve-month period.

- When your payment change is less than 20 percent, there is no cap to the debt-to-income ratio. This means that as long as the lender can verify that you have a source of income, it doesn't matter how much your liabilities are in comparison to your income. When the payment will increase by more than 20 percent, the maximum debt-to-income ratio allowed is 45 percent.
- The lender is not required to review project eligibility standards for condominiums since the GSE already holds the risk. This is a huge benefit. A project that the GSEs would otherwise deem unacceptable due to high delinquencies or investor profiles, for example, may still be eligible for new financing with a lower interest rate with the HARP refinance.
- Depending on certain loan attributes, reduced loan documentation may be acceptable to the lender.

Tip: You can determine whether your mortgage is owned by Freddie Mac or Fannie Mae by checking the websites below. Be sure to enter your property address exactly as it appears on your mortgage billing statement. If you don't, you will receive erroneous information regarding eligibility, because the system will not recognize your property as a match:

- https://ww3.freddiemac.com/loanlookup/
- https://www.knowyouroptions.com/loanlookup

Tip: Make sure that your loan application for the HARP program and the lender's automated underwriting system findings match your property address exactly as listed on the billing statement of your current mortgage. Many lenders use USPS.com to verify the accuracy of the subject property address and will override whatever information was entered by your loan officer on the initial loan application. If you identify this difference, have the loan officer request an override of the system to match the subject property address exactly as it appears on your mortgage billing statement. This is done in back-office operations. If this isn't corrected, and your loan was delivered to the agency before May 2009 (as you can verify by visiting the eligibility website), and meets all other program criteria, you will receive false ineligibility from your lender and be denied access to the HARP program simply because the lender uses USPS.com. This is a systemic challenge.

If you have identified that the printed loan application lists a difference in subject property address and your loan officer tells you that there is nothing they can do about it, request a consultation with their sales manager. While it's true that the loan officer can't do anything to change the system, the system can be changed through higher-level back-office operations—if you demand it. Work with your lender to correct the issue. If your lender adamantly refuses to make the change or refuses to show you the revised automated underwriting system findings with the corrected subject property address, contact the CFPB for further assistance in resolving the matter at 1-855-411-2372.

Tip: Condominiums: When entering the condo unit number on the Fannie or Freddie loan lookup tools, be sure to not enter symbols such as "#," or words such as Apt, No, or Unit. Only enter the unit number as it appears on the mortgage statement. Otherwise, you may receive an ineligibility response in error. Also, ask your loan officer to double-check the automated underwriting system findings to be sure the system is picking up the unit number. If it isn't, you will erroneously receive ineligible findings for what may otherwise be an eligible loan.

Tip: The HARP program has cash-back limitations. Fannie Mae allows the new loan amount to include the payoff of the unpaid principal balance on the existing first mortgage, the origination costs of financing the new loan, prepaid items such as homeowners insurance and setting up your escrow account, and cash to borrower at closing of no more than $250. Freddie Mac limits the new loan amount to no more than $5000 greater than the existing principal balance. With that, you may need to bring cash to closing to make up for any fees not covered under the $5000.

Sometimes, a loan officer will run the loan request through the automated underwriting system without paying attention to how much, if any, money is going back to you, and you will receive ineligible findings due to a simple error in the calculation of needed loan amount. If you've confirmed your loan is eligible for delivery to Fannie or Freddie through the loan lookup tool, and your lender tells you you're ineligible, after confirming they have entered the property address that matches your mortgage billing statement, have them check the loan application to ensure there is no bottom line credit to you in excess of $250 for Fannie or over $5000 for Freddie.

When the program initially rolled out, the occupancy on your existing mortgage (primary, second home, investment) and the occupancy on the new mortgage had to be the same. Under current guidelines, because the loan represents existing Fannie or Freddie risk, there is no requirement that the occupancy has stayed the same. The program has been extended several times and as of this printing, it is set to expire on December 31, 2016 and will hopefully get extended once again. To learn current eligibility standards, check the website www. MakingHomeAffordable.gov. As of this printing, the below guidelines are in place for HARP eligibility:
- The mortgage must be owned or guaranteed by Freddie Mac or Fannie Mae.
- The mortgage must have been sold to Fannie Mae or Freddie Mac on or before May 31,

2009. (I've seen loans originated prior to May 31, 2009 where Fannie is the investor and the eligibility findings are denied because although the loan was originated prior to May 2009 and is owned by Fannie, it wasn't delivered to Fannie by the May 31, 2009, deadline.)

- The mortgage cannot have been refinanced under HARP previously unless it is a Fannie Mae loan that was refinanced under HARP between March and May 2009.
- The current loan-to-value ratio must be greater than 80 percent. (If the LTV on the loan is less than 80 percent, you can apply for a standard refinance product.)
- The original loan was not an Alt-A mortgage (a classification of mortgages with clean credit histories where the risk profile falls somewhere between prime and subprime):
- SISA loans (stated income, stated assets)
- SIVA loans (stated income, verified assets)
- Lo-doc loans (low documentation loans)
- No-doc loans (no documentation loans)
- At the time of refinance application and up until loan closing, there can be no late payments on the mortgage for the preceding twelve-month period.

Home Affordable Modification Program

The Home Affordable Modification Program (HAMP) is a government-initiated program to support loan modifications to eligible borrowers who coordinate a change in loan terms of an original mortgage note with their loan servicer. While I was never involved in the loan modification process, I can direct you to helpful information and share what I've heard from the borrower's perspective. It is a documentation nightmare with a string of endless reassignments of contacts with the mortgage servicer. Here are the guidelines for standard eligibility of HAMP where a borrower must meet all for consideration:

1. You obtained your mortgage on or before January 1, 2009.
2. You owe no more than $729,750 on your primary residence or single unit rental property.
3. You owe no more than $934,200 on a two-unit rental property.
4. You owe no more than $1,129,250 on a three-unit rental property.
5. You owe no more than $1,403,400 on a four-unit rental property.
6. The property has not been condemned.
7. You can exhibit evidence of a financial hardship.
8. If seeking modification of a primary residence, the program requires that you show that you are either currently delinquent or in danger of falling behind on your mortgage payments.

9. If seeking modification for a rental property, program eligibility requires that you currently be delinquent. Strategic defaults do not fare well.
10. You have sufficient documented income to support a modified payment.
11. You must not have been convicted within the last ten years of felony larceny, theft, fraud or forgery, money laundering, or tax evasion in connection with a mortgage or real estate transaction.

Tip: Only mortgage servicers offer loan modifications, not mortgage originators. This means that your local in-market loan officer will not be able to help you with the process because they simply don't offer the loan program. While most loan modification activity occurs online or via telephone, many mortgage servicers will come to your city in an effort to reach borrowers who have difficulty connecting through other methods. Ask your servicer when they will be in your city and make an appointment. Bring every piece of loan documentation that applies to your particular situation.

Tip: If you feel you may be eligible for loan modification, begin conversations with your mortgage servicer as soon as possible. Additionally, contact one of the housing experts recommended by the Making Home Affordable site at http://www.makinghomeaffordable.gov/pages/default.aspx or by calling at 888-995-HOPE (4673). These HUD-approved housing counselors will help you understand your options, design a plan to suit your individual situation, and prepare your application. There is no cost to you for this valuable, around-the-clock service. Help is available in more than 160 languages.

Tip: I will share with you this example. A relative of mine—we'll call him Daniel —had struggled through the modification process on his own for 16 months. He finally decided to enlist my help when he submitted a fifth request and received a FedEx letter from his lender asking for more documentation that read:

Please complete and fax the following required documentation for each borrower listed below using the enclosed fax cover sheet or return using the enclosed FedEx envelope.

Bank Account Statements—Sources of income must be identified from each bank account. Thank you for providing your bank statement(s). Unfortunately, it was not complete. Please contact your customer relationship manager to learn what additional information we need.

Daniel insisted that he had already given them what they asked and he showed me the consecutive bank statements he had provided. I agreed they were complete. We jointly contacted the lender and went through all the security protocol requiring that the lender receive a signed authorization via fax from Daniel allowing the lender to speak to me about the modification request.

The lender representative explained that for all deposit transactions appearing on the bank statement, an explanation is needed identifying the deposit as recurring income or not. I was puzzled. Since I know all about sourcing of deposits for loan applications, I asked, "Ok, you want me to tell you where the money came from?" The lender responded, "No, I only need you to tell me if the deposit was income related or if it was not income related." I nodded in understanding and thought, How interesting. It wasn't that the bank statements were incomplete as the letter delivered via FedEx on his fifth attempt was stating, it was that each deposit was not clearly identified with a pen indicating whether or not it was related to income. Daniel was able to comply with the request and soon thereafter, received an approval for loan modification.

On this day, I learned that when requesting a loan modification, the lender isn't looking to source continuance of income as we require in a regular mortgage, but is instead looking to identify any evidence of additional sources of income not previously reported. And I know why: At that time, if your debt-to-income ratios were less than 31 percent, you were not eligible for loan modification (this has since been lifted). So lenders were looking at loan documentation to identify if borrowers neglected to declare additional income sources in an attempt to defraud them. Because of these terrible communication glitches, many people have hired real estate professionals to help them navigate the modification process.

How the Mortgage Industry Failed at Delivering HAMP

With the initial roll out of HAMP, and the immediate influx of requests received, most lenders were not staffed to handle the volume. Even after placing borrowers on the reduced monthly payment terms, lenders quickly identified that many borrowers were still not making their loan payments on time and, therefore, became ineligible for a permanent loan modification. In an effort to expedite approvals for worthy borrowers and reduce processing costs on borrowers who would not make their lowered monthly payments on time and fail eligibility, lenders decided to take a cursory application. They immediately placed seemingly eligible borrowers on the trial period with reduced payments and only after the borrower showed timeliness did they begin requesting evidence to validate the income as initially reported on the loan modification request. Where borrowers who successfully made timely payments during the trial period were expecting to be placed into long-term modification, many were disappointed when they learned they were later declined because they did not meet the other aspects of HAMP program eligibility. This practice has since changed. Legislation was passed to require income validation along with all other program eligibility requirements prior to the offering of a trial modification period.

Also, in an effort to continue to provide meaningful solutions to the housing crisis, effective June 1, 2012, the Obama administration expanded the population of homeowners that may be eligible for the Home Affordable Modification Program to include:

1. Homeowners who are applying for a modification on a home that is not their primary residence, but the property is currently rented or the homeowner intends to rent it.
2. Homeowners who previously did not qualify for HAMP because their debt-to-income ratio was 31 percent or lower.
3. Homeowners who previously received a HAMP trial period plan, but defaulted in their trial payments.
4. Homeowners who previously received a HAMP permanent modification, but defaulted in their payments, therefore losing good standing.

If you are a homeowner who falls into any of these criteria, you may still be eligible for a modification under the expanded criteria. Please check with your mortgage servicer.

Loan Modifications and FHA Loans

On May 20, 2009, President Obama signed the Helping Families Save Their Homes Act of 2009, which provides additional loss mitigation authority to assist FHA borrowers under the Making Home Affordable (MHA) program. This program provides borrowers with the opportunity to reduce their loan payments through a loan modification through the Home Affordable Modification Program (HAMP). FHA HAMP is designed to help FHA-insured borrowers in default with a greater opportunity to avoid foreclosure by permanently reducing their monthly mortgage payment. If you have an FHA-insured loan, you should contact your current loan servicer to determine if you are eligible for the FHA HAMP or other loss mitigation options.

Portfolio or Non-QM Options

A portfolio option is a loan product that includes features that do not fit GSE guidelines and, therefore, cannot be delivered for guarantee. These loans are either held by the lender or sold in the secondary market as private label mortgage-backed securities. In these products, anything goes. Here are a few examples of product features that can be found in portfolio lending options:

1. Interest only
2. Stated income
3. Jumbo (in excess of conforming loan limits)
4. Super jumbo loans (in excess of $3,000,000)
5. Terms over thirty years
6. Negative amortization
7. Balloon payments
8. Nonwarrantable condominiums
9. Expanded debt-to-income ratios

10. Nonresident aliens
11. One day out of bankruptcy
12. Foreclosures more recent than seven years
13. Financing more than ten properties
14. Loan qualification based on investment property cash flow (debt service ratio)
15. No requirement of IRS Form 4506-T to verify income reported
16. Less than 20 percent down payment without mortgage insurance or guarantee
17. Qualifying income calculations based on average bank deposits for the preceding twelve-month period
18. Qualifying income calculations based on asset dissipation
19. Cash-out in excess of GSE guidelines

09 Managing Expectations

The time constraints prevent loan officers from giving each of you more than a 10,000-mile-high fly-by of the expectations you should have for each milestone in the mortgage application process. In theory, a loan officer is the individual who begins the mortgage application process. In today's reality, the loan officer begins the request for the mortgage loan and shepherds you from application to processing to underwriting and on to closing. Although there are many people working on your file at any given time, at any query or misstep along the way, the loan officer is the one who you call for resolution. As such, you, the loan officer, and the loan processor always have to be on the same page.

What to Expect After Loan Application

EACH LENDER HAS a variable timeline for the completion of each milestone in the process. We call this pipeline management. While not all operating environments work the way I describe here, as a seasoned loan officer having worked in several operating environments, I know that if I don't oversee the transaction—as this list details—regardless of whose responsibility a particular function may be, the loan file will stagger at some point its way to closing. Missing closing dates affects many people and interest rate lock periods expire, so the better loan officer's have systems in place to follow tight pipeline management.

Milestones of the Loan Process

In a perfect scenario, when you bring all required documentation to loan application to ensure a loan commitment is issued with minimal conditions, a purchase transaction goes like this:

1. You contact a loan officer and request program and pricing options.
2. A better loan officer will ask you several questions to uncover your needs before spewing out the day's interest rate. This will ensure the pricing quoted is based on an accurate representation of your particular scenario and loan programs are presented that may satisfy your particular needs.
3. Nonbinding preapplication cost estimates for different loan scenarios are provided and are priced with an estimated credit score and an estimated valuation of the property. You're alerted that final pricing will be based on confirmed credit score, acceptable property valuation, selected loan program, and market pricing as of the day and time you request a rate lock.
4. After reviewing the options and addressing concerns, you make the decision to move forward with loan application and provide your authorization to the lender to pull your

credit report. Some lenders will collect a credit report fee and other third-party fees at this time (such as the fee for the automated underwriting analysis).

5. Loan officer takes a complete application and requests a credit report.

6. Loan officer analyzes credit history and reviews it with you to confirm accuracy of data reported. At this step, it is very important to alert your loan officer if there are debts on the report that someone else pays for. For example, you could have cosigned for your sister's car or your business pays your American Express card.

7. Loan officer runs the file through the automated underwriting system (AUS) where a preliminary automated review of the information entered on the loan application is had—with no actual documentation review. The loan officer receives a recommendation and delivers to you a list of supporting documentation to promptly gather and return, as requested by AUS findings.

8. You deliver all requested documentation within forty-eight hours of loan application and the loan officer will review the items to ensure completeness and identify any potential issues that were not previously identified.

9. Loan officer updates the loan application based on accuracy of credit report and information as gathered by income and asset documentation provided.

10. Loan officer runs the file through AUS a second time with updated information.

11. Loan officer re-prices the loan based on actual credit score, verified assets, and qualifying income and shares new pricing with you. Reminding you again that further changes to pricing may occur once the property valuation has been determined.

12. At this time, you decide whether to lock the interest rate or let it float until, typically, no more than seven days from loan closing.

13. Loan disclosures are provided to you within three days of loan application including a written good faith/loan estimate.

14. You read the loan disclosures, assess the loan application details for accuracy, review the terms listed on the good faith estimate and the Truth-in-Lending forms (both forms replaced by the loan estimate beginning August 2015), and if you wish to proceed with the loan application, notify the loan officer of your consent to proceed. Sign, date, and return loan disclosures to the loan officer or their support staff.

15. Once consent is issued, the loan officer collects any other upfront application fees, as required. Generally, appraisal fee and, depending on the lender, credit report and application fee, if not already collected.

16. Loan officer instructs you on pending items necessary for underwriter review (i.e., signed and dated letters of explanation addressing any loan attributes and additional supporting documents).

17. Loan officer reviews purchase contract, and contacts both the selling and listing agents to share contact information.
18. The lender orders the appraisal.
19. Loan officer writes cover letter to the loan file that tells your story and addresses any areas of concern or compensating factors.
20. Loan officer passes file to loan processor who takes over the next steps in the mortgage loan approval process.
21. Loan processor orders title commitment from your selected settlement agent.
22. If a condo questionnaire is needed, the loan officer or loan processor will contact the homeowner association for completion. If there is a fee to complete the form, you will be contacted to pay the fee directly to the association.
23. Loan processor reviews documentation submitted (ensures clear copies, most current dates, reviews bank statements for large deposits, reviews income calculations, and updates loan application with any new information received).
24. Loan processor contacts you and introduces his- or herself. From this point forward, it is mainly the loan processor who interacts with you, but the loan officer remains diligent in overseeing the milestones to ensure all parties remain on target for meeting the anticipated closing date.
25. In most operating environments, an initial underwriting review is performed within 7 days of submitting a loan.
26. If the underwriter receives the file with insufficient documentation (which shouldn't happen if you've come well prepared) to justify initial approval, the loan file will be suspended until documents come in.
27. If both you and the loan officer worked together to clearly identify and collect the supporting documentation that are necessary for a quick loan approval, a conditional loan commitment is issued by the underwriter. With a conditional loan commitment at hand, the loan processor and loan officer will review the underwriter's additional documentation requests and identify how to best resolve the pending items.
28. Generally, the loan processor reviews pending conditions with you; however, some better loan officers will also engage with you (translating Mortgage Speak) to be sure that you understand, what the remaining conditions are, what exactly needs to happen in order to satisfy them, and by when those conditions need to be turned in so that the anticipated closing date can be met. Some conditions of the loan commitment are only satisfied by the lender, and you will be made aware of those as well.
29. The lender will release a copy of the appraisal to you upon receipt. At this time, you are instructed to shop for property insurance, obtain a quote, compete an application with an insurance agent, and set a date for coverage. The certificate of insurance must

be received by the lender prior to scheduling a closing and must contain the lender's mortgagee clause and your loan number.

30. Once you provide all requested documentation and the appraisal is in, your loan file is resubmitted to underwriting for review. Don't submit items piecemeal, thinking that they are being looked at, because they're not.

31. If the submitted documentation meets the underwriter's expectations, a loan commitment will be issued. This is the document that satisfies the mortgage financing contingency on your sales contract. If the underwriter is not satisfied, additional documentation is requested and another round of resubmission occurs.

32. Back-office operations receives and reviews a title commitment—depending on the lender's size, this function may be completed by the loan processor or by a specific team who specializes in reviewing title documents. The loan processor addresses any related issues.

33. Insurance is received and reviewed by back-office operations. Again, the loan processor addresses any related issues.

34. The loan processor coordinates the closing date with you and the settlement agent and then notifies the loan officer of the time, date, and location of the closing.

35. File is transferred to the loan closer who works with the settlement agent to prepare the final HUD-1/closing disclosure.

36. The settlement agent coordinates with the lender, the buyer, the buyer's agent, the seller, the seller's agent, the seller's lender, outstanding lien holders, and all parties requiring payment in the transaction to ensure final HUD-1/closing disclosure shows accurate fees. Once everyone approves the fees, the HUD-1/closing disclosure is released to the buyer and the seller.

37. The settlement agent gives you the final figures and provides instructions on their preferred method of receiving funds for closing (wire transfer or cashier's check). With the August 2015 release of the closing disclosure, some lenders are opting to take over this function from the settlement agent.

38. The closing package is delivered to the settlement agent, and when all required loan documents are executed (signed) by you and the HUD-1/closing disclosure is executed by both buyer and seller, the lender issues a funding number. This signals to the settlement agent that loan funds can be disbursed. Some lenders don't require a funding number to signal disbursement.

39. Whenever possible, the loan officer attends the loan closing.

And that's not just originating a mortgage, is it?

Turnaround Times

The length of time it takes for you to receive a conditional loan commitment from underwriting is the turnaround time. This should not be confused with the initial automated underwriting system findings that your loan officer shares with you soon after loan application, which detail the documentation required to comply with loan approval. Turnaround times describe the period of time that passes from the lender's receipt of loan documentation to the time an underwriter reviews that documentation. By knowing your lender's expected turnaround time, you'll be able to manage expectations of the loan process and monitor progress to have a clear indication as to whether you will be able to meet the contract closing date or for what period of time you'll need to lock-in your interest rate.

Turnaround times change like the ebb and flow of the ocean tide and are directly proportional to market conditions. When interest rates are low and volume is high, turnaround times are slow. When interest rates are high and volume is low, turnaround times are usually faster. In a stable market, a lender strives to have your initial loan application submitted along with supporting documentation for an initial underwriting review within forty-eight hours of loan submission.

Loan submission is not just the taking of a loan application. Loan submission requires gathering loan documentation, structuring your loan file, and hopefully, a loan officer's analysis of documentation with a cover letter written to address the specific attributes of your loan file.

Local Versus Regional Operations Centers

With the industry's increased focus on cost efficacy, major lenders have moved from local operations in branch offices to regional centralized processing centers. By having local operations centers, each branch office or group of local branch offices is supported by in-market processing, underwriting, and closing functions that are within driving distance of the sales office. Sales offices house loan officers.

With local operations, many lender employees get a broader understanding of how each function is interrelated—they can see how a file progresses from loan officer to file opener, to processor, to underwriter, to closer, to investor. With centralized operations, career trajectories are often linear and employees are often limited in their understanding of the totality of the mortgage loan approval process and how each individual's contribution is truly critical in delivering best in class service. For these reasons, it's important to review proper expectations for each milestone with your loan officer and together, monitor the flow throughout the process. In this way, regardless of distribution channel or cyclical flow of the mortgage markets, you'll be able to identify roadblocks that need to be addressed to keep the file moving forward as scheduled.

Issuing Your Consent

A lender will require your consent to move forward in the application process. Without your specific agreement to proceed, a lender will be stalled. Communication here is key and timeline expectations should be reviewed with your loan officer. Here are a few examples of the point when they'll need your permission to move forward:

- Consent to pull credit
- Consent to collect credit report fee
- Consent to receive edisclosures
- Intent to proceed with loan application
- Consent to collect appraisal fee and any other application fees

Application Fees

In today's high tech electronic environment, most lenders collect the fees for credit report, appraisal, and application through credit or debit cards. Many won't accept a check (neither personal nor cashier's check nor money order). In those cases, a borrower who does not have a credit card may be forced to get a prepaid gift card from one of the major issuers (Visa, American Express, Discover, MasterCard). What is unusual and disturbing for many customers is that the lender is not required to provide an itemized receipt for the fees that are being billed and, in most instances, does not. This is a systemic, regulatory, and lender flaw, as we should be providing applicants with detailed receipts for the amounts billed.

Edisclosure

Edisclosures are an electronic means of delivering loan disclosures via secure email. Not all lenders subscribe to edisclosure. Those that do will provide you with a detailed explanation of how to access the secure documents, which can be a rather complex process. Edisclosure is an expedited means to deliver loan documents that are necessary for your review. I especially like using this method of delivery because it allows the client to immediately receive vital information that is necessary for review and decision-making. Without your consent, a lender is prohibited from using this method of delivery.

Tip: As a best practice, ask your loan officer to send you an email for confirmation of delivery to ensure they correctly spelled your email address. At the same time, ask that they send you written instructions on how to open secure documents. Often, an email containing a link will get caught up in your spam/junk folder. Be sure to check there, as well, when the lender confirms that it has sent the email. Once received, add that sender address to your email contact list so that future deliveries go straight to your inbox.

Consent to Pull Credit

Many lenders will not issue a good faith/loan estimate without knowing your representative credit score, and loan eligibility is difficult to determine without a review of your credit history. Please review the "The Six Basic Steps to Mortgage Approval" section in chapter 1 for an understanding of the processes. If you are averse to having your credit pulled by different lenders in the shopping process and if you have a recent tri-merged credit report in hand, ask for a preapplication cost estimate instead—with the understanding that final loan pricing and program eligibility is directly affected by the representative credit score from the lender's choice of credit-reporting agency not yours. Once you are ready to allow the lender to pull your credit for actual pricing, provide them with your consent to pull credit. I would refrain from providing your social security number to any lender until you are ready for them to pull credit. Some lenders collect a credit report fee prior to your deciding to make loan application.

Notice of Intent to Proceed with Loan Application

The notice of intent to proceed with loan application (NIPLA) is you giving authorization to the lender to charge application and appraisal fees and your acceptance of the terms and fees as listed on the good faith/loan estimate. The NIPLA disclosure is designed to demonstrate the lender's compliance with the requirements of Regulation X, which implements Real Estate Settlement Procedures Act. While the lender is required to obtain your consent to proceed with the loan application, there is no mandate to obtain this consent in a written form. A lender typically chooses to demonstrate the receipt of your consent to proceed with loan application by obtaining your verbal authorization and simply makes a note of it in the loan origination software.

Issuance of Closing Disclosure

As part of the integration of the disclosures for the Truth-in-Lending Act and the Real Estate Settlement and Procedures Act, a lender is required to deliver the final figures for loan closing to you in the form of the closing disclosure no later than three days from loan consummation (closing or funding date). In real estate transactions where the good faith estimate is used and the HUD-1 settlement statement is provided instead of the closing disclosure, the final figures for loan closing are delivered to you no later than twenty-four hours from loan closing.

Note: The closing disclosure can be issued as many days prior to loan consummation as the loan file permits.

Purchase Contract

Before making an offer on a particular property, there are many features and benefits to consider. It's worth your while to take a moment and also analyze the future costs of total housing related to a particular property. Each property has unique characteristics and the monthly cost of utility bills and property insurance will vary based on square footage, age of roof, structure, wear and tear, and other features. Additionally, keep in mind that most property taxes are based on assessed value and not market price, and you shouldn't expect the current owner's property tax bill to be the same for you next year. If you are purchasing the property for an amount greater than what the previous owner paid for it, you should expect to have an increase in your property tax bill the following year. The difference can be significant, and it will impact your monthly mortgage payment if your lender is collecting for property taxes.

Tip: Before you commit to a property, find out the millage rate used by your county property tax assessor to determine an expectation of the future property tax bill. This is also relevant when purchasing new construction with no prior history of property taxes. To determine the amount allocated for monthly property taxes during the qualification process, some lenders will use the current owner's property tax bill while other lenders will use an estimation for the upcoming year's tax bill by multiplying the county's millage rate by the sales price to determine the amount allocated for monthly property taxes.

Tip: If you are concerned with energy efficiency, ask the owner for copies of utility bills for the preceding twelve months to get a full picture of annual expected costs. While it isn't required that the seller turn it over, it may allow for your peace of mind moving forward with your offer.

Tip: As part of the inspection period allowed by your contract, be sure to obtain a four-point inspection on the property. A four-point inspection includes assessment on HVAC (heating, ventilation, and air conditioning), electrical wiring and panels, plumbing connections and fixtures, and roof. Insurance companies have become increasingly reluctant to issue policies on older homes (usually twenty-five years old or more). Their common concern is that there may be conditions in an older home that could become a liability to them. For instance, a home with a roof nearing the end of its reliable service life may fail while under the policy, and the homeowner may seek reimbursement for damages to the home or its contents. Similar concerns extend to the condition of the HVAC, electrical, and plumbing systems. If these elements are in poor condition, in need of being updated or replaced, or were improperly installed, they may fail and cause fire or water damage. Newer homes are assumed by the insurance companies not to have these problems as frequently as older homes.

Tip: If you live in the coastal areas of the southeastern U.S., invest in a windstorm inspection or wind mitigation report. The purpose of a windstorm inspection is to determine the soundness of a given structure in the event of strong winds, such as a hurricane. Windstorm inspections look for construction features that have been shown to reduce losses in hurricanes, such as a hip roof, concrete block construction, the presence of gable end bracing, shutters and opening protections, roof to wall attachments such as toe nails, clips or hurricane straps, and a secondary water resistance barrier. By submitting the results of a windstorm inspection to your insurer, you may be eligible to obtain a discount on your windstorm insurance policy. In Florida, for example, premium discounts for certain favorable wind mitigation features are mandated by state law and can total up to 45 percent of the original policy's premium. In coastal parts of Texas, the state mandates windstorm inspections prior to certifying a new building.

Here are some important details to attend to at this stage:
- Contract closing date: Identify the contract closing date at loan application and ensure your lender has the capacity to meet your closing date.
- Settlement agent: If the purchase contract lists a settlement agent, confirm with your lender that you will be able to use that agent at closing.
- Financing contingency date: Does the lender have the capacity to issue a loan commitment within the time period specified? What is their appraiser's turnaround time?
- Listing and selling realtor information: Have your selling agent work with the listing agent to provide support in obtaining any property related information such as the contact information for granting and scheduling appraiser access, the contact information for the property manager at the homeowner association (HOA), scheduling the HOA interview, coordinating delivery and completion of the lender's HOA questionnaire, and obtaining the master certificate of insurance for condominiums and townhomes (PUDs).
- Closing cost contributions: Are they allowable by the loan program chosen? What do they include?

Purchase of Preforeclosure or Short Sale Properties

Know that in a preforeclosure or short sale, your offer to purchase a home can be agreed to by the seller, but—and here's a big but—without the written agreement of the lienholder, mortgage servicer, or insurer (to which less than the amount owed is being negotiated), the agreement for sale between you and the seller is worth absolutely nothing. These negotiations can take weeks or months to complete and whilst you're in negotiations, it is possible for the property be taken from the seller in foreclosure proceedings.

When negotiating for a property that is a preforeclosure or a short sale, you may be required to pay additional fees, assessments, or payments that are typically the responsibility of the seller or another party. Both the good faith/loan estimate and the HUD-1/closing disclosure must include all fees, assessments, and payments included in the transaction. Examples of additional fees, assessments, or payments include, but are not limited to:

- Short sale processing fees, also referred to as short sale negotiation fees, buyer discount fees, short sale buyer fees (This fee does not represent a common and customary charge and, therefore, must be treated as a sales concession if any portion is reimbursed by an interested party to the transaction.)
- Payment to a subordinate lienholder
- Payment of delinquent taxes or delinquent HOA assessments

When negotiating a contract with a property owner and their mortgage servicer or insurer, be sure to review the following concerns:

- You (the buyer) must be provided with written details of the additional fees, assessments, or payments and the additional necessary funds to complete the transaction. These must be documented and will be included in your underwriting analysis.
- The mortgage servicer that is agreeing to the preforeclosure or short sale must be provided with written details of the fees, assessments, or payments and be given the option of renegotiating the payoff amount to release its lien.
- All parties (buyer, seller, and servicer) must provide their written agreement of the final details of the transaction, including the additional fees, assessments, or payments. This can be accomplished using the Request for Approval of Short Sale or Alternative Request for the Approval of Short Sale forms published by the U.S. Treasury Supplemental Directive 09–09 or any alternative form or addendum. As navigating through Treasury updates can be a bit time-consuming for you, I'm instead providing a link to the USFN.org website. USFN is a nonprofit serving the mortgage industry which keeps links to these forms updated on their website that can be accessed at http://www.usfn.org/Content/NavigationMenu/INDUSTRYRESOURCES/ClientResourceCenter/HAMP_Info.htm.

The Appraisal

When you apply for a residential mortgage loan, the lender will require an independent determination of the market value of the property. Although you are required to pay the appraisal fee, the owner of the appraisal is actually the lender and it is the lender who will select the appraiser and not you. An appraisal is a licensed professional's opinion of value. It does not, however, determine market value. Market value is determined between the buyer and the seller. As no two appraisals are identical, valuation can present significant challenges for you, the seller, and the lender. Not only does the appraisal determine the lender's usable valuation, it is also used as a tool for identifying fraud and provides independent verification of such items as ownership, property taxes, homeowner association dues, special assessments, and occupancy.

Appraisers estimate property values using three different and distinct approaches: market data, cost, and income. The market data approach evaluates the cost to substitute a property; the cost approach analyzes the expenditure to rebuild the property from the ground up; and the income approach determines value based on the ability to collect market rent. Once all three valuations are completed, the appraiser offers an opinion as to which of the three methods most accurately reflects current value.

The most commonly selected valuation approach in residential real estate is market data. Market data analysis takes the comparables (recent closed sales) provided and identifies the differences in property characteristics such as their distance from the subject property, the length of time from the date of sale to present date, location, square footage, number of bedrooms and bathrooms, best conforming use, size of the lot, age of construction, and neighborhood.

Note: Most disputes over value are based on whether or not the buyer or seller agrees with the appraiser's selection of comparables used in the determination of value.

Some people believe that an appraiser is required to remove distress sales from comparables such as short sales, foreclosures, and divorce fire sales—but this isn't entirely true. Yes, in a stable or increasing market, a one-off short sale or foreclosure can and should be excluded from usable comparables. However, in a declining market where the trend shows an increase in availability of short sales and foreclosures (as we saw throughout the Great Recession), those recorded sales will be included in the appraisal as they represent a comparable purchase for the buyer.

Upon assessing the property, if the appraiser identifies any deficiency that makes the property uninhabitable or unsafe, it will note the item on the report. Your lender's underwriter will determine whether or not the deficiency needs to be repaired prior to loan closing. If the deficiency needs to be corrected prior to loan closing, get a move on, as re-inspection will need to take place before loan closing. Many lenders overestimate the appraisal fee by approximately $100 on their good faith/loan estimates because at the time of loan application, they do not know if an additional property inspection will be required. On the final HUD-1/closing disclosure, only actual fees assessed by an appraiser will be listed. Any appraisal fees collected in excess of actual charges will be credited.

Additionally, although the value is met, the appraisal still needs to be reviewed and accepted by the underwriter. If the underwriter doesn't like a comparable that was used and identifies that a more suitable comparable was available, the appraiser will be contacted to justify why they chose not to use the better comp. This back and forth can take a few days. That's why it's very important to get the appraisal ordered right away.

Sometimes neither a full appraisal nor a property inspection is required, and a lender may choose a more simplistic valuation method. Especially when refinancing an existing loan through your current mortgage servicer, your lender may choose to determine market value by using an automated valuation model (AVM) instead of a full appraisal. AVM is a service that provides real estate property valuations using mathematical modeling within seconds. It is a technology-driven report. The product of an AVM comes from the analysis of public records combined with computer decision logic to provide a calculated estimate of the probable selling price of a selected property. An AVM typically includes an indicative market value, the county tax assessor's indication of value, if available, information on the subject property and its recent sales history, and a comparable sales analysis of similar properties. Your lender can use any combination of a full appraisal, drive by, desk review, field review, or an automated valuation model to mitigate risk. The lender's risk manager makes the final determination of value through any combination of these methods.

On Expectations

The person who orders an appraisal is different for every lender and ranges from the loan officer, to the loan processor, to the sales assistant, to the file opener. By any method, the loan file is updated when the appraisal order is sent to the Appraisal Management Company (AMC). The AMC, in turn, notifies the lender of the selected appraiser once the appointment has been scheduled. Ideally, the AMC should be held to a twenty-four-hour turnaround time for setting the appointment with the listing agent, or in the case where there is no realtor, the seller/homeowner. Your loan officer will notify you that the appraisal appointment has been set, and a reasonable expectation for delivery of a completed report is three-to-five business days.

Tip: Do not delay ordering the appraisal.

Tip: At loan application, give your loan officer the direct contact details of the person the appraiser needs to connect with to schedule the appointment to view the property. This would be either the listing agent or the homeowner.

Tip: Ask your realtor to confirm that the listing agent has good comparables to give the appraiser when they come out to view the property. This is the only contact the appraiser will have with anyone directly involved in the transaction. If the property characteristics are different from what is recorded with the county property appraiser's office, this would be the time to let the appraiser know of the differences.

Tip: While having the appraiser and your home inspection team access the property at the same time may seem convenient, don't do it. It is unwise to have these two individuals inspecting the property at the same time as each is tasked to identify different things.

Tip: If the appraised value is lower than the agreed-upon purchase price, an appraisal contingency on your purchase contract gives you the right to withdraw your offer. You also have the option to renegotiate the sales price with the seller or to seek a higher loan-to-value with your lender. Discuss your options with your loan officer and realtor.

Tip: Under no circumstances should you, the seller, or the realtors engage in any type of conversation regarding the value of the property with the appraiser. Any conversation about value with the appraiser can be construed as undue influence. So be careful. If the appraiser feels pressured for value, he will not complete the appraisal and will still bill for his time.

Evidence of Insurance

With a purchase transaction, if you hadn't already received an estimate of insurance prior to negotiating the sale, once you receive a copy of the property appraisal begin shopping for your homeowners insurance policy. When refinancing an existing loan, change the mortgagee clause on your existing policy to match the mortgagee clause of the new loan when you've received the new lender's conditional loan commitment and you are pretty sure you will be able to satisfy all loan conditions.

While just receiving a quote on a new policy may be good enough for you before loan closing, it is not sufficient for your lender to sign off on the insurance contingency that is required to be satisfied prior to scheduling the loan closing. To clear this loan condition, you will need to provide a bound or dated insurance policy. To receive a bound policy, once you accept the provider's quote, your insurance agent will need you to complete an application and will ask for the verbiage of your lender's mortgagee clause and your specific loan number so that the bound policy can have the complete information of your lender. Just because the policy is bound, it doesn't necessarily follow that you need to pay for the policy before you own the property. Most insurance agents will allow you to pay for the policy on the date of closing as listed on and collected for on the HUD-1/closing disclosure.

For condominiums, basic property insurance requirements are usually met with review of the project's master insurance policy, which covers the building and all common areas. Most projects only provide coverage for everything outside of your unit. In those cases, lenders will require that you obtain evidence of an additional HO6 walls in policy. For the HO6 policy, the amount of coverage a lender requires is usually 20 percent of the unit's appraised value and is not based on the purchase price or the loan amount.

Having the mortgagee clause and loan number listed on all insurance certificates is a requirement throughout the servicing of your loan.

You will find your loan specific mortgagee clause and loan number in the lender's disclosure package under the insurance requirements informative piece. Here's an example:

ABC Mortgage Lender

ISAOA (Its Successors And/Or Assigns)

123 Main Street

Anytown, Anystate USA

Loan number: 000123456789

Note: If you will have a piggyback loan at closing (a first and second mortgage), the mortgagee clause for the second mortgage will need to be added to the insurance policy. The second mortgage has its own loan number and servicing address.

Note: It's very important that you begin the insurance process well before loan closing as impending catastrophic events such as a hurricane brewing off the Atlantic seaboard will cause insurance carriers to put a hold on insuring any property until the storm is out of reach. This process is generally referred to as the "black box" or "black hole" of insurance. Assuming a catastrophic event has occurred, such as either two consecutive Atlantic seaboard windstorms, a Florida windstorm, a Gulf of Mexico windstorm, a California earthquake, or an act of terrorism, a reinspection of any property potentially affected by these occurrences will be required by a representative of the insurance agent prior to executing a new policy.

Cleared for Closing, But Are You Really?

Loan officers don't schedule closings; we simply identify your anticipated closing date and monitor the progress of your loan file to move it forward. You and the seller agree to the closing date on the purchase contract, or in the case of a refinance transaction, a date is selected to comply within the lender's expiration date of the interest rate lock period. Once your loan file has cleared the lender's underwriting processes, you'll coordinate with your loan processor in conjunction with the settlement agent to actually secure a closing package.

Typically, it is your loan officer who will call you to give you the great news that your file has been cleared for closing. Hooray for everyone! You can finally wipe the sweat off your brow and jump for joy. You're getting ready to pick up the phone and schedule the movers, but hold on a second. For your loan officer, cleared for closing signals the end of the road in monitoring the flow of your loan application. Most likely, the closing will now take place. Of course, there are those minor instances when other nonlender issues arise, such as the seller backing out of the transaction or a natural disaster damaging the property, but those are generally rare.

A very big word of caution to you here: The only point in time where you can rest assured that the closing will take place is after the closing has actually taken place and the funds have been delivered to the settlement agent. Within ten days of the closing, your lender will run the file through the quality control process. Here, they will do a quick recheck of credit and employment.

Credit Recheck

Your loan officer will typically ask you not to make significant purchases until after loan closing. Some lenders subscribe to a service from their credit-reporting vendor that provides them with updates if any credit provider has made an inquiry on your credit file after your lender did their hard pull. Other lenders will wait until no more than ten days before closing to do this soft pull. A soft pull does not impact credit scores and, therefore, will not change the credit scores with which your loan file was underwritten.

If the credit report is more than 120 days old, then that's a different story. Every piece of documentation in your file has an expiration date. If your credit report is over 120 days old, your lender is required to order another hard pull and your loan file will be subjected to the underwriting standards in place for your new credit score. Either way, if they've identified new debts or an increase in debts, they will pull the file from the closing department and throw it back to the underwriter for a new analysis of your debt-to-income ratio. Hit the brakes, stop right there.

What do you mean my loan file has to go back to the underwriter; what happened?

Yes, it's okay to be nervous here. At this point in the process, you've already signed off on the mortgage contingency and waived your rights to the escrow deposit. If the results of the soft or hard pull significantly impact the loan approval criteria, your loan commitment can be rescinded (taken back to conditional status or even denied).

Reverification of Employment

The other quality control item the lender will check no more than ten days from the scheduled closing is your employment status. If employment information has changed from that listed at the time of loan approval, this could significantly impact the loan decision. Visit the "Verification of Employment" section in chapter 14 to learn about what to expect. Here are a few scenarios that may impact your ability to close as scheduled.

Scenario A: You may have received your loan approval based on the fact that you were an employed mechanic. During the loan approval process, you decided to open up a small business on your own. Fantastic for you. However, you obviously didn't speak to your loan officer about the potential impact of this decision. As an employed mechanic, you probably were paid an hourly rate plus overtime and maybe some bonus income as well. The two-year average of your earned income was used by the underwriter to determine stable earnings that are likely to continue. At the moment you quit your job and went on your own, there was no future predictable income the underwriter could use and, therefore, your loan is denied.

Scenario B: The same mechanic takes a job at another auto dealership that is paying him an hourly rate that is greater than what he was making in his previous job. The underwriter can only use the guaranteed hours per week of his new employer to determine future, stable earnings that are likely to continue because there is no way to predict future overtime and bonus income opportunities with this new employer unless it is guaranteed in writing. If without the overtime and bonus income you exceed the maximum allowable debt-to-income ratio, your loan will be denied (unless you can reduce your monthly liabilities by paying off some debt or lowering your loan amount).

Scenario C: The same mechanic meets the debt-to-income ratio based on his new hourly rate. Approval is still good. However, the closing will be delayed until the borrower can show evidence of a full thirty days of compensation. Yes, the lender needs verification of receipt (pay stubs) of a full thirty days of pay to be able to use the hourly income rate on the new job.

Tip: From the time of mortgage application through to loan funding, refrain from making unnecessary purchases or making any changes to your income stream. If it is absolutely necessary that one or the other takes place, consult your loan officer regarding the potential impact it will have on the credit decision.

Preparations for Loan Closing

Once you've been cleared for closing, your next question is, what do I need to bring to loan closing? Your settlement agent will be able to provide you with specific instructions on what to bring, which will include a form of identification and the remaining funds needed for the transaction. Settlement agents will typically only accept the receipt of funds for closing via cashier's checks made payable to their firm or through bank wire transfer. Ask the settlement agent for bank wiring instructions or the name of the entity to which you will need to have the cashier's check written. Some lenders will require evidence of withdrawal from the account where the money was drawn for loan closing to confirm that funds are coming from an account that was disclosed on the loan application and sourced; others don't. Either way, be sure to withdraw funds from an account that has been sourced by your lender.

At the closing table, you will be presented with a full set of loan disclosures again. While its important to read and understand each document that you are signing, pay special attention to the HUD-1/closing disclosure, which lists all final fees; the promissory note, which confirms the terms of repayment; the final loan application, which details the information the lender has based its approval on; and finally, in real estate transactions where a good faith estimate and HUD-1 are utilized, review the Truth-in-Lending disclosure, which identifies the annual percentage rate (APR).

The Final Loan Application

The initial loan application is updated throughout the processing of your loan with verified income, qualifying assets, and validated employment data. Ultimately, you are responsible for the accuracy of the loan data and can do certain things to control misrepresentation throughout the loan process. If every borrower received and reviewed their final loan application for accuracy prior to attending the closing, post-closing disputes regarding lender misrepresentation would diminish. Unfortunately, you typically won't see this modified loan application until you've reached the closing table and are rushed through it for your signature.

Tip: Ask your lender for a copy of the final 1003 (loan application) once your loan commitment has been issued.

A preliminary review of the final loan application prior to loan closing will help you in many ways. This is not the original one that you received as part of your loan disclosures, but the one that you will be signing at loan closing. Inspect the following items:

- Section I—Type of Property and Term of Loan, to reaffirm final loan program, term, interest rate, and loan amount.
- Section V—Monthly Income and Combined Housing Expense, to identify the proposed monthly housing payment to include principal and interest, property taxes, homeowners insurance, mortgage insurance, and homeowner association dues.
- Section VII—Details of Loan Transaction, to ensure proper application of money held in escrow, lender credits, and/or seller concessions.
- Section X—Information for Government Monitoring Purposes, to verify National Mortgage Licensing System (NMLS) identification of compensated loan officer.

On the final 1003, there are many things you should check. The first of which is identification of the name and the NMLS number of the loan officer. If the person listed is not the same as the person who took your initial 1003, ask why. If you are told that the person who took your initial 1003 is still employed by that organization where you made application, then ask why that person's name is not listed on the final 1003. The only way to maintain the integrity of the profession is by citizens reporting on what they perceive to be potential misrepresentation. If you have identified that potentially you were engaged with someone who is not authorized to conduct mortgage business, it is your responsibility to report this to the Consumer Financial Protection Bureau who will further investigate.

While ideally, loan officers originate loans and back office support processes them through to loan closing, in many organizations, managers know that loans won't necessarily close on time if there is no loan officer watching over them. For this reason, it is common practice for lenders to reassign the oversight of a mortgage to a new loan officer when the original loan officer leaves the organization. But there is a downside to this practice that presents risk for the inheriting loan officer. Not all loan operating systems are sophisticated enough to identify the difference between an originating loan officer and a funding loan officer, nor is there a place on the 1003 to list a difference. Because of this, the loan officer who inherited the loan is now listed as the loan officer who is responsible for the integrity of the representation of the data on the application including your employment, assets, income, liabilities, occupancy, etc., to the investor. If you're loan is reassigned after application, you should expect that the new loan officer review the details of your loan file for assurance of accuracy.

One last thing: Pull out the first payment coupon from your closing package. Sometimes there are delays in delivering your loan to the servicer, and you may not receive a billing statement by the time your first payment is due. This doesn't mean that you can be late on delivering the payment. You are still responsible for its timely delivery. Keep an extra copy of the payment coupon and deliver the one provided with your payment by the due date. Check in with your lender a few weeks later to ensure that you have been properly set up and that the billing statements are being delivered to the address you have requested.

Requests Made After Loan Closing

You've closed the loan and have moved into your new home; all is wonderful. Then one afternoon, you receive notice from your lender requesting that you deliver additional documents. You close it up and throw it out thinking that it must have gone out by mistake since you've already closed. A couple of days later, you receive a telephone call from the lender asking for the same documentation and now you're confused. You ask, "Why is this happening?"

This is happening because in their quality control process, the lender or the investor has identified something that is missing from your loan file that is required for your lender to meet its representations and warranties to deliver your loan to the investor or for guaranty. And guess what? You have to comply with their request because at loan settlement, you signed a document stating that you would. If what they are asking for is something that you are unable to deliver, immediately connect with your lender and discuss other options for satisfying their request. If you don't comply with their requests, they have the right to execute the acceleration clause on the note (see chapter 15 for more information on the acceleration clause).

10 The Uniform Residential Loan Application (The 1003)

The mortgage application is formally called the Uniform Residential Loan Application and is commonly referred to as "the 1003" (ten-oh-three) or "the app". There are ten sections of the 1003 that provide the blueprint for deciding your loan request and no assumptions can be made. I encourage you to familiarize yourself with its questions by reviewing Fannie Mae Form 1003 at https://www.fanniemae.com/content/guide_form/1003rev.pdf. In most cases, your loan officer will be the person who actually completes the loan application based on your answers to their questions. Sometimes the questions on the form aren't necessarily formatted in a way that may call to mind the answer that most accurately reflects the information the lender is seeking. With that, I've broken down each section of the 1003 so that you'll have an understanding of what is really being asked, why it is being asked, how your answers may be interpreted, and your responsibility in confirming the accuracy of the data.

THE FIRST THING you need to know is that the 1003 that you sign at application will be updated throughout the processing of your loan request with data that has either been validated or accepted as true by the lender. We refer to the application that you sign at your first meeting with your loan officer as the initial 1003 and the one that you sign at settlement as the final 1003. Auditors and investors frown upon seeing too many differences between the initial and the final 1003 as these indicate possible attempts at misrepresentation. Although not a requirement to receive a cost estimate, many loan officers will not begin the formal process of loan application without first receiving your supporting documentation, because we don't like dealing with surprises after loan application just as much as you don't like dealing with them.

What separates the better loan officers from the data entry clerks is their ability to accurately detail your story so that whoever sees your file has clear knowledge of any gaps or concerns. This is done by completion of a cover letter. This internal communication of your story is not on any loan document that you will ever see, and that's a shame because the majority of the time, its accurate storytelling that makes all the difference in the speed your loan file is decided. Without the loan officer seeing supporting documentation at application to detail a cover letter and provide a list of any additional documents the lender may need to render a decision, you're setting in motion delays due to a lack of clarity around program eligibility and requirements.

The Danger of Misrepresentation

Documentation has a way of ruining good fiction. In March 2007, in a joint effort to combat mortgage fraud, the Mortgage Bankers Association and the Federal Bureau of Investigations issued a statement requiring each lender to provide a written warning notifying you with the following language:

Mortgage Fraud is investigated by the Federal Bureau of Investigation and is punishable by up to 30 years in federal prison or $1,000,000, or both. It is illegal for a person to make any false statement regarding income, assets, debt, or matters of identification, or to willfully overvalue any land or property, in a loan and credit application for the purpose of influencing in any way the action of a financial institution.

You will receive this FBI warning as part of the loan disclosure set. Unfortunately, loan disclosures are issued only after loan application is made. Loan officers are not police officers, we are not the IRS, we are not the FBI, and we are in no way affiliated with Homeland Security. Our role is to help guide you through the residential mortgage loan approval process. That said, we can't help you when you lie to us, and we most definitely can't help you when you submit fraudulent documentation. What we can do is counsel you on credit and documentation standards.

Don't count on your loan officer informing you that attempts at fraud have been identified because we aren't notified of these identifications during the processing of your loan. Everyone at all levels of mortgage banking is relying on loan officers to effectively represent your particular scenario on the loan application, as we are the frontline mitigators of risk. Licensing and registration requirements are in place for loan officers and our individual NMLS identification is attached to each loan application. Where patterns of misrepresentation are identified, action is taken. Beginning in August of 2015, the new closing disclosure is also monitoring realtors (both listing and selling agents) and settlement agents by tracking their license information on each transaction.

More often than not, an applicant doesn't intend to lie or misrepresent, they are simply following instructions or "helpful advice" from an uninformed source. Here's an example of how a conversation can play out between a misinformed borrower and me:

"I see here on your June bank statement that you have a nonpayroll deposit in the amount of $450. Can you tell me what that was for?"

"Why do you need to know?"

"Lending guidelines require that we source every deposit that is nonpayroll related, so we need to document the file to show where this money came from."

"Well, that's not really your business is it?"

"You're right, I really don't care where you got this money. However, if we don't document the file accordingly, we may not be able to utilize any money from this account and unless you have another account with equivalent funds that have been sourced for the preceding sixty days, your loan request may be declined. So please tell me how you prefer to handle this?" (Kind of mean, I know, but sometimes we have to be in order to compel applicants to speak openly on a particular topic.)

"Well, I was trying to avoid bringing that up because my neighbor told me that if the bank found out that I rented a bedroom out to a college student I wouldn't get my loan approved."

This happened with one of my clients a few years ago. Never assume a friend's negative outcome will be yours as well. Perhaps they didn't seek clarity over how to properly document boarder income with their loan officer and instead, their loan was declined for lack of sourcing. Explain your particular situation—in its entirety—and work with your loan officer to properly document your file and prepare for a successful outcome.

One Final Caveat

Let's say you made application with a bank loan officer and that bank is unable to fund your loan. There are many reasons why one lender can fund your loan and why another cannot. The loan officer at the denying bank may provide you with a referral to a different lender that has a loan program for which you may be eligible, and this is perfectly okay. For expedience, you ask your existing loan officer to copy your loan file and deliver it to the new lender on your behalf. That is not okay, and here's why.

You don't want anyone giving a loan officer information about you except you. Many organizations have policies that prohibit third-party originations and for good reason. A third-party origination means that someone outside of their organization took your information and listed its representation on the loan application. Each originating entity relies on its loan officers to maintain the integrity of the 1003. If you never disclosed your information directly to the new loan officer, how is that loan officer maintaining the integrity of the data listed on the 1003? Your initial thought may be that you don't care because you legitimately believe that your 1003 is accurate; but here's the thing: If the management of the new originating entity identifies that your loan is an unauthorized third-party origination, it may automatically withdraw or deny your loan request with no regard to authenticity of data. Having already been delayed by one lender, I don't think you want to risk being delayed by a second. Third-party originations are allowed by creditors to state licensed mortgage loan originators at nonbank mortgage companies and mortgage brokers where authorized by selling agreements.

If it becomes necessary for you to make application with a second or third lender, I recommend that you take a copy of your 1003 (included in your initial loan disclosure package) along with all the updated supporting documentation (current pay stubs, bank statements, etc.) and deliver it to the new loan officer yourself. A better loan officer won't simply copy the information from another's 1003 to his loan application; the loan officer will ask you questions just as if you did not bring the 1003, and once completed, he or she will look over your copy of the 1003 to identify and address any differences.

Instructions and Signatures

At the top of the loan application is the "Instructions and Signatures" section, where the first sentence reads, "This application is designed to be completed by the applicant(s) with the Lender's assistance." Well, this isn't exactly how it happens. In today's digital environment, most lenders have moved to paperless systems; therefore the reverse is true: Loan officers begin the application process for you on their loan origination software, and then print the completed application for your review and signature.

The form begins by asking that you identify yourself as either a borrower or a co-borrower. Whether you are a borrower or a co-borrower, you are equally liable for the debt. Only married individuals can be listed together on the same 1003. Unmarried individuals are still jointly liable for the debt but must submit separate 1003s. In this question, the co-borrower refers to any nonoccupant co-borrowers. By checking that box, we are saying that the income, assets, and credit of another individual who will not be living in the property are being used for mortgage qualification.

The second box designates whether the subject property is located within a community property state or if the borrower resides in a community property state. This disclosure is relevant for insuring title and doesn't provide any conflict at all in the underwriting process of the mortgage.

Section I–Type of Property and Term of Loan

In Section I—Type of Property and Term of Loan, we list the terms of the loan. The loan program is identified here as VA, FHA, conventional, USDA, or other. The terms of the loan product requested are also listed here. The initial 1003 may or may not have an agency case number listed. This would signify that your loan data has been run through a GSE automated underwriting system for a recommendation (some applications are never run through an automated underwriting system simply because the loan program does not allow delivery to the GSEs). The lender's case number is on the initial 1003, as is the loan number that the loan originator's office has assigned to your application. The final 1003 will list the loan number as assigned by the creditor. For loans originated and funded by banks and nonbank mortgage companies, both loan numbers will generally be the same. For loans originated through mortgage brokers, those loan numbers will generally be different.

Section II–Property Information and Purpose of Loan

Section II—Property Information and Purpose of Loan contains information relating to the subject property that will be used as collateral for the loan. The loan purpose and titling information is also entered. Intended occupancy is the area where fraud is most frequently attempted on a mortgage loan application. Do not ruin your chances of loan approval by lying about your intended use of the property. Aside from slightly higher interest rates, the more significant factors related to the differences in underwriting standards of intended occupancy are down payment requirements and minimum credit scores, which impact loan eligibility between a primary residence, second home, and an investment property.

Subject Property Address

In most loan origination software, the physical property address entered on the loan application is automatically formatted to conform to the United States Postal Service (USPS) address standards for complete addresses (Available online at http://pe.usps.com/text/pub28/welcome. htm). The subject property address must appear consistently throughout all loan documents, including the appraisal.

Something as simple as how the subject property address appears in the lender's loan origination software may hinder program eligibility. If you owe more than your property is worth, visit the "Home Affordable Refinance Program" section in chapter 8 for detailed information to help you assess loan eligibility and for instructions on how to work with your lender to assert accurate loan eligibility information.

Number of Units

The answer to this question may seem straightforward, but its implications cover a wide variety of lending criteria. To be considered a residential loan, the subject property must be in an area that is primarily zoned for residential use and have no more than four units (additional limitations apply to properties located in primarily agricultural zones). The level of risk for a lender in this category progresses from one unit, to two-to-four units, to manufactured housing, with manufactured housing representing the highest risk to a lender.

To mitigate these progressive risks, there are limitations affecting the allowable maximum loan-to-value, down payment requirements, and credit scores based on the number of units, property type, and the selected loan product (varying terms for fixed versus adjustable rate mortgages). For example, the purchase of a single unit principal residence may have a maximum loan-to-value ratio of 97 percent, a minimum credit score of at least 680, and a maximum debt-to-income ratio of 36 percent on a thirty-year fixed rate loan. Where the debt-to-income ratio exceeds 36 percent but is less than 45 percent, a higher credit score will be required. But if the loan-to-value ratio is less than 75 percent, a credit score as low as 620 may be permitted (actual guidelines depend on the lender). This is why credit scores matter. Additionally, minimum post-closing reserve requirements are affected by number of units and minimum contribution requirements from your own funds for down payment.

Sometimes there are discrepancies between the number of units reported on a loan application, on an appraisal, and on county records. These will need to be addressed. For example, I once had a borrower who owned a home that was built in the 1930s, and he was doing a rate and term refinance. This home was originally built as a two-unit property with the second unit serving as in-law quarters. It was built with two separate electric meters to monitor usage for each unit. Through various ownerships, the property was modified into a single-family residence, but these changes were not recorded with the county. My borrower maintained that his family utilized the property as a single-family residence. Because county records showed the property as having two units and because there were two separate electric meters, my borrower was subjected to the tighter lending restrictions of two-unit properties.

Legal Description of Subject Property

While your loan officer could input the legal description of the subject property as listed on the sales contract, this is typically left blank until the lender confirms the legal description via the appraiser or the title commitment, and it will be reflected on your final 1003 at loan closing.

Year Built

This indicates the year county records show the structure was built. If a major renovation was completed since that time, be sure to notify your insurance agent so that a detailed property inspection can be performed allowing lower premiums through compliance with updated building codes.

Purpose of Loan: Purchase, Refinance, Construction, Construction-to-Permanent, or Other

If construction or construction-to-permanent, complete the subsequent section that asks for these further details: the year the lot/land was acquired, the original cost of the (lot/land), the amount of any existing liens on the lot/land, along with (a) your estimate of the present value of the lot/land, (b) your estimated cost of improvements (construction costs) to the lot/land, and finally the total of the present value of the lot/land plus the cost of improving the lot/land (a + b).

If the purpose of your loan is to refinance, complete the subsequent section, which asks for these further details: year acquired (the year you originally acquired the property), original cost (the original acquisition cost of the property), amount existing liens (all loans currently secured by the property), purpose of refinance (Is your intent to lower your interest rate or the remaining term of the existing mortgage? Consolidating debts? Lowering monthly payments?), describe improvements (list the cost of improvements and indicate whether these improvements have already been made or if they will be made).

Under refinance, it's very important to double-check the section marked amount existing liens for accuracy. Here is where you can confirm that the lender has appropriately mapped (matched) existing liens for pay off within the lender's loan origination software. If the lender hasn't mapped the existing liens correctly, quite a few gravely important errors can occur due to the system's erroneous representation of your debt-to-income ratio. For example, let's say you intend to pay off your first and second mortgage liens. If your lender has only mapped your first mortgage and your requested loan amount is indicative of the pay off combination of the first and the second mortgage liens and closing costs, this means that in your debt-to-income calculations, the lender is also including the existing second mortgage lien as an additional debt after loan closing—even though you intend to pay it off at closing with the loan proceeds. This error can cause a falsely inflated debt-to-income ratio and may result in loan denial for excessive debts in relation to monthly income. In the case of borrowers who own multiple properties that have numerous existing liens, if the lender accidentally mapped a lien that is attached to a nonsubject property to the subject property, the settlement agent will receive instructions to pay off the nonsubject lien. That is a much more difficult error to fix once funds have been received by the investor. Be sure to review all intended liens that are to be paid at loan closing with your settlement agent.

Property Will Be (Primary Residence, Secondary Residence, or Investment)

To better help you define occupancy and avert misrepresentation through negligence, I've listed the industry accepted descriptions and am offering additional questions that can help you understand lender concerns.

A primary residence is defined as a property that is occupied by you the majority of the year, is located relatively close to your employer (we'll talk about telecommuters later), and is listed as the address on record for such things as bank statements, tax returns, and pay stubs. It cannot be vacant or tenant occupied, but exceptions apply in new construction and purchase transactions. Fannie Mae's full definition of primary residence (available at https://www.fanniemae.com/content/guide/selling/b2/1/01.html) also includes parents providing housing for physically handicapped or developmentally disabled adult children or children providing housing for parents who are unable to work.

A secondary residence is located a reasonable distance from your primary residence, generally a minimum of fifty miles, is occupied by you for some portion of the year, exhibits vacation-type amenities or access to a major metropolitan area, and may not be a rental or timeshare arrangement. If you rent your second home for a portion of the year and this income is listed on Schedule E of your federal income tax return, the lender may consider the property an investment property (even if you don't need that rental income for loan qualification and even if you only rented it out for two weeks).

It is not required that an investment property receive rental income. An example of this is owning a property that is occupied by a family member who does not pay you rent. Investment properties are charged higher interest rates because the risk of loss is greater than an owner-occupied property. When times get tough, it's more likely that a property owner will stop making payments on their investment property before they stop making payments on their primary residence—as we learned during the financial crisis.

Here are some examples of common application issues that may lead an underwriter to believe misrepresentation has transpired:

1. A secondary residence application is submitted, but the property specifications do not meet second home requirements for distance from primary residence (this happens often in a resort locations, like south Florida, when an out of town underwriter is not familiar with the neighborhoods and doesn't realize the nature of the resort location).

2. An owner-occupied application is submitted, but the applicant only resides in that property a portion of the year.

3. An application is submitted as either owner-occupied or a second home and the prior year's tax return shows the subject property listed on Schedule E with rental income.

All of the above scenarios can be properly addressed on the loan officer's cover letter to loan operations and with supporting documentation submitted with the standard requirements to provide the lender with clarity of intent. Being upfront with the loan officer and providing thorough documentation will ensure the loan goes smoothly through the underwriting process. Although not specifically listed as questions on the 1003, help your loan officer identify potential concerns that can be mitigated by asking yourself some of the following questions:

• Is your commute to work unreasonable for the property to be considered a primary residence? Brainstorm together on how to best document the situation. I see this often when dealing with a high-level executive who resides in one state and travels to work in another. With a little extra detail, it will fly through the underwriting process. Evidence of your primary residence can be documented with a letter written by the HR director of your employer or, in the case of self-employed applicants, by their CPA.

• What property do you have listed on Schedule E of your personal tax return? Schedule E indicates income from nonpayroll sources. If your prior year's tax return shows the subject property as your principal residence and Schedule E indicates receipt of rental income on that same one-unit single-family residence that you are declaring as owner-occupied on the loan application, the lender will want to clarify who is currently renting the property and where you are currently residing. There are many reasons you might declare rental income on an owner-occupied property, such as where you receive boarder income or have an in-law quarter that you rent to a college student. Maybe you didn't occupy the property in the preceding year, but you moved into it this year and going forward it will be owner-occupied. You'll need to have a paper trail that can be submitted to underwriting to justify intent of occupancy. Don't wait until the underwriter questions it. Have a letter of explanation ready for your loan officer at loan application.

If there are address mismatches in the documentation submitted, these need to be properly addressed at loan application as well. For example, your bank statement and pay stub may have one current address and your recently filed tax returns another. Depending on whether you've given them explanation for a discrepancy, these mismatches may only be identified further down the road by an underwriter who may find cause for misrepresentation, if not properly justified and documented.

Title Will Be Held in What Name(s)

Some lenders will require that the borrower name listed on the loan application match the titling name listed on the purchase contract and the name on all loan disclosures. Learn about the multiple concerns this can present in the Borrower Name category below.

Manner in which the Title Will Be Held

By the time you visit a loan officer, you've probably already discussed your titling options with a financial planner, realtor, or real estate, trust, or tax attorney to ensure that titling is set up properly with consideration given to the needs of each owner. This can be of special concern with unmarried co-owners and blended families in the event that one of the owners dies. Mortgages are available not only to single people and married couples, but also to significant others or co-borrowers and corporations.

Hand in hand with titling options is consideration for the estate-planning process that should be an integral part of everyone's financial plan. The benefits of smart estate planning can include tax savings, efficient disposition of assets, end-of-life decisions, financial security for heirs, and a general peace of mind.

In a purchase, the sales contract will identify how you wish to take title to the property, so be sure you've reviewed your options with your selected lender prior to drawing up an offer, as some lenders' eligibility guidelines restrict titling options. The most common titling options for residential real estate are:

- Individual (sole ownership)
- Joint
- Married
- LLC
- Trust (revocable or irrevocable)

Individual or Sole Ownership

Sole ownership is ownership by an individual or entity that is legally capable of holding title. This method of ownership is most commonly held by single men and women, married persons who hold property apart from their spouse, and businesses with a corporate structure that allows for investing in or holding interest in real estate. Married persons requesting sole ownership will need to have their spouse specifically disclaim or relinquish their right to ownership in the property. A concern with sole ownership is the death or incapacitation of the owner. Unless a will exists, the transfer of ownership in these instances can become very problematic.

For married owners, consider estate-planning strategies by consulting a financial planning professional. Upon the death of one spouse, it is common practice that the decedents assets pass to the surviving spouse in order to take advantage of the unlimited marital tax deduction. Doing so will eliminate the immediate estate tax. If the surviving spouse doesn't need or want the inherited money to support their lifestyle, a qualified disclaimer may be an option, so that the decedent's assets can pass to a contingent beneficiary. With a qualified disclaimer, a beneficiary can refuse all or part of an inheritance. For tax purposes, disclaiming an asset is the same as never having owned it.

You may be wondering why you would refuse an asset, but there are many legitimate reasons why you may to consider this. For example, if the deceased is carrying creditors, the inheritance may not be worth the consequences it brings along with it. Another example would be when a beneficiary has such a massive debt load that any estate passing to him would instantly vanish to cover the debt. In order to keep that property in the family, the heir could disclaim it and step out of the line of inheritance altogether.

Married Owners and Joint or Unmarried Partners

For properties with multiple owners, here are some titling options to consider:

1. Tenancy by the entirety: Co-ownership available only to a husband and wife. Both owners must agree before the house can be sold or refinanced. Additionally, when one spouse dies, the surviving spouse automatically inherits complete ownership.
2. Tenancy in common: A type of co-ownership that allows for multiple parties with varying percentages of ownership. The property is owned jointly, but if one owner dies, the deceased

owner's share goes to his or her heir rather than to the surviving owner or owners. If there is a will in place, the property will pass to the heirs listed in the will. In the event that there is no will, the owner's share will be distributed in accordance with the rules in the deceased's state of residence. For unmarried partners, if your intent is to distribute the bulk of your assets to someone other than your partner, then this may be a good choice.

3. Joint tenancy with right of survivorship (JTWROS): An equal, undivided ownership of property by two or more people. During their lifetimes, any of the owners may sell their interest to whomever they choose. This can be one of the best options for unmarried couples who wish to have their ownership transfer to the remaining owner/partner upon their death. If one owner dies, the surviving owner (or owners) automatically gets the decedents share of the property. When considering this option, be cautious to confirm the title reads "with rights of survivorship." In the absence of this wording, the ownership will be deemed as tenants in common. Another consideration with this titling option is the order of ownership as written. Income, gains, and losses will be reported under the Social Security number (SSN) of the first owner. This can prove advantageous when it comes to tax planning if one of the owners is in a significantly lower tax bracket. On the other hand, the owner with the higher tax bracket could use the deductions when filing their taxes. Consult with a tax advisor for all considerations.

Trust Options

In any form of ownership, each individual can create a trust agreement and place their individual assets inside that trust. The trust will spell out the legalities of what would happen if the trustee (the owner of the trust) dies, becomes disabled, or becomes unable to transact on their own behalf. The owner of the trust can designate their partner as the successor trustee, allowing the partner to manage the couple's affairs. While the initial set up of a trust agreement can be costly, the costs of not having one can be significant to your beneficiaries. If you have significant assets and would like to protect not only your partner but also other family members, this is an option you should consider. For example, you may wish your assets to transfer to your partner when you die, but after your partner dies you would like other family members to receive the remainder of your assets. It is important to note that assets and accounts must have the trust named as the beneficiary or be titled in the name of the trust.

In a revocable trust, changes to the trust agreement can be made. In an irrevocable trust, once the grantor contributes property to the trust, the grantor cannot later reclaim ownership of the property or change the terms of the trust. Most lenders of residential real estate will only allow titling in the name of a revocable trust. A lender will require reviewing either the full trust agreement or will allow an attorney's affidavit of trust to confirm certain aspects of the trust in order to consider the agreement as a titling option.

LLC or Corporation

Ownership in real estate can be done as a corporation, whereby the legal entity is a company owned by shareholders and is regarded under the law as having an existence separate from its shareholders. Tax implications of this ownership type can be considerable in instances where corporations undergo double taxation.

Community Property

Property acquired during a marriage is recognized in nine U.S. states as community property, where the husband and wife each own half the property and each can will their half to someone else. IRS Publication 555 (www.irs.gov/publications/p555/ar02.html?_ga=1.21568504.279937 489.1417727172) provides guidance that identifies community property as property that you, your spouse (or registered domestic partner), or both acquire during your marriage (or registered domestic partnership) while you and your spouse (or registered domestic partner) are domiciled in a community property state or that you and your spouse agreed to convert from separate to community property or that cannot be identified as separate property.

If the community property is owned with right of survivorship, the surviving spouse will own the entire property. There are currently nine community property states: Arizona, California, Idaho, Louisiana, Nevada, New Mexico, Texas, Washington, and Wisconsin. Alaska is an opt-in community property state that gives both parties the option to make their property community property.

Estate Will Be Held In: Fee Simple or Leasehold

Most ownership in the U.S. is held fee simple. In fee simple ownership, the buyer acquires the entire property, including improvements, buildings, and land and maintains the rights to possess, use, and dispose of the land in any manner the owner wishes. The property can be sold, mortgaged, leased, or passed to others as beneficiaries of an estate.

Leasehold ownership typically applies to cooperatives (co-ops) where a corporation owns the project and the corporation offers you ownership shares. The buyer enters into a long-term agreement or contract called a ground lease. The buyer of leasehold property does not own the land or even a portion of it. The unit owner of a property held in leasehold will pay a rent to the corporation that holds title until the ground lease expires. The lease agreement will address what happens to improvements upon surrender. The use, maintenance, and alteration of the leased premises are subject to restrictions contained in the lease agreement. Many leases provide the landowner with inspection rights.

Source of Down Payment, Settlement Charges, and Subordinate Financing

Here we identify and list the source of all money that will be used for the real estate transaction. Multiple entries are allowed. Most loan origination software only allows the loan officer to select from a generic dropdown to list an amount and the type of asset where the funds are held with no additional specific details as to the particular asset.

When a gift is entered here as a source of down payment, the gift funds are not automatically included in the lender's calculation of available funds. When using gift funds, the gift amount will also be separately listed in Section VI—Assets as a gift in order to be included in the lender's calculation of available funds for the transaction and to be properly identified for risk assessment by underwriting.

Section III–Borrower Information

In Section III—Borrower Information, we enter the personal information for each applicant on the loan transaction.

Borrower Name

Misidentification of your legal name is a problem on many levels. Avoid using name variations on identification documents such as your social security card, driver's license, passport, and/or U.S. visa. Consistency is key in identifying and deterring financial crimes. Identity fraud is a very real and present threat.

If your full name consists of more than three words, the first issue your loan officer will encounter is how to enter four names into the origination software that only provides for entry of three categories (first, middle, and last). Let them know your preferences. Whether you have four names or three, been married once or five times, take time to review your documentation and update information to reflect one name variation for consistency.

Social Security Number

If you have a U.S. Social Security number, this is where you will list it. Be sure to double-check if it is correctly entered on the loan application before you sign it, as a mistake here will trigger an immediate fraud alert for every aspect of your loan processing. For nonresidents of the U.S., in this section your lender will use 999-99-9999, 111-11-1111, or your taxpayer identification number, whichever their origination software commands.

Home Phone

If you have a landline, that is the telephone number that should be listed. If you prefer to be reached by cell phone, let your loan officer know to document your contact preferences with that information, but the 1003 should list your landline if you have one. If you don't have a landline, list your cell phone.

Date of Birth

This one thing is self-evident; the format used is month, day, and year.

Years of School

List the combined number of years you attended primary, secondary, and postsecondary schooling. For example, if you graduated high school in the U.S., you would list twelve years. If you graduated from a two-year college, you would answer fourteen. If you completed a four-year college degree, you would answer sixteen (even if it took you nineteen years to earn it). If you earned a Juris Doctor, you would list nineteen years.

Married, Separated, Unmarried

If you are legally married, enter married. If you are legally separated (filed a separation agreement with the court), enter separated. If you are not married, enter unmarried.

Dependents (Number and Ages)

List all dependents including minor children, adult children, and adults. If discrepancies exist between what you have listed on the loan application from your most recent year's income tax return, provide an explanation of the discrepancy to your loan officer. For example, has there been a change in custody? If so, address impact on child support, if any. Has there been a separation or a divorce? If so, address impact on alimony, separate maintenance, and changes of property ownership, if any. If the dependent listed on the tax return is an adult, address this at application.

Present Address (Own or Rent?)

This must be a real street address and not a P.O. box. If you've been residing at your present address for less than two years, list all other prior addresses within most recent two-year period along with your ownership interest, if any. If you have a foreign address that does not fit the typical square pegs of the lender's origination software, list the complete foreign address on the continuation sheet of the loan application. Additionally, visit chapter 11 to review specific challenges affecting tourists, immigrants, and U.S. citizens living abroad.

Mailing Address (If Different from Present Address)

If you prefer to have your loan documents mailed to a different address, list it here. Be mindful that if your loan application is for a second home or an investment property, all future communications from your lender on the servicing of your loan will also be sent to the mailing address provided and not to your present address, the address of the second home, or the investment property.

Section IV–Employment Information

In Section IV—Employment Information, the loan application requests that you disclose all sources of employment over the preceding two years including full-time, part-time, temporary, and seasonal jobs as well as all ownership interests in businesses. If you do not have a two-year history of employment and were a full-time student within the preceding two years, provide a copy of your college transcripts. While loan qualification is based on stable earnings that are likely to continue, your loan file needs to document evidence of your employment history over the preceding two calendar years up to and including year-to-date employment. Notice the subtle difference? You can prevent delays in loan processing by not only listing all employment sources, but also providing all supporting income documentation to confirm the sources of all employment as reported to the IRS over the preceding two calendar years along with a signed and dated letter of explanation addressing the discontinuance or instability of any such employment.

Let me share with you how you will be affected by not properly providing to your lender all supporting documentation at loan application (not because you intend to mislead, but simply because you don't understand the intent of the question). Let's say it's August 2015. While the loan application doesn't specifically tell you to list all employment sources, it does state, "If employed in current position for less than two years or if currently employed in more than one position, complete the following: (prior or concurrent employment history)." If you began working for your current employer, ABC Corp, in May 2013, you might think, "Okay, from May 2013 through August 2015, that's two years, so I only need to disclose my employment at ABC Corp." But, you may be wrong and here's why.

In processing your loan request, your lender will execute Form 4506-T. The IRS will return income information as reported by you. In 2013, you received a W-2 income from ABC Corp, but also from Bob's Hardware Supplies where you worked from January through May 2013.

With your supporting documents, you submitted to your lender the W-2s from ABC Corp for 2013 and 2014, but not the W-2s from Bob's Hardware Supplies. The underwriter will see a discrepancy between the income reported on the W-2s in your loan file and the W-2 income reported to the IRS and will condition your loan file with: Provide all W-2s for tax year 2013. Your loan file gets put back into loan processing, and the loan processor contacts you and requests all W-2s for 2013. You go back and pull the 2013 W-2 for Bob's Hardware Supplies and send it to the loan processor. All is good.

Let's say in that same example, that the lender executed the 4506-T to not only document W-2 income, but to also report all information from your previous two year's tax returns (which they can do even though you didn't provide them with your income tax returns). In 2013 you were married. Your spouse also reported W-2 income in 2013. While you provided the additional W-2 from Bob's Hardware Supplies that covers all 2013 W-2 income you earned, when the underwriter reviews the tax transcripts against both your 2013 W-2s, the numbers still don't add up. Again, your loan file will be handed back to loan processing and conditioned: Provide all W-2s for tax year 2013. Now you are mad and wonder, "What the heck is going on? These people don't know what they are doing!"

At this point, if you don't pick up the telephone and have a conversation with your loan officer or your loan processor, you may end up at a standstill and linger in the black hole of loan processing until your loan file is eventually withdrawn by the lender for failure to deliver all supporting loan documentation in a timely manner. Once you clarify with your lender that you were married in 2013 and that your ex-spouse also reported W-2 income in that year, they will be able to tell you that what they need is for you to provide your ex-spouse's 2013 W-2s to support the income as reported through the IRS tax transcripts. Now, know this: Your lender is not using your ex-spouse's income for anything. To avoid having to connect with your ex-spouse over their W-2s, it would be wise for any person's considering divorce to keep copies of tax returns and all supporting schedules that are attached.

So what's the best way to handle this category? Go back to the tax returns that you filed away in the accordion folder and look at every income source (or loss) that was reported. If there are sources that don't belong to you or that are no longer applicable, you should address these in a letter of explanation to your lender at loan application.

Name and Address of Employer

Typically, here we prefer to see information for the location where you actually work. However, if your employer is out of state, or if your pay stubs and W-2's list an employer location that is more than 50 miles away from your primary residence, you will need to write a letter of explanation that clarifies your employment situation. For example, are you contracted to work remotely? Is the employer address listed on the pay stub the corporate main office and you work in a different location? Whatever your situation may be, your lender is looking for clarity.

Self-Employed

You may have permanent employment with one employment source, but additionally have a percentage of ownership in a business or are the beneficiary of a partnership or a trust. For all entities where you hold a 25 percent or greater ownership interest, you are considered self-employed by the lender for that business entity. All borrowers who are considered self-employed will need to provide the lender with personal and business tax returns for the preceding two calendar years and may need to provide additional documentation supporting year-to-date financial information for each business entity such as a profit and loss statement and balance sheet. All income sources reported through IRS Schedule K-1s, 1099s, or 1065s are considered self-employment.

Self-employed borrowers face many documentation challenges in the mortgage approval process. Through the years, I've worked with many self-employed borrowers who own multiple businesses, and it's helpful to coordinate our efforts with their business accountant. There are two recurring entries on business tax returns that negatively impact a lender's calculation of qualifying income for the self-employed. You can help your lender identify opportunities to increase your qualifying income by providing a little bit more documentation. These entries include deductions for net operating losses and mortgages payable in less than one year.

Net Operating Loss and Special Deductions

This information is found on IRS Form 1120-US, Corporation Tax Return, line 82. Not all businesses consistently earn a profit. In years when income earned is less than expenses, the IRS allows the business owner(s) to file a net operating loss (NOL) to reduce their tax liability, which allows for the receipt of a quick cash infusion by applying for a tax refund from previous year's tax payments. By not properly addressing the circumstances that lead to the filing of a net operating loss, better known as a paper loss, a cursory review of income statements is likely to lead to a miscalculation of qualifying income by your lender. In many instances, an NOL can be added back to usable income. To know this, one needs to understand exactly what a net operating loss is.

If you are a business owner who sustained a loss and receive income from other sources, your business loss first applies to reducing this income in the current tax year. If you earn nothing other than business income, or if your net operating losses exceed your other income, you can use the deficit to earn a refund from the IRS for taxes you paid in previous years. This carryback period is usually limited two years, although a three-year rule applies if your net operating loss is the result of theft or a casualty. The IRS sets rules for carryback and carry-forward deductions and these are best addressed by seeking counsel from your certified public accountant.

As it relates to your mortgage application, if no explanation or documentation is provided to the lender, the lender may treat this paper loss as a true deduction to qualifying income instead of adding the amount reported back into the business income. If you are the 100-percent owner of the business, that's an addition of 100 percent of the NOL to your qualifying income.

In its evaluation of qualifying income, the lender will review the documentation provided in reference to the NOL to determine whether the loss was due to a one-time occurrence or to financial mismanagement by the business owner(s). In most cases that are properly documented with a reasonable explanation, the amount of the NOL is added back to the qualifying income determination. However, the loan officer does not set this determination; it is set by the underwriter after reviewing the totality of your loan file. If the lender determines the business has negative income and the NOL is increasing or recurring, both the NOL and the business loss will be deducted from qualifying income.

To expedite the decision-making process of your loan and to allow for the proper calculation of qualifying income when net operating losses are reported, come to loan application meeting prepared with a signed and dated letter (preferably from your CPA) addressing the following questions:

a.   What is the nature of the loss?

b.   In what timeframe did the loss occur?

c.   Is this a one-time loss or is it a recurring loss?

d.   For which tax years has this loss been reported?

e.   For how many years in the future is this loss scheduled to be reported?

f.   If there is more than one occurrence of an NOL, list the complete explanation for each occurrence.

Mortgage or Notes Payable in Less than One Year

These are found on Schedule L of IRS Form 1065-US, Return of Partnership Income, line 55, or IRS Form 1120S-US, Income Tax Return for an S Corporation, line 71. This entry indicates that the business is obligated on a debt that it must pay in full by the end of the year. A lender will see this amount and deduct it from the business cash flow. You can avoid this deduction if you can provide the lender with evidence that the liability regularly rolls over and/or there are sufficient liquid business assets to cover the debt. An example of evidence is a letter from the business CPA stating that the debt regularly rolls over (such as with a one-year revolving line of credit) or a copy of the business checking or savings account statement showing sufficient funds to cover the debt.

Position/Title/Type of Business

Here you will need to list your current position, your title, and the type of business your employment source engages in.

Years on this Job

This question is asking how long have you been at this employment source. If your term of employment is less than one year, list the months in increments of one-twelfth. For example, if you've been at your employer for seven months, you would list .58 years on this job.

Years Employed in this Line of Work/Profession

The answer to this question can cause some thinking. It isn't asking how long you've been in a particular position; it's asking how long have you been working in the same industry. I'll use myself as an example. I joined Savings of America in 1991 as an item processing supervisor. Two years later, I transferred to the mortgage division as a loan officer. If in 1994, I would have been asked to answer this question, my response would be three years—I had been in the financial services industry for three years at that time.

Business Phone (Including Area Code)

Preferably list the main line of your employer. Separately, provide to your loan officer your direct telephone number and the name and contact information of the human resources director that can verify your employment data.

Prior and Concurrent Employment

For all prior and concurrent employment within the preceding two years, list both the to and from dates of each employment and your monthly income from each source.

Section V–Monthly Income and Combined Housing Expense

This is where all the fun happens. Here we list income information separately for each borrower and co-borrower, and we identify the current and future cost of housing. Both the GSEs and, beginning in January 2014, the federal government tell lenders how to calculate income. On the loan application, we list gross monthly income. Gross monthly income (as opposed to net monthly income) refers to pretax dollars. Your sources of qualifying income may be more comprehensive than what initially comes to mind. As such, be sure to thoroughly review the category Other Sources of Income under "Section V-Monthly Income and Combined Housing Expense" later in this chapter to help you identify and document potential sources of additional income outside of employment.

Throughout this section, you can expect to learn the intricacies of how qualifying income is actually calculated by your lender. Only stable earnings that are likely to continue are considered qualifying income. Applicants who change jobs frequently, but who are nevertheless able to earn and document consistent and predictable income, are also considered to have a reliable flow of income.

The biggest thing you need to remember is this: Your loan officer is your storyteller. If you present your loan officer with all the information they need to properly tell your story and calculate your qualifying income early in the process, you are empowering them to have a valuable conversation upfront regarding program eligibility, loan-to-value requirements, and debt-to-income calculations. Together you can strategize on opportunities for expanding loan program options.

If you're not ready to make application—if you haven't gathered all of your necessary documentation to meet with your loan officer as per the Comprehensive Mortgage Documentation Checklist in the "Resources" section—then simply don't. To be able to avert file blowups, loan officers need to have your income documentation at loan application to properly identify and calculate qualifying income and to determine if any further documents are needed to confirm this information to a decision-maker. Federal law tells us that lenders can't require that you deliver supporting documentation before we issue the binding good faith/loan estimate. Here's the thing: This estimate, and not the nonbinding preapplication cost estimate, is delivered with the loan disclosure set that will only print with a full application. Do you want to risk unintentionally misrepresenting your income on the application?

If you neglect to gather the documentation as listed and instead choose to send documentation in piecemeal over the course of three weeks to your lender, your credit decision will be delayed until all standard documents are in. If all loan documents necessary for decision-making are not received by your lender within thirty days of loan application, the lender will either decline or withdraw your loan request due to an incomplete application. And you will have lost your rate lock and will need to begin the entire process again.

Addressing Changes in Income and Expenses From Prior Year's Tax Return

Open up last year's tax return and identify any changes from the last filing forward. For example, let's say Schedule E shows a rental property, but you sold that rental property and no longer have a loss (or income) attributable to the expense carried on that property. You will need to evidence the sale by showing a fully executed HUD-1/closing disclosure. Here are other examples that will require a written letter of explanation and additional supporting documentation from you:

- Did you sell your business last year but remain an employee? You will need to provide your lender with the business contract for sale, your new employment contract, and a letter of explanation. If your employment contract shows variable income as opposed to salaried income, your qualifying monthly income will be subject to the terms of variable income analysis.

- Did you bring on another investor to your business and your percentage of ownership has changed from last year's declarations on your federal income tax return? How will these changes affect future distributions? You will need to provide your lender with the revised shareholder agreement and a letter of explanation.

- Did you claim a deduction for alimony payments and have subsequently fulfilled your financial obligations as per court order? You will need to provide the divorce decree and property settlement agreement along with signed and dated letter of explanation.

The Basics: Hourly and Salaried Applicants

You will need to provide your lender with pay stubs that identify income from the preceding 30-day period. If you are paid via an annual salary, the formula for determining your gross monthly income is by dividing your annual pretax income by twelve to obtain your gross monthly income. Simple. But sometimes people have a hard time identifying what their annual salary is because they only pay attention to their net compensation, their take home pay. To help you determine your monthly gross income, take a look at your pay stubs and follow the calculations listed below:

If paid once per month, use the monthly gross payment amount (pretax dollars).

If paid twice per month, take the twice-monthly gross pay amount and multiply by 2.

If paid every other week, take your biweekly gross pay amount and multiply by 26 pay periods, and then divide that amount by twelve months.

If paid weekly, take your weekly gross pay amount and multiply this by 52 pay periods, and then divide this amount by twelve months.

If you are an hourly worker, take your base hourly rate of pay and multiply this by the number of hours worked in a typical week. If you receive overtime compensation, add the average number of overtime hours worked per week multiplied by the rate of pay for overtime. Add this amount to the weekly base income to determine total weekly income. Take the total weekly income and multiply this by the number of weeks worked each year to determine your annual income. Take your annual income and divide this by 12 to determine your monthly income. The formula is as follows:

[base rate] x [regular hours] = [weekly base income]

[overtime hours] x [overtime rate] = [weekly overtime (OT) income]

[weekly base] + [OT income] = [total weekly income]

[Total weekly income] x [number of weeks worked in the year] = [annual income]

[annual income] ÷ 12 = [monthly income]

A big word of caution: Qualifying income of a salaried or hourly worker will be lowered when you make claims on your federal income tax return for unreimbursed business expenses.

Unreimbursed Business Expenses

The following question is not on the 1003, but it is one that is asked of a salaried applicant at some point in the processing of their loan. The conversation will go something like this:

Loan Officer: "Do you have any unreimbursed business expenses?"

Applicant: "What do you mean?"

Loan Officer: "Do you have any expenses that are related to your work that you have to pay for yourself—expenses that are business related that your employer doesn't pay you back for?"

Applicant: "Oh no, they don't make me pay for anything."

Loan Officer: "Great."

Let's check to see if your answer is indeed, no. Pull out your most recent federal income tax return. Did you file Schedule A? If there was no entry on line 21 of Schedule A, you are good to go. If there is an entry on Schedule A, look down to line 21. Is there an entry there? If yes, find IRS Form 2106 attached to the same federal income tax return. With IRS Form 2106 in hand, write down the amount you have claimed as unreimbursed business expenses. Your lender will divide this amount by 12 and deduct it from your qualifying income.

We get that no one wants to pay more than they absolutely have to in federal income taxes. We understand if you wanted to reduce your tax liability to Uncle Sam, so you told your accountant that you used your car for business use (in addition to getting you to and from work), and you also included a deduction for the cost of your monthly cell phone bill, and miscellaneous charges like dry cleaning and meals and entertainment that were not reimbursed by your employer, but here's the problem. You may have a salary of $55,000 per year, but you deducted $10,000 on IRS Form 2106 of your last year's tax return. The only qualifying income your lender can use in this case is $45,000, unless you've also listed the actual mileage used for business purposes, in which case the per mile deduction for depreciation (as defined by the IRS) can be added back to income.

There are times a client will argue for example, that they've been recently promoted to a new position, with the same or a different employer, and in that new position or new employment they will no longer be required to pay for business expenses out of their own pocket. Your lender must still deduct your qualifying income by the amounts listed on the prior year's federal income tax return because the lender has no guarantee that you won't file the same deductions in the coming year, regardless of your assertions. Fair, or not fair, it is what it is.

Variable Income

Less predictable income sources such as commissions, bonuses, overtime pay, or employment that is subject to time limits (such as for contract employees or tradesmen) will require additional documentation and analysis. All income that is calculated by an averaging method must be reviewed to assess your history of receipt, the frequency of payment, and the trending of the amount of income being received. Two or more years of receipt of a particular type of variable income is standard; however, variable income that has been received for twelve to twenty-four months may be considered as acceptable income, as long as your loan application demonstrates to the lender that there are compensating factors that reasonably offset the shorter income history. For example, a reasonable exception to this is if you have a new job and an employment contract that guarantees bonus income for the next three years; the employment contract can be used to verify both salary and continuance of bonus income.

There is no clear-cut formula to determine usable variable income. Many things affect the final amount the lender will use for loan qualification. For all variable income sources, after the monthly year-to-date income amount is calculated, the underwriter must compare it to your prior years' earnings using your W-2s, signed federal income tax returns and a completed Form 1005 Verification of Employment. If the trend over the most recent two-year period in the amount of income is stable or increasing, the qualifying income amount listed on the loan application should be averaged. If the trend was declining, but has since stabilized and there is no reason to believe that you will not continue to be employed at the current level, the current, lower amount of variable income is listed as the qualifying income amount. If the trend is declining, the income may not be stable. Additional analysis must be conducted to determine if any variable income should be used at all, but in no instance will your lender be able to use the average over the period when the decline occurred.

Bonus Income

To verify receipt and continuance of bonus income, a few things will need to happen. First, your lender will look to your current pay stub to see if you've been paid bonus income this year. If your current pay stub does not report receipt of the yearly bonus income that you claim you are eligible to receive, you will need to add a letter of explanation from your human resources director, business owner, or accountant for the business explaining the timetable for bonus compensation.

For example, if you disclose on the loan application that you receive $18,000 per year in bonus income and it is February and your year-to-date pay stub through current day does not show any bonus income, your HR director will need to send a letter of explanation stating something to the effect of this: "Bonus compensation is scheduled to be paid in June and December. The applicant is eligible to receive bonus compensation based on the production goals as set by their manager." In this same letter, the HR director may want to list the bonus income that was paid to you in each of the preceding two years. Otherwise, the lender will need your employer to complete Form 1005 Verification of Employment. The person completing this form must be an authorized representative of your employer. All too often, small business owners erroneously complete this form at first attempt and create unnecessary loan processing delays. Be sure to review "Verification of Employment" in chapter 14 and share this information with your employer. The verification form will be sent directly from the lender to your employer and receipt of the completed form must be provided directly from your employer to your lender and not pass through your hands at all.

Once the lender has verified the amount of bonus income received for each of the preceding two years and has verified that continuance is likely, it will divide that amount by twenty-four months to determine monthly qualifying bonus income.

Note: Projected bonus income cannot be used as qualifying income; only received bonus or guaranteed income can be considered.

Commission Income

A minimum history of two years of commission income is recommended; however, commission income that has been received for twelve to twenty-four months may be considered as acceptable income as long as there are positive factors to reasonably offset the shorter income history. If the commission income represents less that 25 percent of your total annual employment income, your loan file may be underwritten using standard employment requirements. If commission income represents 25 percent or more of your total annual employment income, your loan file will be underwritten with the self-employment standards and you will need to provide your lender with copies of your signed federal income tax returns for the preceding two years in addition to your most recent pay stub and W-2s.

Other Sources of Income

When asked the income question, many borrowers will simply answer how they are compensated through their current employment—whether they are paid hourly, salary, or on a commission basis. And many forget to report other sources of income such as alimony or child support, automobile allowance, boarder income, capital gains, disability (long-term), employment related severance packages or distributions, future employment contracts, foreign earned income, foster care, housing, interest and dividends, mortgage credit certificates, mortgage differential payments, nonoccupying co-borrower, notes receivable, public assistance, retirement pensions and annuities (401(k)s, IRAs, and Keogh plans), royalties, Social Security, temporary leave (such as maternity, parental, or short-term disability), tips, trust, unemployment benefits, and VA benefits (unrelated to education). In this section, we will review your lender's ability to utilize your other sources of income for income qualification purposes and what you need to do to document their stability and likelihood of continuance. Keep in mind, your lender is looking to determine monthly amount, stability of receipt, and length of continuance.

Alimony, Child Support, or Separate Maintenance as Income

Most lenders have policies in place that prohibit a loan officer from directly asking you if you are the recipient of child support, alimony, or separate maintenance. This direction is given to loan officers to prevent the illusion that the lender may be discriminating against your familial situation. This is one of those things that protects the lender, but I feel it is a disservice to the consumer, as additional sources of verifiable, stable earnings that are likely to continue may help to reduce your debt-to-income ratio and gain mortgage approval. A better loan officer will be sure to ask this question to every loan applicant: Do you have any other sources of monthly income you wish to report?

While there are rules that we must adhere to in order to properly document the stability and continuance of income, we do not need to go to the source of that income to do so—presuming you've kept accurate documentation of receipt. For example, let's say you have a terrible relationship with your ex, but that person makes timely child support payments that match the court ordered documents. If you are consistently depositing those payments into a bank account, you have the ability to document receipt of that income without communicating directly with your ex. Now, if you go to his bank to cash the check, you don't have any record that he paid you. In that case, you'd need to ask him to give you front and back copies of the cancelled checks (cancelled here means cashed).

While your ex would be wise to deliver those payments through checks or money orders (for their own benefit of record keeping), we realize that some people prefer to pay in cash. Cash payments are challenging to source, but if you are consistently depositing that same amount into your bank account every month and if you write a letter of explanation to address that those cash deposits are payments made to comply with court mandated instructions, your lender may be able to utilize that income to support your qualifying income.

Here's how the lender will document the acceptance of child support, alimony, or separate maintenance, as a source of qualifying income:

a. You provide them with a copy of a divorce decree or separation agreement (if the divorce is not final) that indicates payment of alimony or child support and states the amount of the award and the period of time over which it will be received. If you are separated from your spouse, but a legal separation agreement has not been filed that specifies alimony or child support payments, the lender may not consider any proposed or voluntary payments as income. If you were never married to the parent of the child, a court order that addresses the payment terms for child support will suffice along with a signed and dated letter explaining that the parents were never married and, therefore, there is no divorce decree.

b. By reviewing the terms of the decree or agreement, the lender will confirm any limitations on the continuance of the payments, such as the age of the children for whom the support is being paid or the duration over which alimony is required to be paid.

c. The lender will review your receipt of these payments to determine its suitability as stable earnings. To be considered stable earnings, standard guidelines require full, regular, and timely payments received for a minimum of six concurrent months prior to making loan application. Generally speaking, income received for less than six months is considered unstable and may not be used to qualify for the mortgage. In addition, if full or partial payments are made on an inconsistent or sporadic basis, the income is not acceptable for the purpose of qualifying. With other compensating factors present in a loan file, sometimes the GSEs automated underwriting system may condition for the lender to document less than the traditional six months of receipt of income and your lender may in turn, request evidence of only one or three months of receipt of income.

Asset Dissipation

Some lenders will accept the use of documented liquid assets as qualifying income. For example, let's say you have multiple businesses with very complex tax returns and would rather not go through the trouble of producing that much paperwork and explanations. You also have three million dollars in a bank or brokerage account that can more than cover your loan request of $400,000. Under a non-QM loan program, your lender will calculate income based on your liquid assets instead of using the income reported on your tax returns using a formula that allows for market volatility adjustments and an estimated rate of return based on the type of security instrument (e.g., cash, stocks, bonds, annuities). Currently, neither agency guidelines nor appendix Q specifically list this income type as acceptable for loans delivered to the GSEs.

Automobile Allowance

If you need the lender to consider the automobile allowance your employer provides you, you must provide evidence that you have received payments for at least two years in order for it to be considered stable earnings that are likely to continue. The lender will use either the actual cash flow approach or the income and debt approach for calculating qualifying income associated with an automobile allowance and will require copies of your signed federal income tax returns to do so.

In the actual cash flow approach, the lender will review your signed federal income tax return to see if you report automobile allowances on Employee Business Expenses (IRS Form 2106). Funds received in excess of your monthly expenditures are added to your qualifying income, or expenses in excess of the monthly allowance are included in your total monthly obligations. If you used IRS Form 2106 and recognized actual expenses instead of the standard mileage rate, the lender will look at the actual expenses section to identify your costs and make appropriate adjustments. In the income and debt approach, if you do not report the allowance on either IRS Form 2106 or Schedule C, the full amount of the allowance is added to your qualifying income, and the full amount of the lease or financing expenditure for the automobile is included in your total monthly obligations.

Boarder Income

Typically, rental income from boarders in your principal residence or second home is not considered stable earnings that are likely to continue. However, there are two exceptions. When a borrower with disabilities receives rental income from a live-in personal assistant, whether or not that individual is a relative, the rental payments can be considered as stable earnings in an amount up to 30 percent of your qualifying income. Personal assistants typically are paid by Medicaid waiver funds and include room and board, from which rental payments are made to the borrower. Evidence of this will need to be provided to your lender.

Loan programs for low-to-moderate income earners may be eligible for an exception to standard guidelines. In all cases, your loan file must be documented with the boarder's history of shared residency (such as a copy of a driver's license, bills, bank statements, or W-2 forms) that shows the boarder's address as being the same as your address. Additionally, you must provide evidence that you have received boarder rental payments for the most recent twelve months.

Employment Related Severance Packages or Distributions

A severance package or lump-sum payment received from a non-self-employment source may be used as qualifying income when these funds can be documented with a distribution letter from the employer or through IRS Form 1099-R and are deposited into a verified asset account. For 401(k), IRA, SEP, Keogh retirement accounts, you must show unrestricted access to the funds and can only use the same accounts for income qualification if distribution is not already set up or if the distribution amount alone is not enough to qualify. The lender will need to verify the account and its asset composition by receiving the most recent monthly, quarterly, or annual statement. If the employment-related assets are in the form of stocks, bonds, and mutual funds, only 70 percent of the value can be used to determine the income stream to account for the volatile nature of these assets.

Foreign Income

Foreign income refers to income that is earned through a foreign corporation or government and is paid in foreign currency. Foreign income may be used to qualify if it can be documented. There are many issues that are left to interpretation on foreign income, and I go into these with great detail in chapter 11. Be sure to review it in its entirety if you have any foreign earned income you need to use for loan qualification.

Foster Care

Foster income received from a state or county organization for providing the temporary care for one or more children may be considered stable earnings that are likely to continue. The lender will need a letter(s) of verification from the organization providing the income. For unrestricted use of this income source, you will need to evidence a minimum two-year history of providing foster-care services. If you have not been receiving this type of income for two full years, the income may still be counted as stable earnings if you have at least a twelve-month history of providing foster care services and if the income being considered does not represent more than 30 percent of the total gross income that is used to qualify for the mortgage loan.

Future Employment Contracts

A lender may use your employment offer or contract for future employment and anticipated income as evidence of qualifying income. While the GSEs allow a lender to close on your mortgage loan prior to your beginning the new employment, they do require the lender to provide evidence that you have begun employment and must deliver your loan with a pay stub that includes sufficient information to support qualifying income. As this is a high-risk transaction for the lender, typically only lenders who offer portfolio loan products offer this means of documenting future income. If you are working with a lender who is willing to take this risk, be sure to communicate with them as soon as you have begun employment and receive evidence of payment.

Housing Allowance (Nonmilitary)

An employer or a church organization may provide a housing or parsonage allowance to support the cost of their employee's housing. This income may be considered qualifying income if there is documentation that the income has been received for the most recent twelve months and the allowance is likely to continue for the next three years. The housing allowance is added to your qualifying income, but the monthly housing payment is fully included in your debt-to-income calculations. The allowance does not offset the housing payment. This requirement does not apply to military living quarters allowance.

Long-Term Disability

This explanation does not apply to disability income that is received from the Social Security Administration; this refers to disability payments from insurers. Obtain a statement of benefits from the disability income provider (either an insurance company or an employer) that states your current eligibility for the disability benefits, the amount and frequency of the disability payments, and if there is a contractually established termination or modification date. Generally, long-term disability will not have a defined expiration date and is expected to continue. The requirement for re-evaluation of benefits is not considered a defined expiration date.

If you are currently receiving short-term disability payments that will decrease to a lesser amount within the next three years because they are being converted into long-term benefits, the amount of the long-term benefits can be used as qualifying income, if properly documented.

Military Allowances and Special Pay

Military personnel may be entitled to different types of pay in addition to their base pay. Flight or hazard pay, rations, clothing allowance, living quarters allowance, and proficiency pay are acceptable sources of stable earnings, as long as the lender can establish continuance. Income paid to military reservists while they are satisfying their reserve obligations is also acceptable if it passes the same stability and continuity tests as secondary or part-time employment. Veteran's education benefits cannot be used to calculate qualifying income. Provide your lender with either the most recent military Leave and Earnings Statement or a verification of employment through the Defense Manpower Data Center (https://www.dmdc.osd.mil/mla/).

Mortgage Credit Certificates

States and municipalities can issue mortgage credit certificates (MCCs) in place of, or as part of, their authority to issue mortgage revenue bonds. MCCs enable an eligible first-time homebuyer to obtain a mortgage secured by their principal residence and to claim a federal tax credit for a specified percentage (usually 20 percent to 25 percent) of the mortgage interest payments. When your lender is calculating your debt-to-income ratio, it will treat the maximum possible MCC income as an addition to your qualifying income, rather than as a reduction to the amount of your mortgage payment. Available income is determined by calculating the formula:

[(Mortgage Amount) x (Note Rate) x (MCC percent)] ÷ 12 = [Amount added to borrower's monthly income.]

For example, if you obtain a $100,000 mortgage that has a note rate of 4.5 percent and you are eligible for a 20 percent credit under the MCC program, the amount that will be added to your qualifying income would be $75 ($100,000 x 4.5 percent x 20 percent = $900 ÷ 12 = $75).

Mortgage Differential Payments

An employer may subsidize an employee's mortgage payments by paying all or part of the interest differential between the employee's present and proposed mortgage payments. We see this happen when an employer is relocating an employee and the cost of interest on their current mortgage is lower than the market cost of interest on the new mortgage. To confirm this income, the lender will need to receive written verification from your employer of the subsidy, stating the amount and duration of the payments, and confirming a three-year minimum continuance from the date of mortgage application.

Nonoccupying Co-Borrower

Review "Eligibility Versus Qualification" in chapter 4 for detailed information regarding the ability to use nonoccupying co-borrower income based on choice of loan product, loan-to-value and underwriting style (manual versus automated).

Notes Receivable

For a lender to include income received from notes receivable, it must receive a copy of the promissory note to review the terms and will need to verify receipt of interest payments as reported on your federal income tax return and it must confirm continuance of the income stream for the next three years. Payments on a note executed within the past twelve months, regardless of the duration of payments, may not be considered stable earnings.

Public Assistance

Payments received from public assistance may be used as qualifying income where you can document the receipt of public assistance income with letters or exhibits from the paying agency that state the amount, frequency, and duration of the benefit payments. The lender will need to confirm that the income can be expected to continue for a minimum of three years from the date of the mortgage application.

Retirement Pensions and Annuities (401(k)s, IRAs, and Keogh Plans)

The receipt of income from a pension account may be used as qualifying income with evidence of an income statement from the organization providing the income, copies of retirement award letters, signed federal income tax returns, W-2s or 1099s and proof of current receipt. If retirement income is paid in the form of a distribution from a 401(k), IRA, or Keogh retirement account, the lender must document that the income is expected to continue for at least three years after the date of the mortgage application. In addition, the lender must verify that you have unrestricted access without penalty to the accounts. If the assets are in the form of stocks, bonds, or mutual funds, 70 percent of the value that remains after any applicable costs are deducted for the subject transaction are used to determine the number of distributions remaining to account for the volatile nature of these assets.

Royalties

Visit the category Schedule E, Supplemental Income or Loss reviewed a little further down in this section for complete understanding of requirements for using royalty income as qualifying income.

Social Security

Social Security benefits that are nontaxable are not required to be reported on a federal income tax return. The tax-exempt portion of this income can be increased according to the guidelines that address tax-exempt income. Any nonrecurring Social Security benefits will be excluded from the lender's qualifying income analysis. If you have recurring (nonretirement) Social Security benefits, be sure to write a letter of explanation addressing these and provide the lender with a statement of continuance from the Social Security Administration.

Documentation standards for use of Social Security benefits to determine qualifying income varies by the type of benefit received. For retirement or disability benefits drawn on your own work record, provide your lender with the Social Security Administration (SSA) award letter or proof of current receipt such as a bank statement showing direct deposit. If retirement or disability benefits are drawn on another persons work record, provide the SSA award letter, proof of current receipt, and document the expectation of a three-year continuance as evidenced by the beneficiaries age. If you are receiving Social Security survivor benefits, provide the SSA award letter, proof of current receipt and evidence of three-year continuance. If you are receiving supplemental security income (SSI), provide the lender with the SSA award letter and proof of current receipt.

Temporary Leave (Such as Maternity, Parental, or Short-Term Disability)

Temporary leave from work is generally short in duration and for reasons of maternity or parental leave, short-term medical disability, or other temporary leave types that are acceptable by law or by your employer. If you are on temporary leave, you may or may not be paid during your absence from work. If a lender is made aware that you are or expect to be on temporary leave at the time of loan closing and your income is needed to qualify for the mortgage loan, you must provide your lender with a written letter stating your intent to return to work and the agreed-upon date of return. Additionally, the lender will follow standard income verification guidelines to identify your regular employment income and then use a combination of this, your temporary leave salary, your remaining post closing liquidity and the date you're expected to receive regular compensation based on your return to work date to determine qualifying income. Understand that this may require additional effort and documentation from you.

Tips

Tip income is considered variable income and must be underwritten using the variable income guidelines. Please reference Variable Income earlier in this section for detailed information regarding documentation standards and eligibility.

Trust

If you are the beneficiary of a trust and you wish to use the regular income you receive from the trust for qualification purposes, the lender must confirm the trust income by obtaining a copy of the trust agreement or the trustee's statement confirming the amount, frequency, and duration of payments. Additionally, it must verify that the trust income will continue for at least three years from the date of the mortgage application.

Unemployment Benefits

Typically, unemployment benefits are nonrecurring and will be excluded from the underwriting analysis. However, if it is typical for you to be laid off seasonally (for example, a construction worker or landscape laborer), a lender may be able to use this income for qualification. Along with a written letter of explanation, your lender will need to verify unemployment compensation has appeared in the two consecutive years of federal income tax returns and must be relatively consistent. In addition, your current job must be subject to the same seasonally affected layoff.

VA Benefits

For a lender to use your VA benefits as qualifying income, it must review your VA benefits with a letter or distribution form from the VA and verify that the income can be expected to continue for a minimum of three years from the date of the mortgage application. Verification is not required for VA retirement or long-term disability benefits. Education benefits are not acceptable income because education expenses offset them.

Adjustments to Monthly Gross Income from Nontaxable Sources

Special consideration is given to regular sources of income that are nontaxable, such as child support payments, Social Security benefits, workers' compensation benefits, and certain types of public assistance payments. You can assist your lender in verification of nontaxation by providing documentation such as award letters, policy agreements, account statements, or any other documents that address the nontaxable status of the income. If the income is verified to be nontaxable and the income and its tax-exempt status are likely to continue, your lender may develop an adjusted gross income by adding an amount equivalent to 25 percent of the nontaxable income to the portion of your monthly qualifying income that is nontaxable. For example, let's say you report $1,000 per month of child support income. With proper documentation, your loan application can disclose $1,250 per month of child support because this is income that is nontaxable for you.

Schedule A, Itemized Deductions

The lender will review Schedule A to confirm mortgage interest and real estate property taxes paid on owner-occupied properties in prior years. Mortgage interest and real estate taxes paid on investment properties are reported on Schedule E, Supplemental Income and Loss. Unreimbursed employee expenses appear on Schedule A and indicate that you are subject to certain business expenses that must be factored into the qualifying income analysis.

Schedule B, Interest and Dividends

Interest and dividend income is analyzed from income reported on Schedule B of your federal income tax return. Your lender will need to document that the assets producing dividend income still exist and are owned by you. If your lender can verify continuance, it will include this income in your qualifying income. Additionally, it will add any tax-exempt interest income as listed on your federal income tax returns back into your qualifying income. Tax-exempt interest income can be increased by 25 percent or more depending on your tax bracket.

Schedule C, Profit or Loss from Business

An evaluation of IRS Schedule C, Profit or Loss from Business, will allow the lender to identify qualifying income from a sole proprietor, independent contractor, or single-member LLC. Common examples of entities using this form are: Bob's Landscaping (sole proprietor), Sue's Financial Consulting LLC (single-member LLC) or Jill the Realtor (independent contractor). As self-employment income is variable, we follow the standard review of variable income calculation guidelines as discussed earlier. Keep in mind that if the reported income from the most current year federal income tax return is less than the reported income from the prior year's federal income tax return, an average is not used. Instead, the most recent lower year income is used as qualifying income. If there are extenuating circumstances or nonrecurring expenses/losses on your most recent federal income tax return, be sure to address these in a letter of explanation. Where compensating factors exist, the GSEs automated underwriting system may allow for reduced documentation standards and require the lender to only evaluate the most recent year's federal income tax return.

In our evaluation of Schedule C income, the lender is tasked to identify what entries are recurring versus nonrecurring income and expenses. Noncash deductions listed on your federal income tax returns such as depreciation, depletion, business use of a home, and amortization are added back to qualifying income. Documented nonrecurring losses such as casualty losses and net carryover losses from prior years may also be added back to determine qualifying income if your loan file is documented with information that explains those losses are one-time events. The lender will extract the following information from a review of Schedule C:

- Name of owner (very important for us to look here when evaluating married persons so that we separate income for each individual to exclude income or losses from a nonapplicant spouse)
- Address of place of business
- Social Security number of the owner
- Income evaluation begins from the bottom line, Net Profit or Loss. As an example using the 2012 tax forms, Net Profit or Loss can be found on line 31. From this amount, the underwriter will add or subtract the following:
- From line 6 other income. We assume this is a nonrecurring income/expense. As such, we will subtract a positive number or add a negative number. If this entry is income and recurrence is likely and can be documented, this should be addressed with your loan officer.
- Add depletion found on line 12
- Add depreciation found on line 13
- Subtract meals & entertainment found on line 24b. Important note: Since the IRS only allows you to write off 50 percent of the meals and entertainment expenses, we know

that your actual expenses were twice what was reported on this line, and therefore, this same amount is deducted from your qualifying income to represent the total expense.

- Add home expense found on line 30
- Information on your vehicle. If you are using a vehicle for the business, the IRS lets you deduct either actual expenses (retain all receipts) or the standard mileage deduction. The standard mileage deduction is commonly taken and it is listed on line 44a. As depreciation can be added back to qualifying income, the portion of the standard mileage deduction reflecting depreciation is calculated and added. Only the percentage assigned to depreciation, not the full standard mileage rate, is added back. Every year, the IRS redefines the amount allowed for depreciation; in 2012 and 2013, that amount was .23/mile. So, if line 44a says 5,000 miles, the underwriter will add $1,150 (5000 x .23 = $1,150) to that year's usable income.
- Other expenses. One-time casualty losses and amortization can be added back because these represent one-time expenses. For example, the business owner writes off losses incurred due to a fire. The assumption is made that the business will not have a recurring fire year after year. Be sure to include a letter of explanation to your lender to address this type of nonrecurring loss so that it can be considered as an addition to your qualifying income. Without explanation, the lender may assume the loss is recurring.

The summary calculation is as follows:

$_____	+ Net profit or loss (line 31)
$_____	- Other income (line 6)
$_____	+ Depletion (line 12)
$_____	+ Depreciation (line 13)
$_____	- Meals & entertainment (line 24b)
$_____	+ Home expense (line 30)
$_____	+ Calculation for depreciation from mileage deduction (line 44a x .23)
$_____	+ One time casualty loss or amortization
$_____	= Total amount of qualifying income for current year

Schedule D, Capital Gains and Losses

Income received from capital gains is generally a one-time transaction and is, therefore, not typically considered as part of your stable earnings. However, if you need to rely on income from capital gains to qualify, and this type of income is customary for you, your lender will need to confirm the likelihood of continuance by obtaining documentation that supports your ownership of assets that will produce future gains or losses. Additionally, the lender will develop an average income from the last two years' federal income tax returns and use the averaged amount (as per variable income guidelines) to determine your qualifying income.

Note: Capital losses listed on Schedule D do not have to be considered when calculating qualifying income, even if the losses are recurring.

Schedule E, Supplemental Income or Loss

The evaluation of IRS Schedule E, Supplemental Income or Loss, provides the lender with usable qualifying income from rental properties, business partnerships, and royalties. A lender typically will not use the dollar-for-dollar rental income that you receive from your tenant. Instead, rental income is usually determined by an analysis of deductions taken on Schedule E on the federal income tax return. In addition, there are some loan products that have limitations on when rental income can be added to qualifying income. For conventional loans that require private mortgage insurance or that will be sold to Freddie Mac, evidence of a minimum two-year history of managing rental properties (being a landlord) must exist as evidenced by reporting on IRS Schedule E. Loans sold to Fannie Mae do not have a similar requirement of managing rental income property for a minimum of two years when considering use of rental income for loan qualification purposes. For VA loans, a one-year history of managing rentals is required. If you must rely on rental income for loan qualification, be sure your loan officer places you into the right loan product.

For calculation of rental income using Schedule E, follow this formula for each individual property:

On IRS Form 1040—Schedule E, using the lower of Line 21 or Line 22 as the base figure

$_____ + Depreciation (line 20)

$_____ + Property taxes (line 16)

$_____ + Mortgage interest (line 12)

$_____ + Homeowners insurance (line 9)

$_____ = Yearly qualifying rental income or loss

If the final value shows positive income, divide that number by 12 and list this number on the loan application form under the Net Rental Income section. And, very importantly, having listed this positive net rental income calculation, your lender must also exclude the mortgage liability from their debt-to-income calculations in their loan origination software. If this simple, additional, manual function is not done accurately, the automated underwriting system will think your only income from the property is the net rental income reported and will pick up the mortgage liability and hit you again for it in its assessment. I can't begin to tell you how many times I've stepped in on loans for colleagues who had pending declines for an excessive debt-to-income ratio when a simple review through conducting a manual calculation of total liabilities against the system's calculations identified a discrepancy. I would say this systemic challenge leads to the most common errors in qualifying income calculations.

If the final value shows negative income for losses, divide that number by 12 and list that number on the loan application form under the Liabilities section. In this scenario, the mortgage liability remains included in the debt-to-income calculations as do the additional losses incurred.

Tip: How will you know if your loan officer has correctly mapped the information in their loan origination software? Ask them if their manual calculations of debt-to-income match the system generated figures appearing on the Transmittal Summary (Fannie Mae's Form 1008), and passed through to the automated underwriting system.

Note: The net rental income figure is not the same figure that is written further down in Section VI—Assets and Liabilities labeled real estate owned where we list gross rental income for each investment property. In that section only, is where you will list the actual amount of monthly rental income received from your tenant.

There are three instances where review of Schedule E rental income is not required.
a. When the full housing payment is included in the debt-to-income ratio, and no credit is given for rental income.
b. When the rental property was purchased in the current year—instead, a copy of the HUD-1/closing disclosure from the purchase, the fully executed lease agreement, and evidence of receipt of a security deposit are required.
c. When the departure residence is being converted to a rental and there is evidence to support the property has at least 30 percent equity (through an independent property valuation). By meeting all lender requirements, proposed rent can be included in qualifying income by providing the valuation evidencing 30 percent equity, a copy of the lease agreement, and evidence the security deposit has cleared the homeowner's account.

For calculation of rental income not found on Schedule E, use the following formula:
[Monthly rent per lease agreement x 75 percent] – [PITIA] = [monthly qualifying rental income/loss]

Tip: When the rental property was purchased in the preceding year and Schedule E reports less than twelve months of rental income, be sure to point this out on a written letter of explanation.

Otherwise, the lender may miss this point and will assume twelve months of rental income is being reported and the qualifying rental income calculation will be incorrect.

Partnership Schedule K-1 (Form 1065)

On line 35 we find ordinary income (loss). Ordinary losses are subtracted from your qualifying income. With ownership interests less than 25 percent, ordinary income will be added to qualifying income. With ownership interests greater than 25 percent, ordinary income will be added to your qualifying income only if the business has a positive earnings trend, the business has adequate liquidity to support the withdrawal of earnings, and you can document ownership and access to the income through a partnership resolution. As such, ownership interests greater than 25 percent will require the lender's review of business tax returns.

On Line 36, we find net income (loss). Ongoing losses will be reduced from your qualifying income. Continuous and ongoing income can be added to your qualifying income if the three conditions listed above are met and the income is not reported elsewhere in your tax returns. Portfolio income (such as interest, dividends, and royalties) listed on Schedule K-1 is reported elsewhere on the 1040; therefore, no adjustment to qualifying income is required. Amounts listed on line 37, guaranteed payments to partner, are included in qualifying income only when you have evidenced at least a two-year history of having received them.

S Corporation Schedule K-1 (Form 1120s)

Line 38 shows us ordinary income (loss). Ordinary losses shown on Schedule K-1 are deducted from your qualifying income. Ordinary income is added to your qualifying income only if the business has positive sales and earnings trends, the business has adequate liquidity to support the withdrawal of earnings, and you can document ownership and access to the income through a corporate resolution. The lender will need to review the history of distributions and the S corporation's financial position and liquidity to determine the ability of the business to support your withdrawal of earnings.

On line 39, we find net income (loss). Ongoing losses will be subtracted from your qualifying income. Continuous and ongoing income can be added to your qualifying income if the three conditions listed above are met and the income is not reported elsewhere in your tax returns. Portfolio income (such as interest, dividends, and royalties) listed on Schedule K-1 is reported elsewhere on the 1040; therefore, no adjustment to qualifying income is required.

Royalties

Royalty income must be verified as ongoing and consistent before it can be included in qualifying income. Provide your lender with supporting documentation that asserts royalty payments will continue for a minimum of three more years.

Current and Future Cost of Housing Expense

In the current and future cost of housing expense section, you will list only your present monthly housing expense, based on your current primary residence. Notice current primary residence and not subject property residence. Regardless of the property for which you are seeking a mortgage, the lender is asking here to list your current monthly housing expenses for your principal residence. The lender will complete the future cost of housing expense section and information here is based on the subject property future monthly housing expense.

Section VI–Assets and Liabilities

In Section VI—Assets and Liabilities, we list all information relating to assets (both liquid and illiquid), liabilities, and real estate owned. I'll break down the sections in great detail accordingly.

Depository Assets

A question not explicitly asked and one whose answer your lender will need to know is: What account will you be using to cover down payment and closing costs? Disclosing this information upfront to your loan officer can avert so many issues. Will you be liquidating stock accounts? Receiving gift funds? Taking a loan against your 401(k) or IRA? Will you be selling an asset? In each of those instances, additional documentation aside from bank account statements will be required.

Allowable Funds for Loan Transaction

Funds you have in a depository account may be used as evidence for source of funds. These liquid or near liquid assets are funds that are easily converted to cash by either drafting or withdrawing funds from an account, selling an asset, redeeming vested funds from a retirement account, or by obtaining a loan secured by assets from a fund administrator or an insurance company. Examples of liquid assets include:

a. Checking or savings accounts
b. Investments in stocks, bonds, mutual funds, certificates of deposit, money market funds, and trust accounts

   c. The amount vested in a retirement savings account

   d. Assets held in a 1031 exchange

   e. The cash value of a vested life insurance policy

Unacceptable funds for use in a real estate transaction include:

1. Cash on hand
2. Cash advances from credit card accounts
3. Personal unsecured loans
4. Stock options and nonvested restricted stock
5. Stock held in an unlisted corporation
6. Funds that have not been vested
7. Funds that cannot be withdrawn under circumstances other than your retirement (where you are not of retirement age), employment termination, or death
8. Sweat equity (any work done prior to owning the property)

Sourcing Nonpayroll Related Deposits

Lenders seek the source of all nonpayroll deposits to identify if they have been derived from borrowed funds, which may have an impact on the debt-to-income calculations. In addition, the lender is looking to verify that no interested parties have contributed to the transaction to falsely enable your loan qualification. Before handing in your bank statements, look at them and identify each deposit that was made. If you have any nonpayroll deposits, be sure to gather copies of each deposit transaction and prepare a letter of explanation addressing the source of those funds.

Earnest Money Deposits

The deposit given on a sales contract is known as earnest money or an escrow deposit. Where a copy of the canceled (cashed) deposit check is used to document the source of funds, the bank statement provided must cover the period up to (and including) the date the check cleared the bank account. At the time of loan application (usually within five business days of executing a contract), the check provided for the escrow deposit has typically not cleared your account. Through the processing of the loan, you will need to provide a transaction history from the date of the last statement through the date the escrow deposit cleared your account. It is not sufficient to only provide a front and back copy of the deposit check. Evidence is needed for the period of time (between thirty and sixty days) before the check was cashed. Before presenting these new statements to the lender, review if any nonpayroll deposits were made into the account during that time, and be prepared to provide evidence of the source of those funds (copy of deposit transaction and a letter of explanation, signed and dated).

Tip: Be certain that your lender has properly credited you for the full amount of all escrow deposits in their cash-to-close estimates by reviewing "Section VII - Details of the Transaction" on the loan application.

Receipt of Gift Funds

Individual loan programs and individual investors have different rules regarding acceptance of gift funds. Agency allows the borrower of a mortgage loan secured by a principal residence or second home to use funds received as a personal gift from an acceptable donor. Agency does not allow gift funds on an investment property. An acceptable donor is defined as the borrower's spouse, child, or other dependent, or by any other individual who is related to the borrower by blood, marriage, adoption, or legal guardianship, or is a fiancé or domestic partner. The donor may not be, or have any affiliation with, the builder, the developer, the real estate agent, or any other interested party to the transaction. Non-QM loan programs may allow for gifts on investment properties, consult with your lender.

Gift funds may be used for all or part of the down payment, closing costs, or financial reserves subject to the loan program's minimum borrower contribution requirements. It is important that the gift amount is identified separately as a gift on the 1003, even if the funds have already been deposited in a liquid asset account that is owned by you (such as a checking or savings account). The balance of the liquid asset account entered in the loan application must be adjusted accordingly to prevent duplicate entry of funds. For example, if your verified checking account reflects a balance of $15,000, and $5,000 of that amount came from an eligible gift donor, the lender will adjust the checking account balance on the loan application to reflect $10,000, and the $5,000 will be entered separately as a gift.

The use of gift funds must be evidenced to the lender by receipt of a completed gift letter. If your loan officer did not provide you with a preformatted gift letter at application, ask them or the loan processor for one immediately. Do not make your own; the lender will not be able to use it. The gift letter must include:

1. The specific dollar amount of the gift (don't estimate here as the lender will require the final gift amount to match identically to what was listed on this letter)
2. The specific date the funds were transferred (see my tip below)
3. A donor's statement that no repayment is expected. Oftentimes, loan applicants who are receiving gift funds are inclined to tell their loan officer that although their mom is giving them the money for the closing, as soon as they can, they plan to pay her

back. In my experience, people offer this tidbit because they're a little embarrassed they haven't saved the monies themselves. Don't be so inclined. Many first-time homebuyers receive financial support from their parents who are happy to offer their assistance. It's either a gift, or it is a loan; it cannot be both. If it is a loan, you will need to provide the terms of repayment, and the monthly payment will need to be included in your debt-to-income calculations.

4. Indicate the donor's name, address, telephone number, and relationship to the borrower.

When a gift from a domestic partner is being used, the following items must also be included:

a. A certification from the donor stating that he or she has lived with the borrower for the past twelve months and will continue to do so in the new residence.

b. Documents that demonstrate a history of borrower and donor shared residency (the lender will be looking for the donor's address to be the same as the borrower's address). Examples of documents that can be used to evidence domestic partnership include, but are not limited to, a copy of a driver's license, a bill, or a bank statement.

c. Verifying donor availability of funds and transfer of gift funds. If the domestic partners share bank accounts and the non-borrower deposits into an account that is being used for closing, evidence of the deposit source will be required—including copies of deposit transaction.

For each gift letter provided, the lender must verify that the gift funds are already in the borrower's account, the donor's account contains sufficient funds to cover the gift or that the gift funds have already been transferred to the settlement agent. The lender confirms transfer of the asset in the form of a certified check, a cashier's check, or other official check that clearly identifies the donor as the remitter. Acceptable documentation supporting the transfer of gift funds to the borrower includes the following:

a. A copy of the donor's check and the borrower's deposit slip (not recommended to do near the closing date as you will then need to wait until those funds have cleared your account)

b. A copy of the donor's check payable to the settlement agent (this is the best option) with the preliminary HUD-1/closing disclosure evidencing a credit for the gift amount.

c. A copy of the donor's request for a wire transfer from their depository institution to the settlement agent's depository institution along with a copy of the settlement agent's evidence of receipt of those funds in their depository account.

Tip: Avoid transferring gift funds from the donor into your account (unless those funds were needed for the escrow deposit). If you wait until the last minute to move the monies, the lender will delay sending the closing documents to your settlement agent because evidence of receipt of gift funds is a prior-to-closing condition.

Retirement Funds Used in the Transaction

Vested funds from individual retirement accounts (IRA, SEP, and Keogh accounts) and tax-favored retirement savings accounts (401[k] accounts) are often overlooked in the loan application process. These are valuable sources of funds, as most plans allow for distribution without penalty (taxes are withheld) of up to $50,000 for use on the purchase of a primary residence. If you have a loan against your retirement funds, the monthly payment is not included in calculating debt-to-income ratios. Accessing these funds where necessary for down payment can also reduce your monthly housing expense if their use eliminates or reduces the requirement of monthly mortgage insurance.

If you will be taking a distribution or obtaining a secured loan from your retirement accounts for closing costs and down payment, you must begin the paperwork with your plan administrator at least one month before closing and provide evidence to the lender of your actual receipt of the funds before your loan can be scheduled for closing.

Retirement Funds as Reserves

When funds from retirement accounts are used only for reserves, liquidation is not required. However, to be considered for reserves, valuation will be discounted by 30 percent to account for market volatility. In addition, if you are not of retirement age (typically 59.5) and are subject to an early withdrawal penalty, that penalty (10 percent unless confirmed otherwise) will be included for a total valuation discount of 40 percent. IRAs are taken at face value, as these are after tax contributions. IRS tax penalties may apply for early distribution. Seek advice from your certified public accountant.

For clarification, let's say you are forty-four years old and you provided a retirement account statement to meet the lender's reserve requirement, and in that account, you are fully vested for $200,000. The loan officer will list retirement assets on the loan application of only $120,000 because consideration is only given for 60 percent of the asset.

Tip: When providing your retirement account statement, also provide a copy of the Terms of Withdrawal from the plan administrator. These can usually be accessed online through your plan administrator's website. The Terms of Withdrawal will list the circumstances under which you are allowed to access the funds prior to age 59.5. Without this verification, the lender will not be able to use any funds from the retirement account for reserves or down payment.

Assets Held in a 1031 Exchange

The U.S. tax code recognizes the importance of home ownership by providing certain tax breaks when you sell your home. IRS Code section 1031 provides a powerful protection of assets by deferring capital gains taxes, facilitating significant portfolio growth, and potentially increasing return on investment allowing re-investment to occur up to 180 days from the sale of an asset. (IRS publication 523, Selling Your Home: http://www.irs.gov/uac/Publication-523,-Selling-Your-Home-1). Assets held in a 1031 exchange are also considered trade equity. According to the 2014 tax rules, the sale of like-kind property may qualify for exclusion up to a $250,000 gain for a single person or $500,000 for those who are married and filing a joint return.

In a properly structured 1031 exchange, a real estate investor defers capital gain taxes by selling a property and reinvesting the proceeds in a new property. Here's a simplified example of how this works. An investor buys a property for $100,000 and five years later, sells it for $300,000. The sale provides a $200,000 capital gain on the initial investment. Under the 2014 U.S. tax code, an individual's tax rate will vary by at least four different rates on earnings, depending on how much income and gain the particular investor sees in any year. In our example, the capital gains earned incur a tax liability of approximately $70,000 in combined taxes when the property sold. Only $130,000 remains to reinvest in another property. Assuming a 25 percent down payment and a 75 percent loan-to-value ratio, the seller/investor would only be able to purchase a $520,000 new property. If the same seller/investor structures a 1031 exchange, the entire $200,000 of equity could be reinvested in the purchase of $800,000 in real estate, assuming the same down payment and loan-to-value ratios.

A taxpayer must make careful preparations prior to the sale of a qualified asset in order to assure compliance with the tax code. Setting up a 1031 exchange is not a do-it-yourself project; its completion is complex so you should consult experts. If documents are prepared incorrectly, the IRS will disallow the exchange. Sellers cannot touch the money between the sale of their old property and the purchase of their new property. By law the taxpayer must use an independent third party known as an exchange partner or intermediary to handle the change.

A seller who wants to complete an exchange will list and market a property in the usual manner. When a buyer steps forward and the purchase contract is executed, the seller enters into an exchange agreement with a qualified intermediary who, in turn, becomes the substitute seller. The exchange agreement usually calls for an assignment of the seller's contract to the intermediary. The closing takes place, and because the seller cannot touch the money, the intermediary receives and holds the proceeds due the seller. The taxpayer must either close on or identify in writing a potential replacement property within forty-five days of the closing and transfer of the original property. Titling on the new property must be a mirror image of the titling on the relinquished property. Once a replacement property is selected, the taxpayer has 180 days from the date the relinquished property was transferred to the buyer to close on the new replacement property. However, if the due date on the investor's tax return, with any extensions, for the tax year in which the relinquished property was sold is earlier than the 180-day period, the exchange must be completed by that earlier date.

Tip: To document assets held in a 1031 exchange, provide your lender with a title search of the land records to verify ownership of the relinquished property, proof of title transfer, the exchange agreement, HUD-1/closing disclosure, and proof of satisfaction of any liens.

Offshore Asset Accounts

Properly validated offshore accounts are allowable sources of funds for a real estate transaction. The lender must verify that you are the account owner and all sourcing requirements apply to these accounts as well. While many lenders will accept a verification of deposit form in lieu of foreign language bank statements, many foreign banks will not complete the verification of deposit form because it is only provided in either English or Spanish. A bank reference letter may be acceptable in lieu of foreign language bank statements or the standard verification of deposit form. Please review the instructions for bank reference letters in the "Verification of Depository Assets" section in chapter 14 for clarity on acceptable processes.

Sales Concessions

The seller, builder/developer, real estate agent, or broker may incentivize a buyer by providing a sales or financing concession. These are called interested party concessions. Allowable concessions vary by occupancy, loan program, and investor. Use of these funds is not permitted to make the down payment, meet financial reserve requirements, or meet minimum borrower contribution requirements. Based on the below listed loan-to-value percentages, standard guidelines for conventional financing allow the following concessions (lender overlays may apply):

Principal residence or second home:
Greater than 90 percent 3 percent maximum
75.01 percent–90 percent 6 percent maximum
75 percent or less 9 percent maximum

Investment property:
All LTV ratios 2 percent maximum

Allowable uses of funds from sales/financing concessions includes payment of origination fees, discount points, commitment fees, appraisal costs, transfer taxes, stamps, attorneys' fees, survey charges, title insurance premiums, real estate tax service fees, interest charges (for a maximum of thirty days), real estate taxes covering any period after the settlement date (only if the taxes are being impounded/escrowed), hazard insurance premiums (for a maximum of fourteen months), homeowner association assessments covering any period after the settlement date (maximum of twelve months), and initial or renewal mortgage insurance premiums.

Tip: If the sales contract is written with a concession that exceeds the lender's allowable limits or if dollar amount of contribution exceeds the dollar amount of allowable costs, the loan officer must submit the file with a reduction to sales price for the excess solely for the purposes of the lender's calculation of loan-to-value ratios. If the loan officer does not submit the file this way, the loan will be denied due to excess seller concessions.

Tip: Prior to entering into a sales contract with specific verbiage regarding sales or financing concessions, be sure to review with your loan officer the maximum interested party contributions for your specific loan program as limitations vary with each loan program and each investor.

Note: It is generally advised to word any seller credits on minor repairs or replacements as a generic closing cost contribution instead of specifically stating the reason why the concession was offered. For major repairs, a contract would call for let's say, a sales concession of $10,000 for roof repairs. In such case, the lender will require the appraiser to take photos of the damaged area and will also require a roof inspection and an estimated cost to cure from a general contractor. If the item being repaired is considered hazardous to living, the lender will prohibit the closing from taking place until the repairs are made and the appraiser returns to retake photos to ensure correction.

Net Proceeds from Sale of Real Estate

If you are counting on the proceeds from the sale of your current home as funds to purchase your next home, the lender calculates available funds using one of two formulas. If you have a buyer and the sales price has been established, the estimated net proceeds are calculated by taking the sales price and subtracting all costs associated with the sale (commissions, liens, etc.). If all you have is a listing agreement (no buyer yet), the lender will calculate net proceeds by taking 90 percent of the asking price and reducing all costs associated with the sale to arrive at estimated net proceeds. To issue a loan commitment, the lender will require evidence to support final net proceeds with a copy of the HUD-1/closing disclosure from the sale of your departure residence. If a simultaneous closing will take place, and if the contract for the sale of your home had a financing contingency, your lender may require a copy of your buyer's loan commitment prior to closing and then make it an at-closing condition to evidence the HUD-1/closing disclosure proceeds from the sale.

If you are moving due to a corporate relocation and your employer is assuming responsibility for paying off the existing mortgage in connection with a corporate relocation plan, provide your lender with a copy of the executed buyout agreement to document the source of funds. No actual HUD-1/closing disclosure from the sale of the property is needed in this case.

Assets Held "In Trust For"

Funds in an account that is held "In Trust For" you, do not belong to you (this situation is not equivalent to being the beneficiary of a trust). They belong to the trustee and, therefore, cannot be considered your own funds. If the trustee chooses to give you the funds, then documentation standards for verifying gift funds are followed.

Beneficiaries of Trust Accounts

Where you are the beneficiary of a trust, funds disbursed from a trust account are an acceptable source for the down payment, closing costs, and reserves provided you have immediate access to the funds. To document trust account funds, you must provide the lender with a signed and dated letter from the trustee documenting the current value of the trust account and stating the conditions under which you have access to the funds, and the effect, if any, that the withdrawal of funds will have on future trust income (as used on loan application for qualification purposes).

Cash Value of Life Insurance Policy

Proceeds from a loan against the cash value or from the surrender of a life insurance policy are an acceptable source of funds for a loan transaction. To document availability of funds, provide your lender with an account statement. To document your receipt of funds from the insurance company, you must provide your lender with a copy of the check from the insurer and a copy of the payout statement issued by the insurer.

Sale of Personal Assets

Proceeds from the sale of personal assets are an acceptable source of funds, provided the individual purchasing the asset is not an interested party to the sale. In order for the lender to accept proceeds from the sale of a personal asset, you must provide the following:

1. Evidence of your ownership of the asset
2. Valuation of the asset, as determined by an independent and reputable source
3. Transfer of ownership of the asset, as documented by either a bill of sale or a statement from the purchaser
4. Your receipt of the sale proceeds from documents such as deposit slips, bank statements, or copies of the purchaser's canceled check

Secured Borrowed Funds

Borrowed funds secured by an asset owned by you are an acceptable source for down payment, closing costs, and reserves, since borrowed funds secured by an asset represent a return of equity. The lender must verify your account ownership. Borrower-owned assets that may be used to secure funds include automobiles, artwork, collectibles, real estate, or financial assets, such as savings accounts, certificates of deposit, stocks, bonds, and 401(k) accounts. Unsecured borrowed funds are not an acceptable source of money for a real estate transaction.

When calculating debt-to-income ratios, the lender must consider monthly payments for secured loans as a debt. However, when the loan is secured by your financial assets (such as stocks and retirement accounts), monthly payments for the loan do not have to be considered as long-term debt.

Here are two examples to help clarify. In the first scenario, you need additional funds for closing and decide to take out a loan on a car previously owned free and clear. The terms of the new loan need to be provided to the lender and the monthly payments must be included in debt calculations because a car is not considered a financial asset. For new loans not yet reported to the credit repositories, you must provide the lender with the following:

1. The terms of the secured loan
2. Evidence that the party providing the secured loan is not an interested party to the sale
3. Evidence that the funds have been transferred to you

In the second scenario, you have a vested retirement account with $100,000. In your accumulated savings, you have $20,000. You find a home you like for $200,000. To avoid paying monthly private mortgage insurance, you decide to take a loan from your 401(k) for $30,000. The $30,000 can be used for down payment, closing costs, and reserve requirements. Because the loan is secured by a financial asset, the monthly payment of the loan is not included by the lender in the debt calculations. It's important to note that if the remaining portion of the financial asset is used as part of financial reserves, the lender will reduce the value of the asset by the amount of proceeds and related fees for the secured loan.

Gift of Equity to Be Used for Down Payment

A gift of equity is the value of the portion of the seller's equity in the property that is being transferred to the buyer as a credit in the real estate transaction. This is typically only permitted for principal residence and second-home transactions. The acceptable donor requirements for gifts also apply to gifts of equity. A completed gift letter is required and the HUD-1/closing disclosure must also list the value of the equity being transferred.

For example, let's say your parents are selling their home to you. The home value is $500,000. You apply for a loan in the amount of $400,000. Your parents are giving you $100,000 of the equity they hold as a gift. No actual money is exchanging hands. You and your parents will be required to complete the standard gift letter form and the HUD-1/closing disclosure will show a credit to you, the buyer, for $100,000 of equity, and it will also show a debit to the sellers, your parents, for $100,000. For underwriting purposes, your loan is evaluated with a loan-to-value of 80 percent.

A Seller Credit for Rent Received from a Lease Option

While a rent/lease option credit is an acceptable source of funds, I'm somehow always surprised to find the renter/buyer who thinks that all money paid during the rental agreement will go toward the down payment on the purchase of the home. Credit for the down payment is actually determined by calculating the difference between the market rent and the actual rent. For example, let's say market rent is $1000 per month. In your agreement, you elect to pay the property owner $1100 per month to allow you to secure the property at a specific purchase price one year from today. This difference between market rent and actual rent of $100 each month is applied as a lease option credit for a total of $1200.

In addition to a market rent analysis, the lender will require a copy of the lease option agreement evidencing a minimum original term of at least twelve months (which can have month-to-month extensions beyond original term), clearly stating the monthly rental amount and specifying the terms of the lease. The lender also requires copies of your canceled checks or money order receipts for the last twelve months evidencing the rental payments. It is not required to evidence sourcing of rental payments to be credited toward the down payment.

Employer Assistance with Funds for Transaction

Employer assistance funds are only allowed on the purchase of a primary residence. Funds must come directly from the employer to the settlement agent. The lender will review a copy of the terms of the assistance. If the secured second mortgage or unsecured loan does not require regular payments of either principal and interest or interest only, the lender does not need to calculate an equivalent payment for consideration as part of your monthly debt. If regular payments are required for the secured second mortgage, the payments must be included in the debt-to-income calculation. If your move is based on an employment transfer and your employer is buying out the equity in your departure residence, see the guidelines for acceptable assets under the Net Proceeds from Sale of Real Estate category earlier in this section.

The very few times I've had an applicant tell me that his employer is helping him out with the down payment, there's immediate cause for concern. This is usually an indication that the applicant works for a family-owned business, which requires a whole other way of documenting their income. In the rare instance that the borrower has no relationship to his employer and the employer does offer this benefit to its employees, employer assistance for the purchase of a primary residence may be in the form of:

  a. A grant
  b. A direct, fully repayable second mortgage or unsecured loan
  c. A forgivable second mortgage or unsecured loan
  d. A deferred-payment second mortgage or unsecured loan

Use of Business Funds for Real Estate Transaction

When a self-employed borrower will be using business funds in the real estate transaction, the lender will need to analyze how the depleted funds will affect the soundness of the business. Lenders will analyze the business cash flow to determine whether a business is able to meet its monthly obligations. To determine the soundness of your business, a lender will want to see that it has more cash coming in each month from income than it has going out from expenses and loan repayments. We perform a cash-flow analysis to derive a ratio often called a minimum debt-service-coverage (DSC). A good rule of thumb is to shoot for a minimum DSC ratio of 1.25. That means that for every $1,000 of debt repayment your business has to make each month, it should have $1,250 of cash available after expenses. By having more income than you need to pay the bills, you create a buffer that protects your business from the unexpected, like rising costs or falling prices. This ratio gives your lender a good indication of the soundness of your business and an expectation of reliability for future income. If your DSC goes below the recommended amount after depleting business funds for your real estate transaction, the lender will be concerned about the soundness of your qualifying income from that business.

Liabilities

Your lender does not view all liabilities and debts the same way. Some liabilities listed on your credit report are not included in your lender's calculation of debt-to-income ratio (DTI). Sadly, sometimes your credit report will list a debt twice, and you and your lender may not catch that on the initial loan application and your debts will be falsely inflated along with your DTI, decreasing your chances of loan eligibility.

If you're DTI is excessive, the lender will not make a downward adjustment to the amount of money they can loan to you. Instead, they will simply decline the loan. This is not the result you want. In this section, we will identify the lenders definition of debt and provide you with the tools to review the loan application to ensure false data is not impeding your chances of obtaining a mortgage approval.

Tip: If your loan application is correctly showing all your debts and your loan officer says your DTI is too high, you may want to consider looking at options to reduce your recurring monthly obligations. Here are two immediate options that may be available to you.

a. Installment debt: If you have an installment loan that you can afford to pay off and close with funds that aren't needed for down payment, cash-to-close, or reserve requirements, your lender will be able to eliminate the monthly debt from your DTI calculations.

b. Credit card/revolving debt: For a lender to be able to exclude the minimum monthly payment from your DTI, it will need evidence that you have the funds available to pay off the account at or before loan closing.

In both scenarios, the lender will reduce your available funds for closing by the amounts due to extinguish the debt and will require the account be paid off prior to or at loan settlement. Until recently, the lender would also be required to show that the revolving account was closed in order to exclude the payment from the debt-to-income ratio, but this policy changed in May of 2015 and closure of a credit account is no longer required.

It is recommended that no account be paid off prior to loan settlement, in anticipation of loan settlement. Instead, have your settlement agent pay the creditor at loan closing and have that payment reflected on the HUD-1/closing disclosure. This is the most effective manner of evidencing pay off. If you pay the debt prior to loan closing, you will need to provide evidence from the depository account where the payment has cleared and in that process, that depository account may show additional deposits or withdrawals that will now need to be sourced causing additional delays, or worse yet, may show a reduced balance that would make your prior verified cash-to-close look inadequate. People are constantly transferring monies from one account to another. If this happens to you, you will now need to provide the lender with updated bank statements for all accounts. Additionally, expect the lender to also do a soft pull on your credit as well to determine if any new debt was obtained for funds to pay off the debt in question. See how messy this can get?

Tip: The lender's credit report may show a minimum monthly payment for a revolving credit card that is in excess of the range you normally are required to pay. You'll know this when comparing the payment amount listed on the printed loan application to the amount on your billing statement. This may happen in that snapshot of time when the creditor has not received your prior month's payment and the next month's payment is already due, so the minimum amount due includes both months' payments. In this case, bring the billing statement for the most current month, so that the lender can confirm the lower required minimum payment and update your loan application accordingly. Note that the lender will process an internal request to update your credit report with the submitted data and this may take some time.

Tip: Sometimes, an account that you believe to be closed with no amounts due appears as an open trade line on your credit report, with a pending amount due. Your loan application will reflect the payment due and your debt-to-income ratio will be impacted. This happens frequently at the crossroads of trading in an automobile lease for a new automobile lease or loan, and your credit report picks up both the extinguished lease and the new lease/loan payment. To resolve this, you will need to provide your lender with a letter from the extinguished creditor (whoever holds the debt that you believe is being inaccurately reported) showing the account is closed and has a zero balance due. With that letter, your lender will send an internal request to their credit-reporting vendor and have them update the report provided to show that account as closed and paid in full. Note that your lender's credit-reporting vendor does not and will not update the repositories. That is the responsibility of the creditor.

Installment Debt

All installment debt that is not secured by a financial asset (i.e., cash or marketable security)—including student loans, automobile loans, and home equity loans—must be considered part of your recurring monthly debt obligations if there are more than ten monthly payments remaining. So if you own your car and you have more than ten monthly payments remaining to complete your obligation on the loan, this debt will be included in your debt-to-income ratio.

If you are in the early stages of considering a mortgage loan, and you identify that your buying ability will be significantly impacted by an installment loan, consider paying it down to no more than ten months remaining of payments. You have to do this well before you make formal loan application so that when the credit report is pulled, the debt appears as having less than ten months remaining. Do not wait to reduce the debt until after loan application, as some über-conservative lenders will not allow a reduction in debt to improve your debt-to-income ratio. Most lenders will allow the pay off and closure of an installment or revolving debt during the process to reduce your debt-to-income ratio.

Tip: You don't want to assume an account has been paid in full and then have delinquencies show up on your credit history when you still owed $3, because the payment arrived one day later than expected. So a few days after loan closing, be sure to communicate with your extinguished creditor to confirm payment was received and the account has been paid in full.

When you're using your own financial assets such as the cash value of your life insurance policy, or the vested amount of your 401(k) accounts or individual retirement accounts, or certificates of deposit, stocks, or bonds as the security (collateral) for a personal loan, this loan is considered a contingent liability. The lender is not required to include this contingent liability as part of your recurring monthly debt obligations provided the lender obtains a copy of the applicable loan instrument that shows your financial asset as the collateral for the loan. If you intend to use the same asset to satisfy financial reserve requirements, the lender must reduce the account balance of the asset by the proceeds from the secured loan and any related fees to determine your remaining reserve funds. Therefore, if you borrowed against your 401(k) or you have a margin loan against your marketable securities, this installment debt is not included in your debt-to-income calculations.

Student Loans and Other Deferred Installment Debt

Agency guidelines require deferred installment debts to be included as part of your recurring monthly debt obligations. These are loans that have an initial period requiring no monthly payment and include such things as student loans or furniture and electronics plans by retailers. If your credit report does not indicate the monthly amount that will be payable at the end of the deferment period, the lender will request copies of forbearance agreements so that a monthly payment amount can be determined based on the actual terms of the note used in calculating your total monthly obligations. Otherwise, for a student loan, in lieu of obtaining forbearance agreements, the lender can calculate a monthly payment using a minimum of 2 percent of the outstanding balance as your recurring monthly debt obligation. That said, there are some depository institutions who offer specialized loan programs to recent college graduates (often limited to medical or law, but not always) who will exclude the student loan liability from the debt-to-income ratio because they want to attract these college-educated clients as depository customers. Inquire about these programs from your personal bank or from the college alumni benefits administrator.

Home Equity Lines of Credit

While not a best practice, many homeowners rely on the equity in their homes as their savings and tap into this equity by obtaining and using a home equity line of credit (HELOC). Prior to the financial crisis, many homeowners were counting on these funds for sending their children to college. When banks began to see property values decline, they froze access to or closed the equity lines altogether, even for people who were never delinquent. This presented a big dilemma about financial planning for many families.

A HELOC is a hybrid loan because it initially acts as a revolving account where you can tap into money as often as you'd like, but then at a predetermined date repayment is required and the line changes into a fixed term of repayment, while still having a variable interest rate. We call these two periods a draw period and a repayment period. During the initial draw period, you are able to access the funds in the account, are usually only required to make interest-only payments, and have a variable interest rate. Take money out, pay it back, take it out again, pay it back, and so on—whatever you want. During the repayment period, you are no longer allowed to withdraw funds and are required to make monthly payments that fully amortize during the remainder of the term. Going from interest-only payments to fully amortizing payments —usually requiring full repayment within ten years—catches many people off guard with the increase in the monthly payment. Plan accordingly.

Tip: Before you sign the loan documents, be sure you know how long the initial draw period lasts, if you are required to make interest-only payments or fully amortizing payments, and what happens at the end of the draw period. Are you given the option of fixing a portion of the available funds during the initial draw period and then keeping open access to the remaining funds during the draw period?

Of importance in handling of debt-to-income calculations: Agency guidelines say that if a HELOC does not require a payment—in cases where the line is open but has no outstanding balance and therefore, no payment is required in that month—there exists no recurring monthly debt obligation. As such, the lender does not need to develop an equivalent payment amount to include in their calculation of DTI and overall assessment of your financial capacity. However, to be conservative, most lenders will calculate the fully amortized payment assuming full use of the amount available on your line with a monthly recurring payment calculated using the highest possible note rate that can be charged during the lifetime of the loan, at the remaining term to conservatively calculate the highest possible payment should you draw on those funds and will include this amount as a recurring liability in your DTI calculations. The lender will ask you for a copy of the HELOC loan agreement, specifying the terms of repayment, to complete its assessment and make its decision on your loan request.

Tip: If you have an open line that is making your DTI is too high, prohibiting you from receiving a loan approval, consider closing the line. The lender will modify its calculated monthly recurring payment to reflect your outstanding balance, if any. Before doing this, review with your loan officer to ensure the new payment will indeed bring your DTI within the lenders guidelines. You will need to provide your lender with evidence the line has been closed.

Know that no prior lienholders can prohibit or restrict your future access to the equity in your home. Keep in mind that new subordinate liens can be a bit more challenging to obtain because they naturally carry higher risks to the lender due to lien priority. Expect more conservative loan amount limitations, combined loan-to-value restrictions, and higher interest costs, which will all vary by lender.

Tip: If there is sufficient equity in your home and your selected loan program guidelines allow for cashing out, consider closing your existing HELOC and including the outstanding balance into your new mortgage. Many times, this option allows you to have a much smaller total monthly housing obligation—especially when you are in the repayment period of a HELOC where the term is shorter and the interest rate is higher. In this case, evidence of HELOC closure does not have to take place before closing. The settlement agent will ensure the line is paid off and closed to comply with the lenders funding requirements.

Departure Residence and Proposed Rental Income

When the mortgage crisis hit in 2008, a new phenomenon occurred that we now call buy and bail. To get out of a primary residence that was underwater or that the owners could no longer afford, homeowners misled lenders by claiming a new purchase would be an investment when they really intended to occupy it as their primary residence. At that time, proposed market rent for the new property would be used as qualifying income to offset the cost of the monthly housing payment, whether or not the property was currently tenant occupied. Once they got into their more affordable home, they stopped paying the mortgage on their departure residence. Due to buy and bail, underwriting guidelines for departure residences have become much stricter so that lenders can better determine the financial soundness of the buyer.

Prior to recent changes, when a homeowner claimed they were downsizing into a smaller home and intended to become landlords of their departure residence, most lenders only required borrowers to provide a copy of a proposed lease agreement on the property they were vacating, and they could use that proposed rental income alone to offset the housing expense. Those days are no more. However, most lenders will still allow for a partial offset of the current mortgage payment (75 percent of the proposed rent) based on how much equity you have in your home.

Borrowers who currently own their home typically have three options when they decide to purchase a new principal residence. They can:

a. Sell the current residence and pay off the outstanding mortgage
b. Convert the property to a second home, assuming they can qualify with both the existing and new mortgage payments
c. Convert the property to an investment (depending on several circumstances, new loan qualification will either include or exclude the departure residence housing payment)

When the departure residence will not be sold prior to settlement on your new home, the amount of equity in the departure residence will determine the specific underwriting guidelines that will apply to you.

Guidelines for Departure Residences that Have Less than 30 Percent Equity

1. You must qualify with both the subject property and the departure residence full housing payments.
2. You must have six months of the subject and departure residence total housing payment or principal, interest, taxes, insurance, and homeowner association (PITIA) in post closing reserves.
3. You may not use the rental income to offset the departure residence PITIA.

Guidelines for Departure Residences that Have More than 30 Percent Equity

To document 30 percent equity, a property valuation is required and can be satisfied by submitting a full appraisal, automated valuation model, or a broker price opinion. Consult your loan officer to determine which format is acceptable to your lender.

1. You may use 75 percent of rental income from a qualified proposed lease agreement (fully executed lease agreement with evidence the security deposit has been deposited into your bank account). Note that a particular loan program may prohibit the use of any proposed rental income for loan qualification, consult with your loan officer.
2. If a qualified proposed lease agreement has not been provided, you must qualify with the subject property and departure residence's full PITIA in your debt-to-income calculations.
3. You must have two months of the subject and departure residence PITIA in post closing reserves.

If you have a confirmed pending sale on the departure residence and meet the reserve requirements of six months (or two months with documented 30 percent equity), the monthly PITIA of the departure residence may not be counted against you, it depends. Your lender may additionally require a copy of your buyer's loan commitment for a contract that is subject to financing and if that isn't available before the settlement date of your intended purchase, the closing will be delayed (be cautious of expiring rate lock periods).

Name Variants Under Which Credit Accounts Have Been Opened

In the final portion of Section VI you're asked to, "List any additional names under which credit has previously been received and indicate appropriate creditor name and account number." I can tell you that it is very rare that a borrower will remember the name variation she used to open a credit card ten years earlier. However, this section is where all name variations should be listed.

COMMONLY MISHANDLED DEBTS

Authorized User on Revolving Credit Accounts

An authorized user of a credit account is not the account owner. This person, typically a family member who is managing credit for the first time, is permitted by the owner to have access to and use an account. Generally speaking, the lender will omit these monthly payments from the debt-to-income ratio; however, some lenders require the monthly payment on the account to still be considered if, as the authorized user, you are the spouse of the account owner and your spouse is not a borrower in the mortgage transaction.

Lease Payments

Lease payments are considered recurring monthly debt obligations regardless of the number of months remaining on the lease, because the expiration of a lease agreement for an automobile typically leads to either a new lease agreement or the purchase of a new vehicle.

You'll often hear people say, "Don't get any new credit if you're planning on buying a house." It's not that you shouldn't, because clearly, if you trade in a lease where you are paying $725/month for a car and instead get a new car where you are paying $325/month, you've just increased your home buying power by $75,000 on a thirty-year fixed rate loan priced at 5 percent. But making a new purchase in the midst of buying a home creates a documentation hazard that you need to keep mindful of to clarify with your lender.

Cosigned Loans

When you cosign for a loan to enable another party (the primary obligor) to obtain credit—but you are not the party who is actually repaying the debt—the debt is considered a contingent liability. To exclude contingent liabilities from the debt-to-income ratio, you must provide a twelve-month history of timely payments made by the primary obligor (shorter payment histories may be considered on a case-by-case basis). Only payments that are made from an account where you are not an owner (i.e., not a joint checking account) can be considered for exclusion. If there is a history of delinquent payments for that debt, this could be an indication that you might be called upon to assume the obligation in the future, and the lender may choose to include this liability in your debt-to-income calculations.

Business Debt

When a self-employed borrower claims that a monthly obligation that appears on his or her personal credit report is being paid by their business and wishes to have this debt excluded from the debt-to-income calculations, the lender will request documentation to verify that the obligation was actually paid out of company funds and that this recurring debt was considered in the cash flow analysis of the borrower's business.

The account payment does not need to be considered as part of your individual recurring monthly debt obligations if:

a. The account in question does not have a history of delinquency
b. The business provides acceptable evidence that the obligation was paid out of company funds (such as twelve months of canceled company checks)
c. The lender's cash flow analysis of the business took payment of the obligation into consideration.

The account payment does need to be considered as part of your individual recurring monthly debt obligations in any of the following situations:

a. If the business does not provide sufficient evidence that the obligation was paid out of company funds.
b. If the business provides acceptable evidence of its payment of the obligation, but the lender's cash flow analysis of the business does not reflect any business expense related to the obligation. It is reasonable to assume that the obligation has not been accounted for in the cash flow analysis.
c. If the account in question has a history of delinquency. To ensure that the obligation is counted only once, the lender will adjust the net income of the business by the amount of interest, taxes, or insurance expense, if any, that relate to the account in question.

Court-Ordered Assignment of Debt

Let's say you got a divorce. You owned a home jointly and in the marital separation agreement, the house and the mortgage were assigned to your ex. Ideally, as part of the court order, the judge will require that the retaining spouse refinance any mortgages to remove you from the liability within a specified time period. While the ex still owns the property and the joint mortgage is in effect, you decide to get a new home. The lender for your new mortgage application will exclude the housing liability from the marital residence because it is considered a contingent liability. The lender is not required to count this contingent liability as part of your recurring monthly debt obligations as long as you provide the court order showing the assignment of property and debt to your ex.

As an aside, things can get pretty messy when you quitclaim the property to the ex without also removing yourself from liability on the house.

Although by court order you are not responsible for the debt, the creditor will not physically release you from liability and it will still appear on your credit report. Although the lender is not required to evaluate the payment history for the assigned debt after the effective date of the court-ordered assignment, delinquencies will be reported by the creditor to the repositories and will negatively impact your credit score. It's a mistake to stop making mortgage payments during divorce proceedings. Don't let anger and ego impact your future access to and cost of credit. The lender cannot disregard your payment history for the debt before the court-ordered assignment date.

Child Support, Alimony, or Separate Maintenance as Debt

When you are required to pay alimony, child support, or separate maintenance under court order by divorce decree, separation agreement, or any other written legal agreement, those obligations must be factored into your monthly debt payments to calculate your total debt-to-income ratio—if they will continue in excess of ten months into the future. If the obligation will end within ten months of making mortgage application, the lender can exclude this debt from your debt-to-income calculations, provided you've given them the right documentation and accompanied it with a letter of explanation. The underwriter will request to review a copy of the divorce decree and the marital settlement agreement. If you were never married to the parent of the child, a court order that addresses the payment terms for child support will suffice along with a signed and dated letter explaining that the parents were never married and, therefore, there is no divorce decree.

If you happen to make voluntary payments in excess of what is mandated by court order, the underwriter does not take that excess into consideration as a recurring monthly debt. However, you will be asked to write a letter of explanation addressing why payments are being made in excess of mandate. I've seen borrowers huff and puff at the very audacity of being asked why they are contributing additional funds to support their children, and I've seen very colorful letters written stating things like "Because I feel like it," "Because I can," "Because I'm a great dad," "Because I can spend my money however I want," "Because I choose to contribute to my son's college expenses," or "Just because." Just write it, sign, date it, and move on.

Real Estate Owned

For each real estate property owned, you must provide the lender with a complete picture of contingent liabilities. Follow the instructions for real estate owned on the Comprehensive Mortgage Documentation Checklist found in the "Resources" section to gather all necessary items to deliver to your lender at loan application to avoid unnecessary delays in loan processing. Aside from asking, "Do you own any residential real estate?" a better loan officer will help you bring to mind all the real estate that you actually own. These questions may look something like this:

1. Do you own any property jointly with another party? For example, did you cosign a mortgage loan for your child ten years ago? You might forget to mention it because your child has been making full payments, and you are completely out of the payment making process.

2. Have you inherited any property, or are you titled on any real estate for estate-planning purposes? For example, you may be titled on your parents' home and not occupy the property or receive rental income from the property, so this address would not appear on your tax return. But the lender will need to know about your ownership interest and will include any liabilities on that property such as property taxes and property insurance as well as any mortgage payments unless you can show that your parents (or another person) have made those payments directly to the creditor for the preceding twelve month period.

3. Do you own vacant land or a lot with a mobile home on it? Sometimes a borrower doesn't consider a mobile home owned real estate, but it is. In this case, you need to provide the lender with the tax bill and association dues, if any.

4. Does your business own any property or pay any expenses on any individually owned property or liabilities? Answers to this question may help reduce your debt-to-income ratio. Typically, commercial real estate is titled in the name of a corporation. If it is and if the corporation pays the loans and property taxes on the property, and if this is evidenced by tax returns, that contingent liability can be excluded from your debt-to-income ratio. In cases where the commercial asset is privately titled, it will appear on your personal tax returns under Schedule E and the underwriter will analyze any debt and income received as it would with a residential property.

Free and Clear Properties: Disproving the Existence of a Liability

Sometimes you may receive an unusual request from your lender to disprove the existence of a liability on a property that is owned free and clear of encumbrances. You may be wondering, "How am I supposed to prove the property doesn't have a mortgage if it simply doesn't have one?" Leave it to us lenders to make such unusual requests. Evidence can be shown by requesting that your settlement agent provide a lien search on the property in question (usually not the subject property) or, if there is a homeowner association, a lender may accept a signed and dated letter from the property manager asserting no liens are in existence.

Section VII–Details of Transaction

In Section VII—Details of Transaction, your lender enters the details of the financing structure of the purchase or refinance transaction. On line P you will find your total cash required for closing. This figure is not explicitly listed on the 2010 version of the good faith estimate, which has long been contended as a failure of design because borrowers prefer to have this amount displayed prominently for assurance. Make sure the details below listed agree with your understanding of the transaction, and pay careful attention to the amounts the lender has identified for money held in escrow, seller credits, and lender credits.

Often, borrowers confuse prepaid items with closing costs. Prepaid items would be paid regardless if you borrowed with this particular lender or not, and normally include days of interest, property taxes, and homeowners insurance. Unlike rent payments, monthly mortgage payments are paid in arrears, meaning that when you have a payment due on the first of the month, you are actually paying the principal, interest, taxes, and insurance for the previous month. Therefore, a closing that occurs on the last day of the month would only have one day of prepaid interest expense. A closing on the fifteenth of the month, would have the number of days from the fifteenth to the end of the month, including the fifteenth. Again, this cost is not specific to the lender you choose, but instead, to the day of the month you close.

Itemization of Section VII
- A. + Purchase price
- B. + Alterations, improvements, and repairs
- C. + Land acquisition costs
- D. + Refinance—debts to be paid from loan proceeds (including mortgages, liens, installment loans, and revolving debts)
- E. + Prepaid items such as prepaid interest, property taxes, and homeowners insurance
- F. + Estimated closing costs
- G. + Upfront mortgage insurance or VA funding fee

H.   + Borrower paid loan discount fees (reductions to interest rate by paying origination points at loan closing)

I.   = Total of costs (the addition of items listed in lines A through H)

J.   - Subordinate financing (including home equity line of credit, second mortgage, or seller-held second mortgage)

K.   - Closing costs paid by the seller (these amounts are identified on the sales contract)

L.   - Other credits (including money held in escrow and such additional contributions as lender or developer credits)

M. The loan amount that is being financed

N.   Any mortgage insurance premium or VA funding fee that is being financed

O.   Total loan amount—the totality of amounts listed in section M and N

P.   Subtract J, K, L and O from line I to obtain the expected amount you will need to bring to closing to consummate the transaction. This is your estimated cash you are required to bring to the closing table.

Section VIII–Declarations

In Section VIII—Declarations, using your answers to these questions, your lender will identify additional supporting documentation that will be required to determine your creditworthiness. Pay special attention to the explanations listed below for a full understanding of what is really being asked.

a.   Are there any outstanding judgments against you? While these generally appear on the credit report, timing may prevent these from popping up, so a lender will specifically ask this question. If the answer is yes, you will be required to provide a copy of the judgment so that the lender can review whether it will take a first lien position against the loan. If it does, the lender may require that the judgment be satisfied prior to closing on its loan.

b.   Have you been declared bankrupt within the past seven years? If the answer is yes, the lender will need to review a copy of the bankruptcy and discharge papers.

c.   Have you had property foreclosed upon or given title or deed in lieu thereof in the last seven years? Same as above, and its important to note here that the filing of an action of foreclosure is treated the same as having executed on a foreclosure. This means that if a lender files a foreclosure action (invoking its right to acceleration) for default or misrepresentation or any other violation of the mortgage, even though your loan is reinstated or paid up to date, future possible lenders will view the action of foreclosure a derogatory event and will underwrite your loan request as if the property had been taken back by the lender.

d. Are you a party to a lawsuit? Are you suing anyone? Is anyone suing you? The lender will need to review the details of the litigation to discern whether possible action would impede on their lien priority. Have ready an attorney's opinion letter listing details of the litigation.

e. Have you directly or indirectly been obligated on any loan that resulted in foreclosure, transfer of title in lieu of foreclosure, or judgment? Note that there is no specific time period for this question and your lender expects a truthful answer—even if credit repositories stop reporting foreclosures after ten years. If the answer is yes, you will need to write a letter addressing the circumstances that led to the default. This question also allows you to bring forth information on various situations like being an heir to an estate that has defaulted on a loan secured by an asset of the estate. Although you didn't directly take the mortgage, you became indirectly responsible for both the assets and the debts of the estate. Or let's say you had a divorce and the marital settlement agreement called for a particular debt to be paid by your ex-spouse and your ex-spouse defaulted on the debt. Although by court order, you became no longer responsible for the debt, it may still appear on your credit report. You will need to clarify with your lender by showing the court order.

f. Are you presently delinquent or in default on any federal debt or any other loan, mortgage, financial obligation, bond, or loan guarantee? Your response here applies to any financial obligation including child support and alimony delinquencies. If the answer is yes, provide details, including the specifics of the obligation and the reason for your actions.

g. Are you obligated to pay child support, alimony, or separate maintenance? If the response is yes, provide a copy of the court order listing the obligation.

h. Is any part of the down payment borrowed? For all borrowed funds, the lender will need to review the terms of the promissory note and the monthly obligation will need to be included in the lender's calculation of your debt-to-income ratio.

i. Are you a co-maker or endorser on a note? This is asking if you cosigned for anyone on a loan. For any contingent liability, the lender will need to see a copy of the promissory note, and if another party is singularly making payments and you need to have this debt excluded from your debt-to-income ratio, provide your lender with evidence of third-party payments for the preceding twelve-month period. Otherwise, the lender will include this debt in your DTI calculation.

j. Are you a U.S. citizen? A better way a loan officer might ask this question is, "What is your immigration status?" because this allows you to provide a clear depiction that will allow your lender to identify which identification documents are necessary.

k. Are you a permanent resident alien? If so, provide a copy of your Immigration and

Naturalization Service card. If the INS expires before loan closing, you will need to provide evidence that the federal government has approved its renewal.

l. Do you intend to occupy the property as your primary residence? If yes, answer question M. Self-explanatory.

m. Have you had an ownership interest in a property in the last two years? Self-explanatory.

1. What type of property did you own? Primary residence, second home, or investment property?

2. How did you hold title to the property? By yourself, jointly with spouse, or jointly with another person?

Section IX–Acknowledgement and Agreement

In Section IX—Acknowledgement and Agreement, you acknowledge that you have received and read various loan disclosures and provide authorization for the lender—and any subsequent investor—to verify or re-verify any information provided on the loan application and through any other source including a consumer reporting agency. You also provide your assertion that all information on the application is true and correct and that no intentional or negligent misrepresentation has been made—which Section IX states would result in civil liabilities, monetary damages, fine, or imprisonment for any resulting losses to the lender. This is a good time to review the printed application and double-check everything you have represented. If something appears unclear, work with your loan officer to clarify, either through updating the loan application or by providing a letter of explanation.

Section X–Information for Government Monitoring Purposes

The mortgage industry is mandated by the Home Mortgage Disclosure Act to collect information regarding your race and ethnicity in Section X—Information for Government Monitoring Purposes to ensure compliance with Equal Credit Opportunity and Fair Housing laws. We recognize the inaccuracy that is sometimes inherent in labeling any person and rely on your representation of ethnicity in groupings by white, black, Hispanic, and Asian. While supplying this information is strictly voluntary, when you choose to not respond and the loan application has been made in person, know that regulations require your loan officer to make an educated guess based on our visual observation or your surname. But why leave it up to us to guess in the first place? Prior to loan settlement, you can make changes to the loan officer's responses. Here you will also find the license number and identification details of your loan officer.

Continuation Sheet/Residential Loan Application

In the Continuation Sheet/Residential Loan Application, we enter any additional information that didn't fit on the standard form such as additional employment, liabilities, assets, real estate owned, detailed explanations, or foreign address and telephone numbers when required.

11 Challenges Affecting the Immigrant Community

Foreign nationals, nonpermanent resident aliens, and similar groups face additional systemic challenges to homeownership that are not present for natural born U.S. citizens. My hope is that with a better understanding of the effects of an impaired system, service providers and mortgage executives can collaborate on technological advances and process improvements that may lessen the struggles that create unnecessary barriers to homeownership. If you are a non-U.S. citizen, the most important thing that you need to know in the mortgage application process is that you must connect with a lender who has loan programs that cater to your situation. Seek a referral to a mortgage professional from an immigration attorney, certified public accountant, financial advisor, or a global realtor.

***Note:** If you have a Social Security number that was issued after June 2011, be sure to review the "Social Security Randomization" section in this chapter.*

Immigration Status and Loan Options

I N MORTGAGE LENDING, we differentiate program eligibility by immigration status including the following groups:

- U.S. citizen and permanent resident aliens
- Nonpermanent resident aliens
- Nonresident aliens (NRA) or foreign nationals

A permanent resident alien is someone who has qualified to live and work in the U.S. and has been issued a Permanent Resident Card INS Form I-551 (a "green card"), which is issued by U.S. Citizenship and Immigration Services (USCIS). The issuance is valid for ten years and is renewable. In mortgage underwriting, we treat permanent resident aliens exactly as we do U.S. citizens. A permanent resident—like a U.S. citizen—is eligible to purchase an owner-occupied, second home, or investment property.

Nonpermanent resident aliens (NRAs) are citizens of another country who reside in the U.S. under a Conditional Resident Alien Card, Temporary Resident Card, work visa, student visa, or some other permit for some specified period of time and who have a valid Social Security number. Many employers in the U.S. routinely need and search for highly skilled temporary workers outside of our borders. For these workers, temporary employment visas such as an H1B or L1 (L1A or L1B) are available to live and work within the United States. These types of visas are widely accepted by lenders under their full product offerings for conforming loans because these visas cover a three-year life span and are renewable, thereby meeting the eligibility standards for delivery to the GSEs. A nonpermanent resident is sometimes limited to financing an owner-occupied property.

Mortgage lenders will not lend to any individuals with diplomatic immunity because those with diplomatic immunity cannot be sued unless their home state (country) allows it. In other words, diplomats are generally beyond the reach of civil process with few exceptions granted under the Vienna Convention. While a diplomat may offer to waive their immunity as it relates to property laws, immunity can only be waived by the diplomat's own government as the immunity belongs to the nation not to individuals.

A foreign national is not a nonpermanent resident alien, permanent resident alien, or a U.S. citizen. The term foreign national refers to individuals who are citizens of another country who hold a valid visa to live or visit in the U.S. Visas are not required of individuals from certain countries participating in the Visa Waiver Program, which allows citizens of participating countries to travel to the U.S. without obtaining a visa, for stays of ninety days or less for business, tourism, visiting, or pleasure. Citizens of the following countries are eligible: France, Germany, Greece, Ireland, Italy, Japan, Netherlands, Norway, Spain, and citizens of the United Kingdom with the unrestricted right of permanent abode. Canadian citizens are not required to obtain either a visa or visa waiver in order to enter the U.S., and Canadians who enter the U.S. without establishing any other status are presumed to be in the country for pleasure.

Many lenders prefer not to lend to nonresident aliens because this group presents a higher risk transaction in many regards. One of the greatest risks with lending to NRAs lies with enforcement. A loan dispute with a nonresident alien could be brought in federal court, and that court would have jurisdiction. The problem would not be with obtaining a favorable judgment; the challenge would be with enforcing that judgment. Some lenders will make loans to nonresident aliens only when a co-borrower is either a U.S. citizen or a permanent resident alien. There are many lenders in the marketplace who understand the risks inherent in foreign national lending and are eager to provide these individuals with mortgage financing, while appropriately pricing and labeling these loans for sale in the secondary market.

Challenges In Meeting Loan Eligibility Standards

The GSEs can accept delivery of all of the above types of borrowers under certain conditions. In addition to meeting legal residency and documentation requirements, the GSEs require that all borrowers have a valid Social Security number or an individual taxpayer identification number (ITIN). But only lenders who have negotiated a variance to the agency's selling guide under their master agreement can deliver mortgage loans for borrowers without Social Security numbers or ITINs.

One common issue is the borrower classification under lending program. Lenders' guidelines will list eligible borrower types for each specific loan program. For example, an NRA program may exclude any borrower with a Social Security number, and a conforming loan may exclude foreign-earned income that is not reported on a U.S. federal income tax return. But a borrower may have a legitimate reason for having a Social Security number and still be a tourist in the

U.S., and a nonpermanent resident may have legitimate income outside of the U.S. that is not subject to U.S. taxation.

Just because an individual is in the U.S. on a tourist visa, a lender cannot assume he doesn't have a valid Social Security number. Sometimes, a foreign national may have a Social Security number because they applied for one while they lived and studied in the U.S. and these individuals may have an established credit history. This can be a good thing or a bad thing for mortgage underwriting. If an individual fails to report that they have a Social Security number, a lender may still be able to identify that one exists and may presume that the borrower intended the misrepresentation because many lenders will enforce loan eligibility standards using the representative credit score where one exists. If the foreign national who studied in the U.S. fifteen years earlier has not utilized U.S. credit in that time, their representative credit score may be low. This lower score—though not a true depiction of an individuals credit habits outside of the U.S. and within the past twenty-four months—will be used to judge program eligibility standards.

Tip: For borrowers who fall into this category, be sure to discuss this with your loan officer, as with a written explanation and proper supporting documentation, your loan request can be submitted to risk managers for credit exception review, which would allow the use of nontraditional credit in place of or in addition to a U.S. credit report. Be sure to review considerations given to nontraditional credit or low credit scores in the "No Credit?" section in chapter 6.

By definition, a foreign national purchasing a property outside of his home country is generally affluent. Most are self-employed in more than one business and are often shareholders in multiple businesses in different countries. Because of the complexity of their income sources, lenders have historically relied upon the assertion of foreign income earned through a licensed or certified public accountant from the borrower's country of origin. Traditionally, this has been an acceptable alternate source of income verification and is not to be confused with a stated income loan where no third-party income verification is obtained. A foreign national can expect higher down payment requirements and is usually limited to financing a second home or an investment property, but there are exceptions. The exception that allows for a foreign national to finance an owner-occupied home lies with a group of borrowers that I refer to as either hybrids or recent Immigrants, and we'll get to those after we review U.S. tax law differentiations by immigrations status.

With the January 2014 roll out of the final rules of the Dodd-Frank Act, many lenders have limited foreign national lending to only those seeking financing for investment properties and prohibit the financing of both second homes and owner-occupied properties. The reason for this may be due to assumptions made under the supporting income documentation standards as set forth under the Ability-to-Repay (ATR) rule. Under ATR, a lender is instructed to follow accepted income documentation methods as listed in the Federal Register under Appendix Q to Part 1026—Standards for Determining Monthly Debt and Income or those issued under GSE guidance.

Neither in Appendix Q nor under GSE guidance is there a specific entry for acceptable methods of documenting non-U.S. sourced foreign income. All that is mentioned is that for foreign income to be used, it must be reported on federal income tax returns. Neither specifies if what they really mean is U.S. federal income tax returns or any government's federal income tax returns. Many lenders assume compliance with only U.S. federal income tax returns and exclude from qualification any income not reported. Some lenders assume compliance with review of any government's federal income tax returns and require the analysis of foreign income tax returns instead of the traditional accountant's letter.

Note: Our underwriters face enough challenges with following U.S. tax laws. When we throw in the mix that they need to evaluate foreign federal income tax returns, well, that's just an unrealistic expectation.

The regulators left it open on purpose so individual lenders decide what income verification sources they wish to rely upon. The caveat is that the lender must disclose their alternative methods on program guidelines and ensure proper labeling for sale in the secondary markets. But lenders are afraid because of the lack of clarity surrounding the acceptable use of an accountant's letter. They fear that its use would imply the loan to be a stated income loan. Stated Income loans are not deliverable to the GSEs. Without clarity, a lender would have to park the loan in their portfolio or find a private investor to free up their funds.

Let's revisit ATR and QM. The Ability to Repay (ATR) and Qualified Mortgage (QM) rules apply only to transactions secured by owner-occupied and second homes. Loans that have a business purpose are not covered by the Truth-in-Lending Act, and so would not be covered by the Ability-to-Repay provisions (Reference page 145, http://files.consumerfinance.gov/f/201301_cfpb_final-rule_ability-to-repay.pdf.) Therefore, the Truth-in-Lending Act does not regulate loans made to individuals that are secured for investment properties, and a lender is not required to comply with ATR definitions for qualifying income. What this means is that a lender will still make a good faith determination of loan qualification, but it has much more flexibility in determining what documentation it uses to base its assumptions. It is for this reason, many lenders have chosen to only lend to foreign nationals who are financing investment properties so as to avoid the dangers of possible noncompliance.

Foreign Income Earned

U.S. tax law differentiates responsibilities by immigration status. If you are a U.S. citizen or a resident alien of the United States and you live abroad, you are subject to taxation on the entirety of your worldwide income. However, you may qualify to exclude an amount of your foreign earnings from income. The allowed amount is adjusted annually for inflation ($91,500 for 2010, $92,900 for 2011, $95,100 for 2012, and $97,600 for 2013). (Guidelines available at www.irs. gov/Individuals/International-Taxpayers/Foreign-Earned-Income-Exclusion.) Exclusion does not mean nonreporting as you are still required to file IRS Form 2555 or Form 2555-EZ to declare the foreign income earned. If you fail to report, and you seek financing from a traditional lender, that nonreported income will be excluded from qualifying income calculations even if you can prove receipt of foreign income sources.

The income of a U.S. resident alien is generally subject to tax in the same manner as a U.S. citizen. If you are a U.S. resident alien, you must report all interest, dividends, wages, or other compensation for services, income from rental property or royalties, and other types of income on your U.S. tax return—whether they are earned inside or outside the United States.

When a nonpermanent resident alien has legal authorization to work in the U.S. through Immigration and Naturalization Service sponsorship given by a U.S. corporation, in which the NRA has no substantial interest, a borrower can make mortgage application and use the salary received in the U.S. as qualifying income (subject to regular underwriting criteria). This person does not have to wait two years to establish stability of employment. A lender can use their two-year history of foreign employment to meet this underwriting standard. If the nonpermanent resident alien is sponsored by a U.S. corporation in which he or she has a substantial interest or that is an affiliate of a foreign-based corporation in which the borrower has a substantial interest, qualifying income will be subject to self-employment guidelines.

A nonresident alien is a non-U.S. citizen or U.S. national who has not passed the green card test or the substantial presence test. Regardless of immigration status, you will be considered a U.S. resident for tax purposes if you meet the substantial presence test for the calendar year. To meet this test, you must be physically present in the United States on at least thirty-one days during the current year, and 183 days during the three-year period that includes the current year and the two years immediately before that. A nonresident alien is usually subject to U.S. income tax only on U.S. source income. Under limited circumstances, certain foreign source income is subject to U.S. tax. If you are any of the following, you must file a U.S. tax return:

- A nonresident alien individual engaged or considered to be engaged in a trade or business in the United States during the year. However, if your only U.S. source income is wages in an amount less than the personal exemption amount, you may not be required to file. (See IRS Publication 501, Exemptions, Standard Deduction, and Filing Information at www.irs.gov/publications/p501/index.html.)

- A nonresident alien individual who is not engaged in a trade or business in the United States and has U.S. income on which the tax liability was not satisfied by the withholding of tax at the source.

NOTE: If you were a nonresident alien student, teacher, or trainee who was temporarily present in the United States on an F, J, M, or Q visa, you are considered engaged in a trade or business in the United States. You must file IRS Form 1040NR, U.S. Nonresident Alien Income Tax Return, or Form 1040NR-EZ, U.S. Income Tax Return for Certain Nonresident Aliens With No Dependents, only if you have income that is subject to tax, such as wages, tips, scholarship and fellowship grants, dividends, etc. (Refer to IRS publication, References for Foreign Students and Scholars at http://www.irs.gov/Individuals/International-Taxpayers/References-for-Foreign-Students-and-Scholars.)

Understanding Which Nonresident Alien Income Must Be Reported

A nonresident alien's income that is subject to U.S. income tax is generally divided into two categories: income that is effectively connected (ECI) with a trade or business in the United States, or U.S. source income that is fixed, determinable, annual, or periodical (FDAP). Generally, when a foreign person engages in a trade or business in the United States, all income from sources within the United States connected with the conduct of that trade or business is considered to be effectively connected income (ECI). Anyone who is performing personal services in the United States is generally considered to be engaged in a U.S. trade or business. Deductions are allowed against ECI, and it is taxed at the graduated rates or lesser rate under a tax treaty. In limited circumstances, some kinds of foreign-source income may be treated as effectively connected with a trade or business in the United States. (Refer to IRS Publication 519, US Tax Guide for Aliens at http://www.irs.gov/uac/Publication-519,-U.S.-Tax-Guide-for-Aliens-1.)

You are considered to be engaged in a trade or business in the United States if you are temporarily present in the United States as a nonimmigrant on an F, J, M, or Q visa. The taxable part of any U.S. source scholarship or fellowship grants received by a nonimmigrant in F, J, M, or Q status is treated as effectively connected with a trade or business in the United States. If you are a member of a partnership that at any time during the tax year is engaged in a trade or business in the United States, you are considered to be engaged in a trade or business in the United States. If you own and operate a business in the United States selling services, products, or merchandise, you are, with certain exceptions, engaged in a trade or business in the United States. For example, profit from the sale in the United States of inventory property purchased either in this country or in a foreign country is effectively connected trade or business income. Gains and losses from the sale or exchange of U.S. real property interests (whether or not they are capital assets) are taxed as if you are engaged in a trade or business in the United States. You must treat the gain or loss as effectively connected with that trade or business. Income from the rental of real property may be treated as ECI if the taxpayer elects to do so.

Note: If your only U.S. business activity is trading in stocks, securities, or commodities (including hedging transactions) through a U.S.-resident broker or other agent, you are not engaged in a trade or business in the United States.

Note: Effectively connected income is reported on page one of IRS Form 1040NR, U.S. Nonresident Alien Income Tax Return and FDAP income is reported on page four of the same form.

Hybrids or Recent Immigrants with Non-U.S. Sourced Income

A newly emigrated self-employed borrower is a hybrid of sorts. This person is authorized to work in the U.S. through an L visa and draws a salary, but also earns self-employment income from outside the U.S. that may not be sourced from U.S. trade or business. Because they are neither a permanent resident of the U.S. nor do they qualify under the substantial presence test, they are not required to report foreign earned income not derived from U.S. sources. It is in this space where many lenders fail newly emigrated borrowers. Typically, this borrower owns a foreign entity and establishes a U.S. affiliate of that entity and then applies and holds a valid INS authorization to work for the affiliate owned by his foreign parent company. While technically a U.S. employee with salary income, lenders may or may not use that salary for income qualification, it depends.

If the borrower has a two-year history of reporting the U.S. sourced income, then that U.S. income can be used subject to regular underwriting standards. But if the borrower doesn't have that two-year history yet or needs to show foreign-sourced income for qualification, he or she faces a challenge. While immigration status makes the person technically eligible for most conforming loan programs, the need to use foreign-sourced income may make it necessary to make application under a nonresident alien loan program. In addition to the higher down payment and pricing requirements, the loan request would need to be submitted for a credit exception to allow a nonpermanent resident to make application under a loan program that is strictly for nonresident aliens. It depends. It depends if they've fallen into the hands of a lender who understands the predicament and that has a loan program to accommodate it.

Foreign Address and International Telephone Input

Most loan origination software systems hard code the need for a five digit zip code for all street addresses entered, have only one line to enter the street address, and don't accept more than ten digits for a telephone number—this is all in order to follow the U.S. universal mailing address and telephone standards and prevent input errors. This presents a problem when entering foreign contact information for mailing addresses and employment information, and is a challenge in mortgage servicing. This challenge isn't specific to loans to nonresident aliens. U.S. citizens living abroad, and recent immigrants will have prior residence and employment histories that need to be reported and verified.

Different lenders use different workarounds to record accurate foreign mailing addresses and international telephone numbers. Many will list the full details on the continuation sheet of the loan application, but this doesn't automatically transfer into loan servicing. Most lenders who offer financing for nonresident aliens have modified their input screens to allow for adjustments that ensure accurate delivery of loan disclosures and contact details for transfer into loan servicing to set up delivery of mortgage billing statements. But there are plenty of lenders who don't have the volume in that segment and haven't made the investment to upgrade their systems. For those, an adjusted process of delivering loan disclosures is necessary.

Most but not all lenders today use an edisclosure service that allows you to receive highly sensitive documents in a secure manner via email. You will need to give your lender permission to use this delivery method, and I encourage you do so because it eliminates time delays from regular postal service and because it protects you against manual errors in mailing address data.

Before edisclosures were around, some lenders who originated loans for nonresident aliens required the loan officer to enter the branch sales office as the borrower's mailing address and then printed loan disclosures and set up delivery through DHL or FedEx to the borrower's foreign primary residence. This system assumed that the borrower was at the residence to receive it or that someone else was there to sign for it. The problem is that most foreigners purchasing real estate in the U.S. stay here for an extended period through loan closing, and many never saw the full disclosure set until loan closing because not all documents require borrower signature and regulations only call for lenders to record evidence that disclosures were sent. It isn't required that the borrower evidence receipt nor understanding.

It was also assumed that the investor would input the accurate foreign contact information at some point for mortgage servicing. As would be expected, with a manual process, errors occur. Many loans to nonresident aliens defaulted on the first payment because the borrower never received their billing statement because somebody, somewhere didn't update the loan data from the continuation sheet into the mortgage servicing software system. We can argue that all borrowers receive a copy of the first coupon (billing statement) in the closing documents, but how many people remember to look there? Many loan officers will, as a courtesy to their clients, set up an alert to remind them of their first payment due date and will deliver an additional copy of the coupon just in case the servicer hasn't set up their loan by the due date.

As technologies advanced, many lenders began requiring that the nonresident alien set up automatic draft payments from a U.S.-based bank to prevent first payment defaults. Personally, I'm not a fan of any creditor automatically accessing my checking account because I prefer to see what I'm being billed to ensure accuracy. If your lender doesn't give you a choice but to set up automatic draft (some will let you waive this by adding a one time fee at closing usually between twenty-five and fifty basis points), be sure to view your billing statement every month as changes will occur to amounts escrowed and, therefore, to the amounts being subtracted from your checking account.

Lack of a Traditional Credit File

Most foreign buyers have traditional credit cards and can document payment histories. As accounts opened outside of the U.S. are not reported through the U.S. credit repositories, foreigners can work with their loan officers to build a nontraditional credit report to satisfy lender requirements of having a minimum of three to four credit accounts (depends on the lender). To evidence account ownership and payment history, provide to your lender a credit reference letter from the creditor (American Express, Visa, MasterCard, auto loan, etc.). For specific instructions on credit reference letters, please review the "Credit Reference Letter" section in chapter 14.

Social Security Randomization

In the U.S., a Social Security number (SSN) is a nine-digit number issued to U.S. citizens, permanent residents, and temporary (working) residents. Although its primary purpose is to track individuals for Social Security purposes, the Social Security number has become a de facto national identification number for taxation and other purposes. Since its inception, the SSN has always been comprised of the three-digit area number, followed by the two-digit group number, and ending with the four-digit serial number. Virtually every employer, volunteer organization, or landlord that utilizes background checks to screen their applicants has a Social Security verification process (often known as an SSN trace or address history verification) built in to their background screening package. It is a valuable tool that validates an applicant's Social Security number through a multistep process that involves:

1. Determining the state of issuance via the area number
2. Determining the approximate time of issuance via the group number
3. Revealing a history of name, date of birth, and address history associations via several proprietary databases

The Social Security Administration (SSA) changed the way Social Security numbers (SSNs) are issued on June 25, 2011. This change is referred to as randomization. The SSA developed this new method to help protect the integrity of the Social Security number, and it has affected the assignment process in the following ways:

1. It eliminated the geographical significance of the first three digits of the SSN, referred to as the area number. Area numbers are no longer allocated for individuals in specific states.

2. It eliminated the significance of the highest group number and, as a result, the high group list (which identifies the period of time that an SSN was issued) is frozen in time and can only be used to see the area and group numbers SSA issued prior to the randomization implementation date.

3. The change introduced previously unassigned area numbers for assignment, excluding area numbers 000, 666, and 900-999.

In 2011, lenders that frequently provided lending to recent immigrants who had a newly issued Social Security, found that they were suddenly unable to verify the existence of the borrower's identity and Social Security number in the verification stage of loan processing. In automated underwriting systems (AUS), the algorithm pulls the social security number reported from the loan application and verified through the credit repository. Where the credit repository is unable to verify your Social Security number, AUS findings will automatically issue a refer or critical error message to your loan request. Being unable to verify the existence and matching of a social security is an immediate red flag and presents additional delays in loan processing. Due to the mandates of the Equal Credit Opportunity Act, a lender may be forced to decline a loan within thirty days of application, if verification cannot be quickly resolved.

The only current solution to verifying that an individual's name and date of birth match the Social Security number provided during an applicant background check is to utilize the Consent Based Social Security Verification System by executing Form SSA-89. But getting this form to you may be a challenge as well. Many lenders don't automatically include this disclosure in their loan packages. And even when they do, disclosures print with only one name variation throughout, and the name on your Social Security card may not match the loan documents detail exactly, and when this happens, the lenders request for validation to the Consent Based Verification System is returned as "unable to verify."

Even after verifying the validity of the social security number, some underwriters were unaware of the additional steps required to obtain accurate AUS findings and loan files were systemically discriminated and subjected to the tighter lending criteria of manual underwriting standards. For loans run through Desktop Underwriter, the underwriter must add Special Feature Code 162 when the SSN has been positively validated through the Social Security

Administration and re-run the AUS to deliver accurate findings. For loans delivered to Freddie Mac, the underwriter must ensure that the Taxpayer Identifier Type (Sort ID 613) and Taxpayer Identifier Value (Sort ID 614) are complete and accurate for all borrowers.

The GSEs issue instructions for the handling of verification of identity in AUS and offer instructions for proper execution, but if your loan file never makes it to an underwriter (as in the case of a manufacturing model where a borrower may make application at a kiosk or online and who has little, if any, interaction with a human), an automatic denial will be issued.

This is a systemic challenge that negatively impacts both young people and immigrants.

Tip: Loan officers in areas of the country that don't typically handle recent immigrants may not be familiar with the recent changes. If your loan officer tells you that your loan request has received a critical error or refer message on the initial AUS findings due to an inability to validate your identity, please remind them to have you complete form SSA-89 and have it quickly executed to validate your identity so that your loan request can be analyzed for compliance with AUS guidelines.

12 HOAs: Condos, Co-Ops, and PUDs

Communities form homeowner associations (HOAs) as a means of regulating the consistent maintenance of properties within their neighborhoods, setting rules with the hopes of preempting many problems before they happen, and creating amenities that enhance the value of each home in the community. Covenants, conditions, and restrictions (CC&Rs) are commonplace for condominiums and planned unit developments (PUDs) and are increasing in popularity with newly constructed single-family homes.

MANY ASSOCIATIONS OFFER a variety of services and amenities, from pools and tennis courts, to golf courses and marinas, to equestrian facilities and fitness centers and even airstrips for landing small planes. Very few people can afford such benefits without the shared responsibility enabled by community associations. To pay for these amenities, monthly assessments are collected from homeowners. The collective assessment fund also provides for many essential association obligations which customarily include professional management services, utilities, security, insurance, common area maintenance, landscaping, allocation for capital improvement projects and reserves.

While large associations are usually professionally managed, many smaller associations are managed by one of the homeowners who may have very little experience in property management. According to the Community Associations Institute, between 30 and 40 percent of homeowner associations are self-managed, meaning they may use professional assistance for specific projects, activities, and services, but they do not employ a professional manager or management company for day-to-day services. (You can read the full report at http://www.caionline.org/info/Documents/2014%20Stat%20Review.pdf.)

Representations and Warrants

Borrowers purchasing in communities with HOAs are usually eligible for the same types of loan programs as offered in communities without HOAs with one caveat: The association must provide evidence that it is well managed. The GSEs require lenders to make certain project warranties (claims) regarding each mortgage that is secured by a property governed by an HOA. An underwriter documents warranties after thorough review of a questionnaire completed by the HOA property manager, the project insurance coverages, and the subject property appraisal. Fannie Mae and Freddie Mac each have their own project warranty requirements, as do FHA and VA.

For loans sold to Fannie or Freddie, your lender must document evidence in every file to prove it conducted a thorough analysis of the financial health of the project at the time the loan is made. On the other hand, FHA and VA maintain an online list of their approved projects and your lender may comply with less documentation in each loan file (usually just insurance). In certain cases, your lender may be able to obtain a waiver of representations and warrants from Fannie or Freddie in projects that don't meet the minimum standards evidencing financial health, as is the case with a HARP refinance where there is no new risk because Fannie is the investor on the existing loan and will be the investor on the new loan.

For financing of existing units, the level of scrutiny the lender is required to undertake for Fannie and Freddie project approval will vary on a loan-by-loan basis and is determined by loan-to-value and the occupancy status (primary, second home, investment) of individual loan files. In new projects where the developer is seeking initial agency approval, the developer is required to seek a sponsoring lender to initiate their request (to act as the intermediary) with the GSEs to deliver the paperwork that ensures the project meets its warranty requirements. Typically, a lender will sponsor a project review if it deems the investment worthy of future business (financing transactions in the project). Inclusion on the FHA or VA approval list does not require lender sponsorship and may be initiated at the request of homeowners through the board of directors or by the property manager, depending on the size of the association.

HOA and Your Mortgage

At your initial interview with your loan officer, be sure to give them the contact information for the homeowner association so that the lender may request completion of a condo questionnaire, delivery of the project's operating budget, balance sheet, and audited financial statements, and be provided with the contact information for the insurance agent to order a copy of the master certificate of insurance for the project and any supporting explanations, as applicable. If you leave this until the last minute, you risk not identifying that a project is nonwarrantable. Some associations charge between $100 and $300 to complete a questionnaire, so be prepared to pay this fee.

If the project isn't financially healthy (nonwarrantable), your financing choices are very limited, and while non-QM lending alternatives may be available to you, the costs of financing will be significantly higher. If you are determined to buy a unit in a nonwarrantable project, seek a lender who offers a loan program for this collateral. Down payment requirements for nonwarrantable condos are usually 25 percent or greater while healthy projects (warrantable) with conventional financing options may allow for as little as 3 percent down payment and government programs with as little as 0 percent down payment.

If you already live in a community governed by an association, know that a reduction in available financing options will impact the marketability of your property and subsequently drive down its value. Mandating that your association comply with GSE warranty requirements is key. Get and stay involved in your homeowner associations.

Make it a point to attend the HOA meetings and become an active participant. Don't assume that you don't have a voice or that the "condo commandos" have your best interests at heart. Push for changes that will make or keep the project within warrantable standards. If not, your unit will be less saleable as the number of persons able to buy it will be reduced to cash buyers or those with significant down payments.

With almost 50 percent of new loans being backed by the FHA and the cost of application for project review with FHA and VA being relatively low, it's probably a good idea for associations to comply with FHA/VA project standards and seek approval to increase the marketability of properties within their communities. Complying with and independently seeking FHA and/or VA project approval is a choice that is left up to the board of directors of the HOA.

Tip: If you represent an HOA and are seeking to have your community approved through the FHA, visit the HUD.gov portal and search for the "Condominium Project Approval and Processing Guide" to learn HUD's requirements. Additionally, there are private companies that can help process your request with HUD.

Note: A word of caution to the HOA board: As no board director has the unilateral authority to control the assets of others, decide which families can and can't purchase in their development, or determine what types of mortgages are acceptable, by denying member requests to seek FHA or VA project approvals, board members may be risking judicial charges of negligence and discrimination.

Prior to 2010, FHA allowed spot approvals or individual unit approvals when an eligible borrower wished to obtain FHA financing on a unit located within a project that was not on FHAs approved list. Due to elimination of spot approvals, an entire project must now obtain FHA approval status for any single unit owner or buyer to be considered for eligibility of FHA financing. There's talk of spot approvals coming back in some fashion in the third quarter of 2015. Ask your lender to review HUD mortgagee letters being issued around that time for an update.

Tip: If you are seeking VA financing, the project must be approved the VA. To find VA approved projects, visit the VA homepage for approved condos and PUD communities at https://vip.vba.va.gov/portal/VBAH/VBAHome/condopudsearch. Limit the search criteria to state so as not to exclude any projects input with spelling errors.

Tip: If you are seeking FHA financing, the project must be approved by the FHA. To find FHA approved projects, visit https://entp.hud.gov/idapp/html/condlook.cfm. Limit search by zip code or state so as not to exclude any projects input with spelling errors. Also, pay special attention the approval expiration date on the far right column.

Tip: Many newly constructed condominiums are not eligible for financing from Fannie or Freddie because they simply do not yet comply with agency guidelines for the number of closed unit sales. For this reason, when buying a unit in a newly constructed condominium, be sure to either seek the referral of a lender from the developer or ask your lender of choice if they finance in new construction projects (or have a nonwarrantable product offering). Aside from the requirement of closed sales, the agency may also require that the management of the homeowner association have been transferred to the homeowners a minimum of two years prior.

Condo and Co-Op Distinctions

From the outside looking in, you won't be able to tell the difference between a condo and a co-op by their structures. The major difference lies in how the individual units are owned. When you buy into a condo, you buy real property and the individual unit is yours. When you buy into a co-op, you buy shares of a corporation. These shares entitle you to a proprietary lease, and usually the larger the apartment, the more shares you will have in the corporation. The building then leases the co-op to you under a long-term proprietary lease.

Both co-ops and condos require board approval, hold regular board meetings and develop an ever-changing set of rules for living. For co-op buildings, potential occupants are more intensely scrutinized by board members for approval and require intimate financial and familial details to be shared much as you do when you apply for a mortgage loan. In a co-op, property taxes are billed to the corporation instead of the individual unit owner as in condos and in all other real property. Many co-ops specifically prohibit renting of apartments, while there is some flexibility with renting condo units. Often established condominiums with healthy financials can be financed with down payments less than 20 percent. The board of directors for a cooperative typically requires potential shareholders to invest a minimum down payment of at least 25 percent (regardless of lender financing minimums).

You'll find that most major lenders limit co-op financing to properties located in New York City. If you're looking for co-op financing outside of New York, try searching the smaller community banks for loan programs. The processing time from loan application to funding is usually longer for co-ops—lasting about ninety days due to the amount of time it takes to receive and review project documentation.

Building and Law Ordinance

A recent development that has led many projects to be deemed ineligible for guaranty by the GSEs is a lack of building law and ordinance insurance coverage. Here's the problem: Let's say that a fire causes major destruction to a building. Because more than 50 percent was damaged, local building codes require the building to be torn down and rebuilt to comply with current building codes. While the master certificate of insurance may have replacement cost value on the policy, you may not be fully covered and here's why. Property insurance policies generally have an ordinance or law exclusion, which means that the policy covers the building as it exists, but it does not cover the cost to upgrade the building to current building codes and ordinances after a loss. Building codes and zoning laws affect every piece of property no matter how big or small. These laws are continually changing, requiring new or improved features such as better wiring, handicap access, sprinkler systems, and more. If a loss situation triggers code upgrades, it could be financially devastating unless there is additional ordinance or law coverage. Because of these risks, the agencies have recently added the requirement for inclusion of a law and ordinance policy in order to consider delivery of a loan and many lenders have adapted this policy within their guidelines.

Law and ordinance policies provide coverage for the undamaged part of your building. The master insurance policy typically only protects against actual damage caused by a covered cause of loss to a building. It doesn't cover the cost to replace an undamaged portion of the building that is required to be torn down and rebuilt because of a local ordinance. The ordinance or law coverage, listed under Part A of the declarations page provides this protection based on the coverage limit selected. While property insurance covers debris removal for a portion of property damaged by a covered peril, it doesn't cover demolition expenses for an undamaged portion of a building that has to be removed. Part B of ordinance or law provides this coverage. Since demolition costs vary based on building size and other factors, coverage amounts should reflect the building's structure. It's wise to assess exactly what types of upgrades could be required if you had a major loss (i.e., sprinkler systems, elevators, wiring, septic system, etc.). The limit set for Part C requires serious consideration and talking with a contractor may be helpful in determining the appropriate level of protection.

Issues That May Deem a Condominium Project Nonwarrantable

a. Budgeted line item for annual reserves: The guidelines call for the minimum line item entry for reserves to be equal to or greater than 10 percent of the total annual budget. If the annual budget does not show a line item entry of at least 10 percent of the total budget, ask the property manager if they have a separate savings account for excess reserves from prior years. Sometimes they do, and this can be presented to show evidence of sufficient reserves. It's also important for lenders to note that the GSEs allow exclusions of certain items from the 10 percent minimum reserve calculation. These include:

o   Incidental income on which the project does not rely for ongoing operations, maintenance, or capital improvements; income collected for utilities that would typically be paid by individual unit owners, such as cable TV or Internet access; income allocated to reserve accounts; and special assessment income.

o   The lender may use a reserve study in lieu of calculating the replacement reserve of 10 percent provided that the lender obtains a copy of an acceptable reserve study from the property manager and retains the study and the lender's analysis of the study in the project approval file, the study demonstrates that the project has adequate funded reserves that provide financial protection for the project equivalent to Fannie Mae's standard reserve requirements, the study demonstrates that the project's funded reserves meet or exceed the recommendations included in the reserve study, and the study meets GSE requirements for replacement reserve studies. Note: The GSE requirements for a budget review, replacement reserves, and reserve study are not applicable to two to four unit condominium projects.

b.   For condominium projects in which the units are not separately metered for utilities, the lender must determine that having multiple units on a single meter is common and customary in the market where the project is located and confirm that the project budget includes adequate funding for utility payments. Again, these requirements are not applicable to two to four unit projects.

c.   Delinquencies must be less than or equal to 15 percent: This one is a little tricky. Guidelines say that there can be no more than 15 percent of the units delinquent on their monthly association dues. First, agency allows properties that are in foreclosure to be excluded from this calculation. Second, the property manager completing the questionnaire will list how many units are presently delinquent and usually makes no distinction against foreclosed units. When the lender's condo project review team analyzes the questionnaire and the balance sheet, it will run the dollar amount listed on the balance sheet for pending dues with the total units listed on the questionnaire and identify disparities.

d.   Greater than 51 percent owner-occupied: Owner occupants pose a smaller risk to lenders than properties occupied by tenants because when the unit owner is in financial trouble, he is more inclined to allocate his limited funds to preserving the roof over his head instead of making payments on the second home or the investment property he owns. Hence, lenders view projects with a high concentration of rental units as an elevated risk.

e. One individual/entity owning 10 percent or more of the total units: High concentration can be defined by projects in which a single entity (the same individual, investor group, partnership, or corporation) owns more than one unit in a project that has two to four units, owns more than two units in a project that contains between five and twenty units, or owns a 10 percent interest in projects containing twenty-one or more units. The concern here is if the owner with the high percentage of ownership comes under financial distress, the entire association can be at financial risk if that owner stops paying the monthly dues. These concerns also apply where homeowner associations own set number of units.

f. Pending litigation: If there is pending litigation against the project, the lender doesn't like it. To potentially remedy the dislike, obtain a copy of the suit from the attorney representing the HOA so that the lender's condo review team can assess potential losses and whether or not the condos liability coverage is sufficient to sustain the claim and whether or not the budget shows sufficient funds to pay the deductible on the claim. Be forewarned: Some lenders won't bother to request review of the legal documents and will immediately decline the project. If a project is denied, ask your lender for the reasons and work with your loan officer and the homeowner association to remedy the cause. Many times, simple clarification will turn a denial into an approval.

g. Percentage of project allocated for commercial use: In most states, commercial square footage cannot exceed 20 percent of the entire project. In New York State, that amount can be no higher than 30 percent.

h. Failure to maintain adequate insurance coverage: See chapter 13 for homeowners insurance essentials. Once the lender receives a copy of the master certificate of insurance and completes coverage analysis, it may identify that the project is insufficiently covered by their existing policies. In my experience, this usually happens with errors calculating the square footage of common areas, when separate policies are in place for separate buildings within the same project, or when flood maps show one building is in a flood zone while the one right next to it is not in a flood zone, or if the lender does not accept gap insurance (requires master policy to show replacement cost coverage of 100 percent).

Tip: When you run into insurance issues with your lender, ask the property manager for a copy of the project appraisal their insurance agent used in determining proper coverage for the building. This is not the appraisal your lender does on your particular unit. This is the appraisal on the entire project. With that, the condo reviewer should be able to adjust their calculations and confirm proper coverage.

Common Issues That Cause a Co-Op Project Denial

a.   Total reserve amount is less than 10 percent of annual budget.

b.   The number of units that are owner occupied is less than 51 percent.

c.   Flip tax exceeds 3 percent of the sales price. The term flip tax is actually not a state, city or federal tax, but instead a fee paid to the co-op when a property is sold. It is typically paid by the seller and is usually no more than 2% of the sales price. It is a form of revenue collection used to offset maintenance costs.

d.   The project has underlying mortgages with these features: Balloon payments in less than three years; adjustable interest rate mortgages.

e.   Depending on the lender, the maximum space allowed for commercial use is between 20 percent and 30 percent.

f.   Properties less than 70 percent owner occupied and taller than three stories, require twelve months of rent loss coverage.

g.   Properties less than 70 percent owner occupied and up to three stories, require six months of rent loss coverage.

Monitoring HOA Dues

There's no doubt that the economic downturn afflicted many households. As we learned in the Great Recession, when homeowners in communities found themselves with little or no income, they rarely kept up with their HOA dues. As such, many HOAs quickly saw their funds depleting and reserve funds evaporate—assuming it had allocated any at all in their budgets to begin with—and communities had no choice but to defer maintenance. Communities suffering from excessive delinquencies quickly found that their projects were deemed nonwarrantable for sale to the GSEs. Associations came under a lot of pressure to meet their obligations to the rest of the homeowners who continued with timely payments, and often special assessments were added to make up for the difference of lagging maintenance, which further perpetuated delinquencies in a time where most homeowners were already struggling to make ends meet. While the Great Recession brought mass devaluation to properties all across the country, condos were hardest hit because not only was it difficult to find qualified buyers but condos located in nonwarrantable projects were also limited for sale to either cash buyers or only to those who were willing to pay premium dollars for portfolio or private money financing. Values plummeted.

Note: When you don't pay the monthly dues or special assessments imposed by your homeowner association, in most cases, an assessment lien is filed with the court, which usually attaches to your property automatically. That lien will stay with the property until you settle the debt or until the property is transferred. If the property is transferred in foreclosure, the HOA assessment lien is usually extinguished.

Time out.

Let's learn some background on the interactions of originators, investors, and servicers.

Investors are those who invest money in mortgage-backed securities, using third-party service providers to handle the servicing requirements of your loan including collection and foreclosure activities. As the mortgage industry was faced with overwhelming defaults, it scrambled to begin foreclosure proceedings or negotiations on short-sale agreements (accepting less than what was owed on their investment) to get the nonperforming assets off their books. The sheer magnitude of the nation in crisis had servicers completely unprepared to handle the volume of properties in distress and they began to outsource labor to expedite foreclosure proceedings. Much has already been reported in the news about the mistakes and failures that ensued from unskilled labor cutting corners to rush the process.

Mortgage servicers are also tasked to handle the negotiation of short sales on behalf of the investor. The investor relies on the servicer to let it know what amount will be recaptured through the sale. Meaning, it is up to the servicer to provide a detailed analysis of any existing liens, encumbrances, or claims against the property and to include this amount with the presentation of the buyer's sales offer. As these negotiations can take months, many times from the date of submission to the closing date, an HOA assessment lien is filed against the property for nonpayment of delinquent dues and neither the servicer nor the investor have any prior knowledge that HOA delinquencies even exist.

This is where problems and unforeseen liabilities mount for lenders, investors, and servicers. An HOA is often managed by resident owners who lack the expertise or time to find and connect with the right department in the foreclosing institution and, without this, has little ability to present payment claims. Even when managed by a professional HOA management company, the job of finding out where to turn for payment of HOA fees can be daunting. Because of this disconnect, HOA claims and liens oftentimes surface at the last minute, causing delays and failures in sales and title transfers.

How Is it that the Loan Servicer Doesn't Know an HOA Lien Exists?

For a variety of reasons, the mortgage industry has typically not tracked the payments of HOA dues on its mortgaged properties. While this is counterintuitive, keeping track of the HOA contact information has never been deemed a task of the originator nor is it regarded as the responsibility of the mortgage servicer. That was before delinquent HOA obligations became an obstacle to timely, profitable, or easy disposition of a property through a short sale or foreclosure sale. (For more on these obstacles, read "Resolving Unpaid HOA Accounts Before it's Too Late" by Steve Bergsman at www.inman.com/2012/09/21/resolving-unpaid-hoa-accounts-its-too- late.) With servicing rights changing hands frequently through loan ownership transfers and subsequent securitizations, many declarations of covenants, conditions, and restrictions (CC&Rs) have been lost in the shuffle. The resulting effects have been that subsequent servicers are generally unaware of the HOAs that are involved with their loans.

The lack of a unified database for HOAs and loan servicers to connect with one another presents an enormous challenge for the entire real estate and lending community and has led to an emerging crisis for all parties. HOAs need payment to keep their communities functioning and lenders and servicers of bank-owned properties desire to stay current on their HOA obligations to avoid problems arising during resale activities. In a short sale, delinquent borrowers almost never have the capacity (or willingness) to pay the totality of their HOA debt prior to transferring ownership, and the new buyers of the property have no desire to pay the delinquent dues of the seller. So it is usually left up to the investor to satisfy the outstanding dues, further reducing the recapture amount—dollar for dollar—or the sale is off.

When there are no buyers prior to foreclosure, the next option on a delinquent loan is for the investor to take back the property in foreclosure. The foreclosure process typically begins once a homeowner is 120 days delinquent on mortgage payments, although it can technically begin earlier or later. Depending on the property state, the foreclosure process may proceed in one of three ways:

1. Judicial sale, which requires that the process go through court
2. Power of sale, which can be carried out entirely by the lender
3. Strict foreclosure, which is only available in a few states and requires the servicer, acting on the lender's behalf, to file a lawsuit against the titleholder

Foreclosure's Affect on the HOA

During the time it takes for a servicer to take back a property from a homeowner, no one is making payments to the HOA for the monthly dues, and the association is getting pulled deeper and deeper into financial crisis. When foreclosing investors take ownership, they become responsible for making payment on HOA dues from the time they take ownership, just as is required of all the other owners in the association. The point here is this: Foreclosure is a lengthy and costly process for all parties and the prevailing thought that "banks just want to take the property" simply doesn't hold true.

Lien Priority

Priority of liens is generally established by their recording date, and in the event of a foreclosure sale, lien priority determines the order in which lien holders are paid from sale proceeds. As most people do when buying a home, you'll probably take out a mortgage, which gets recorded first and becomes the first lien. In some cases, you might take out a second mortgage, which is then recorded behind the first lien and therefore, becomes the second lien. In most cases, all of the proceeds from a foreclosure sale will go to satisfy the debt of the first mortgagee, and if there is remaining equity in the property, it will be distributed to junior lien holders in order of priority.

HOA Assessment Lien and Super Lien States

An HOA assessment lien is a lien that is attached to your property records when you become delinquent in paying the monthly dues or any special assessments. The lien typically automatically attaches to your property, commonly as of the date the HOA's declaration of covenants, conditions, and Restrictions (CC&Rs) was recorded or as of the date the assessments became due. Often the CC&Rs will contain a provision stating that any HOA lien is subordinate to a first mortgage, even if the mortgage was recorded after the assessment lien was perfected. In this manner, HOA liens are most often subordinate to first mortgage liens. State laws may also determine the priority of an assessment lien.

A super lien is a category of lien that, pursuant to state statute, is given a higher priority than all other types of liens. An example of a super lien is one that is placed against delinquent property taxes. Nonpayment of property taxes presents a threat to first mortgage priority. As such, loan servicer's have long subscribed to tax monitoring services for alerts of nonpayment. A loan servicer may make payment of delinquent taxes to preserve the integrity of its first mortgage priority lien and will adjust your monthly housing payment to reflect the amount they paid on your behalf. Adjustments to escrow are also made in instances where homeowners insurance coverage has lapsed, as nonpayment of this critical item that protects the collateral that secures the mortgage and has long been understood to carry serious consequences.

In response to the tumbling effect of the Great Recession, homeowners began pushing for legislation in their states to protect their associations from being ignored by titleholders and mortgage servicers. Today, there are approximately sixteen states that have passed legislation that gives HOA assessment liens priority over a previously recorded mortgage, and that number is growing. These super lien states currently include Alabama, Alaska, Arizona, Colorado, Connecticut, Florida, Massachusetts, Minnesota, Nevada, New Jersey, New York, Oregon, Pennsylvania, Rhode Island, Washington, and the District of Columbia. Now, just like property tax liens, HOA assessment liens in these super lien states can be used to take ownership of a property and the prior first lien mortgage is extinguished. With that, it's no surprise that HOAs in super lien states are more than twice as likely to file and record a lien on delinquent dues, as they know that these claims can take precedence over first mortgages. (For more on this issue, read "The Hidden Threat of HOA Dues: Why Delinquent HOA Accounts are a Threat to Investor ROI and First Mortgage Lien Positions" at http://marketing.housingwire.com/acton/attachment/4321/f-00d2/1/-/-/-/-/Sperlonga%20 -%202014%20-%20HOA%20lien%20threat.pdf.)

If the HOA forecloses in a super lien state, it may, in some cases, eliminate the first mortgage. For example, in Nevada, the supreme court has ruled that an HOA super lien can extinguish a first deed of trust in a foreclosure. Consequently, when a lender is notified that a foreclosure has been initiated by the HOA for unpaid assessments in a super lien state, in most cases, the lender pays off the super lien amount to preserve its position as the first lien holder. When the first mortgage holder forecloses in a super lien state, the HOA is repaid first up to the allowable amount of the super lien, which is commonly a certain number of months of overdue assessments. Generally, if the first mortgage holder forecloses, but it is not a super lien state, the HOA assessment lien gets extinguished in the foreclosure (making special assessments necessary to make up for lost dues).

Mitigating Future Risk of Nonpayment of HOA Dues and Assessments

As a result of increased legislation and an understandable concern over losing their investment, in April 2012, Fannie Mae announced (and HUD quickly followed) that servicers are now required to protect the integrity of their mortgage lien by proactively resolving HOA delinquencies that could result in endangerment to their first mortgage positions. (Read the full announcement at www.fanniemae.com/content/announcement/svc1205.pdf.) Servicers are instructed to advance funds when they are notified by an HOA that the borrower is sixty days delinquent in the payment of assessments or charges levied by the association if such a payment is necessary to protect the priority of Fannie Mae's mortgage lien. The GSE will provide for reimbursement to the servicer for up to six months of such advances in super lien states. Additionally, in cases of foreclosure or acceptance of a deed-in-lieu of foreclosure, Fannie also requires servicers to ensure that any priority liens for delinquent HOA dues and assessments on acquired properties are cleared immediately, no later than thirty days after acquisition. Clearing the priority liens within this time frame will ensure that Fannie Mae's lien position is preserved and costly delays are avoided when selling the property.

As to whether servicers are equipped to monitor HOA delinquencies, I think we all understand that it is difficult to track what cannot be seen, and its going to take some time for them to build effective systems or to partner with third-party service providers that can streamline the process. While the GSEs know there is currently no connection between HOAs and mortgage servicers, it's tasking the industry to find a way. It's quite possible that a servicer completely misses the HOA problem and the lender loses the property. If the servicer allows this to happen, Fannie has threatened that the servicer will not only incur a penalty, but may be required to buy the entire loan. While improved communications between loan servicers and HOAs is welcome, an increase in homeowner participation in associations, and the resulting improvements in the financial health of projects all around the country, is even more vital.

13 Homeowners Insurance Requirements

When you take out a loan to buy or refinance your home, the lender will require insurance to protect the dwelling. If you custom build a home, you will need to have special coverage during the construction period known as builder's risk. There are many variations to requirements of insurance coverage by property type, ownership and location. Lenders usually follow GSE guidelines in determining basic requirements. When there is a lapse of coverage on an existing loan, the servicer of your mortgage will force place an insurance policy with any company it chooses for required protections.

SOMETIMES, HOMEOWNERS ELECT to cancel insurance policies once their mortgage has been paid off. But if you do this, you need to consider whether you have the financial resources to repair or replace your home and its contents in the event of a fire or major damage. This happens most often with homes that are inherited. The beneficiaries often fail to recognize the value in insurance coverage when they themselves don't have the financial resources to repair damages. Even mini-disasters like lightning strikes, theft or vandalism, or heating, plumbing, or other home system failures can create significant financial hardships. If someone is injured at your home or if you are sued for causing injury or damage to someone else's property in a situation that doesn't involve a motor vehicle—a home, condo, or renters policy can provide coverage for damages and defense costs. Even if you're not found liable, the attorney's fees alone could be financially devastating unless you have protection.

There are many different kinds of homeowners insurance that cover varying perils. Deciding which one is best for you can be confusing if you don't understand the insurance designations. Each type of homeowners insurance has a numerical designation that indicates its purpose. Work with your lender and your insurance agent to learn which policy your home needs. Here is a list of the basic types of homeowners insurance and their designations:

Basic named perils policy (HO1): This is the basic policy for homeowners. It covers the cost of replacement of the house, its contents, and any outbuildings. The HO1 policy only protects you from ten specific perils: fire and lightning, windstorm or hail, explosion, riot or civil commotion, aircraft, vehicles (unless it is caused by the insured), smoke, vandalism or malicious mischief, theft (may have limits), and volcanic eruption. If something else happens to your home it will not be covered.

Broad named perils policy (HO2): This is a more comprehensive policy in terms of coverage. In addition to the basic causes of damage or destruction covered in an HO1 policy, damage from the following pearls are also covered: falling objects; weight of ice, snow, or sleet;

accidental discharge or overflow of water or steam; sudden and accidental tearing apart, cracking, burning, or bulging; freezing; and sudden and accidental damage from artificially generated electric current.

Basic open perils policy (HO3): This is the most common type of home insurance policy. The contents of your home are covered for the same sixteen perils that are in the HO1 and HO2 policies and are covered at market value unless you get replacement cost for an extra charge. This policy covers your dwelling for anything and everything that could possibly happen to it other than explicitly excluded events, while your contents are covered for all sixteen perils covered in the HO2 policy. The exclusions to the dwelling protection are: earth movement; ordinance or law (some coverage may be provided in your policy); water damage (sudden and accidental water damage is automatically included); power failure; neglect; war; nuclear hazard; intentional loss; government action; collapse (some coverage may be provided in your policy); mold, fungus, or wet rot (some coverage may be provided in your policy); birds, vermin, rodents, and insects; typical wear and tear; and deterioration. If something happens to your home that is not specifically listed as one of the exclusions, then it should be covered under your HO3 policy.

As you can see from the third exclusion above, water damage is normally excluded from HO3 policies. However, there are four types of water damage that can be added as endorsements to your policy. Note that most agents will automatically include an endorsement for sudden and accidental discharge of water coverage but not for the others.

- Sudden and accidental discharge of water: This is protection from water damage resulting from a pipe bursting.
- Water backup: This is protection from water damage resulting from a backup in a sewer system that causes water to pour out of your toilets and sinks into the house.
- Foundation coverage: This is protection to your foundation if it has to be destroyed in order to fix a water problem in or under the foundation. This is typically only an important coverage if you have to tear up the foundation to get to pipes. A good example of this is a slab foundation.
- Continual and repeated seepage: This is protection from water damage resulting from a slow leak in the home, which damages the home over time.

Renters policy (H04): If you rent, your landlord's policy will not cover your personal property. If you're renting in an apartment building, the insurance policy that covers the building where you live does not cover your possessions inside the dwelling. A renter or tenant's policy covers your personal property, liability, and medical payments to others, and includes no coverage for the dwelling, other structures, or loss of use. It covers the same perils in the HO1 and HO2 policy. All of the contents are covered at replacement cost. An aside, while not a criterion that is considered in mortgage underwriting, it has been identified that person's who rent who have adapted the responsible personal financial habit of maintaining renter's insurance, have an increased probability of becoming future homeowner's.

Full open perils (HO5): This is a very comprehensive policy. This policy covers almost anything that can happen to your home unless it is excluded by the policy. All contents of the home are covered at market value for their replacement cost, even clothing and appliances. The main difference is the contents are covered the same as the dwelling not just the sixteen perils like the HO3 policy. However, the HO5 policy is only available to newer homes built in the past thirty years or completely renovated within the past forty years.

Walls in/unit owners (HO6): A condo association's master policy generally covers only from the exterior walls out and not any of your personal property. A walls in/unit owner policy is specifically designed for owners of condominiums or cooperatives and covers certain semi-permanent structures, such as carpeting, wallpaper, built-in appliances, and kitchen cabinets, but it does not cover the structure itself or common areas. Most HO6 policies also cover living expenses if you are forced to temporarily vacate the building due to damage of some kind, and it will also cover you if someone is injured in your condo unit.

Basic market value policy (HO8): This policy is for very old homes that are too old to get regular homeowners insurance coverage. This policy is generally used on historic homes that have not been renovated. The home and its contents are covered as if they were under the same perils as the HO1 policy. The bad thing about this policy is that the home is covered for actual cash value and not the standard replacement value that most policies offer.

Classifications of Coverage

In each policy type listed above, there are different classifications of coverage identified below:

Coverage A—dwelling: Covers the value of the dwelling itself, but does not include the land. Typically, a coinsurance clause states that as long as the dwelling is insured to 80 percent of actual value, losses will be adjusted at replacement cost, up to the policy limits. This is in place to give a buffer against inflation. HO4 (renters insurance) typically has no coverage A, although it has additional coverage for improvements.

Coverage B—other structures: Covers other structures around the property that are not used for business, except as a private garage. Typically limited at 10 percent to 20 percent of coverage A, with additional amounts available by endorsement.

Coverage C—personal property: Covers personal property, with limits for the theft and loss of particular classes of items such as money and coins. Typically 50 to 70 percent of the amount of coverage A is required for contents, which means that sometimes, you may be paying much more insurance than is necessary. There are two types of policies for personal property: cash value policy and replacement cost policy. Cash value policy will pay the cost to replace belongings, minus depreciation. Replacement cost policy will reimburse for the current full cost of replacing belongings.

Coverage D—loss of use/additional living expenses: Covers additional living expenses as when you must vacate the property for repairing damage or for reimbursement of fair rental value resulting in loss of use of insured property due to covered damages.

Additional coverage: Covers a variety of expenses such as debris removal, reasonable repairs, damage to trees and shrubs for certain named perils (excluding the most common causes of damage, wind, and ice), fire department charges, removal of property, credit card/identity theft charges, loss assessment, collapse, landlord's furnishing, and some building additions.

Exclusions: In an open perils policy, specific exclusions will be stated in this section. These generally include earth movement, water damage, power failure, neglect, war, nuclear hazard, septic tank backup expenses, intentional loss, and concurrent causation. The concurrent causation exclusion excludes losses where both a covered and an excluded loss occur. In addition, the exclusion for building ordinance can mean that increased expenses due to local ordinances may not be covered. Mold damage is usually excluded, as it is typically not covered if the water damage occurs over a period of time, such as through a leaky pipe.

Floods: Flood damage is typically excluded under standard homeowners and renters insurance policies. Flood coverage, however, is available in the form of a separate policy both from the National Flood Insurance Program (NFIP) and from a few private insurers.

Coverage E—personal liability: Covers damages that the insured is legally liable for and provides a legal defense at the insurer's own expense. About a third of the losses for this coverage are from dog bites.

Coverage F—medical payments to others: Reasonable charges for medical expenses for events resulting in bodily injury occurring on the insured location, caused by activities of the insured or by an animal owned by or in the care of an insured. These may include charges for medical, surgical, x-ray, dental, ambulance, hospital, professional nursing, prosthetic devices, and funeral services. This coverage does not apply to you or regular residents of your household except residence employees.

Commonly Added Riders

Riders are special additions to the policy provisions that offer benefits not found in the original contract, or that make adjustments to it. These special provisions are, in effect, attached to the policy. Riders are not necessarily found in all policies but when they are, an extra premium may be charged because they provide the policyowner with some kind of additional benefit. Below is a sampling of some of the most common riders that can be added to or purchased along with a Homeowners insurance policy.

Windstorm: Windstorm protects against damages resulting from windstorms such as hurricanes and tornadoes.

Flood: Most homeowners are four times more likely to sustain a loss from a flood than a fire. While a lender will only require flood coverage if your property is located in a high risk area as designated by FEMA, careful consideration should be given to whether you have the financial resources to cover flood damage if your policy excludes coverage.

A Word of Caution: There exist many riders that can be added to your homeowners insurance policy. Be mindful that each carries additional monthly costs to your total housing expense. When calculating your debt-to-income ratio, your lender will include the totality of charges for insurance costs—regardless if the coverage provided is necessary to the lender or not. Examples of additional riders that drive up your costs and are not necessary to the lender may include: scheduled personal property (e.g. itemized jewelry, coins, etc), computer, home business, additional theft, sewer and drains backup, watercraft and recreational vehicle, and worker's compensation, among others.

Requirements for Condominiums and Cooperatives

The homeowner association master policy usually covers most lender requirements. Walls in coverage is typically not covered. For this, the unit owner will be required to purchase a separate HO6 policy (as described above). The master insurance policy for the building usually includes coverage for the following:

- Fidelity coverage in an amount to equal a minimum of one-month maintenance income plus all cash funds available.
- Liability coverage of a minimum amount of $1,000,000 is required. If the building contains an elevator, minimum coverage required is $3,000,000.
- Hazard coverage at 100 percent replacement cost (the project must be named as the insured).
- Flood coverage is required on each building within the project that is in a flood zone with 100 percent replacement cost or the National Flood Insurance Program (NFIP) maximum. The project must be named as the insured and a maximum deductible is $25,000.
- Building law and ordinance coverage to increases in the cost of construction, repair, or demolition of the project or other structures on the premises that result from enforcement of ordinances, laws, or building codes.
- Directors and officers liability coverage protects a director, officer, or property manager who participates in the planning, directing, and reviewing of organizational activities from risk for being named in lawsuits related to alleged breaches of duty, errors in

judgment, and other situations that caused a third party to suffer a financial loss. Without a directors and officers policy in place, individuals performing these roles have unprotected liability exposures that carry serious financial risks.

Requirements for Planned Unit Developments

Properties located within planned unit developments will carry individual homeowner insurance policies as listed above and the lender will also require evidence from the property manager that coverage is in place for all common areas within the project.

14 Standard Forms and Sample Letters of Verification

This chapter discusses some typical forms and letters almost every borrower will encounter, each having its own nuances that can present delays in the processing of your loan application. You'll learn their proper completion and the significance of timely delivery.

4506-T

IRS FORM 4506-T is included as part of your mortgage disclosure set and is a request from you to the IRS to release transcripts to your lender, or to an authorized third party vendor for the lender, of your filed and processed federal income tax returns or other information on record for specified financial years or periods. The form is completed and signed by you, the taxpayer. In cases of jointly filed federal income tax returns, either spouse may sign the form (divorced people do not need to obtain the signature of an ex-spouse to release the tax information). In case of corporations, an authorized officer of the company may sign. The IRS will issue the transcripts to the party authorized by you on this form.

Typically, your lender will pre-fill Form 4506-T with the information of the third party vendor it uses to obtain your tax transcripts. As this form is also pre-filled at loan application with the version of the name you provided on the loan application and will automatically list your current mailing address, don't be surprised if you are asked to sign several versions of this same form with differing addresses or versions of your name usage to match information as listed on filed federal income tax returns.

IRS Form 4506-T allows the lender to independently verify your income and determine if the information on the loan application and the documentation is consistent with the tax returns. This review will uncover any misrepresentation on the loan application or supporting documentation. Therefore, the tax information obtained from the use of IRS Form 4506-T serves multiple purposes for the lender including:

- Fraud prevention: The transcripts of the tax returns can be used to proactively detect and prevent any fraud on the mortgage application.
- Identify a difference between tax returns and financial statements: It is possible that the taxable income can be different on the federal income tax return from the income reported on financial statements. This difference is generally due to differences between tax laws and generally accepted accounting principles. However, the

difference may reveal that the financial statements submitted are misleading. A person is more likely to misrepresent facts on a financial statement than on a tax return submitted to the government.

- Quality control and compliance with investor guidelines: The tax returns can be used as part of quality control at the time of loan application, prior to loan closing, or after the loan has closed. When this is executed depends on the lender's policies.
- Filing status: The tax returns can be reviewed to ensure you have filed the tax returns on time or to confirm that you're still on extension.
- Employment status: The employment status, such as self-employed or W-2 employee, can be confirmed.
- Income documentation: Infrequently, some lenders may use the IRS Form 4506-T to obtain tax transcripts and use those instead of requesting and obtaining a copy of the full tax return from you.

Note: In order for the IRS to release the information requested, Form 4506-T must be an identical match to the information it has recorded for you under the name and address listed on the filed federal income tax return and W-2 form.

Tip: To prevent delays in the processing of your loan, take a moment to look at your loan documentation and request that you are provided several pre-filled forms to match the address and name variations exactly as they appear on your filed IRS federal income tax returns and W-2 forms. This can cause major delays in processing loan request.

Tip: Also note that transcripts for amended tax returns are not provided unless the box marked section 6B Account Transcript or 6C Record of Account is checked. If you have filed amended tax returns, be sure to point this out to your loan officer at application so that IRS Form 4506-T can be properly executed. In a rushed processing environment, the lender may not notice that the return you provided says amended, and when it receives the tax transcript for the original filed return, it may make the presumption of fraud.

When tax returns are submitted to the IRS, the IRS estimates processing times between ten to forty-five days in order for the information on the tax return submitted to be made available through a request by Form 4506-T. Delays in underwriting and closing can occur when final loan approval is dependent on confirmation of filed federal income tax returns.

Through the execution of Form 4506-T, the IRS provides your lender with the following documents, as requested:

- Transcripts for Form 1040 series: U.S. Individual Income Tax Return. Records are available for up to four years.
- Transcripts for Form 1065: U.S. Return of Partnership Income. Records are available for up to four years.
- Transcripts for Form 1120, 1120A, 1120H, 1120L, and 1120S: U.S. Corporation Income Tax Return. Records are available for up to four years.
- Account transcript: Provides current status of the taxpayer including payments, penalty assessments, and adjustments.
- Record of account: Provides combination of line item information and later adjustments to the account. Records are available for up to four years.
- Verification of nonfiling of tax returns. Available for any year.
- Transcripts for Form W-2: Wage & Tax Statement. Records are available for up to ten years.
- Transcripts for Form 1099 series: Dividends, Interest, Miscellaneous Income, Government Payments, Cancellation of Debt, etc. Records are available for up to ten years.
- Transcripts for Form 1098 series: Mortgage Interest, Student Loan Interest, and Tuition Statements. Records are available for up to ten years.
- Transcripts for Form 5498 series: IRA Contribution Information. Records are available for up to ten years.

SSA-89

Form SSA-89 is an authorization form for the Social Security Administration (SSA) to release Social Security number (SSN) data to the lender (or its delegated third party) and is used to verify if the name and the SSN combination match the data in the SSA's records. The lender uses SSA-89 to prevent identity fraud. Although execution of this form is not mandated by federal law and is not a required disclosure, many lenders will use this verification for quality control purposes. The lender will provide a pre-printed form where it has entered the information for the vendor it uses and who you are authorizing to handle the verification process for the lender.

It is critical that Form SSA-89 is completed with your name matching exactly as it appears on your Social Security card. Otherwise, it will be returned, no match found/unable to verify, and your loan request will be escalated for possible fraud and you may experience tighter lending standards, closing delays, or even worse, loan denials for preventable reasons. Therefore, please pull out your Social Security card to see if the name listed matches how you want your name to appear on the loan application and title documents. If it doesn't, be sure to point this out to your lender and have them provide you with the SSA-89 consent form and request that they execute the form as quickly as possible.

How It Works

Upon receipt of the completed Form SSA-89, verification will be requested by using the SSA's Consent Based Social Security Number Verification Service (CBSV). SSA matches the SSN, name, date of birth, and gender code, if available. Each SSN and name combination submitted to SSA is returned with either a yes or no indicating an exact match. If applicable, SSA will report a death indicator when their records reflect that the SSN holder is deceased. There are only two very important things you need to be concerned with on the form:

1. Complete all personal details: Complete the name, date of birth, SSN, address, and personal phone. Be absolutely certain you have entered your name exactly as it is registered under the records of the Social Security Administration.
2. Signature and date: Sign and date the form. An undated form will not be processed.

Tip: If your Social Security number was issued prior to June 2011, be sure to request that this form is executed at loan application. Review the "Social Security Randomization" section in chapter 11 for further details on systemic challenges that may inadvertently disqualify you or subject you to tighter lending standards.

Notice of Incomplete Application (NOIA)

If your lender has not received critical documents to render a loan decision within thirty days of the date of loan application, it will send you a written notice of incompleteness. Once this letter is printed, most lenders will halt all activities on your loan file until the requested documentation is received. If the requested documentation is not received within the time constraints of required loan decision-making as dictated by federal law under Regulation B, your loan file may be either withdrawn or denied by the lender without any further contact. As a withdrawal is not a denial, it is not recorded as such under Home Mortgage Disclosure Act statistics. Application fees are generally not refunded when a loan file is withdrawn due to incompleteness. The NOIA letter will specify the following information:

*   Information/documentation being requested
*   Due date the information must be received by the lender
*   A disclosure that the lender may deny the application in the event of nonreceipt of information by the due date

Tip: If you receive a NOIA notification, you should respond immediately by providing the missing information or documentation well before the due date. Don't put this off. You may send in one thing thinking that it will satisfy the request, but the lender actually needs something completely different. To avoid delays, pick up the phone and contact your lender to confirm what exactly it is they need and ask why they need it. This is not because it could be a point for you to argue, but instead so you know the purpose of the request—sometimes we ask for an item thinking that it will provide what we are looking for, but it won't. This confusion happens often when money is moved between bank accounts, and we need to trace the source.

Written Verifications

Lenders will verify your loan data through third-party service providers. While the GSEs offer guidance on who it deems an acceptable source, each lender's compliance and credit policy makers determine what sources of verification are acceptable to them. For example, some lenders will allow a verification of deposit form provided by a depository institution, while other lenders require actual account statements. This interpretation is what will potentially disqualify an applicant from approval with one lender yet gain approval from another lender with no misrepresentation.

Blanket Authorization Form

Rather than having you sign multiple forms, the lender may have you sign a borrower's signature authorization form, which gives the lender blanket authorization to request the information it needs to evaluate your creditworthiness. When the lender uses this type of blanket authorization, it will attach a copy of the authorization form to each form it sends out (i.e., verification of deposit, employment, rent, or mortgage). The lender must request this information directly from the depository institution, employer, landlord, or private mortgage holder. The completed form(s) must be signed and dated, and must be sent directly from the verifying entity.

Verification of Depository Assets

Funds or money held in a checking, savings, money market, certificate of deposit, or other depository accounts may be used for the down payment, closing costs, and financial reserves as long as they can be verified and are liquid. Liquidity refers to whether or not the funds are considered cash or easily convertible into cash. For example, if you own stocks and you plan to use funds from the sale of stocks for the transaction, a lender may only give you credit for 60 to 70 percent of the current market value of those stocks (depending on GSE guidance). Only when you have sold the stock and converted it to cash can a lender use the full 100 percent value of the liquidated stock. That said, do not liquidate stocks that you have no intention of using as available funds for the real estate transaction.

Unverified funds are not acceptable for the down payment or closing costs unless they satisfy the GSE requirements for borrowed funds. The lender will investigate any indications of borrowed funds. These must be identified separately on the loan application. The lender can generally use any of the following types of documentation to verify that you have sufficient funds for closing, down payment, and financial reserves:

- Verification of Deposit, Form 1006 or Form 1006(S): The information must be requested directly from the depository institution, and the complete, signed, and dated document must be sent directly from the depository institution. You can have no handling of this document. That said, while the lender initiates the request, many bank representatives will not release information to a third party service provider without your specific instructions to allow it. Therefore, if your lender will request a written Verification of Deposit be sure to alert your personal banker and provide your prior approval so that the request can be expedited.

- Copies of bank statements or investment portfolio statements. As a standard measurement, your lender will generally request statements that cover account activity for the most recent two-month period (or, if account information is reported on a quarterly basis, the most recent quarter). The statements must:
  o Clearly identify you as the account holder
  o Include the account number
  o Include the time period covered by the statement
  o Include all deposit and withdrawal transactions (for depository accounts)
  o Include all purchase and sale transactions (for financial portfolio accounts)
  o Include the ending account balance

If the lender is the holder of your depository account, it may produce a printout or other alternative verification of the asset(s) directly from its system. The printout or alternative verification is acceptable as long as all required data (above listed) is supplied and documented.

Date of Information

If the latest bank statement is issued more than forty-five days earlier than the date of the loan application, the lender may ask you to provide a more recent, supplemental, bank-generated transaction history that shows the account number, balance, and date. The transaction history may be computer-generated forms, including online account or portfolio statements downloaded from the Internet. Any documents that are faxed to the lender or downloaded from the Internet must clearly identify the name of the depository or investment institution and the source of information—for example, a listing of the Internet or fax banner at the top of the document.

Sourcing Large Deposits

When the lender reviews the bank statements provided, and it identifies deposits that are inconsistent with payroll income, you will need to provide a signed and dated letter of explanation along with the supporting documentation to verify the source of all nonpayroll deposits for each statement provided. The source identifies where you got the money.

Note: If the source of a large deposit is readily identifiable on the account statement, such as a direct deposit from an employer (payroll), the Social Security Administration, or IRS or state income tax refund, the lender does not need to obtain further explanation or documentation. However, if the source of the deposit is printed on the statement, but the lender still has questions as to whether the funds may have been borrowed, the lender may request additional documentation.

Bank Reference Letter in Place of a Verification of Deposit Form

A lender may choose to send Fannie Mae Form 1006 Verification of Deposit to verify amounts held in U.S. or foreign bank accounts as disclosed on your loan application or in place of obtaining bank statements. By signing the required borrower's signature authorization form, the lender does not need to get an additional signature from you to verify any information on your loan. When assets are held in overseas accounts and the banking officer is unable to understand English and, therefore, cannot complete this form, a lender will instead accept a bank reference letter. To expedite this process, you may want to request an original signed and dated letter from your banker typed on depository institution letterhead that includes the following:

1. Date of completion
2. Name of account holder
3. Type of account
4. Date opened
5. Account number (some depository institutions may have privacy laws that prevent them from listing the full account number)
6. Current balance (to list currency type)
7. Average balance maintained for the preceding sixty days
8. Contact information for the bank officer completing the form (name, title, telephone, email, and street address)
9. Bank stamp by signature line

Letters written in a foreign language will be translated by your lender's choice of translation service and these costs will be relayed to you. If the depository institution omits any of the above, the reference letter may not be usable by the lender, and your lender won't know that something is missing until after it receives the translated document. Keep in mind that when dealing with foreign language documents, the cost of translations can be exorbitant if resubmissions are required, and time delays may prevent you from closing by contract date.

Verification of Employment

At loan application, a lender may require the completion of a verification of employment form. This is especially required when an applicant discloses overtime or bonus income for qualification purposes. This is the form that is most often completed incorrectly, not because your employer wants to misrepresent your income, but because they simply do not know how to complete it or understand the importance of breaking compensation into each category. Additionally, a verbal verification of employment/self-employment is required on all loans no more than ten days prior to loan closing. As mentioned in "Cleared for Closing, But Are You Really?" in chapter 9, this is where you could run into trouble if income or employment information has significantly changed during the processing of your loan request.

Verification of Employment to Confirm Overtime, Bonus, Salary, and Commissions

When a lender is considering variable income, it needs to confirm the breakdown of the receipt of this income for the preceding two year period and will send the standard written verification of employment form (Fannie Mae form 1005) to your employer. All too often, a small business owner incorrectly completes this form. Of special significance on this form are sections 12A, 12B and 14.

Section 12A asks for the measure of your base income. Is the employee being paid a salary? An hourly wage? Weekly or biweekly? Your employer must identify the measure and list the amount. Section 12B asks for the year-to-date and previous year's breakdown of total income. How much of the employee's total income was base pay? Overtime? Commissions? Bonus? On the final line in this section, the dollar amount listed should match the employee's year-to-date income and the prior year's income as reported on their W-2. Section 14 asks if the employer anticipates the borrower will have the opportunity to earn overtime or bonus income in the future. If these sections are not accurately completed, the lender will not be able to use the variable income.

Verbal Verification of Employment for Employed Borrowers

If you work at a small business where anyone can answer the main line, be sure to alert the staff that your lender will be calling to verify employment so that they can be promptly directed to the responsible party. Often, people go by a nickname or they'll use their middle name instead of their given name and when the loan processor calls to verify employment for let's say William Todd Smith, and she asks to speak with someone who can verify William's employment, the receptionist will say, "I'm sorry we don't have anyone here by that name." Poor Todd in accounting just got his loan red-flagged and sent to QC for an all-out investigation.

The loan processor will independently verify through a third party source the existence of the employer (e.g., Yellow Pages, Google, website for State Business Licensing) and when they call your employer, they will ask for the following:

1. Your hire date
2. Your job title/position
3. Your current employment status (full-time, part-time, inactive)
4. Details of the individual who verified employment to include full name, job title, and telephone number

Verbal Verification of Employment for Self-Employed Borrowers

A lender may require an active business license to affirm continuity of business, or it may accept from your certified public accountant (CPA) a letter to independently verify your continued self-employment status. The CPA letter (better known in the accounting industry as a comfort letter) for verification of self-employment is prepared by your tax preparer and provides affirmation that they prepared your most recent income tax return and that you currently remain self-employed. In this regard, the CPA cannot be asked to make assurances about a business's future performances or an individual's future earnings capacity as this is beyond the scope of a comfort letter. The lender will usually require that the letter be delivered in hard copy format (no emails), on the CPA's letterhead, and include:

1. Your name
2. Your business name, address, and phone number
3. Nature of the business
4. Number of years you have been in this business
5. Your percentage of ownership
6. Time since the CPA has prepared your tax returns
7. Confirmation that you reviewed the tax returns prior to the CPA filing them with the IRS
8. Signature of the CPA

Credit Reference Letter

When a U.S. credit report does not list at least four traditional credit accounts held for a minimum twenty-four month period, you will need to show your lender proof of credit history for other types of credit accounts to build a nontraditional credit history. These accounts can generally include utilities, gym memberships, daycare, tuition, auto insurance, health insurance, and things of that nature. For these accounts that are not reported to the credit bureaus, including foreign-opened credit accounts, a lender will generally accept a credit reference letter from the creditor to confirm account existence, terms of credit, and payment history to build your credit file.

You will need to request a reference letter from your creditor written on company letterhead, signed, and dated by an authorized representative of the creditor and with that person's contact information listed (name, title, telephone number, email address, street address). The letter should include the following:

1. Date account opened
2. Type of account (revolving or installment)
3. Name of account owner(s)
4. Terms of credit
5. Amount of credit offered
6. Current balance
7. Minimum required monthly payment
8. Current monthly payment
9. Twenty-four month payment history

Letter of Explanation

Any time a lender needs an explanation from you about anything in the file, you'll be asked to write your explanation in a signed and dated letter. This is so that the lender can document your explanation. With email and texting being today's preferred form of written communication, many borrowers feel uneasy having to write a formal letter. Often they'll say, "Can you just write it for me?" And the answer is, " While we physically can write it for you, ethically, we can't." It has to come from you to maintain the integrity of the loan file. So we'll do the next best thing. We'll send you a model letter of explanation listing the specific questions that you're being asked in the format that the lender needs. You can modify it to fit your responses, but the answers must be yours and it must be printed and contain your original signature. You can scan and email the signed letter or fax it to your lender. Either way, confirm they have received it and that it contains a thorough explanation.

Generally, most borrowers can expect to write at least two letters of explanation (LOX) in the mortgage process. The first will be the standard one that everyone must write. In this LOX, you will be asked to write an explanation of your relationship with addresses identified on your credit report and the result of any recent credit inquires. What we are really asking is:

a. Have you ever resided in this property? If so, list the dates. Do you have an ownership interest in this property?

b. What was the purpose of the credit inquiry? Did you open a new account? If so, attach a copy of the most recent billing statement.

The second LOX will likely have to do with your addressing any employment gaps, movement of money in bank accounts, payments that are made by third-parties, nonpayroll deposits into your bank account, or any other number of things that were reviewed as we moved through each section of the loan application. I've provided a model letter of explanation for you to download and modify at www.MortgageMattersBook.com.

15 Loan Servicing

Your loan servicer is the entity that handles the administrative functions of your loan from loan closing through loan payoff. This includes preparing and delivering monthly billing statements, collecting monthly mortgage payments, properly applying amounts to principal and interest and mortgage insurance (if any), maintaining records of payments and loan balances, following up on delinquencies, and, when an escrow account is set up, collecting for and paying property taxes and homeowners insurance. Here you'll find the typical queries that borrowers have during the servicing of their loan.

Acceleration Clause

ACCELERATION CLAUSES ARE terms in loan agreements that require you to pay off the loan immediately (usually within thirty days of notice). Home mortgages often include acceleration clauses that are triggered by failure to make regular payments, attempts to sell or transfer the property (without settlement of the debt), failure to pay property taxes, failure to maintain proper insurance on the property, or failure to make payments on a separate mortgage on the same property.

As an example, a lender may invoke an acceleration clause when you miss too many payments. This will require you to immediately pay the unpaid balance of the loan's principal, as well as any interest that accumulated before the lender invoked the acceleration clause. Few acceleration clauses will trigger automatically. Instead, after the conditions in the clause occur, the lender may choose whether or not to invoke the clause. Typically, the lender will work with you to cure the default within a specified period of time. Although in recent years foreclosed properties were commonplace, know that your lender is not interested in the business of selling real estate; a foreclosure costs the lender too much money. It would rather be profitable by collecting the interest payments on your loan.

Since death and taxes are certainties, know that the survivability of property title liens after the owner's death are also nearly certain. Property liens are attached to property titles, not to the owners of those properties. If you have a mortgage lien on your home and you die, that lien will live on. Once you die, though, your mortgage loan and any other debts you have become your estate's responsibility. This is where consideration should be given to securing adequate life insurance. With proper coverage, what you are doing is planning for the succession of your family unit. Succession planning is a term typically used to describe the transitioning of owners in a family-owned business. But the same principles need to be applied to the care of your surviving family once the head of household passes. How will the loss of your income affect their living?

The word estate tends to conjure images of palatial mansions, but it's just a way of saying, "the whole of one's possessions." Your home and its mortgage are two of your possessions. The acceleration clause written into most mortgage loans contains language allowing lenders to foreclose in the event of the borrower's deaths. But lenders don't want homes; they want money. Foreclosure is expensive for mortgage lenders, so your lender may negotiate with your estate, or the heirs inheriting your mortgaged home to determine a time period within which to pay off the mortgage.

Note: After you die, the estate or the heirs to your estate should continue making your mortgage payments while your home is awaiting distribution to the heirs to avoid any rush foreclosure process from your lender.

It's also common for inherited homes to pass to heirs with the mortgage still attached. When you die, your mortgage lender will expect your heirs to eventually do something about paying off your mortgage. In most cases, inheritors of mortgaged homes have several options. Generally speaking, relatives inheriting mortgaged homes will have the option of continuing to make payments on the mortgages as long as they also live in those homes. Nonrelatives inheriting mortgaged homes usually need to pay off or refinance those mortgages in their own names.

If you die without a will, the probate court handling your estate will decide what to do with your mortgaged home. If nobody inherits your mortgaged home, your lender will usually choose to foreclose on its loan.

Tip: Homeowners reading this, please, please, please: get your estate in order; you don't need to wait until you're ninety-two years old to do so. If you own property, prepare a will. And if no one has a copy of your will, what's the point of having it drawn up? I can't stress to you enough the importance of spelling out how you wish to have your assets distributed upon your death. Don't leave this matter to your children or to your extended family or to the whim of the courts. I've witnessed the greed of some, and it's a very painful process for the family members to have to take up arms against another family member. Often, one relative has more resources and education than the other and you may inadvertently be leaving one heir out in the cold because you didn't go through the simple process of defining your wishes.

Tip: When the obligor on a note dies and there are no other obligors on the note, any joint owner or heirs to the estate should immediately contact the lender's loan servicing department and begin discussions on options to transfer the obligation to the heir or to discuss timeframe allowed for sale of the asset and payment options.

Principal Reductions/Recasting

It isn't always necessary to refinance your current mortgage to obtain a lower monthly payment when all that you want to do is pay down your loan balance. Ask your loan servicer if they have an option to allow a payment recast which allows you to reduce your monthly payment based on making a significant reduction to the principal balance. Significant is relative to the loan size and a benefit is usually incurred in principal reductions of at least 10 percent of the existing loan amount. A servicer typically charges a fee somewhere around $250 for this service, but sometimes you can negotiate a reduction or waiver of this fee. With a recast, your original interest rate and mortgage term remain unchanged. Your monthly principal and interest payment is revised to reflect the reduced loan balance. No need to refinance.

Before exercising this option, check if your loan has a prepayment penalty. If it does, most are written so that the penalty applies only within the first three years when a principal reduction is made in excess of 20 percent in each of the three years. Additionally, most government loans (FHA, VA, or USDA) do not allow you to recast. For these, consider a streamline refinance into a new government product that allows for reduced documentation, or if market conditions are such that with the new loan amount you'll reach an 80 percent loan-to-value, look at your options to refinance into a conventional loan product. To be eligible for a government streamline refinance, your loan payments must have been timely for the twelve months preceding the date of application.

Escrow Analysis

Not all borrowers have an escrow account set up to collect property taxes and insurance. Some borrowers have an escrow account to collect only for property taxes. Some borrowers have an escrow account to collect only for insurance. Some borrowers have an escrow account to collect for only flood insurance and not for hazard or windstorm insurance. Any combination can exist depending on the lender's requirements and your wishes.

Federal law allows your lender to set up and collect a reserve amount to maintain a cushion in your escrow account for unexpected property tax or insurance premium increases and other costs. Each lender must comply with an annual analysis of your escrow account to adjust your monthly payments for the next year's billing expectations. Billing expectations are based on the current year's amount charged by the property tax assessor's office and any amounts billed to your lender for property insurance coverage.

The property tax assessor's office adjusts your property tax liability once per year, so your lender will typically analyze your escrow account in November and mail notification to you in December of their estimated changes to your monthly billing beginning in January. On this annual escrow analysis, there are a few things you need to identify.

a. Bills for which your lender will make disbursements from your escrow account (property taxes, hazard insurance, flood insurance, windstorm insurance, etc.).

b. The yearly amount needed to pay for each category included in your escrow account will be listed here separately (i.e., Property taxes, hazard insurance, flood insurance, windstorm insurance, etc.).

c. The projected carryover balance of your escrow account based on the assumption that from the time of that notice through the January billing statement, you will continue to make timely and full mortgage payments. We call this the beginning balance that will be used to calculate for next year's projections.

d. Determination of your lowest projected balance: You will find a monthly listing of the anticipated activity in your escrow account based on the due dates for every item your lender is being billed on your behalf. The lowest monthly escrow balance during the year projection is the low point.

e. The excess cushion collected by your lender is capped at 16.6 percent of the current year's projected lowest balance.

The Insurance Dance

I can't tell you how many times I've received notice from the servicer on my personal mortgage stating that I didn't have insurance on my property, and unless I provided evidence of coverage within thirty days, they would force place a new policy and bill me for it. I would think to myself, "These people are crazy. I have insurance, and they receive a copy of my policy from the agent every year upon renewal. They are a disaster!" Very frustrated, I'd go to my filing cabinet, pull out a copy of the most recent declarations page of my insurance policies, fax it to them, call them at the number they gave me on the letter, and confirm they received the fax and that the coverage listed was adequate. When I finally get someone on the phone to confirm they had received the fax, they tell me one of these two things:

a. Our mortgagee clause has changed and your agent needs to update the policy to reflect the current mortgagee clause.

b. Your loan number was changed and the insurance agent needs to reflect the current loan number on the policy.

Okay, so my lender changed their servicing address on my loan and they reassigned my loan number and now they are going to force place insurance on me because I haven't given them evidence of insurance. "Yes, Ms. Gutierrez, we mailed notice to you three months ago of the upcoming change. Did you not receive the notice?" There is silence on my end, because I don't want to say what I do with the billing statements when they come in. She continues, "Let's confirm the mailing address we have on file for you."

So she reads off my address and I say, "Yes, that's correct. But I didn't receive any notice." And of course, I'm not going to tell her that I don't open my billing statements because, after all, I'm trying to make the point that they are the idiots. I don't open my billing statements because I've set myself up on automatic payments from my checking account to the lender to be certain I never accidentally forget to pay the mortgage. I should know better than to not open my mortgage billing statements. After a few years of going through this insurance dance, I began opening my billing statement every month to look for anything of importance, and you should do the same. Here are some other tips.

Tip: If you have an adjustable rate mortgage, note that your monthly payment will be adjusted on an annual basis on the anniversary of your promissory note. Be sure to open your billing statements to account for the changes in your new monthly payments.

Tip: When you receive the annual notice of your insurance policy, review the declarations page to confirm the correct mortgagee clause and loan number for all mortgages and lines of credit tied to your property. All this must be included on the declarations page. If you've closed a lien against the property, be sure to have that mortgagee clause removed from your declarations page, as well, because in the case where you have a claim, you will be required to have all listed lenders sign off on claims reimbursement money, and if you've left a closed lien on the declarations page, you will be delayed in receiving the claim until you can evidence the closed lien was in fact satisfied.

Tip: If you find that the servicer has force placed insurance on your property (whether in error or legitimately), take immediate action. Know that the policy they've obtained carries a premium that is usually 25 to 40 percent higher than what you can obtain yourself. Get your evidence of insurance with the correct mortgagee clause and loan number to them as quickly as possible so that they cancel the force placed policy.

Tip: Pay special attention to late fees. If they've changed the billing amount of the monthly escrows and you've continued to send in the amount due for the lower escrows, they may be showing you as delinquent on your payment because you haven't paid the full amount due. Call the servicing desk, pay the amount due over the phone, and very nicely request that they please reverse the reporting of delinquency. Yelling and screaming isn't an effective method to get the servicer to do what you need them to do.

Tip: When shopping for homeowners insurance, be sure to ask your agent about any discounts you may be eligible to receive. Note that not every agent is eager to sell you a policy with a lower premium. If you live in an older home, ask about obtaining a four-point inspection or a mitigation report. If you've recently replaced your roof or installed hurricane shutters or impact windows, you're entitled to a discount. The agent will send someone to inspect the property, and then you can have the discount.

Tip: One note on flood insurance: Flood maps change every few years. Just because you didn't need flood insurance the last time you applied for a mortgage doesn't necessarily follow that you won't need it this time. To save money on the premium for flood insurance, be sure to provide your agent with the elevation certificate. The elevation certificate is provided by the surveyor with the property survey (not by your lender or the appraiser).

Tip: When you are in the process of refinancing, your loan processor will request that you update your declarations page to reflect the new lender's mortgagee clause and your new loan number. Don't initiate this process until you've received the initial loan approval. But be sure to do so immediately after, as it can take a few days to update the policy.

Recognizing Foreclosure Scams

If you are in danger of foreclosure, it is understandable that you're nervous about speaking to your loan servicer, but you must set aside your fears in favor of open and constant communication. Connect with your loan servicer as soon as you're having trouble paying the totality of your mortgage payment. Only your loan servicer can set you up on a short-term reduction of monthly mortgage expenses to accommodate for temporary setbacks. Keeping open lines of communication with your servicer is critical. Avoid any business, organization, or person who promises to prevent foreclosure or guarantees you a new mortgage. Some will make a promise to find mistakes in your loan documents that will force your lender to cancel or modify your loan. Know that lenders are not required to modify your loan so that it is more affordable to you simply because of mistakes in your loan documents.

Scammers will advise you to stop paying your mortgage company directly and begin making payments through them. Never do this. Additionally, some will advise you to stop speaking with your loan servicer because they'll be speaking on your behalf; this is a big mistake as some scammers will offer to handle financial arrangements for you and then pocket your payment instead of sending it to your mortgage company, and you may not find out until it's too late. Send your mortgage payments only to your loan servicer. If you fear that you are a victim of a foreclosure scam, contact the Consumer Financial Protection Bureau for guidance at

1-855-411-2372. If you are looking for help to prevent foreclosure and prefer to speak to a local authority, visit the Department of Housing and Urban Development's (HUD) website for a list of approved local counseling agencies (www.hud.gov/offices/hsg/sfh/hcc/hcs.cfm) or call 1-877-HUD-1515 (1-877-483-1515) for more information.

Mortgage Industry Challenges

In this section, you'll find key information on the issues that plague the mortgage industry and the efforts from all sides to move us forward. Links are provided to documented studies and I offer my experiences and personal opinions on polarizing topics. Some will agree with my views on the effects of certain policies and others won't. That's okay. Everyone has a voice and everyone should use it.

The Financial Crisis

Many Americans have very little understanding of the events that led to the financial crisis and of the decisions our government made to intervene with taxpayer dollars to bail out some of the players in the financial markets. Those of us on the mortgage frontlines began witnessing the events leading to the meltdown of the mortgage market at the beginning of 2007 and the world learned of it by September 2008. The failure of the mortgage giants—Fannie Mae and Freddie Mac—presented a systemic risk that government officials were compelled to act upon to avoid a collapse of the financial markets.

Understanding Systemic Risks and Systemic Events

Some feel that bigger isn't always necessarily better. As a result of banking deregulation in the early 1990s, and the subsequent consolidation of financial firms with traditional banks, the differences blurred between commercial banks, investment banks, insurance companies, and other types of financial intermediaries. A general concern with consolidation is how to minimize the threat of moral hazards.

As with many groups of interrelated or interdependent living things, a breakdown in the functioning of one thing can spread to many others and cause sufficient damage to harm the well being of the system as a whole, as when both of our kidneys fail and this corruption leads to the failure of all other organs in our bodies. The sudden failure of a very large financial or nonfinancial firm, or a large group of small firms, is a systemic risk that may lead to a catastrophic systemic event. A systemic event is a financial crisis that leads to a substantial reduction in total economic activity. That possibility was of concern when Enron was near bankruptcy in 2001. At that time, U.S. government officials and the private sector assessed the potential for Enron's failure to disrupt the markets for wholesale electricity and credit derivatives, and whether such a disruption would damage the economy as a whole.

A 2001 Group of Ten market study suggested that some nonbank financial institutions could be sources of and transmission mechanisms that lead to systemic events. (See the full "Consolidation in the Financial Sector" report at www.bis.org/publ/gten05.htm.) The study identified there was a relatively strong desire to limit the federal safety net to insured depository institutions, and our relative lack of experience with financial conglomerates raised a number of difficult issues that stemmed from the results of complex corporate structures from mergers and acquisitions. The group study raised concerns with the extension of supervision that should be applied to the various legal entities within a single organization and expressed a high level of concern with operational risks. It called for enhanced supervisory and regulatory actions that could support both operational risk and market discipline. Additionally, the study identified the probabilities of both an individual firm experiencing severe financial difficulties and of a systemic crisis could be lowered by setting risk-based capital standards, which tie more closely to economic risk. Capital standards refer to a firm's basic requirement of liquidity to offset potential losses.

The Mortgage Crisis

On September 7, 2008, Henry M. Paulson, Jr., Secretary of the U.S. Treasury, issued a statement announcing the conservatorship of the GSEs. (The full statement is available at www.treasury.gov/press-center/press-releases/Pages/hp1129.aspx.) Prior to the establishment of the conservatorships in 2008, investors assumed that the GSEs would meet their obligations to provide timely principal and interest payments with the financial support of the U.S. government, if necessary. And as a result of this implicit guarantee, the GSEs were generally able to price their fees only slightly higher than those charged by the U.S. Department of the Treasury on securities with similar maturities.

During the housing boom of 2004 through 2007, it was found that the Enterprises' guarantee fee rates were too low to cover the risks associated with their mortgage purchase and securitization practices that included higher risk mortgages. ("Estimated Impact of the Federal Reserve's Mortgage-Backed Securities Purchase Program" by Johannes Stroebel and John B. Taylor, issued in December 2009 by the National Bureau of Economic Research, gives more insight: www.nber.org/papers/w15626.) Ultimately, many of these higher risk mortgages defaulted and the Enterprises suffered $218 billion in losses. These losses exceeded their available capital of about $78 billion at the beginning of the conservatorship by nearly three times. Moreover, the financial models failed to predict the drastic decline in house prices caused by the collapse of the housing bubble. Starting in late 2007, the Enterprises began to increase their guarantee fees to better protect themselves against potential credit losses.

On November 25, 2008, the Board of Governors of the Federal Reserve System issued a press release announcing the mortgage-backed security (MBS) purchase program for quantitative easing and stated "this action is being taken to reduce the cost and increase the availability of credit for the purchase of houses, which in turn should support housing markets and foster improved conditions in financial markets more generally." (Full press release available at www.federalreserve.gov/newsevents/press/monetary/20081125b.htm.) On January 13, 2009, Ben S. Bernanke then Chairman of the Federal Reserve System gave a speech at the Stamp Lecture, London School of Economics, where he provided an explanation of the collapse of the financial markets, our government's plan of action for improving financial stability through what he referred to then as credit easing instead of quantitative easing, and laid out the government's exit strategy. (Read the speech at www.federalreserve.gov/newsevents/speech/bernanke20090113a.htm.)

By the fall of 2010, one of every eleven outstanding residential mortgage loans was at least one payment past due but not yet in foreclosure, and by the end of 2011 over one million homes were foreclosed upon (according to The Financial Crisis Inquiry Report: The Final Report of the National Commission on the Causes of the Financial and Economic Crisis in the United States, Including Dissenting Views, published by the U.S. Government and the Financial Crisis Inquiry Commission in May 2011. The full report is available at http://www.gpo.gov/fdsys/pkg/GPO-FCIC/pdf/GPO-FCIC.pdf). Many things contributed to the mortgage crisis of 2008, including, but not limited to:

- Ease of originator licensing
- Inadequate education of loan officers
- Inadequate systems to detect misrepresentation
- Inability to verify the validity of tax returns submitted
- Inability to detect the legitimacy of loan documents
- Loan products requiring no verification of income or assets
- Loan products sold in the secondary market without proper categorization and ratings

Of importance and seldom mentioned, is the effect of the introduction of credit scoring models and how this changed the trajectory of loan underwriting from a manual to an automated process. Credit scoring models may have provided a more automated way to analyze creditworthiness, but the benefits of this technology didn't necessarily decrease the relative costs. (See Group of Ten, Consolidation in the Financial Sector report from January 2001 at http://www.bis.org/publ/gten05.htm.) In 1995 in an effort to remove lender bias from the loan approval equation, Fannie and Freddie issued a recommendation for use of FICO scoring. But far too much weight was put on past credit performance as an indication of future credit performance, and investors began loosening their debt-to-income requirements or removing them altogether for borrowers who showed they maintained an excellent credit history. This gave rise to a group of mortgage products called stated income/stated asset (SISA) or no income/no asset (NINA).

For many years to come, very smart people will be monitoring the effects of government intervention to assess whether it was a success. If you're interested in learning more about the events that led to the mortgage crisis, the Mortgage Bankers Association recommends these books:

- Reckless Endangerment by Gretchen Morgenson
- All The Devils are Here by Joe Nocera and Bethany McLean
- The Weekend That Changed Wall Street by Maria Bartiromo

Governance

The mortgage industry must comply with several laws and is regulated by several federal and state agencies with overlapping oversight. Here's an idea of how many agencies are overseeing the mortgage industry: On October 22, 2014, I listened in on a Federal Interagency Fair Lending Hot Topics webinar offered by the Federal Reserve System and produced in conjunction with the quarterly newsletter Consumer Compliance Outlook. Speakers identified lenders' policies have potential to violate the Equal Credit Opportunity Act or present risk of a fair lending violation, such as discretionary policies without sufficient controls or monitoring to control fair lending risk, insufficient documentation for pricing and underwriting exceptions, and data inaccuracies that impair the institution's fair lending self-assessments. In attendance were representatives from Department of Justice, Consumer Financial Protection Bureau, Federal Deposit Insurance Corporation, Office of the Comptroller of the Currency, Federal Reserve Board, Department of Housing and Urban Development, and National Credit Union Administration—all of whom help oversee the industry.

A lender must comply with all applicable laws that address fair housing, fair lending, equal credit opportunity, truth in lending, wrongful discrimination, appraisals, real estate settlement procedures, borrower privacy, data security, escrow account administration, mortgage insurance cancellation, debt collection, credit reporting, electronic signatures or transactions, predatory lending, anti–money laundering, terrorist activity, ability to repay, state community and marital property, and the enforcement of any of the terms of a mortgage loan. Lenders must also confirm that no borrower or principal is listed on the Specially Designated National and Blocked Persons list that is maintained by the Office of Foreign Assets Control, and we are required to report instances of mortgage fraud and money laundering activities through the Banking Secrecy Act. In a recent survey conducted by Fannie Mae, it was reported that in just the short period from 2013 to 2014 alone, 72 percent of lenders believe that their compliance costs have increased by nearly 30 percent. (The full survey is available at www.fanniemae.com/resources/file/research/mlss/pdf/mlss-oct2014-presentation.pdf.)

The U.S. Department of Justice (DOJ) enforces the laws that prohibit discrimination. The Housing and Civil Enforcement Section of the DOJ works to protect our fundamental rights as individuals, including the right to access housing free from discrimination and the right to access credit on an equal basis, among others. The DOJ is authorized to bring federal lawsuits to enforce various civil rights statutes, including the Equal Credit Opportunity Act and the Fair Housing Act.

Title X of the Dodd-Frank Wall Street Reform and Consumer Protection Act, established the Consumer Financial Protection Bureau, an independent agency with the authority to implement and enforce federal consumer financial law as set forth in the Act, also including the Equal Credit Opportunity Act and the Home Mortgage Disclosure Act. The Act established an Office of Fair Lending and Equal Opportunity within the CFPB, which is authorized to conduct hearings and adjudication proceedings and commence civil actions to enforce federal consumer financial law. Its functions include overseeing and enforcing federal fair lending laws and coordinating these laws with other federal agencies to promote consistent, efficient, and effective enforcement of federal fair lending laws. Section 1052 of the Act authorizes the CFPB, where appropriate, to engage in joint investigations with, and requests for information from, the DOJ in matters relating to fair lending.

Both the CFPB and the DOJ are authorized to file civil actions to enforce ECOA. These agencies also have a shared interest in ensuring that enforcement of federal fair lending laws is consistent and not duplicative. The CFPB along with DOJ, HUD, and the FTC (Federal Trade Commission) conduct investigations on fair lending.

In March 2012, Assistant Attorney General Thomas E. Perez testified before the Senate Judiciary Committee at a Hearing on Fair Lending in Washington, D.C. where he shared the result of a complaint charged against Countrywide Financial Corporation alleging systemic discrimination over a four year period violating the Equal Credit Opportunity Act and the Fair Housing Act that impacted more than 200,000 African-American and Latino families. The $335 million settlement is the largest fair housing discrimination settlement in U.S. history. The complaint against Countrywide alleges that if you were African-American or Latino, you likely paid more for a Countrywide loan than a similarly qualified white borrower. In addition, if you were African-American or Latino, you were far more likely to be steered into an expensive and risky subprime loan than a similarly situated white borrower. Borrowers who were steered, paid on average tens of thousands more for their loans, and many subprime loans came with prepayment penalties that carried an increased risk of default and foreclosure.

Here's a section of his commentary: "One of the insidious aspects of these practices is African-American and Latino borrowers who walked into Countrywide's door had no idea they could have gotten a better deal. That is discrimination with a smile." (Read the full speech at www.justice. gov/crt/opa/pr/speeches/2012/crt-speech-120307.html.) It is wrong to place any borrower into a product that is more costly to the borrower yet monetarily more beneficial to a loan officer, and the Dodd-Frank Act prohibits this activity. But whose fault is it exactly that the borrower "had no idea they could have gotten a better deal"? The comment implies it is on the lender to educate the consumer on whether and where a better deal can be obtained. I've never heard of a salesperson at any retail outlet be required to tell a consumer that they can get the same product cheaper two stores down. Does our government offer the same direction to auto dealerships, retail vendors, supermarkets, bakers, restaurants, or lemonade stands? I don't think so.

With the CFPB, DOJ, HUD, and the FTC coming at lenders from all directions, loan officers, stakeholders, and everyone in between are paralyzed with fear from possibly violating the laws that are regulated by multiple agencies. I'm going to share with you some of the significant ways our fear translates to you.

Fair lending means providing consumers fair, equitable, and nondiscriminatory access to credit. The Fair Housing Act prohibits lenders from discriminating against borrowers applying for residential mortgage loans based on the protected classes. A lender cannot discourage you from applying for a mortgage or reject your application because of your race, color, religion, national origin, sex, marital status, age, or because you receive public assistance.

Title VIII of the Civil Rights Act of 1968, as amended in the Fair Housing Act, prohibits discrimination in the sale, rental, or financing of dwellings and in other housing-related activities on the basis of race, color, religion, sex, disability, familial status, or national origin. HUD has long interpreted the Act to prohibit practices with an unjustified discriminatory effect, regardless of whether there was intent to discriminate. (Read the full "Implementation of the Fair Housing Act's Discriminatory Effects Standard" at http://portal.hud.gov/hudportal/documents/huddoc?id=discriminatoryeffectrule.pdf.)

If a lender is charged with discrimination, it has the burden of proving that the challenged practice is necessary to achieve one or more substantial, legitimate, nondiscriminatory interests of the lender. A prohibited practice is failing or refusing to provide to any person information regarding the availability of loans or other financial assistance, application requirements, procedures or standards for the review and approval of loans or financial assistance, or providing information which is inaccurate or different from that provided others because of race, color, religion, sex, handicap, familial status, or national origin. That said, the law does not prohibit a loan officer from sharing with you the eligibility standards for a particular loan. And here is where things get sticky for loan officers: If we share those things with one borrower, we must take the time to share them with all borrowers. Therefore, many lending institutions have adapted a practice that prohibits the loan officer from having any conversation about loan qualification/ eligibility prior to a decision maker's review of a complete loan file, as telling the loan eligibility standards may discourage you from making application, and if you happen to belong to one of the protected classes, it may appear that the loan officer potentially violated fair lending. It is for this reason that some lenders require their loan officers to accept loan applications when they know that an applicant does not qualify.

The Enterprises publish their guidelines on their respective websites and access is not restricted to consumers. These agencies want both investors and borrowers to know the adhered to credit standards. But lenders don't publish their specific program guidelines to the general public. Let's put aside for a moment any actual discriminatory practices and discuss the impact of a lender's policy to neither publish nor discuss eligibility standards.

If during the loan application process a loan officer identifies a potential issue, and they don't want to risk being fined, fired, losing their license, or going to prison, the conversation will go something like this: "It appears that we may have an issue with XXXXX. I won't know for sure until an underwriter reviews the complete file." But guess what? They probably do know but aren't allowed by company policy to tell you. Is that fair? Is it fair of the lender to collect a nonrefundable application and appraisal fee when the loan officer knows that the file does not conform to program eligibility requirements, but you still want to apply? Here's the thing: Every file is unique. There may be a component of a file that may not meet the qualification standards for a particular loan program, but the review of the entirety of the file may identify compensating factors that indicate it would make sense to offer the loan. In the industry, we call this commonsense underwriting.

If you feel you have been discriminated against based on a protected class, gather all of your records and report the event through the CFPB hotline at 1-855-411-2372. But don't give up on the mortgage process. You may have been subjected to the bias of a particular lender, go find another lender.

Anti-Steering

One of the issues brought up in the mortgage crisis was the charge that loan officers steered applicants to loan products that were riskier due to higher incentive compensation to the loan officer (as we saw in the Countrywide settlement). The Dodd-Frank Act prohibits this activity under the Qualified Mortgage rule. To comply with anti-steering regulation, Fannie Mae published this statement in their December 16, 2014 Selling Guide:

"Borrowers should be offered the lowest-cost product with the lowest-risk loan terms for which they qualify. Lenders must not steer borrowers toward a particular loan program to qualify the borrower for a mortgage loan in an effort to misrepresent the borrower's true credit and/or income related qualifications. Lenders also must ensure that their loan originator compensation practices comply with the loan originator compensation provisions of the Truth in Lending Act and Regulation Z, and that loan originators comply with these requirements when presenting loan options to consumers."

An unintended consequence of this prohibition is that interpretation of that law indicates the lender, or the lender representative, cannot suggest a change in terms to the applicant's loan request. What this means for you is that although the lender may see a potential opportunity to structure the loan in a different way that will allow loan approval, the lender will not communicate this to you, unless you specifically ask about alternative options. This lender policy makes no sense to me now that the industry is mandated to compensate loan officers under a predetermined pay structure. If the loan officer isn't directing you to an appropriate loan program, then how does anyone expect you to know what programs you may qualify for, since no lender publishes credit criteria for the general public?

Underserved Borrowers

Through the granting of its charter from Congress, there is an implicit presumption that the very existence of the GSEs will improve the primary mortgage market. Although the GSEs do not originate loans, since 1994 the U.S. Department of Housing and Urban Development (HUD) has explicitly set goals that require the GSEs to make targeted purchases of mortgages to underserved borrowers. Many support the view that its activities have resulted in improved homeownership opportunities for minority and low-income families. (Find out more in "Have the Doors Opened Wider? Trends in Homeownership Rates by Race and Income" by Raphael Bostic and Brian J. Surette, published by the Journal of Real Estate Finance and Economics in 2001: www.researchgate.net/publication/5151650_Have_the_Doors_Opened_Wider_Trends_in_Homeownership_Rates_by_Race_and_Income.). N. Edward Coulson and Maurice Dalton have collected and studied data, and observed certain factors as creating a difference across ethnic groups to include actual income, the components of permanent income (e.g., education), wealth, age group, family structure, immigration status and location. (Read their full study, "Temporal and Ethnic Decompositions of Homeownership Rates: Synthetic Cohorts Across Five Censuses" at www.smeal.psu.edu/ires/documents/temp-ethnic-decomp.)

Minorities represent the growing share of first-time homebuyers and demographic forces in the period between now and 2025 will drive household growth of 11.6 to 13.2 million with minorities accounting for 76 percent of net household growth. Despite a growing presence in the homeownership market, minorities still struggle to obtain loans. In 2011 and 12, lending to

Hispanics was up just 7 percent and only 5 percent among African-Americans, in contrast with an increase of 15 percent or more in the volume of loans extended to both white, Asian, or other borrowers. In 2011 and 12, HMDA reported denial rates for conventional purchase mortgages among Hispanics at 25 percent and for blacks 40 percent. These figures are two to three times the denial rate among whites, and the recent HMDA data published for 2012 and 2013 shows no strides in improvement to shorten the gap.

The Harvard study "State of the Nation's Housing 2014" shows that the housing recovery has been far from even within metro areas, as declines in value are found to be three times more severe in minority neighborhoods. Over a quarter of mortgaged homeowners in both high-poverty and minority neighborhoods were underwater in 2013, nearly twice the amount of both white and low-poverty neighborhoods. Why have these homeowners not benefitted from the Home Affordable Refinance Program to reduce their overall monthly payments and utilize the benefit to either reduce their principal balances or invest in the maintenance or repair of their homes?

Perception Isn't Always Reality, But it Can Be a Deterrent

It's true that the vast majority of low-income, high-achieving students do not attend selective colleges (according to "The Missing 'One-Offs': The Hidden Supply of High-Achieving, Low-Income Students" by Caroline Hoxby and Christopher Avery: www.brookings.edu/~/media/projects/bpea/spring 202013/2013a_hoxby.pdf) Why is this? While the Ivy's have large endowments and offer needs-based financial aid, many low-income high achievers don't believe an Ivy League education is within their reach; therefore, they don't make application even when most colleges provide application fee waivers to eligible students. It is these same limiting beliefs that prevent minorities and low-income wage earners from applying for a home mortgage with a prime lender. Many believe they only have access to credit through the subprime channel. Predatory lenders abuse creditworthy borrowers by feeding upon these fears.

A 1994 Gallup Poll commissioned by the Mortgage Bankers Association of America examined racial and ethnic differences in borrowers' experiences, satisfaction levels, and knowledge of the mortgage application process. It also studied whether racial discrimination was a significant factor in why potentially qualified buyers had not attempted homeownership. Eighty-three percent of black homeowners and 60 percent of Hispanic and white homeowners said they think mortgage discrimination exists. Among those who had never applied for a mortgage, race or ethnic background was the most frequently cited reason for their believing they would be discriminated against. This was true among 53 percent of blacks, 50 percent of Hispanics, and 15 percent of whites.

We don't live in a perfect world. There will always be unscrupulous people who take advantage of the uneducated and misinformed. How can we empower the underserved with the tools to know whether they are creditworthy so they become unafraid to seek financing at prime interest rates? The first step toward defeating predatory lending is the financial education of the consumer. If you have an interested audience, reach out to a financial service professional in your local community and organize a course that defines responsible financial habits. As more minorities come to believe that lenders will deal with them fairly—and as the treatment they are accorded confirms those beliefs—the gap in homeownership rates that currently exists between ethnic groups should narrow substantially.

A Note on Character Assessments

It doesn't make sense that a loan officer would discriminate against any group of people as we are paid on closed loan volume. Why wouldn't we want to help a creditworthy applicant? We push the system for creditworthy applicants. As an originator, I have not had anyone say to me that a loan is being denied based on an applicant's age, gender, race, or sexuality. Discriminatory practices occur more subtly.

I'll share a story: I came across an underwriter who questioned how a recently divorced housewife receiving alimony and child support income would be able to manage a household on her own. I said, "Excuse me, I don't understand your question." Was he unaware of the guidelines? First, no applicant takes a test to measure their ability to manage a household; we have other credit criteria that we evaluate to determine creditworthiness. Facts are facts. By court order, the borrower would be receiving alimony payments for the next six years and child support for the next seven years. Bank statements verified that the borrower had already been receiving this income for the last twelve months. Agency guidelines state that if the lender is able to verify continuance of income for the next three years, it can be used for qualification. That's it.

But I was foolish. I wasn't arguing with an inexperienced underwriter who didn't know the guidelines, I was fighting someone who was discriminating against a single woman. At the mercy of their authority, I gently reminded the underwriter that there was no room for prejudice on this salable loan, as we had properly documented the file to meet agency guidelines. With further pushback and subsequent escalation to senior management, my recently divorced borrower closed on her new home thanks to her loan officer who wouldn't sit back and allow the personal bias of this particular underwriter get in the way. It is on all of us, at every level in mortgage lending, to name discriminatory practices when we see them.

I can identify one situation when I didn't go out of my way to push for an applicant. I was relatively new to the business and had a client with an unpaid judgment for child support in arrears exceeding $10,000 who worked for a small business who helped him hide his income. He had plenty of cash in an account he had set up in his father's name and he could have easily settled the claim but had chosen not to. I have zero compassion for loan applicants who fail to report their income to the IRS and then expect a lender to extend credit at the prime rate based on their unreported and unverifiable income, and you'll be hard pressed to find one underwriter who will approve a borrower who denies their children basic living needs. The logic here is this: If you can walk away from fulfilling the obligations to your own children, what compels you to think that a lender will extend you credit? The non-QM/subprime/hard equity market exists for people like this. There are investors who are willing to lend to these individuals, and the smarter investors will require larger down payments and higher interest rates to offset the risk of poor credit habits.

Discriminatory Practices

In conducting research for this book, I was very fortunate to have industry professionals speak freely, openly, and off the record about the challenges they face. As I've explored discriminatory practices and researched Home Mortgage Disclosure Act statistics as published by the CFPB on their website, I recognize that there is a disparity in lending among ethnicity and race. I acknowledge that we all have preconceived notions about groups of people, we are human after all, and we each struggle to make sense of where these notions come from and how to change our mindset about them. What we think about other people isn't always because they look different from us. Sometimes people discriminate against people who look just like them. In my role to expand the conversation and identify the practices that contribute to discrimination, I too have done some soul searching.

While I don't consider myself a racist, I know a few people who clearly are and don't recognize it within themselves, so it got me thinking. I'll share with you what I've learned about my own preconceived notions as I attempt to help others identify theirs. I am of Cuban descent. My parents emigrated from Cuba to the U.S. in 1962, a short time after the communist revolution. I was born in New York and have lived the majority of my life in south Florida. As I write this passage, it was announced this week that the U.S. has negotiated with the Castro regime to reopen diplomatic relations between our two countries after more than five decades of silence.

Here's a little lesson on history that provides an explanation of the nature of my own prejudices. Prior to the 1959 revolution, it was customary for Cubans to name their children after other family members or in honor of the Roman Catholic saint associated with the child's birthdate. After the revolution, Cuba declared itself officially as an atheist state and all kinds of religion were abolished (Cuba ceased being officially atheist in 1992). Without religion, official baptisms couldn't take place. To renounce their religion or avoid appearing to practice it, Cuban nationals began using monikers to name their children. The islanders born during the Cold War whose parents were inspired by the Russians, began creatively naming their children with a Y with names like Yuniesky, Yadinnis, Yilka, Yiliannes, or Yonersi, to name a few.

As names provide images of a country, when I meet a Cuban immigrant with an unusual moniker beginning with the letter Y, I make an automatic assumption that this person must be the child of a communist. While I was not directly affected by communism, my elders were and I have been indoctrinated about the many atrocities that occurred, which communism represents to the exiled community. While unprovoked by this new person that I just met whose name begins with the letter Y, I immediately think that they are someone I should fear. Because I am able to recognize this trigger in myself, I am able to contain my automatic assumption, and I don't respond with immediate fear, but its still there. By this method, we can insert any trigger and draw a conclusion of any demographic and this is how discriminatory practices occur. We need to recognize these triggers and fight our natural instincts to apply our misconceptions to those who have not shown that they are untrustworthy.

Buyback Risk/Compare Ratio

There are few terms that invoke more anxiety from a lender than the word repurchase. Buyback or repurchase risk endangers the loan originator's survival. A mortgage buyback is generally defined as the forced repurchase of a mortgage by the originating organization from the entity that currently holds the note (the investor). This risk applies to bank, nonbank, and broker organizations alike. Many mortgage brokers assume that their repurchase obligations are limited to instances of fraud or gross negligence. While many nonbanks believe their repurchase risk is significantly lessened when the creditor performs the underwriting on the loan.

As sellers of mortgage loans, the originating organizations sign contracts with the buyers of their loans (creditors or investors). When they enter a selling relationship with a creditor, the creditor may choose whether to grant the organization underwriting authority. When the creditor grants this authority, we say the originating organization has delegated underwriting authority. In the selling contracts, we find language that sometimes limits repurchase risk to instances of fraud or gross negligence, but many transfer most, if not all, of the credit risk to the originating organization regardless of which entity performed underwriting responsibilities. When the risk of loan default has been placed on the originator, every closed loan represents a contingent liability that may not expire for years.

When an originator agrees to deliver your loan to a creditor or an investor, it signs a loan sale agreement in which it recognizes instances where the investor has a right to demand a repurchase of your loan and seek indemnification remedies when it believes the originator breached or violated the representations and warranties it made when delivering your loan. These agreements were traditionally designed with the intent to enforce underwriting discipline but not to transfer risk of loss.

This is how it can play out: A loan officer takes your loan application and submits it to the creditor for underwriting with your supporting documentation and the property appraisal. The loan is approved and funded, and the creditor or an affiliated third-party vendor assumes loan servicing. Several years later the originating organization (bank, nonbank, broker) receives a repurchase letter, notifying them (for the first time) that the loan is in default, and in many cases by the time of notification, the property has been liquidated at a loss. The current investor on the note—who suffered the loss—is demanding repurchase, and the originator must choose to defend itself against the claim or settle the demand—either option is costly.

Since the financial crisis, billions of dollars have been at stake for the industry, the GSEs, and taxpayers to bring greater clarity to an otherwise gray area of the mortgage business. With declining valuations and deficiency claims for dollar-for-dollar losses when the collateral (property) on a defaulted loan is sold, more and more investors are making repurchase demands. Recent legislation has more clearly defined the circumstances under which an originating organization will have to repurchase a loan by setting a time limit, from funding through a specified date, in cases when the borrower defaults, or at anytime where it is determined that there was fraud on the application.

Note: With a rise in buyback risk, underwriting guidelines become tighter and spreads grow wider. Mortgage spread represents the difference in interest rate between the ten-year United States Treasury bill and the average rate on a conventional thirty-year mortgage. Additional return is demanded by investors for assuming higher risk. (For a full understanding of the primary-secondary market spread, view http://www.ny.frb.org/research/epr/2013/1113fust.pdf.)

When going through difficult times, I often hear people say, "The bank doesn't care about me; they just want to take my property." This simply isn't true. Banks aren't in the business of recovering assets. Lenders deplete their capital reserves through losses taken from nonperforming assets or repurchasing loans when early default, misrepresentation, or fraud is identified. Potentially, a small originator could be wiped out by having to buyback just one loan.

With the crash of the financial markets giving rise to borrower default and repurchase demands, credit risk has risen sharply. With a rise in credit risk and intense risk aversion by stakeholders who saw their capital being depleted and were at risk of shutting down, credit spreads rose to unprecedented levels. The private markets for securitized assets with no government guarantees essentially disappeared. If your loan wasn't deliverable to the agencies, there were simply too few investors for it and the cost of taking on the risk without guarantee caused those creditors to demand higher interest rates for the additional risk.

I've often heard, "Banks simply don't want to lend money." Banks have traditionally made money through money lending—so what that statement is missing is the right ending. I would offer: Banks don't want to lend money to people they believe are a high credit risk.

Lenders Have to Watch Their Compare Ratio with FHA

Another kind of troubling conversation I've had is when decision-makers struggle with making judgment calls due to fear of buyback risk and fear of losing their underwriting authority for FHA loans—when loans default and the lender runs the risk of exceeding FHA's compare ratio. To understand what a compare ratio measures, we need to first understand how HUD and lenders work together. While this explanation is a bit technical, it provides background and understanding of why and how your character is measured and what our industry and government is doing to combat discriminatory practices.

FHA-approved lenders underwrite and close a loan and then send the closed loan file to HUD to endorse it for FHA insurance. The ability to expedite FHA loan approval and closing is given to lenders who apply for and maintain direct endorsement (DE) authority. Unconditional DE authority is granted to the lender by a regional FHA Homeownership Center (HOC). A lender's DE authority can be pulled by HOC when their compare ratio is excessive.

The compare ratio is part of FHA's Neighborhood Watch Early Warning System. The system identifies and analyzes patterns in loans, by geographic area or originating lender, that became ninety days delinquent during their first two years. Technically speaking, the compare ratio is a numerical value used by HUD that reveals the largest discrepancies between a lender's default and claim percentage and the default and claim percentage to which it is being compared. A higher ratio is indicative of an area (or lender) that has an unusually high default percentage in comparison with that region or lender's surrounding area. For example, if a lender has an 8 percent default rate in California and 4 percent of all California loans defaulted, then the lender's compare ratio equals 200 percent. One FHA default can cost a lender tens of thousands of dollars in buyback fees and companies can quickly go out of business if they face too many. While it seems the intent of the FHA was to come up with a way to identify lender's who were making poor underwriting decisions, it appears through what I've been hearing, that it may have inadvertently made access to credit tougher for underserved borrowers.

Rob Chrisman is a secondary market mortgage professional—a capital markets guy who follows the buying and selling of debt and equity instruments. Five or six times a week, he dispenses colorful commentary on the inner workings of the mortgage industry and provides those who subscribe to his newsletter with a platform to share, question, or vent—with attribution or anonymously. In a January 2012 post on his blog, I found the best layman's explanation of the unintentional consequences of FHA's Neighborhood Watch Early Warning System from an anonymous contributor, which Rob has graciously granted permission to reprint. (The full post, "California says 'no thanks'; FHA, more FHA, thoughts on the compare ratio, and lender FHA changes that can't be ignored," is available at http://robchrisman.com/archives/a1327683600.htm.)

"I wanted to share a thought on FHA's compare ratios and their "hard coding" of 150% as the max to be eligible for LI (lender insurance). The problem with this approach is quickly evident using a bit of math. A compare ratio is a peer based metric. In other words, everyone's compare is based off of the entire group's average 90 day delinquent figures. When a hard cap is placed at 150 - with death penalty type consequences if that cap is exceeded, the results are very predictable. Any company that is moving toward 150 will quickly clamp down hard on their FHA lending. They will put FICO score minimums, DTI maximums, etc., in place. They will tell their underwriters to be very, very careful. They will move away from areas of the country that are experiencing economic challenges. And, in doing so, those companies will see their 90 day defaults drop. And that will drop the average that calculates everyone's compare ratio, so when the average goes down, any company whose 90 day delinquents didn't go down by an equal amount, will see their compare ratio go up. Those companies will then tighten - which will mean the average will again drop - which means that any company whose 90 day delinquents remained static - will have their compare ratio rise. And so on. Just watch – my guess is that after a few years FHA lending will become extraordinarily tight. Taken to its logical conclusion, if average 90 defaults fall below 1.0%, any firm that has 1.51% (an extraordinarily clean book) would have a 151% compare ratio and would be terminated by FHA. A compare ratio is a useful tool - but to wrap draconian penalties around it is a terrible mistake. Those who the FHA program is meant to help, the borrower who isn't, by definition, 'perfect', is going to be the big loser."

Enforcement of this metric and the subsequent fear of an organization losing its authority as granted by the FHA, compels decision-makers to toe the line of fair lending. Redlining is a discriminatory practice that involves refusal to lend money or extend credit to borrowers in certain "struggling" areas of town. Redlining became known as such because lenders would draw a red line around a neighborhood on a map, often targeting areas with a high concentration of minorities, and then refusing to lend in those areas because they considered the risk too high. Depository institutions are subject to anti-redlining provisions mandated by the Community Reinvestment Act, as such they must lend in the communities where they take in deposits (we call these areas our footprint), but nonbanks are subject only to Fair Housing and Equal Credit Opportunity laws.

When an underwriter is faced with a high-risk file that contains negative factors that fall below the particular lender's credit standards but within the minimum standards set by the GSEs, these can be offset by other compensating factors. When this happens, the underwriter must review the totality of the file and make a judgment call based on your character. What can you do to prevent a negative automatic assumption of your financial character? Exhibit the behaviors that evidence responsible financial habits. Control what is within your control. Get your financial house in order, clean up your credit, and don't be lazy with your paperwork. Strive to make your loan application so solid that an underwriter has no reason to doubt your timely repayment of the loan.

Mortgage lending is highly politicized, but at the end of the day, it is a for profit business. Underwriters must protect the interests of stakeholders. While prejudice and stereotypes exist everywhere, we must continue to fight against automatic assumptions.

The Face of Mortgage Lending

Under Section 342 of the Dodd-Frank Act, Congress established new statutory requirements to enhance diversity policies and practices within the financial services, such as the mortgage industry. The Consumer Financial Protection Bureau and other federal financial agencies responded by developing proposed standards covering four key areas: (1) organizational commitment to diversity and inclusion, (2) workforce profile and employment practices, (3) procurement and business practices and supplier diversity, and (4) practices to promote transparency of organizational diversity and inclusion.

The trade associations that support our industry are seeking ways to connect with members and industry professionals to identify and respond to not only overt but also (and more likely) implicit, subconscious, and subtle discrimination that prevents access to credit on prohibited factors such as race, religion, color, national origin, gender, sexual orientation, marital status, familial status, disability, maternity, or age. Organizations that represent themselves as either minority-owned businesses or women-owned businesses, or both, appear to have greater diversity within their workforce and within their customer base. While the ability to effectively communicate is critical in mortgage lending, sometimes commonality in culture—more than just language alone—allows for quicker opportunities for trust building. As such, the industry is actively seeking to expand the cultural diversity of its workforce for expanded opportunities within the mortgage industry.

Rightsizing the Business

All lenders will "right size" their business depending on volume expectations. The mortgage industry struggles with the consequences of cyclical layoffs and subsequent re-hirings and trainings to adjust back-office operations to fit sales force productivity. And it struggles with building up or breaking down distribution channels based on the demand for refinance or purchase activity. This constant back and forth rightsizing of a business can affect the quality of the talent pool that our industry attracts and the mindsets of the staffers who are retained. To provide you with an understanding of how these cyclical changes affect you, I'd like to briefly share some statistical data.

The third quarter of 2013 saw thirty-year fixed rate mortgages climb from 3.54 to 4.49 percent, according to the Freddie Mac Primary Mortgage Market Survey. This increase of 95 basis points marked the end of the largest refinance boom in U.S. history. The uptick's impact was immediate. In 2012, mortgage originations peaked at $2.1 trillion, and for 2014, the Mortgage Bankers Association (MBA) expects lenders will struggle to generate even $1 trillion of originations. A 50 percent market contraction hits any industry hard; however, the mortgage market's highly skilled workforce not only contracted but is also reshaping in other significant ways. Fully 70 percent of 2012's originations were refinanced mortgages. By contrast, 80 percent of originations in 2015 are expected to be purchase transactions. (Purchase share projections vary: 65 percent, 75 percent, and 80 percent based on third quarter 2014 forecasts by the Mortgage Bankers Association, Fannie Mae, and Freddie Mac, respectively.) This is significant because purchase loans are harder for lenders to originate because they require their having loan officers on the ground developing relationships with realtors to support the finding and educating of homebuyers, which is considerably more challenging than mining your servicing portfolio for streamlined refinances or sitting at an inbound call center desk waiting for the telephone to ring.

During the financial crisis and the refinancing boom that followed, the mortgage industry lost a generation of seasoned mortgage loan officers, largely through attrition. These loan officers had strong relationships within their local real estate community and were adept at self-sourcing leads and shepherding transactions through to closing. In 2014, the average age of a loan officer is fifty-four years old, and we are struggling to find new blood to enter the business. Read the full commentary at http://www.nationalmortgagenews.com/news/origination/recruiting-the-next-generation-of-loan-officers-1042981-1.html.

Why Are We Losing Mortgage Professionals Through Attrition?

If you work in mortgage operations and the ability to feed your family is dictated by something other than your performance at work, how long will you stay in that career? How often will you speak up when something isn't right if you fear that you might be layered in the next round for not just blending in? How many times will you be willing to uproot your family to comply with the industry's need to migrate from local operations centers to large regional operations centers? Organizations that value skilled processing, underwriting, and closing teams hesitate to bring on new staff when volume increases because they don't want to layoff skilled workers when volume is slow. Instead, they do the best they can by offering overtime and hiring temporary workers to support low-level functions.

As organizations grow, many of the steps to getting your loan to the closing table are broken down into handling by specialized teams. When the mortgage process is too decompartmentalized, it can become very challenging to navigate the mortgage approval process because there are many hands in the kitchen. With each function limited by the training and experience of the worker, the flow of the loan file can actually become even slower. More quality loan files seem to fall through the cracks when unskilled workers are handed seemingly menial tasks with little, if any, understanding of how mortgages work and of how each function flows to another. This causes frustration to all of us who seek excellence in workflow.

There are things that matter and there are things you can control. While you can't control who is handling your file, you can only control the accuracy of the data on the loan application, the completeness of your file at loan submission with supporting documentation, your knowledge of the decision-making process, and your responsiveness to your lending team.

Loan Officers Move Around a Lot

When selecting where we hang our license, what most of us care about is which product offerings are at our disposal so that we can find the one that best matches our clients' needs, the knowledge of our support staff to ensure a smooth process, the timeliness of execution to deliver on our borrowers' commitments to the sales contract, and competitive pricing so that we won't spend a single second justifying our value to a potential client. That's it. When any one of those things suffer, our income is negatively affected, and we start entertaining conversations with recruiters. Additionally, when a lender imposes overlays that are more restrictive than those imposed by comparable lenders, a loan officer will eventually grow tired of referring clients to a competitor and will take a meeting with that competitor's sales manager. If you've dealt with a loan officer in the past that you really liked and have lost touch, you can search for them on the NMLS Consumer Access website at www.nmlsconsumeraccess.org.

Misconceptions About Millennials

The Millennial Generation (or generation Y) are the demographic that follows Generation X. There are no precise dates when the generation starts and ends, but commentators use birth years ranging from the early 1980s to the early 2000s. Some journalists say the mortgage industry has priced Millennials out of homeownership. I disagree. The programs in place today are very much like those in place twenty years ago. What has changed significantly is the perception of credit accessibility. This mindset doesn't apply exclusively to Millennials; it applies to everyone affected by the financial crisis or who has struggled with financial security.

The industry is trying to understand what motivates Millennials. They've identified that skepticism exists in this generation's DNA. Previous assumptions were that Millennials are transient, don't save their money, aren't fiscally responsible, and, therefore, don't have the means to invest in homeownership. This belief simply doesn't hold up over the long haul. I have found

Millennials to be business savvy, independent thinkers, and fiscally conservative. They come better prepared to mortgage application—harboring a keen understanding of responsible finance because they've witnessed the financial sufferings of the Great Recession, have more access to information, and ask better questions.

This generation appears to be more socially responsible. Social responsibility is an ethical framework that suggests that an individual has an obligation to act to benefit society at large. For example, if an investor has a moral objection to smoking, that person may not invest in a tobacco company. Millennials might be feeling they are acting socially responsible when they exhibit a passive resistance to Wall Street by avoiding engagement with potentially harmful acts of investment such as obtaining a mortgage. They are struggling with this psychological block that prevents them from developing a fully productive relationship to investing. Historically, the quickest way to build wealth is through homeownership, so this generation must overcome a paradox in order to move toward homeownership. There is an internal struggle to maintain balance that must be addressed, both theirs and the industry's.

The reality is that it is difficult to obtain mortgage loan approval even for those who have wealth and exceptional credit histories. The perception that exists throughout the country is that one lender is the same as another lender, while in actuality, there exists gargantuan differences among all lenders in product availability, underwriting standards, and distribution channels. These differences—and your interaction with them—can make or break the homeownership experience.

Supply List for Enhancing Your Mortgage Experience

1. Highlighter
2. Post-it tabs
3. Notebook
4. Accordion-style file folder (with pockets)
5. Flash drive
6. Monthly Budget Spreadsheet (available at www.MortgageMattersBook.com)

Break out your highlighters and Post-it tabs and mark any important items that may apply to you and need to be reviewed with your loan officer throughout this book. Buy a flash drive specifically for scanning and saving loan related documents and a notebook specifically to record all mortgage related activities, events, questions, and contacts. As you begin to pull your supporting documentation together, place them in the accordion file. While you may not need to deliver all these documents to your loan officer, it's important to keep the information together for ease of access during the process.

Label the accordion file as follows:

1. Credit Report
2. Identification Documentation
3. Address History and Employment Contact information
4. Checking/Savings/Brokerage Statements (label and keep statements separated by month)

5. Quarterly Retirement Account Statements (401(k)s, IRAs)
6. Life Insurance (for cash valued policies)
7. Pay Stubs (keep in order by date)
8. Additional Sources of Income (include child support, alimony, pension, annuity, trust, Social Security, etc.)
9. W-2s (for the most recent two years)
10. Personal Tax Returns (for the most recent two years)
11. Letters of Explanation
12. Billing Statements (for recurring monthly installment and revolving credit accounts)
13. Real Estate Owned (label a tab for each property owned, and collect the mortgage statement, yearly property tax bill, declarations pages of homeowners insurance policies, and billing statement for the homeowner association dues, if any)

Only as applicable:
1. Business Tax Returns (for the most recent two years)
2. IRS Schedule K-1 (for beneficiaries of partnerships, S corporations, trust, and estates; for the most recent two years)
3. Miscellaneous (divorce decree, marital settlement agreement, separate maintenance agreement, trust document, bankruptcy discharge papers)
4. School Transcripts
5. Debts Paid by Others (twelve month evidence of payment of recurring installment and revolving credit accounts)
6. VA Eligibility (certification and supporting documentation)
7. Homebuyer Counseling Certificate

Once you have selected a property, continue to make use of your accordion folder by adding the following labels:
a. Purchase Contract
b. Contact Information (for selling agent, listing agent, closing agent, loan officer, loan processor, insurance agent, and home inspector)
c. Evidence of Escrow Funds
d. Appraisal
e. Property Inspections
f. Insurance Quotes
g. Estimates for Repairs
h. Closing Documents (keep a copy of your first payment coupon)

Ideally, you'll also have these items scanned onto a flash drive so that your lender receives the clearest available copies. Most lenders have moved away from paper files and use a document imaging system to record every aspect of your loan file, so that any document submitted for loan processing is recorded, viewable, and permanent to the file. Here are some tips on scanning documents:

1. Be sure to set the scanner to save documents in PDF format. Be careful not to save in JPEG or TIFF formats as these are not easily uploaded into mortgage origination software systems.

2. Scan and label each item individually (following the organization of the checklist).

3. Keep all pages of a singularly dated document in one scanned file. For example, your 2014 tax return includes thirty-two pages. All thirty-two pages should be in one file. But if you've been asked to deliver four pay stubs; as each pay stub is issued on a different date, you will have four files labeled accordingly.

4. If you are scanning documents that have two sides, program your scanner to read both sides so that page numbers stay in order. If your scanner doesn't have this capability, print one side of each page, then commingle the original with the backside copy so that all numbered pages stay in order. Then scan the document.

5. Don't be tempted to scan documents all together because this creates difficulty for the lender on many levels. If the file size is too big, it may get rejected or get caught in the lender's virus scanning system. The item you deliver may not be the item that the lender needs to satisfy the condition, and if you've labeled each individual document correctly, you'll be able to have a smart conversation with the loan officer or loan processor to quickly direct them to the document you feel was submitted to satisfy a particular condition—speeding the process of finding a resolution.

Delivering the Documents to the Lender

1. Bring your accordion folder to you loan application meeting so that you can review each document with your loan officer for completeness and accuracy. This is your best opportunity to mitigate the risks associated with the timing expectations for processing your loan request and obtaining a loan commitment.

2. Under no circumstances should you ever leave your originals with the lender. Your lender will let you know what, if any, original letters of explanation they need to have.

3. Bring your flash drive with all document files properly labeled, and let your loan officer upload onto his system. Take back your flash drive.

4. If you're handling the transaction virtually, your loan officer will tell you how you can deliver the supporting documentation to their document imaging system. Personally,

I prefer that I or someone on my team to upload the client's documentation because misfiling can easily occur when a person is unfamiliar with which loan condition a document satisfies. If we're communicating virtually, I'll have my client email to me the labeled files.

Tips for Additional Readiness

Now that you've gathered all of your financial documentation in one place, you've also readied yourself for the following very important life tasks:

a. Determination of life insurance needs

b. Preparation of your will

c. The college financial aid application process

Take advantage of your financial readiness at this time and schedule a meeting with a financial planner to protect your heirs from financial hardship and delays in the probate courts. This isn't a process that only benefits the wealthy. Whatever your assets, big or small, you're going to want to protect them for your loved ones. If you've set up your estate planning needs before, call in for a quick check, as your financial needs change over time, and adjust your estate plans needs accordingly.

Comprehensive Mortgage Documentation Checklist

Here's a detailed list of supporting documentation that will be needed along with a suggestions for labeling individual item PDF files. (You can download a printable copy of the Supply List and Comprehensive Mortgage Documentation Checklist at www.MortgageMattersBook.com.) Handle the organization and delivery of these items as instructed in the Supply List above.

Be ready to deliver these items to your loan officer at loan application:

1. Driver's license or government issued ID. (Jane-DL-exp 10-15-2020)
2. Social Security card. (John-SSN)
3. If you are a permanent or a nonpermanent resident, your alien registration card or permanent resident card (INS Form I-551). (John-INS exp 10-15-2018)
4. If you are a nonresident alien, your valid U.S. nonimmigrant visa and unexpired passport from your country of origin. (Jane U.S. Visa exp 10-15-2018)
5. A list of all addresses where you have lived during the preceding two years. If you use a mailing address, provide both where you actually live and where you'd like your mail delivered. (Jane and John - home and mailing addresses)
6. Landlord information: If you were renting a property within the last two years, bring

the contact information for the landlord including name, telephone number, email, housing fee, and length of time lived in the property. In some cases, lenders will require evidence of payments for the preceding twelve months so keep track of those payments. (Jane and John Landlord Info)

7. Employment information: Bring a list of all contact information for any employers within the last two years including name of company, address, telephone number, position, salary, hiring date, and ending date, if applicable. (Jane -Employer contact info)

8. Assets: The most recent two months statements for all bank, brokerage, and retirement accounts (include all numbered pages). (Chase x4538 ending June 2019 —the x4538 signifies the last four digits of the account number)

9. Income: Annual Social Security awards letter, pension, and annuity statements, as applicable. (ex. John SSN Awards 2016)

10. Pay stubs: Individual paystubs for the most recent thirty days; for military personnel, include Leave and Earnings Statement (LES). (John pay stub ending 5-15-2016)

11. Two most recent W-2s. (Jane 2015 w2 for ABC company)

12. Two most recent personal tax returns: All schedules, all pages, page 2 with client signature—most people never sign their copy of the tax return, so please be sure to sign yours before you scan the copy for your lender. (John and Jane 2014 personal tax return)

13. For all real estate owned, provide the following:
    a. Most recent mortgage and/or home equity line of credit billing statement, if any. (BofA mtg stmt 123 Main St Aug 2015) (Greentree HELOC stmt 456 Elm Aug 2015)
    b. Declarations page of your homeowners insurance policies including hazard, wind, flood, etc., as applicable. (dec page 123 Main St) (flood 123 Main St)
    c. Property tax bill. (Prop Tax Bill 123 Main St)
    d. Homeowner association (HOA) billing statement, if applicable. (HOA billing 456 Elm St)
    e. In cases where you own more than two properties, you may want to include an Excel spreadsheet for your lender for ease of transferring information to the loan application and matching liabilities to collateral under the real estate owned section. (Complete REO schedule)

14. Letters of Explanation for any elements requiring explanation. All letters must be signed and dated (LOX for credit inquiries, LOX for large deposits).

After loan application, you'll be asked to deliver the following:

1. Purchase agreement/sales contract. (Purchase Agreement)
2. Funds held in escrow: For each deposit, as required by the sales contract, you'll include a copy of the check and a printout of the transaction history from the date of the last statement up to and including when the escrow check cleared your account. If money was wired, you will need a copy of the wire transfer and evidence of receipt by the escrow agent. ($5,000 first escrow deposit 2-11-15) ($10,000 second escrow deposit 2-28-15)
3. Certificate of homeowners insurance. (COI bound on _____ [Est. closing date])
4. Application for flood Insurance and evidence of payment, as required. (Flood app and payment)

Special Circumstances Requiring Additional Paperwork

1. Although it is a general standard that a lender is not to request or include any documentation from a nonapplicant in your loan file, if you have been required to deliver your tax returns and are married and filed joint income tax returns with your spouse (who is not an applicant on your loan yet who has made contributions to your income tax returns), you will need to present your lender with your spouse's supporting documentation to evidence the declared income or losses as they apply directly to your spouse, so that in your qualifying income analysis, an underwriter can properly distinguish between what's yours and what's not yours. (2013 Evidence of nonborrower income on joint return)
2. For the self-employed: Two most recent business tax returns (all businesses, all schedules, all pages, page 2 with client signature). (XYZ Corp 2014 return)
3. If your tax returns show income or losses that are not continued in the current year (nonrecurring), come prepared with a written letter of explanation as to why those losses/income will not continue into the future. Additional documentation may be required after initial review. (Signed LOX for income variation)
4. Year-to-date profit & loss statement and balance sheet for all businesses owned with greater than a 25 percent share. (XYZ Corp ytd 9-thirty-2015 P&L)
5. For all beneficiaries of partnerships, S corporations, trusts, and estates, provide IRS Schedule K-1 for the preceding two years. (John 2014 Schedule K-1 ABC Revocable Trust)
6. For any revolving debts or recurring liabilities that are in your name but paid by another individual who can evidence they have been the sole payer on the account for the most recent twelve months (a relative or friend, your employer or business), we can exclude that payment from your debt-to-income ratio. Supporting evidence includes front and back copies of twelve months of cancelled checks, or in the case of auto draft

payments, a transaction history from the payer's account. (Evidence of payments of Chase auto loan paid by XYZ corp.)

7. If a car loan or lease is traditionally paid by your business, and in the preceding twelve month period, the term of your existing loan/lease ended and you replaced that vehicle with a new one whose loan/lease payments are being paid by your business and that you would like excluded from your debt-to-income calculation, you will need to provide evidence of payment by the business on both vehicles to show a combination supporting a total twelve month history. Additionally, you will need to write, sign, and date a letter of explanation clearly describing the replacement. (LOX for twelve month history on totality of business paid auto debt to exclude Chase auto payment)

8. If responsible for paying child support, alimony, or separate maintenance, provide a copy of the divorce decree, marital settlement agreement, or maintenance agreement. (John - Court order evidencing child support)

9. If you'll be receiving child support, alimony, or separate maintenance for at least three more years and wish to submit this income source for qualification, provide a copy of the divorce decree, marital settlement agreement, or maintenance agreement in addition to evidence you have been receiving such income for at least twelve months. In some instances, evidence is only needed for 6 months. (Jane - Evidence of receipt of Child Support) AND (Jane - Court order evidencing continuation of child support)

10. If receiving Social Security income, provide copy of the Social Security awards letter. If funds are directly deposited into your checking account, provide a copy of a complete bank statement (all numbered pages). (John - Evidence of receipt of Social Security income)

11. If seeking financing under a Veteran's Affairs (VA) loan product, submit a certificate of eligibility. (John VA COE)

12. If you've filed for bankruptcy in the preceding seven years, provide a copy of the final bankruptcy and discharge. (John 2009 Bankruptcy court order and discharge papers)

13. If seeking loan programs that require evidence of prior completion of an approved homebuyer counseling course, a certificate of completion will be needed for all borrowers evidencing attendance. (John Counseling Cert) (Jane Counseling Cert)

14. If you do not have a two-year history of employment and were a full-time student within the preceding two years, provide a copy of your college transcripts. (Jane college transcripts)

Glossary of Mortgage Industry Terms

Here's a list of common terms that are interchangeable:

1. A document that contains facts as reported by the borrower or as validated by the lender: Loan Application, Uniform Residential Mortgage Application, the 1003, or App.
2. The person to whom you give all of your financial data to complete the mortgage application: Mortgage Loan Originator, Loan Officer, Mortgage Broker, Loan Consultant, and Account Executive.
3. All refer to you: Borrower, Applicant, Client, Buyer, and Mortgagor.
4. A recurring monthly payment that will continue for more than ten months: Obligation, Debt, or Liability.
5. The underwriting standards of a particular lender: Credit Policy, Eligibility Standards, Rules, or Guidelines.
6. The credit-reporting agencies whose information the lender relies upon to evaluate creditworthiness: Repositories, Credit Bureaus, Nationwide Consumer Reporting Companies, Equifax, TransUnion, and Experian.
7. The generally accepted guidelines for underwriting mortgage loans: Agency, Selling Guide, AllRegs, Conforming, Fannie Mae, and the GSEs.
8. The property that the mortgage loan is secured against: Subject Property, Collateral, Security.
9. A borrower's signed and dated letter confirming their intent to occupy a property that is being financed as their primary residence: Letter of Intent, Letter of Intent to Occupy, Letter of Intent to Occupy Subject Property.

10. Signed and dated letter addressing any issues on the transaction ranging from additional addresses found on the credit report and not listed on the loan application to credit inquiries to nonpayroll deposits in your bank statements, or any other thing to lender needs your explanation: Letter of Explanation, LOX, Credit Explanation Letter.

11. The document received at closing that details all fees and credits and debits due the seller and buyer: HUD-1, Settlement Statement, Closing Statement, Closing Disclosure.

Acceleration Clause

A provision in a loan agreement allowing a lender to demand the entire balance of a loan to be repaid in a lump sum under certain circumstances. A lender may invoke their right of acceleration for triggers such as misrepresentation, ownership transfers, breaches of contract, or loan defaults.

Appraisal

A document from a licensed professional that gives an estimate of a property's fair market value based on the recent sales of comparable homes in the area and the specific features of the subject property.

ARM (Adjustable Rate Mortgage)

A mortgage loan in which the interest rate periodically changes. The changing interest rate is based upon the upward and downward movement of an index, such as the current yield on ten-year treasury securities or the one-year average London Interbank Offered Rate (LIBOR), and a fixed margin above that index. Provisions to the security instrument or the mortgage note are amended through the use of a rider or an addendum to identify the terms for reassessing the interest rate.

Amortization

The gradual repayment of a mortgage loan through both principal and interest payments. An amortization schedule breaks down each payment to reflect the portion that is allocated to principal and that which is allocated to interest.

Annual Percentage Rate (APR)

Like the interest rate, the APR is expressed as a percentage. Unlike the interest rate, the APR takes into account the annual cost of credit including charges and fees such as mortgage insurance (where necessary) to reflect the total cost of the loan. Your monthly payment is not based on the APR; it's based on the interest rate as identified by the lender on the interest rate lock agreement and as recorded on your promissory note at loan closing.

Automated Underwriting System (AUS)

Loan processing completed through a computer-based system that evaluates loan details such as past credit history, reported income and assets, and estimated value to systematically determine if a loan is recommended for approval.

Automated Valuation Model (AVM)

A service that provides an estimated property valuation by using mathematical modeling tools combined with a database of recent closed sales that can be obtained in a manner of seconds. An AVM report typically includes an indicative market value, tax assessor's valuation, recent sales history, and bed, bath, and square footage.

Broker's Price Opinion (BPO)

Typically ordered by a lender in cases where they've foreclosed on a property and are looking for current market valuation to determine resale price. The report is provided by a licensed realtor and typically provides values of similar surrounding properties, sales trends in the neighborhood, the amount of repair or preparation the property requires to be put up for sale. BPOs are different from appraisals: They are generally completed by real estate professionals and not licensed appraisers, and they are less thorough than a full appraisal valuation.

Back-End Ratio

The sum of your total monthly housing payment including principal, interest, taxes, insurance, and association dues, if any, and all other monthly recurring debts (credit cards, car payments, student loans, etc.) divided by your monthly gross (pretax) income.

Balance Sheet

A financial statement that shows assets, liabilities, and net worth as of a specific date.

Cancelled Check

A front and back copy of a check written and executed that is provided to your lender as evidence that the deposit money on a purchase transaction has cleared your (or the donor's) account.

Capacity

The ability to make mortgage payments on time, dependent on assets and the amount of income each month after paying total housing costs, and other recurring debt obligations.

Capital

An individual's usable or qualifying savings, investments, or financial assets. Capital investment refers to the dollar amount a buyer places as a down payment on a purchase transaction.

Cash-Out Refinance

A financial transaction where a borrower refinances an existing mortgage at a higher loan amount than their existing mortgage debt (or on a property that has no debt) to convert the equity into cash. For example, if a home has a current value of $100,000 and an outstanding mortgage of $60,000, the owner could refinance $80,000 and have additional $20,000 in cash.

Chain of Title

The chronological order of conveyance of property ownership from one owner to the next.

Change of Circumstance

An action that affects the originally disclosed settlement costs.

Chapter 7 Bankruptcy

A bankruptcy that requires the liquidation of assets (the sale of a debtor's nonexempt property) with distribution of the proceeds to creditors in exchange for the cancellation of debt.

Chapter 13 Bankruptcy

A bankruptcy that allows a debtor to keep property and pay debts over time, usually three to five years.

Charge-Off

A debt that is deemed to be uncollectible by the creditor and is written-off as an expense on their income statement.

Clear Title

An unencumbered or unrestricted legal ownership of real property.

Cloud on Title

Any document, claim, unreleased lien or encumbrance that might invalidate or impair the title to real property or make conveyance doubtful.

Collateral

Security in the form of money or property pledged for the payment of a loan. For example, on a home loan, the home is the collateral and can be taken away from the borrower if mortgage payments are not made.

Collection Account

An unpaid debt that has been assigned by the creditor to a collection agency to collect on the bad debt. This type of derogatory account is reported to the credit bureau and will show on the borrower's credit report.

Combo Loan

A concurrent first and second mortgage.

Combined Loan-to-Value (CLTV) Ratio

The total amount you are borrowing in mortgage debts divided by the home's fair market value. Someone with a $50,000 first mortgage and a $20,000 equity line secured against a $100,000 house would have a CLTV ratio of 70 percent.

Compensating Factors

An element of a credit application that is so strong that it may counter a concern that would otherwise negatively impact loan approval. Compensating factors may include: larger than necessary down payment, existing housing payment greater than proposed housing payment, or excess liquid reserves after loan closing.

Compensation

How a person is paid: base salary, overtime, commissions, or bonuses (guaranteed dollar amount or percentage-based).

Conditions

Loan conditions are additional required documents needed either prior to the lender issuing a loan commitment (full approval) or at loan closing. Conditions are mostly standard for all loans, such as that you obtain proper homeowners insurance coverage and others are specific to your individual financial characteristics.

Condominium

A form of ownership in which individuals purchase and own a unit of housing in a multiunit complex. The owner also shares financial responsibility for the maintenance of common areas.

Conforming Loan

A mortgage that meets the requirements for purchase by the GSEs. Requirements include the loan amount, type of loan product, term and specific underwriting criteria. Loans that exceed the conforming loan limits are considered nonconforming or jumbo mortgages.

Conveyance

A transfer of ownership in real property from one party to another party.

Cosigner

A person who signs a credit application with another person, agreeing to be equally responsible for the repayment of the loan.

Consent

The borrower's confirmation of their intent to proceed with the loan application after loan disclosures have been received. The method of delivery of disclosures can be in person, via U.S. mail, or email. Without consent, the lender cannot move forward with its analysis of the loan request.

Consummation

The moment in time that a consumer becomes contractually obligated on a credit transaction. This period usually equates to the date of loan funding.

Contingency Clause

A clause in a purchase contract that defines a condition or action that must be met in order for the contract to become binding. Types of contingencies can include dates for completion of appraisal, inspections, obtaining financing, or the sale of the buyer's primary residence. A contingency becomes part of a binding sales contract when both parties (i.e., the seller and the buyer) agree to the terms and sign the contract.

Conventional Loan

A mortgage loan that does not have an explicit guarantee by the U.S. government, falls within the guidelines of the Government Sponsored Enterprises (GSEs), and is below the conforming loan limit.

Cost to Cure

This term refers to the one of two things. As it relates to the HUD-1/closing disclosure, it means the cost a lender will incur to ensure the final fees charged to the customer are within the tolerance levels as mandated by law. See "Why Do I Keep Receiving Another Copy of the Good Faith/Loan Estimate?" in chapter 5 for tolerance levels. If the final figures exceed the tolerance levels allowed from the original good faith/loan estimate, the lender will bear the cost of the excessive fees and the amount of excess will be listed on the final HUD-1/closing disclosure as a lender credit to the borrower. Additionally, cost to cure can refer to an estimate of the amount to repair a fault of the property or deferred maintenance. In this regard, where the estimated cost to cure figure exceeds 3 percent of the appraised value, or if the lender believes the repairs are required for safety and livability, the lender will typically require the repair before loan closing. If the lender allows for the repair to take place after loan closing, it will require the closing agent to hold one and a half times the estimated repairs in their escrow account at loan closing.

Counter/Counteroffer

An offer that is made by the lender to the applicant based on different terms than what the applicant originally requested.

Creditworthiness

The lender's measurement of the borrower's ability to qualify and repay a loan through an extensive analysis of both credit and noncredit risk factors. The underwriter will review installment and revolving payment histories, credit utilization, delinquencies, public records, foreclosures, collections, and lender inquiries. Noncredit risk factors include equity and loan-to-value, liquid reserves, loan purpose, loan term, amortization, occupancy, debt-to-income ratio, and property type.

Credit Bureau

An agency that provides financial information and payment history to lenders about potential borrowers. Also known as a national credit repository. They include Equifax, TransUnion, and Experian.

Debt-to-Income Ratio

The relative value representing monthly debts to income used by lenders to determine a borrower's financial ability to repay a loan. Qualifying ratio's consist of a maximum front-end and maximum back-end ratio; amounts varying by lender and loan program. A front-end ratio, expresses the total monthly housing expense (PITIA) compared to the borrower's gross monthly income. The back-end ratio, expresses the PITIA plus other recurring monthly debts compared to the borrower's gross monthly income.

Deed in Lieu of Foreclosure

Where a lender/servicer/insurer accepts a homeowner's deed to a property in exchange for the cancellation of the mortgage debt to avoid the high cost of foreclosure proceedings.

Default

Instances when a borrower fails to meet a debt obligation. A default can include a debt service default or a technical default. In a debt service default, a borrower fails to make a scheduled payment of interest or principal. In a technical default, the borrower fails a covenant of the terms of a loan.

Down Payment

The portion of a home's purchase price that is paid in cash and is not part of the mortgage loan. The amount required for down payment varies based on the loan type, but the amount is always the difference of the sale price and the actual mortgage loan amount. Mortgage insurance is typically required on mortgage loans where a down payment of less than 20 percent is made. The money for down payment is not required to come from the borrower's own funds. Different loan programs specify the amounts that are required to come specifically from the borrower's own savings, if any are required at all.

Due on Sale Clause

A provision of a loan allowing the lender to demand full repayment if ownership is transferred.

Disclosures

A set of loan documents that detail relevant information about the selected loan program and related costs issued within three business days of loan application.

Divorce Decree

In an uncontested divorce, the final decree grants a divorce effective at the date of signing. In addition, both parties will have signed a marital settlement agreement that addresses the division of property, assets and liabilities, the custody of children, visitation arrangements, and any other such things. In a contested divorce, where a husband and wife can't or won't agree to a division of items, there is no marital settlement agreement. In this case, a final decree signed by the judge will determine the disposition of marital assets, liabilities, and issues surrounding children of the parties. A lender may require that a borrower provide a copy of the marital settlement agreement or divorce decree to review obligations.

Elevation Certificate

A tool used to ensure compliance with community floodplain management ordinances and to determine the proper insurance premium rate. The elevation certificate measures a structure's elevation in relation to the base flood elevation (BFE). The base flood is a flood with a 1 percent chance of occurring in any given year. The BFE identifies how high the water is likely to rise (also called water surface elevation) in a base flood. The land area of the base flood is called the special flood hazard area, floodplain, or high-risk zone. Flood insurance rates vary according risk zones. Premiums in a high-risk zone (a zone beginning with the letter A or V) are based on a building's elevation above, at, or below the BFE. An elevation certificate is usually provided by a property surveyor.

Eligibility

A term used to describe whether the loan characteristics meet the minimum guidelines of a specific loan program.

Encumbrance

A claim, charge, liability, or regulation against a property that usually impacts transferability of ownership and can restrict its free use until the claim is removed. An encumbrance can take several forms: mortgages, claims by other parties, court judgments, pending legal action, unpaid taxes, restrictive deed or loan covenants, easement rights of the neighbors, or zoning ordinances. It may diminish the value of property, but may not prevent transfer of title.

Escrow Deposit/Earnest Money/Amounts Held in Escrow

The security deposit given by the buyer as a good faith intention of purchasing a property. This money becomes part of the down payment if the offer is accepted, is returned if the offer is rejected, or is forfeited if the buyer pulls out of the deal after the contract specified contingency date. During the contingency period, the money may be returned to the buyer if the contingencies are not met to the buyer's satisfaction. It is best to provide this money to a third party (such as the real estate broker, attorney, or settlement agent) and never directly to the property seller.

Escrow Account

Funds included in the monthly mortgage payment to accumulate the amounts necessary for the future payment of county taxes and any of the following, when applicable: private mortgage insurance, homeowners insurance, flood insurance, and property taxes. Using the funds in the escrow account, the lender makes these payments as they become due.

Execution

A measure of a lender's effectiveness as it relates to its processes, timeliness, accuracy, and delivery. For example, "ABC Bank has great products and loan pricing, but their execution is horrific."

FICO

The pioneer credit score company, Fair, Isaac and Company (FICO), founded in 1956 by engineer Bill Fair and mathematician Earl Isaac. FICO scores are the most widely used representative credit score in U.S. mortgage loan underwriting. This three-digit number, ranging from 300 to 850, is calculated by a mathematical equation that evaluates many types of information in your credit report. Higher FICO scores represent lower credit risks, which typically equate to better loan terms.

Fannie Mae/Federal National Mortgage Association (FNMA)

A federally chartered government-sponsored enterprise owned by private stockholders that guarantees residential mortgages and converts them into securities for sale to investors. By purchasing mortgages, Fannie Mae supplies funds that lenders loan to potential homebuyers. Loans delivered to Fannie Mae do not have an explicit guarantee of the U.S. government. The GSEs are supervised by the Federal Housing and Finance Authority.

FHA/Federal Housing Administration

The Federal Housing Administration is a U.S. government agency created as part of the National Housing Act of 1934. It sets standards for construction and underwriting and insures mortgage loans made by banks and other private lenders. Its goals are to improve housing standards and conditions, and advance homeownership opportunities by providing mortgage insurance to lenders to cover most losses that may incur when a borrower defaults. This encourages lenders to make loans to riskier borrowers who might not qualify under the traditional conventional mortgage guidelines.

Financial Asset

Liquid assets—cash or those funds readily available for conversion to cash. These include cash deposits such as in checking, savings, certificates of deposit, and marketable securities such as stocks, bonds, annuities, and cash value of insurance policies and mutual funds. May also include assets held in retirement accounts.

Flip Tax

Not an actual tax payable to a state, city or federal taxing authority, but instead a form of revenue collection used by co-operatives to offset maintenance costs that is assessed upon the sale of a unit.

Flood Insurance

Insurance that protects homeowners against losses incurred from a flood. If a property is located within a flood plain that is determined to carry risk as recorded by Federal Emergency Management Agency, the lender will require verification of a flood policy before closing a loan transaction. The cost of flood insurance will vary by the measurements of an elevation certificate.

Foreclosure

The act of enforcing a mortgage lien by the judicial sale of a property. A lien is created when there is a loan contract for money borrowed under a promissory note. This loan is secured by the mortgage lien upon real property. When the debt is not paid according to the terms of the promissory note, or when other contract terms are violated, a lender can pursue its lien on the property through the act of foreclosure.

Forbearance

An agreement that allows a homeowner to pay less than the full amount of the mortgage payment for a given period. A forbearance period is usually followed by and requires either a repayment plan or a loan modification that adds the amount in arrears to the principal amount either by increasing the monthly payment or extending the loan.

Form 2106 of Federal Income Tax Return

IRS Form 2106, Employee Business Expenses, indicates employee deductions for ordinary and necessary expenses of their job. An ordinary expense is one that is common and accepted in your field of trade, business, or profession. A necessary expense is one that is helpful and appropriate for your business. An expense does not have to be required to be considered necessary.

Freddie Mac/Federal Home Loan Mortgage Corporation

Freddie Mac was chartered by Congress in 1970 with a statutory mission to provide liquidity, stability, and affordability to the U.S. housing market. It is a government-sponsored enterprise whose primary business is to purchase loans from lenders to replenish their supply of funds so that lenders can make more mortgage loans to other borrowers.

FSBO (For Sale by Owner)

A home that is offered for sale by the owner without the benefit of a real estate professional.

Fund (to)

To execute the mortgage by delivering loan monies to a settlement agent.

GSE/Government-Sponsored Enterprise

Privately held corporations with public purposes created by the U.S. Congress to enhance the flow of credit to targeted sectors of the economy in order to make those segments of the capital market more efficient and transparent and to reduce the risk to investors and other suppliers of capital. GSEs carry the implicit backing of the U.S. government, but they are not direct obligations of the U.S. government. Examples include: Federal National Mortgage Association (Fannie Mae), Federal Home Loan Bank, Federal Home Loan Mortgage Corporation (Freddie Mac), Federal Farm Credit Bank and the Resolution Funding Corporation. The Student Loan Marketing Association (Sallie Mae) was originally chartered as a GSE in 1972. In 1995, the U.S. congress allowed Sallie Mae to relinquish its government-sponsorship and become a fully private institution via legislation.

Ginnie Mae/Government National Mortgage Association

A U.S. government corporation within the U.S. Department of Housing and Urban Development ensuring liquidity for government-insured mortgages from the Federal Housing Administration, Veterans Affairs and the Rural Housing Administration.

Gross Income

The total amount of money earned before taxes and other deductions. Sources of income may include those derived from salary, self-employment, rental property, alimony, child support, public assistance payments, and retirement benefits, among others.

Hard Pull

A term used to describe a type of credit inquiry that identifies that an individual is actively seeking credit. These types of inquiries require your consent to the institution who will receive a credit report. A hard pull of your credit report includes credit utilization information about lines of credit, late payments, bankruptcies, and defaults; discloses your credit score; lowers your credit score slightly; and will be listed on your credit report for at least 120 days.

Hazard Insurance

Protection against certain hazards such as damage through fire, wind, theft, and vandalism, among others that is provided by your homeowners insurance policy.

Home Equity Line of Credit

A type of loan that allows a borrower to convert home equity into cash over a period of time and up to a predetermined limit. Repayment is of the amount drawn plus interest costs.

Home Inspection

An examination of the structure and mechanical systems to determine a home's quality, soundness, and safety. A completed report alerts a potential homebuyer of any repairs needed and is often accompanied by an estimate of the cost to cure (remedy/fix) the defect.

Homeowner Association (HOA)

An elected group of individuals who govern a subdivision or a planned community. The association exists to enforce the covenants, conditions, and restrictions of the properties it governs and collects fees from owners to maintain common areas. An HOA is a corporation that is usually initially formed by a real estate developer for the purpose of marketing, managing, and selling homes, units, and lots in a residential subdivision. The developer will exit financial and legal responsibility by transferring ownership of the association to the homeowners after selling off a predetermined number of units.

HOA Coupon

A billing statement that identifies the monthly charges of the homeowner association for the specific home, unit, or lot.

HUD-1/Closing Statement/Settlement Statement/Closing Disclosure

A document that provides an itemized listing of all parties that are providing or receiving payment in a real estate transaction. Items that appear on the statement include sales price, real estate commissions, loan amount, origination points and fees, settlement agent fees, transfer taxes, property survey, home inspections, and funds to set up an initial escrow account. The totals at the bottom of the statement provide net funds received from the buyer at consummation and net funds distributed to the seller.

Homeowners Insurance

An insurance policy that combines protection against damage to a dwelling and its contents, including fire, storms, or other damages, with protection against claims of negligence or inappropriate action that result in injury or property damage. All property secured by a mortgage lien will require homeowners insurance and monthly prorations may be collected by the lender and held in an escrow account. A separate flood insurance policy is required for property located within a special flood hazard area and is optional, but recommended, for all other properties.

Homeownership Counseling (Education Classes)

Informative sessions that prepare consumers for homeownership through lessons in budgeting, loan programs, insurance, property maintenance, and mortgage requirements.

Homestead Exemption

Property tax credit program, offered by some state governments and mandated by others, that provides reductions in property taxes to eligible households. A Homestead Exemption can be claimed on the one property that is the primary residence of a person.

HUD (U.S. Department of Housing and Urban Development)
Established in 1965, HUD works to create decent housing and suitable living environments for all Americans by addressing housing needs, improving and developing American communities, and enforcing fair housing laws.

Inquiry or Hard Pull on a Credit Report

A credit report request known as a hard pull will retrieve a new credit score and may impact your representative credit score that is used for deciding your loan. A soft pull will not impact the credit score, but will provide your lender with updates of any new credit opened or information on creditors who have pulled your credit report within the preceding 120 days.

Jumbo Loan

A loan in an amount that exceeds the conforming loan limits.

Lease Agreement

A written agreement between a property owner and a tenant (resident) with provisions that stipulate the security deposit, duration of the lease, amount of rent, payment due dates, penalties for late payments, renewal policy, responsibility of utilities, pet policies, and conditions for termination, among other things.

Legal Description

Refers to the written description of a property that identifies the subject piece of property by county or parish, the judicial district within that county or parish, and may include such specifics as fractional designation, metes and bounds, courses and distances, reference, blanket, name designation, and part of a tract or subdivision lot.

Lender's Title Insurance

Protects the lender against any claims that may arise from prior liens against the property or title defects such as errors or omissions in deeds, mistakes in examining records, forgery, or undisclosed heirs. A similar policy is available for purchase by homebuyers. Most lenders will require the buyer to purchase the lender's title insurance policy.

LIBOR Index (London Interbank Offered Rate)

A measure of the average interest rate at which a select group of large, reputable banks that participate in the London interbank money market can borrow unsecured funds from other banks. The LIBOR index is among the most common internationally recognized benchmarks used by mortgage lenders for calculation of variable interest rates on adjustable rate mortgages.

Lien

A legal claim against property that must be satisfied on or before a transfer of property ownership.

Listing Agreement

A contract between a seller and a real estate professional to market and sell a home providing terms such as: listing price, broker's duties, seller's duties, broker's compensation, terms for mediation, termination date, and additional terms and conditions. Under the provisions of real estate license laws, only a broker can act as an agent to list, sell, or rent another person's real estate.

Liquid Asset

An asset that is readily convertible to cash or with minimal impact to the price received. Liquid assets include most stocks, money market instruments, and government bonds.

Liquidity

A measure of the extent to which a person or organization has cash to meet immediate and short-term obligations or assets that can be quickly converted to do this.

Loan Commitment

A lender's approval of a loan request subject only to at closing/funding conditions.

Loan Officer

An individual mortgage loan originator who is registered with the National Mortgage Licensing System (NMLS) and who is responsible for soliciting borrowers for mortgage loans.

Loan Modification

A written agreement between the investor/servicer and the borrower that permanently changes one or more of the original terms of the note such as: mortgage product type (adjustable rate mortgage to a fixed-rate), interest rate reduction, principal reduction, maturity extension, or increasing the unpaid principal balance by capitalizing the delinquent amounts.

Loan Servicer

The company that administrates the day-to-day management of your mortgage loan by collecting interest, principal, and escrow payments. Loan servicers also monitor nonperforming loans, contact delinquent borrowers, and notify insurers and investors of potential problems. Loan servicers may be the lender or a specialized company that handles loan servicing under contract with the lender or the investor who owns the loan.

Loan-to-Value (LTV) Ratio

Expressed as a percentage, representing the ratio derived by dividing the amount borrowed by the sales price or by the appraised value (generally, whichever is less).

Lock In

To secure an interest rate and origination points for a specific period of time. A loan will need to fund within the lock-in period for the lender to honor the offered terms.

Loss Mitigation

A lender's process to support collection efforts and avoid borrower default that may result in loan foreclosure. A loan servicer will work with borrowers who are experiencing a temporary setback and wish to stay in their homes by mitigating, or arriving at an agreement to resolve, past-due mortgage payments by setting up options such as repayment plans, forbearance, and loan modification with eventual reinstatement. If the borrower doesn't wish to stay in the property, a short sale or deed in lieu of foreclosure can be arranged.

Marital Settlement Agreement

A written statement accepted to by both parties dissolving a marriage reflecting their desires as it relates to the division of property, child custody, visitation, and any other matters involved in the divorce action. A settlement agreement is incorporated into a divorce decree usually by reference to it in the decree.

Market Value or Estimate of Market Value

The amount a willing buyer would pay a willing seller for a home. While market value is determined by the negotiated price of a buyer and seller, the lender will use an independent appraiser's opinion of value to determine a valuation for loan underwriting purposes.

Misrepresentation

The action of giving a false or misleading account of information contained on a loan application.

Mitigation Report

A property inspection that identifies specific construction features that have been shown to reduce losses in hurricanes, such as a hip roof, concrete block construction, the presence of gable end bracing, shutters and opening protections, the presence of roof to wall attachments such as toe nails, clips, or hurricane straps, and the presence of a secondary water resistance barrier. The results of a windstorm inspection can be presented to an insurer for premium discounts, which can total up to 45 percent off the original policy's premium. Also referred to as a windstorm mitigation report.

Mortgage

A debt instrument, secured by the collateral of specified real estate property, that the borrower is obliged to pay back with a predetermined set of payments. In this legal agreement, owners of a property convey a conditional right of ownership to a lender as security (collateral) for a promissory note that allows a lender to foreclose on the property if the loan obligations are not met. The lender's security interest is public information, recorded in county records, and is voided when the loan is repaid in full.

Mortgagee and Mortgagor

The mortgagee is the lender; the mortgagor is the borrower.

Mortgage Broker

An origination company that intermediates the origination of mortgage loans between borrowers and lenders through state licensed and nationally registered mortgage loan originators. The mortgage broker is regulated to ensure compliance with banking and or finance laws in the jurisdiction of the collateral. A mortgage broker does not use their own funds to loan money. Instead, they deliver a loan to a creditor through its wholesale channel, and the loan is funded in the creditors name. A creditor is the entity that funds a loan whether it is a bank or a nonbank mortgage company.

Mortgage Insurance

Protection for the lender against some or most of the losses that can occur when a borrower defaults on a mortgage loan. Premiums are paid by the borrower. Mortgage insurance is usually required for borrowers with a down payment of less than 20 percent of the home's purchase price. Mortgage insurance is available through private mortgage insurers or through a government agency, such as the Federal Housing Administration.

Multifamily Housing

In residential lending, a building with less than four residential units that has one legal description.

Net Income

An individual's take-home pay, or the amount of money that is received in your paycheck after deductions, credits, and taxes are factored.

No Cash Out Refinance

A loan transaction that extinguishes or replaces an existing loan in an amount that is no greater than the remaining balance on the existing loan plus allowable closing costs. Also referred to as a rate and term refinance.

No Cost Loan

A loan where no fees are charged to the borrower. This lessens the need for up-front cash during the buying process, but generally carries a higher interest cost (rate).

Nonbank Mortgage Company

An organization that does not take in customer deposits, but only originates loans and resells them to banks or secondary market mortgage participants, like Fannie Mae or Freddie Mac. Nonbank mortgage companies use their own funds or funds borrowed from a warehouse lender to fund mortgage loans.

Nonconforming Loan

A loan amount that is above the conforming loan limit as established under the terms of the Housing and Economic Recovery Act of 2008 (HERA) and re-calculated each year or a loan whose features do not comply with GSE guidelines.

Note (Promissory)

A legal document obligating a borrower to repay a mortgage loan at a stated interest rate over a specified period of time.

Note Rate

The simple interest cost of a loan used to calculate the monthly principal and interest mortgage payment.

Notice of Commencement

A term used to describe the recording of a legal document within county records, which signifies that a property owner has begun construction, improvements to, alteration of, or repair of real property.

Obligor

The person who is legally responsible for payment of a debt.

Occupancy

Identifies the intended use of the property as either owner-occupied, second home, or investment.

Origination

The process by which a borrower makes loan application and a lender evaluates creditworthiness.

Origination Fee

Costs that a creditor or mortgage broker charge the borrower for making a loan. These include costs associated with taking and processing a loan application, underwriting and funding a loan, and other administrative services.

Owner's Title Insurance Policy

An insurance policy that protects the homeowner from prior liens against the property or title defects such as errors or omissions in deeds, mistakes in examining records, forgery, or undisclosed heirs.

Overlays

Stricter rules that an individual lender places on top of the guidelines as set forth by the government-sponsored enterprises.

Partial Payment

A payment made that is less than the total amount owed on a monthly mortgage payment. Normally lenders do not accept partial payment unless the reduced amount has been preapproved through the loan servicer.

Payment Shock

A term used to describe an increase of over 125 percent of a borrower's current monthly housing expense and the proposed monthly housing expense on a loan request. To offset the lender's risk with increases over 125 percent, it will generally require that a borrower show additional reserves in excess of the program minimum requirements of approximately two to six months of mortgage payments to include principal, interest, taxes, insurance and homeowners association dues, if any.

PITIA

Acronym for the five elements of a mortgage payment to include: principal, interest, taxes, insurance, and homeowner association dues, if any.

Prequalification Letter

A nonbinding cursory evaluation of a prospective borrower's finances to determine how much can be borrowed and under what terms. A prequalification letter is less formal than a preapproval letter because the lender has not verified any income or asset documentation as communicated by the borrower.

PITIA Reserves

An amount representing the totality of liquid funds that a borrower has available after allocation for down payment and closing costs. This amount is expressed by dividing the monthly housing payment to include principal, interest, taxes, insurance, and homeowner association dues by remaining funds. Each loan program has varying minimum requirements for required reserves. Reserve requirements typically range from zero to twelve months, with two months being the standard.

Planned Unit Development

A real estate project in which individuals hold title to a residential lot and home while the common facilities are owned and maintained by a homeowner association. With ownership, monthly dues are collected by the homeowners association.

Post-Closing Liquidity (Reserves)

A term referring to a borrower's remaining liquid funds available after down payment and closing costs.

Preapproval

A preliminary assessment of a formal loan application that is made where no subject property is identified, a credit report is pulled, and a borrower's estimations of income and assets are run through an automated underwriting system for recommendation to meet program guidelines. This is not the same as a loan commitment. A loan commitment is issued by the lender once an acceptable property valuation has been reviewed and a borrower meets all underwriting conditions of the preapproval.

Project Eligibility Standards

The standards by which a lender or the government-sponsored enterprises determine if projects such as condominiums, co-ops, manufactured homes, and PUDs are acceptable. A loan request from an otherwise qualified borrower will be denied if the property used as collateral fails to meet project eligibility standards.

Public Record Information

Court records of events that are a matter of public interest such as credit, bankruptcy, foreclosure, judgments, and tax liens.

Purchase Agreement/Sales Contract

A legal document where a buyer agrees to purchase certain real estate and a seller agrees to sell under the stipulated terms and conditions.

Qualifying Income

A lender's determination of stable earnings that is likely to continue.

Quality Control (QC)

Processes followed by the broker, creditor and final investor that occur both before and after loan closing to ensure data integrity.

Real Estate Settlement Procedures Act (RESPA)

The Act requires creditors, mortgage brokers, or servicers of home loans to provide borrowers with pertinent and timely disclosures regarding the nature and costs of the real estate settlement process. The Act also prohibits specific practices, such as kickbacks, and places limitations upon the use of escrow accounts.

Release of Lien, Satisfaction of Mortgage, or Reconveyance of Deed

A document that is recorded in the county public records to show evidence a loan has been paid in full.

Repayment Plan

An agreement that gives a borrower a fixed amount of time to bring delinquent mortgage payments current by paying the normal monthly payment plus an additional amount to cover amounts not previously paid in full.

Revolving Debt

Credit accounts whose balance and required monthly payments fluctuate each month.

Schedule C of Federal Income Tax Return

Schedule C, Profit or Loss From Business, indicates income and losses sustained through business ownership.

Schedule E of Federal Income Tax Return

Schedule E, Supplemental Income or Loss, indicates income reported from nonpayroll sources.

Seller Concessions or Credits

Monetary credits from a seller to a buyer provided at the closing (settlement) of a real estate transaction. When determining the maximum loan amount, credits provided in excess of lender allowances are reduced from the sales price in compliance with loan-to-value guidelines for a specific loan program.

Short Sale

An agreement to sell a property for less than the total amount owed on existing liens.

Soft Pull

A term used to describe a type of credit inquiry that alerts lenders of any new attempts to seek credit. Soft pulls do not require your consent and do not affect your representative credit score. A lender will request a soft pull before loan closing to confirm a borrower has not opened new accounts that may affect the debt-to-income ratio.

Subject Property

The home being used as collateral for the loan.

Subordination Agreement

A legal document that is generally used to grant first lien status to a lienholder who would otherwise be secondary to another party; it makes the claim that the prior lienholder approves of taking an inferior position to the claim of another.

Survey

A lot drawing performed by a licensed surveyor that indicates the location of the land, its dimensions, and any structural improvements. It also checks for easements of record, encroachments, and building line violations.

Suspense/Suspended

An action that causes a loan application to hit the pause button in processing and underwriting. No further actions are taken by the lender until clarity is received regarding the item causing suspense.

Tax Proration

The distribution of seller's proceeds to the buyer to cover county taxes that are owed but not payable at the time of the title transfer.

Third-Party Origination

When a lender uses another party to completely or partially originate, process, underwrite, close, fund, or package the mortgages it funds.

Title

The right of ownership, control, and possession of property.

Title Search

The process of retrieving documents evidencing events in the history of a piece of real property to determine relevant interests in and regulations concerning that property by identifying encumbrances and chain of ownership.

Trade Lines

Active credit accounts (installment or revolving) that appear on your credit report.

Transfer Taxes (also called Conveyance Fees)

Taxes imposed by states, counties, and municipalities on the transfer of ownership of real property within the jurisdiction.

Underwriting

The process of reviewing a loan request to measure an applicant's creditworthiness as determined by their credit habits in meeting past debt obligations, the capital investment into the transaction (down payment), the condition of the collateral (property), the capacity to repay the debt (income), and the overall financial character.

Up-Front Charges

Origination fees charged to applicants by the lender at the time of loan application. This generally includes fees for a credit report, application, processing, and appraisal.

VA Loans (U.S. Department of Veterans Affairs)

Loans that have the explicit guarantee of the U.S. federal government helping service members, veterans, and eligible surviving spouses become homeowners.

Verification of Employment (VOE)

A document provided by the lender and completed by an employer disclosing an applicant's hire date, position, yearly salary or hourly rate, overtime or bonus income, and likelihood of continued employment.

Verification of Deposit (VOD)

A document provided by the lender and completed by a depository institution providing account ownership information, account opening date, type of account, current balance, and average balance for the previous sixty days.

Verification of Mortgage (VOM)

In cases where a mortgage payment history is not reported to the credit repositories, this document is provided by the lender and completed by a mortgage servicer with details regarding payment history, payment amount, amount owed, and current balance.

Verification of Rent (VOR)

A document provided by the lender and completed by an applicant's current or former landlord to provide the lender with details regarding payment history and payment amount.

SYLVIA M. GUTIÉRREZ is a mortgage professional. A loan officer since 1993, Sylvia has assisted thousands of families in the mortgage application process. She earned a Bachelors of Business Administration degree from Florida International University majoring in Finance and further expanded her knowledge in the field of Education by subsequently completing teaching requirements to comply with the Florida Department of Education standards. In her chosen field, it seems she's always educating someone about responsible personal financial habits or the workings of the U.S. housing finance system and what an individual needs to do to prepare for homeownership, so she decided to take it one step further and introduce the basic concepts and deliver a plan of action in this broader platform.

At publication, Sylvia serves as a director on the board of the South Florida Chapter of the Mortgage Banker's Association and on the Diversity & Inclusion Committee for NAMB - the National Association of Mortgage Professionals as Vice Chair for Fair Lending topics. In these roles, she partners with industry-wide real estate finance professionals to deliver education to both mortgage professionals and the community at-large.

SylviaGutierrez.com
MortgageMattersBook.com
Twitter.com/Gut2bMe
Facebook.com/MortgageMattersBook
Instagram.com/Mortgage_Matters

Made in the USA
Coppell, TX
19 August 2020